In This Fragile World

Islam in Africa

Editorial Board

Mauro Nobili
Rüdiger Seesemann
Knut Vikør

Founding Editor

John Hunwick †

VOLUME 25

The titles published in this series are listed at *brill.com/isaf*

In This Fragile World

*Swahili Poetry of Commitment
by Ustadh Mahmoud Mau*

Poetry by

Ustadh Mau (Mahmoud Ahmed Abdulkadir)

Translated and edited by

Annachiara Raia
Clarissa Vierke

In collaboration with

Jasmin Mahazi
Azra Ahmad Abdulkadir

BRILL

LEIDEN | BOSTON

This is an open access title distributed under the terms of the CC BY-NC-ND 4.0 license, which permits any non-commercial use, distribution, and reproduction in any medium, provided no alterations are made and the original author(s) and source are credited. Further information and the complete license text can be found at https://creativecommons.org/licenses/by-nc-nd/4.0/

The terms of the CC license apply only to the original material. The use of material from other sources (indicated by a reference) such as diagrams, illustrations, photos and text samples may require further permission from the respective copyright holder.

Research for this book was supported by the German Research Foundation (DFG) at the University of Bayreuth as part of the project *Poetry as Aesthetic Practice* (VI 622/3-1) and the Modern Endangered Archives Program (MEAP cohort 3 0058) hosted by the University of Leiden and the Lamu Museum. This publication is also part of the project *Forging Transoceanic Muslim Histories: Swahili Literary Networks in the 20th century Indian Ocean* (VI.Veni.211C.027) of the NWO Talent Programme 2021, financed by the Dutch Research Council (NWO).

Cover illustration: Ustadh Mahmoud Mau in front of his books
Back cover illustration: The madrasa al-Najah where he studied
Photos from Ustadh Mau's private archive

The recordings referred to in this book are freely available online at
http://dx.doi.org/10.6084/m9.figshare.c.6074855.

The Library of Congress Cataloging-in-Publication Data is available online at http:/catalog.loc.gov
LC record available at http://lccn.loc.gov/2022040953

Typeface for the Latin, Greek, and Cyrillic scripts: "Brill". See and download: brill.com/brill-typeface.

ISSN 1570-3754
ISBN 978-90-04-52571-9 (hardback)
ISBN 978-90-04-52572-6 (e-book)

Copyright 2023 by Ustadh Mau, Annachiara Raia and Clarissa Vierke. Published by Koninklijke Brill NV, Leiden, The Netherlands.
Koninklijke Brill NV incorporates the imprints Brill, Brill Nijhoff, Brill Hotei, Brill Schöningh, Brill Fink, Brill mentis, Vandenhoeck & Ruprecht, Böhlau, V&R unipress and Wageningen Academic.
Koninklijke Brill NV reserves the right to protect this publication against unauthorized use.

This book is printed on acid-free paper and produced in a sustainable manner.

Contents

Foreword   IX
   Rayya Timammy
List of Figures   XIV
Abbreviations   XVI
Notes on Contributors   XVII

Introduction   1
   Annachiara Raia and Clarissa Vierke

PART 1
Poetry as Intellectual Practice

Ustadh Mahmoud Mau, *Mtu wa watu* ("A Man of the People"): Poet, Imam, and Engaged Local Intellectual   11
   Kai Kresse and Kadara Swaleh

Shaping and Being Shaped by Lamu Society: Ustadh Mau's Poetry in the Context of Swahili Poetic Practice   30
   Jasmin Mahazi

"Born on the Island": Situating Ustadh Mau's Poetic Practice in Context   41
   Clarissa Vierke

Seeking *'ilm* on Lamu: Ustadh Mau's Library and Services for the Benefit of His Community   69
   Annachiara Raia

How Ought We to Live? The Ethical and the Poetic in Ustadh Mahmoud Mau's Poetry   95
   Clarissa Vierke

Mabanati in Search of an Author: Portable Reform Texts and Multimodal Narrative Media among Swahili Muslim Communities   133
   Annachiara Raia

PART 2
Poems by Ustadh Mau

Introduction to Part 2   171

Jamii: Topical Issues on Lamu   175
1   *Amu* ("Lamu")   175
2   *Bandari ina mawimbi* ("The Port Makes Waves")   186
3   *Jahazi* ("The Dhow")   190
4   *Tupijeni makamama* ("Let Us Embrace")   192

Ilimu: The Importance of Education   196
1   *Mwalimu* ("Teacher")   196
2   *Kilio huliya mwenye* ("Change Begins at Home")   200
3   *Kiswahili* ("Swahili")   206
4   *Za Washirazi athari* ("The Influence of the Persians")   214

Huruma: Social Roles and Responsibility   218
1   *Mama msimlaumu* ("Don't Blame My Mother")   218
2   *Jilbabu* ("Veil")   223
3   *Mchezo wa kuigiza* ("Play")   228
4   *Haki za watoto* ("Children's Rights")   235
5   *Wasiya wa mabanati* ("Advice to Young Women")   274

Matukio: Biographical Poems   319
1   *Hafi asiye timiwa* ("No One Dies before His Time Is Up")   319
2   *Mlango* ("The Door")   324

Maombi: Personal Poems of Supplication   328
1   *Hapo zamani za yana* ("Once upon a Time")   329
2   *Tunda* ("Fruit")   355
3   *Kipande cha ini* ("Piece of My Liver")   356
4   *Mola zidisha baraka* ("God Increase Your Blessings")   360
5   *Yasome na kukumbuka* ("Read and Remember")   365

References of Part 2   371
Index   373

FIGURE 1   Ustadh Mahmoud Mau at the British Institute in Eastern Africa in Nairobi, 2009

Foreword

First and foremost, I wish to profoundly thank God for giving me the honor of writing the foreword to this book. God has been kind to me, and my prayers have been answered with the publication of this book. The readers, without a doubt, may wonder exactly how my prayers have been answered with this publication. In 2012, I presented a paper on Ustadh Mau's work entitled "Mahmoud Ahmed Abdulkadir (MAU): Mshairi mcheza kwao lakini asiyetuzwa" ("Ustadh Mau: The Unsung Poet at Home," published in 2017).[1]

This book answers those prayers, for the writers of this book about Ustadh Mau's works have not only made him known at home, but exposed him to a worldwide audience.

It has not been an easy task for me to write this foreword. This is not because I have nothing to say about Ustadh Mau, but rather because what I would have said has already been written in great detail by the writers of this book, thus providing the reader with extensive information about him and his works. Despite this, I have been able to write briefly about him due to my having grown up in Lamu and my personal engagement with him.

I do not wish to repeat what is already written about Ustadh Mau in this book. However, my experiences with him may make this inevitable to some extent. I have known Ustadh Mau since my primary-school days in Lamu. My friends and I used to pass by his bakery and take in the sweet scent of his confectioneries while he worked in the bakery. Another, earlier memory of him is when I used to sing his *Kimwondo* poems[2] in the 1970s, during the electioneering periods when Madhubuti and Mzamil were vying for the Lamu parliamentary seat. Because our family supported Mzamil, we used to recite Ustadh Mau's poems in favor of him (the poem *Amu*, "Lamu," presented in this volume is also about the politics of that time).

When I left Lamu to enter high school, it is as if, for some time, I forgot Mau and his works until many years later, when I began teaching at the university. A student of mine from the coast of Kenya gave me a copy of two of Mau's narrative poems. After reading them, I became curious to read more of his works,

---

1 Rayya Timammy, "Mahmoud Ahmed Abdulkadir (MAU): Mshairi mcheza kwao lakini asiyetuzwa," in *Lugha na fasihi katika karne ya Ishirini na Moja. Kwa heshima ya marehemu Profesa Naomi Luchera Shitemi*, ed. Mosol Kandagor, Nathan Ogechi, and Clarissa Vierke (Eldoret: Moi University Press, 2017), 231–242.

2 Assibi Amidu, "Lessons from Kimondo: An Aspect of Kiswahili Culture," *Nordic Journal of African Studies* 2, no. 1 (1993): 34–55. See also Kai Kresse's contribution in this volume.

analyse them, and have a book published; that is when the title of the above-mentioned essay came to mind: Mau was a poet whose works were unknown or not acknowledged in his home country of Kenya. This excludes his hometown of Lamu and the Swahili people there; it includes non-native speakers of the Kiswahili language, many of whom might not have been aware of his works, or if they were, might have ignored them or considered them "just some Swahili poetry whose main concern is Islamic religious teachings." However, on reading the poems in this book, one is inclined to believe that Ustadh Mau's poetry is more than just the propagation of religious teachings. Being a Muslim, Ustadh Mau draws his philosophy and worldview from Islam but, as Clarissa Vierke and Annachiara Raia have shown, there is more to the writer's poems and his poetry than religious pedagogy. The two writers have been very successful in exposing Mau as a great, multifaceted artist, and thus have fulfilled my wish of seeing his works published, thereby contributing to the great tradition of Kiswahili metrical poetry.

When I decided to study Mau's works, I wanted to meet him so that I could interview him about his works. I traveled to Mombasa and mentioned this to my father. Coincidentally, Mau had traveled to Mombasa and met my father, who told him of my intention to meet him. I was so humbled when he came home with my father to meet me instead of me going out to meet him. Such a great but humble soul! I talked to him at length, and he made a promise to supply me with all the works of his that he could lay his hands on. And whenever he composed a poem, he would send it to me along with books, magazines, journals, and essays on the Kiswahili language and its literature. I have nothing to repay him for his generosity and his trust in me; my prayer is that God showers him with His abundant grace. Ustadh Mau has also been an important advisor to researchers (especially foreign ones), and has gladly guided many in their research without expecting recompense of any kind. Mau has also been active in offering his poetry as a service to the community, and has composed works both for individuals in need of topical poems for marriage ceremonies, the hajj (pilgrimage to Mecca), and funeral ceremonies, as well as for social service groups in order to publicize their missions and visions. I warmly remember how, when my daughter was set to sit her KCSE (Kenya Certificate of Secondary Education) exam, Ustadh Mau composed and sent her a poem wishing her success in the endeavor. What I wish to reiterate is that Ustadh Mau is a selfless man of the people: always ready to offer advice and guidance, and all this without hesitation or red tape.

I have a lot to say about Ustadh Mau and his poetic works. But my task here is to write a foreword to this book. The book is divided into an introduction, six chapters, and a second part featuring some of his poems. I have opted to

FOREWORD

summarize the contents of the chapters all together—i.e., the introduction by Raia and Vierke, who have each contributed two chapters, and the chapters of Mahazi, Kresse and Kadara who each wrote one chapter—because they all have written about Mau's poetry. The introduction and the first four chapters talk about Ustadh Mau. The chapters describe Mau's life and works at length: he is a husband, father, a teacher, a sheikh (religious leader/scholar), and, first and foremost, a renowned poet of Lamu. All the writers revisit his life history and acknowledge the fact that he was the first sheikh or religious scholar to deliver the Friday sermon in the Kiswahili language in order to reach a wider audience of Muslim adherents. In these chapters, we learn what inspired the writer, his experiences, and his challenges, and how he contributed to the well-being of Lamu residents and how they affected him and his poetry in turn. Mau is portrayed as a self-made scholar through his reading of works by scholars who had a great and lasting impact on him and his life as a poet. His home library is described in great detail, and his love for books reiterated.

An important characteristic of Mau's works and sermons, as mentioned by all the writers, is his eagerness to educate and guide Lamu residents to pursue an education for their own economic well-being. He feels it is his incumbent duty as an artist to impart morals as he draws his inspiration from the day-to-day life of the Lamu people. Some of the themes he engages in are the AIDS scourge, drug abuse, politics, and the effects of adopting negative foreign cultural traits. Religious instruction is also a central theme in Mau's poetry, as evidenced by the traditional structure of his narrative poems, which start and end with thanksgiving and prayer. Mau believes that poetry and the arts are a powerful medium of mass education, but he is saddened by the lack of a reading culture in his society. The Lamu people are accustomed to the oral word, which is the reason why most of his works are not published, but recorded in audio and video formats. Since traditional poetry is sung, word of mouth is more effective than the written word (at least in traditional society), while the meaning of the words is clearer when uttered or sung by talented balladeers. The editors of this book have explained why Mau's poems are recorded in audio and video media and sung by talented artists (see Raia's contribution on the *Wasiya wa mabanati* in this volume); as Abdilatif Abdalla puts it, "[M]ore than the fact that words in a poem have sound and meaning, they also portray certain images, feeling, smell and taste and these will only be realized when the poem is read or sung aloud rather than have it pasted on paper."[3] The writers of

---

3 Abdilatif Abdalla, "Dibaji II," in *Shuwari*, ed. Haji Gora Haji, Flavia Aiello, and Irene Brunotti (Paris: DL2A Buluu Publishing, 2019), 30.

XII   FOREWORD

this book have successfully portrayed Mau as both the servant and representative of his people.

The chapters by Vierke, "How Ought We to Live," and Raia, "*Wasiya wa mabanati* in Search of an Author," analyze one narrative poem and three others, viz. *Haki za watoto* ("Children's Rights"), *Mama msimlaumu* ("Don't Blame My Mother"), *Mlango* ("The Door"), and *Wasiya wa mabanati* ("Advice to Young Women"). The characteristics of Mau's language feature in each chapter. He writes in the Kiamu dialect in order to "preserve" it for future generations, not forgetting that it was the language of most classical Swahili poets. By using his mother tongue, Mau is able to command a powerful diction, full of figures of speech and imagery. Despite this, his language is simple, fluid, as his objective is to reach his audience without any impediments. Mau's poems are a testimony to his coastal origin and environment; thus, many poems feature themes related to the sea and marine life and economy, like the poems *Amu* ("Lamu") and *Jahazi* ("Dhow"). This quality is what distinguishes great poets from ordinary poets. It is evident that Mau is very familiar with both his social culture and his geographical environment, as evidenced both by the form and themes of his poetry. Ustadh Mau lives his culture and is an active participant in its daily life.

The writers have explicated Ustadh Mau's use of language and how he employs metaphorical language whenever he treats issues intended only for a particular adult audience, thus adding to the aesthetic and thematic appeal of the poems. In the poem *Ukimwi ni zimwi* ("AIDS Is a Monster"),[4] his language enables the reader to see the disease for what it is, that is, an ogre "eating away" at human life and comfort. He has explored the different verse meter and genres, like the *Dura Mandhuma* and the *Tathlitha*, among others. In other poems, he has used a dialogic style in which two or more characters interact, as in *Jilbabu* ("The Veil") and *Wasiya wa mabanati* ("Advice to Young Women").

Concerning the second part of the book, which consists of different poems of Ustadh Mau, I would like to laud the editors for their efforts in this making this selection. It would have been an uphill task for any reviewer or critic to choose from Mau's many beautiful compositions. The book comprises twenty compositions: five narrative poems and fifteen poems in other forms and styles. These have been picked from a total of fifteen narrative poems by Ustadh Mau,[5] while his shorter verses are more than eighty in number. I congratulate the editors on

---

4   [Remark by the editors: This poem is not included in this volume.]

5   See the list in Ahmad Abdulkadir Mahmoud and Peter Frankl, "Kiswahili: A Poem by Mahmoud Ahmad Abdulkadir, to Which is Appended a List of the Poet's Compositions in Verse," *Swahili Forum* 20 (2013): 1–18, https://nbn-resolving.org/urn:nbn:de:bsz:15-qucosa-137405.

FOREWORD XIII

accomplishing the difficult task of choosing which verses should be included in the anthology and which should be left out.

The writers have categorized the poems into five parts: social themes comprise the first part, in which they include poems about Lamu, while the second is about education and its importance to society. The third part features poems on generosity and mercy; then follow verses about his life experiences, and last, poems about supplication. Another valuable contribution of the volume editors is that every verse has an introduction and analysis, enabling the reader to understand the background of the composition, and hence its message, in a better way. Lastly, the verses have all been translated, thus enabling the non-Kiswahili speaker to understand them.

Ustadh Mau's pictures form part of this volume, thus enabling those who haven't met him to at least have a glimpse of this great Lamu poet. There is much more to say about Ustadh Mau and his works, but let me not preempt your curiosity, for you will get the full picture as you read this book. Finally, I wish to laud the editors for this great endeavor. Let us all celebrate this book.

Rayya Timammy

References

Abdalla, Abdilatif. "Dibaji II." In *Shuwari*, edited by Haji Gora Haji, Flavia Aiello, and Irène Brunotti, 30. Paris: DL2A Buluu Publishing, 2019.

Amidu, Assibi. "Lessons from Kimondo: An Aspect of Kiswahili Culture." *Nordic Journal of African Studies* 2, no. 1 (1993): 34–55.

Mahmoud, Ahmad Abdulkadir, and Peter Frankl. "*Kiswahili*: A Poem by Mahmoud Ahmad Abdulkadir, to Which is Appended a List of the Poet's Compositions in Verse." *Swahili Forum* 20 (2013): 1–18. https://nbn-resolving.org/urn:nbn:de:bsz:15 -qucosa-137405.

Timammy, Rayya. "Mahmoud Ahmed Abdulkadir (MAU): Mshairi mcheza kwao lakini asiyetuzwa." In *Lugha na fasihi katika karne ya Ishirini na Moja. Kwa heshima ya marehemu Profesa Naomi Luchera Shitemi*, edited by Mosol Kandagor, Nathan Ogechi, and Clarissa Vierke, 231–242. Eldoret: Moi University Press, 2017.

Figures

All pictures belong to Ustadh Mau's private archive unless otherwise indicated.

1 Ustadh Mahmoud Mau at the British Institute in Eastern Africa in Nairobi, 2009 VIII

2 Ustadh Mahmoud Mau during a reading at the Iwalewahaus, University of Bayreuth, 2015 XIX

3 Ustadh Mahmoud Mau at home reading the *Texas Review* given to him by his American neighbour 10

4 The District Commissioner awards Ustadh Mahmoud Mau a medal for his outstanding commitment for education on the Kenyan Jamhuri Day 29

5 The poet at the entrance of Asilia Bakery on Lamu in 2000 40

6 Ustadh Mahmoud Mau at the beach on the island in 1967. Behind him the motorboat of the District Commissioner 68

7 A bookshelf in Mahmoud Mau's private library 94

8 Ustadh Mahmoud Mau as a small boy in 1963; next to him a *kiti cha enzi*, a prestigious, commonly shared Indian Ocean piece of furniture from the epoch of Portuguese rule 132

9 Excerpt from the booklet *Yā-bintī* by al-Ṭanṭawi, EG 1406/AD 1985, 28 141

10 The cover art for the three *Wasiya* tracks available on SoundCloud 148

11 Original first (right) and last (left) page of Ustadh Mau's *Wasiya wa mabanati*, composed and handwritten in Roman script in a notebook 151

12 Barka Aboud, Ustadh Mahmoud Mau's mother, in 1968 168

13 Ustadh Mahmoud Mau and his photo album 171

14 Ustadh Mahmoud Mau giving a speech to motivate adults to have their children vaccinated against polio during the time of the *maulidi* celebration around 2010 175

15 Ustadh Mahmoud Mau visiting a school in the village of Barigoni on the mainland 196

16 Ustadh Mahmoud Mau reading *Mama Musimlaumu* at the Jukwaani Festival in Nairobi in 2009; in his hands the newspaper report which inspired his poem 218

17 First page of the manuscript of "Haki za Watoto" in Ustadh Mau's handwriting 273

18 First page of the manuscript of the "Wasiya ya Mabanati" in Ustadh Mau's handwriting 318

19 Ustadh Mahmoud Mau sitting in front of the oven in his bakery in 1988 319

FIGURES

20 Ustadh Mahmoud Mau with his children Aboud (in the middle), Hannan (on the right), and Azra (behind)   328

21 The young Mahmoud in 1964   369

Abbreviations

Abr.	Arberry, Arthur, J. *The Quran Interpreted*[1]
Am.	Kiamu dialect
Ar.	Arabic
Baj.	Kibajuni dialect
Bak.	Bakhressa, Salim K. *Kamusi ya maana na matumizi*[2]
Eng.	English
Krp.	Krapf, J.L. *A Dictionary of the Suahili Language*[3]
Kak.	*Kamusi Kuu ya Kiswahili*[4]
Kiung.	Kiunguja dialect
KNUT	Kenya National Union of Teachers
lit.	Literal meaning
Mau	Mahmoud Ahmed Abdulkadir Mau
meth.	methali "proverb"
Mv.	Kimvita dialect
Nab.	Ahmed Sheikh Nabhany *Kandi ya Kiswahili*[5]
OUP	Oxford University Press
Qur.	Qur'ān
RISSEA	Research Institute of Swahili Studies of Eastern Africa
Scl.	Sacleux, C. *Dictionnaire swahili-français*[6]
Std.	Standard Swahili
stz.	stanza (Sw. *ubeti*)
syn.	synonym

---

1 Arthur J. Arberry, *The Quran Interpreted* (Oxford: Oxford University Press, 1984).

2 Salim K. Bakhressa. *Kamusi ya maana na matumizi.* (Nairobi [etc.]: Oxford University Press cop. 1992).

3 John Ludwig Krapf. *A Dictionary of the Suahili Language: With Introd. Containing an Outline of a Suahili Grammar.* (London: Trubner, 1882).

4 John Mwaura Gicharu, Benjamin Nyangoma and Chris Oluoch. *Kamusi Kuu ya Kiswahili* (Nairobi: Longhorn Publishers Limited, 2015).

5 Nabhany Ahmed Sheikh, *Kandi ya Kiswahili* (Dar es Salam: Aera Kiswahili Researched Products, 2012).

6 Charles Sacleux, *Dictionnaire swahili-français* (Paris: Inst. d'Ethnologie, Univ. de Paris, 1939).

Notes on Contributors

Annachiara Raia
Ph.D. (2018), is assistant professor in African literature at Leiden University (The Netherlands). Specialised in Swahili Muslim textual traditions and interested in the question of archive and collection, she is currently researching on vernacular print networks in the 20th-century Indian Ocean.

Clarissa Vierke
Ph.D. (2010), is professor of Literatures in African Languages at Bayreuth University (Germany). She is an expert of Swahili poetry, manuscript cultures and has been working on travelling texts in East Africa and literary entanglements with the Indian Ocean.

Kai Kresse
is Professor of Social and Cultural Anthropology at Freie Universitaet Berlin and Vice-Director of Research at Leibniz-Zentrum Moderner Orient (ZMO). He has conducted fieldwork on the Kenyan Swahili coast since 1998, working on and with local thinkers, and on internal debates of the Muslim community. His publications include the monographs 'Philosophising in Mombasa' (Edinburgh University Press, 2007) and 'Swahili Muslim Publics and Postcolonial Experience' (Indiana University Press, 2018), the edited translation of Sheikh al-Amin Mazrui's *Uwongozi* (Guidance) (Brill, 2017), and the edited volume 'Struggling with History: Islam and Cosmopolitanism in the western Indian Ocean' (Hurst/Columbia University Press 2007/2008).

Jasmin Mahazi
holds a PhD in Social Anthropology from the Berlin Graduate School Muslim Cultures and Societies (BGSMCS, FU Berlin) on the textual corpus and social dimensions of vave oral poetry and its ritual performance. Currently she is an associate researcher at the Leibniz-Zentrum Moderner Orient (ZMO) in Berlin working on a matrifocal anthropological study of oral archives and embodied knowledge practices along the Swahili coast.

Kadara Swaleh
is Research Fellow at Leibniz-Zentrum Moderner Orient (ZMO) in Berlin, Germany from April 2021 in a transnational group project titled De:link:Re: link focusing on transnational infrastructure projects such as China's Belt and Road Initiative (BRI). He is concurrently pursuing a Ph.D. at Freie Universität Berlin

in the Cultural and Social anthropology Institute, examining the impact and repercussions of China's BRI projects in Mombasa, Kenya. He is published in peer-reviewed journals and contributed to book chapters on diverse topics like Islamic proselytizing, inter-faith relations, Swahili culture, Swahili poetry, and women's rights in Islam.

Rayya Timammy
Ph.D. is Associate Professor in the Department of Linguistics, Languages and Literature, Faculty of Arts, University of Nairobi. For the last 17 years, she has been the chairperson in the Department of Kiswahili. Her areas of specialization are Kiswahili Language and Literature and Muslim Women issues. Prof. Timammy is also a Kiswahili fiction writer and composer of poems.

FIGURE 2 Ustadh Mahmoud Mau during a reading at Iwalewahaus, University of Bayreuth, 2015

Introduction

Annachiara Raia and Clarissa Vierke

This book brings together poems by one of the most outstanding Muslim poets and intellectuals from Kenya, namely Mahmoud Ahmad Abdulkadir (commonly called Ustadh Mahmoud Mau). The volume is the first published anthology of poetry by Ustadh Mau, which strives toward filling an important gap in our current scholarship: the accessibility of African-language texts by individual poets and intellectuals in Africa, which are important sources for African intellectual and literary history. Ustadh Mau's broader scholarly reception and recognition is still only in its early stages, and this volume intends to lay the groundwork for further research with and on local poets and intellectuals from the Swahili coast for a better understanding of intellectual discourse outside of Western frameworks. Our investigation into Ustadh Mau's poetic practice and his active involvement in his own community—ranging from his daily social interactions, to his poetic works answering to local circumstances and struggles, to the Friday sermons he delivered in the oldest mosque in Lamu—also places emphasis on the Lamu archipelago as a yet-neglected Swahili Islamic hub. Thus far, poetry as a genre of debate and critical reflection in Islamic Africa has not received enough attention: on the so-called "Swahili coast," however, it has been the most highly valued intellectual genre of critical Muslim discourse in Swahili for centuries. Moreover, for Ustadh Mau, poetry is the most important means of addressing topical political concerns and burning social issues. In his poetry, he re-explores poetic forms and tropes that one can trace back to Lamu's nineteenth-century "golden age" of Muslim poetic and cultural production, which itself has even older roots.

Mahmoud Ahmad Abdulkadir was born on the island of Lamu in northern Kenya in 1952. Unlike his own children, he never attended a secular state school; he received all his education in Swahili and Arabic from very renowned Islamic teachers at the local madrassa and Islamic institutes. He became a baker to earn his living, but also an imam at the oldest mosque on Lamu, where he began teaching and preaching in the early 1980s. On Lamu, he was the first imam to give his Friday sermons in Swahili. For him, Swahili is linked with his struggle for change. Influenced by the writings of reformist scholars that he imbibed in his early twenties, he has been promoting an agenda of progress, of which one can find strong echoes in his own poems. The notion of reform Islam or even more his self-identification as Salafi may sound alarming in the present

© ANNACHIARA RAIA AND CLARISSA VIERKE, 2023 | DOI:10.1163/9789004525726_002

This is an open access chapter distributed under the terms of the CC BY-NC-ND 4.0 license.

global and local context where Salafism has been increasinly associated with fundamentalism and a whole spectrum of groups opposing local Sufi practices and traditions but also suppressing and apply increasing violence against people considered leaving the 'right path'. As our contributions show, although Ustadh Mau has read many classical reformist scholars, Ustadh Mau's search for reform and change is too complex to be translated into a dichotomy of 'traditional' versus 'reformist' Islam. Far removed from the aggressive moral agendas of reformist currents of the last decades, his writings are characterized by tolerance and understanding toward people's everyday struggles and diverse ways of living. He stands up for the weaker classes of his society and has, for instance, courageously championed the rights of women and children. Furthermore, he does take keen interest in local Swahili poetic traditions rooted in Sufi context, which also influenced his own poems.

In his early twenties, Ustadh Mau began composing his own Swahili poetry. In fact, the first poem he composed came into being almost on the spot, on the occasion of the tenth anniversary of Kenya's independence, when one audience member enjoyed his performance so much that he paid him one shilling as a reward—a promising sign that encouraged him to continue composing poetry. While, on the one hand, the composition of political verses, like *Kimwondo* ("Shooting Star") and the *Wasiya wa mabanati* ("Advice to Young Women"), earned him a reputation in the Lamu community as well as a broader coastal audience, scholarly contributions by Rayya Timammy[1] and Kai Kresse[2] have made important first steps toward situating his writing and thinking in the broader Swahili Muslim context of poetic debate. Furthermore, Ustadh Mau coedited the *utendi* poem *Kiswahili* with the late British scholar Peter J. Frankl, who was living in Mombasa at the time. *Kiswahili* was published by the journal *Swahili Forum* in 2013, which represents the first time that an original manuscript of one of Ustadh Mau's poems—handwritten on lined paper in

---

1 Timammy, "Thematising Election Politics in Swahili Epic: The Case of Mahmoud Abdulkadir," in *Song and Politics in Eastern Africa*, ed. Kimani Njogu and Hervé Maupeu (Dar es Salaam, Tanzania: Mkuki na Nyota, 2007), 303–314; "Shaykh Mahmoud Abdulkadir 'Mau': A Reformist Preacher in Lamu," *Annual Review of Islam in Africa* 12, no. 2 (2015): 85–90; "Mahmoud Ahmed Abdulkadir (MAU): Mshairi mcheza kwao lakini asiyetuzwa," in *Lugha na fasihi katika karne ya ishirini na moja. Kwa heshima ya marehemu Profesa Naomi Luchera Shitemi*, ed. Mosol Kandagor, Nathan Ogechi, and Clarissa Vierke (Eldoret: Moi University Press, 2017), 231–242.

2 Kresse, "Knowledge and Intellectual Practice in a Swahili Context: 'Wisdom' and the Social Dimensions of Knowledge," *Africa* 79, no. 1 (2009): 148–167; "Enduring Relevance: Samples of Oral Poetry on the Swahili Coast," *Wasafiri* 66 (2011): 46–49.

INTRODUCTION 3

Arabic script—was included, together with its typed transliteration in Roman script and an English translation. The article also offers an appendix with a first inventory of Ustadh Mau's poems.

The poems presented in this volume are composed in Kiamu, the dialect of Lamu, which is considerably different from standard Swahili. In the nineteenth century, poetic production was so vibrant on Lamu that Kiamu became almost synonymous with "poetic language." Poets from Lamu, including Ustadh Mau, take great pride in their dialect and its tradition. We also stick to Kiamu variants, including spelling conventions (often derived from Arabic script), in the rendition of the texts, but make reference to their equivalents in standard Swahili. In our presentation and readings of the texts, we make abundant use of the poet's own commentaries and reflections on literature, religion, language, and education, about which we have had conversations with him at various times and places. All the contributors to this volume have cherished memories of time spent with Ustadh Mau, who hosted us at his place in Kenya or came to visit Germany and Italy.

The other contributors to this volume have known Ustadh Mau much longer than its editors: Rayya Timammy, professor of literature at the University of Nairobi, was not only among the first scholars to work on his poetry and biography, but was also born on Lamu; Jasmin Mahazi, who played an important role in translating his poetry, holds fond memories of Ustadh Mau from her childhood on Lamu; and since the late 1990s, Kai Kresse has been in dialogue with Ustadh Mau as part of his wider project on Swahili thinkers. His contribution to this volume emerged from a discussion with Kadara Swaleh, who, himself from Lamu, has known Ustadh Mau for many years.

Clarissa Vierke first became acquainted with Ustadh Mau at a conference on popular culture in East Africa organized by Andrew Eisenberg and Ann Biersteker in Mombasa in 2006, where she presented on an earlier important Muslim poet from Lamu, Muhamadi Kijuma (1855–1945), who had left behind a large number of Swahili poems in Arabic script. Always interested in and knowledgeable about Lamu's poetic history, Ustadh Mau invited her to his house for further—and still ongoing—conversations about Swahili poetry. In 2009, Clarissa Vierke invited Ustadh Mau to contribute to the Jukwaani poetry festival in Nairobi, whose Swahili section—which brought together the most renowned coastal poets, including Ahmad Nassir Juma Bhalo, Abdilatif Abdalla, and Ahmed Sheikh Nabahany—she curated for the Goethe Institut. The Jukwaani festival was one the few public occasions where Ustadh Mau read his own poetry—in this case, *Mama msimlaumu* ("Don't Blame My Mother")— aloud, as he regards himself as a composer (*mtungaji*), but not a reciter or singer. Instead, important Swahili reciters and singers like Muhammad Kadara, el-Shatry, and Bi Ridhai have given voice to his compositions, ensuring their wide circulation along the coast.

Ustadh Mau is not only a poet, but has also become a scholar of and reference person for the Swahili poetic tradition. He has been a part of a working group translating early nineteenth-century dance poetry from Lamu, and also helped Annachiara Raia decipher manuscripts of the *Utendi wa Yusuf* ("The Poem of Joseph") in Arabic script. Raia first met Ustadh Mau in August 2014, when she first came to Lamu. Later, in 2018, Annachiara Raia began research on the contents of Ustadh Mau's home library on Lamu, and in 2019, she met him again in Mombasa, when they not only selected the photos for this volume, but also expanded the corpus of poems with *Amu* ("Lamu"), which now opens this anthology. It was among his first poems, composed in response to a shipwreck that shocked Lamu in 1979. They translated the poem in July 2019, exactly forty years after the calamity occurred. The other poem is *Hapo zamani za yana* ("Once upon a Time"), one of the oldest existing poems in his collection— composed by Ustadh Mau's father, Ahmad Abdulkadir Abdulatif (1915–1970), around the time Ustadh Mahmoud Mau was born in 1952. His father wrote the poem with didactic intent, typical of the *wasiya* genre, to provide his son with guidelines on how to live, drawing from his own experience as well as the existing lore of instructional poetry, Islamic literature, and popular wisdom.

In April 2015, together with Ustadh Mau—who had come to Bayreuth— Annachiara Raia, Clarissa Vierke, and Jasmin Mahazi began working on the translation of his poetry. The more than fifty manuscripts of poems that he shared with us were neither bound nor organized in a single notebook, but rather constituted loose sheets of paper. For some poems, there was already a transliteration typed in Roman script and, for very few, a rough translation in English, thanks to previous editorial works done mainly by two people very close to Ustadh Mau: his daughter Azra and Mohamed Karama. The selection of twenty poems to be translated and included in this volume was made by the poet himself, who singled out the poems he considered his most important, because they either addressed critical issues in the community or commemorated pivotal events in his own life. With the help of student assistants (Janina Buck and later Duncan Tarrant and Melissa Deiß), we began scanning the material and typing the poems, which until then had only been handwritten. While we have been able to archive further poems digitally, Ustadh Mau has written and continues to write more poetry, which we also want to preserve. Annachiara Raia is currently working on a digital archive program in cooperation with the Lamu Museum and Ustadh Mau himself, which aims to include the increasing number of vocal renderings of his poems; this initiative is con-

INTRODUCTION   5

tributing to spreading his words more widely and in multimodal formats (i.e.,
printed and aural).[3]

The fragile state of the poetry manuscripts that Ustadh Mau brought to
Bayreuth impressed on us the urgency to begin both digitizing the original
manuscripts in Arabic script, but as well as translating them to make them
more widely available. In a culture where orality and recitation and spontan-
eous, sharp-witted rhetorical intervention are so highly valued, the written and
printed are often of little priority. As elaborated further in the contributions in
this volume, Ustadh Mau has always considered his people more receptive and
accustomed to listening rather than reading. This makes written manuscripts,
which are such unique documents of Swahili intellectual history, precarious
and highly endangered. Moreover, the practice of writing Swahili in Arabic
script, as Ustadh Mau commonly does, is all but extinct on Lamu nowadays.
Thus, this book not only intends to make his poetry more widely accessible, but
also to offer an idea of the manuscripts' beauty as a vanishing Swahili Muslim
heritage. Lastly, besides reproducing some of the manuscripts, the book also
presents rare and valuable photographs of from Ustadh Mau's personal library,
which adds to the portrayal of the poet. Ustadh Mau allowed us to digitize these
photographs and to store the digital copies in the Africa Archive of Bayreuth
University, which has been generous in its technical support (thank you to Ben-
jamin Zorn!).

Besides offering a collection of Ustadh Mau's poetry, the book's foreword,
by Rayya Timammy, and its first part, with contributions by Kai Kresse and
K. Saleh, Jasmin Mahazi, and both editors, situate the poet and his poetics
within the social and intellectual context of Lamu. As Ustadh Mau himself con-
siders poetry so deeply grounded in social practice, all of the contributions in
this volume illuminate facets of his modus vivendi.

Kai Kresse and Kadara Swaleh's portrayal of Ustadh Mau highlights his
emphasis on social responsibility and personal engagement in relation to the
local concept of a *mtu wa watu* ("man of the people"). In an attempt to position
Ustadh Mau within the wider social field of intellectual practice in Lamu and
the intellectual history of the Swahili Muslim coast, Kresse and Swaleh draw
parallels between Ustadh Mau and other Islamic intellectuals who have taken
on key roles in society because of their respective agendas, speeches, and acts

---

3 Ustadh Mau Swahili Muslim Library is among the UCLA Library 29 international cultural
   preservation projects (MEAP-3-0058). This project is supported by the Modern Endangered
   Archives Program at the UCLA Library with funding from Arcadia, a charitable fund of Lisbet
   Rausing and Peter Baldwin. https://www.ascleiden.nl/research/projects/ustadh-mau-digital
   -archive-umada-maktaba-ya-kidijitali-ya-ustadh-mau

toward and within their own communities—viz., three renowned East African ulama: Sheikh Al-Amin Mazrui (d. 1947), Sheikh Abdalla Saleh Farsy (d. 1982), and especially Sayyid Omar Abdalla (d. 1988).

Along the same lines, Raia, in her outline of books and thinkers that shaped Ustadh Mau's personal education and knowledge, brings to the fore a Cairene network that the poet—despite being a lifelong resident of Lamu—has been in close contact with, as attested, for instance, by the books and scholars he knows well. For instance, the Egyptian Islamic theologian Yūsuf al-Qaraḍāwī (1926–) used to address Ustadh as "al-ʿAqqād," after the Egyptian writer ʿAbbās Mahmoud al-ʿAqqād from Cairo—whose writing and modus vivendi Ustadh Mau admired so much that, when he was just sixteen years old, he adopted "ʿAqqād" as his nickname (before becoming "Mau").

Ustadh Mau's close relationship with his hometown Lamu and the island's longstanding poetic tradition are elements that Jasmin Mahazi and Clarissa Vierke both outline in their own contributions. The poet's personal genealogy is inevitably entangled with the ancestral roots of poetic discourse on the island, but also related to more far-reaching Indian Ocean connections: Ustadh Mau's grandfather came to East Africa from India.

Two further contributions, by Annachiara Raia and Clarissa Vierke, zero in on Ustadh Mau's poetry and poetics. Ustadh Mau's poetry covers a wide-ranging spectrum of topics, from political issues to social, didactic, and religious ones, not to mention his shorter compositions composed on behalf of others on the occasion of a graduation ceremony, wedding, funeral, or pilgrimage. With her interest in the relationship between morality and poetry in Ustadh Mau's poetic practice, Vierke offers a close reading of his oeuvre as a major site of "doing ethics." Annachiara Raia draws on the *Wasiya wa mabanati* ("Advice to Young Women") to explore how narratives and their related media frame and shape social and religious discourse in coastal Kenya. According to her reading of the poem, the *Wasiya*—besides being an outstanding example of Ustadh Mau's experiments with the didactic genre and its media—hosts a polyphonic community whose familiar drama, as told in its stanzas, mirrors Lamu's own societal drama at a time when customs were considered in danger of being corrupted. Rather than treating poetry purely as the vessel for a social message, Vierke and Raia highlight the specific Swahili poetic forces that can affect audiences through the use of prosodic patterns, sharp, sermon-like language in some parts, or veiled, metaphoric language (*mafumbo*) in others. Ustadh Mau's poetry provides unique viewpoints, mostly on issues troubling the community, by enacting highly mimetic plots that unfurl daily dramas that no one would dare speak publicly about, if not the poet—who, through an almost Dostoyevskian realism, morphs into and voices his characters, imparting to his

INTRODUCTION

poetry a prophecy-like character and making scenes palpable to listeners. If there is one talent that the authors in this work are committed to highlighting in various ways, it is certainly the poet's ability to plumb the depths of human frailty.

Many individuals and various institutions have assisted us in the course of researching and writing this book, and it is our pleasure to offer our sincere and heartfelt thanks first of all to Ustadh Mau, who never tired of and was ever at our disposal in answering our numerous questions and sharing portions of his life and island with us. Furthermore, we are very grateful to all the contributors to this book—Kai Kresse and Kadara Swaleh, Jasmin Mahazi, and Rayya Timammy—whose contributions have vastly enriched and expanded the scope of the current study.

We also owe much gratitude to Mohamed Karama and Azra Mahmoud Ahmad, who allowed us to amend and publish in this volume their poetic translations of *Mwalimu*, *Za Washirazi Athari*, and *Yasome na Kukumbuka* (Karama) and *Mchezo wa Kuigiza* and *Mola Zidisha Baraka* (Ahmad). While Jasmin Mahazi worked on most of the translations with us, Azra Mahmoud Ahmad helped us enormously to improve some of the translations presented in this volume, like the *Wasiya wa mabanati* and others. Kristen de Joseph accompanied us from the beginning. She put an enormous effort into this book and proofread the English translations.

Furthermore, we are grateful to several institutions: first and foremost, the University of Bayreuth, but also the African Studies Centre Leiden, without which trips to Kenya as well as Germany and Italy would have been difficult.

Speaking in the name of all contributors to this book, we are grateful to all close colleagues and friends—too numerous to mention by name—who helped us in improving our contributions. Thank you to all the children who accompanied us: Freya, Giulia, Martina, Giada, Ivan and Nicoló.

We wonder whether or not to consider it a coincidence that we've found ourselves completing the last stages of this book, titled *In This Fragile World*, at a time where human connections and frailty have indeed been put to the test. Besides the global challenges of war and corona pandemic, we, all of us editors and authors here, also as friends and fellow human beings, particularly feel with Ustadh Mau, whose son Yasir, an ambulance-driver, was abducted in mid 2021 by policemen and imprisoned without trial. As in other parts of the world more broadly, in Kenya specifically, the ideology of a 'war on terror' has been used to cast Islam as a whole as associated with terrorism. Under these circumstances, in such a fragile world, being a Muslim from the coast is enough to raise suspicion; and basic human rights become suspended. We are glad that, despite everything, Ustadh Mau has always been with us. *Mola akubariki, Ustadh.*

References

Kresse, Kai. "Knowledge and Intellectual Practice in a Swahili Context: 'Wisdom' and the Social Dimensions of Knowledge." *Africa* 79, no. 1 (2009): 148–167.

Kresse, Kai. "Enduring Relevance: Samples of Oral Poetry on the Swahili Coast." *Wasafiri* 26, no. 2 (2011): 46–49.

Timammy, Rayya. "Thematising Election Politics in Swahili Epic: The Case of Mahmoud Abdulkadir." In *Song and Politics in Eastern Africa*, edited by Kimani Njogu and Hervé Maupeu, 303–314. Dar es Salaam: Mkuki na Nyota, 2007.

Timammy, Rayya. "Shaykh Mahmoud Abdulkadir 'Mau': A Reformist Preacher in Lamu." *Annual Review of Islam in Africa* 12, no. 2 (2015): 85–90.

Timammy, Rayya. "Mahmoud Ahmed Abdulkadir (MAU): Mshairi mcheza kwao lakini asiyetuzwa." In *Lugha na fasihi katika karne ya Ishirini na Moja. Kwa heshima ya marehemu Profesa Naomi Luchera Shitemi*, edited by Mosol Kandagor, Nathan Ogechi, and Clarissa Vierke, 231–242. Eldoret: Moi University Press, 2017.

PART 1

Poetry as Intellectual Practice

∴

FIGURE 3   Ustadh Mahmoud Mau at home reading the *Texas Review* given to him by his American neighbour

Ustadh Mahmoud Mau, *Mtu wa watu* ("A Man of the People"): Poet, Imam, and Engaged Local Intellectual

Kai Kresse and Kadara Swaleh

1 Introduction

This chapter seeks to provide a brief character portrayal of Ustadh Mahmoud Ahmed Abdulkadir, commonly known as Ustadh Mau. "Mau" is a peculiar nickname, and Ustadh Mau himself has given me two differing accounts of its origin.[1] According to the first account, he began being called after Chinese Communist Party Chairman Mao for his egalitarian and socialist leanings. According to the second, people in Lamu started using this name for him as they linked his attitude with the activities of the anti-colonial Mau Mau fighters.[2] I have known Ustadh Mau for many years, having first met him in 1999 when, as a PhD student, I was based in Mombasa's Old Town for fieldwork. I went to Lamu to witness the popular Maulidi celebrations, and sought him out specifically to discuss his poem *Wasiya wa mabanati* ("Advice to Young Women"), which I had come across in Mombasa. Friends in Mombasa had called my attention to this composition as one that offers deep thought and philosophical reflection upon

---

1   This chapter is based in part on Kai Kresse's many (mostly informal) conversations with Ustadh Mau and on information he collected on research visits to Lamu between 1999 and 2019; Kresse's perspective supplies the main narrative voice of this text. It is also based on Kadara Swaleh's long-term familiarity and many informal conversations with Ustadh Mau. Swaleh also interviewed several of Ustadh Mau's former students as well as his former mentor, Ustadh Harith, by phone in early April 2019. Kadara is Ustadh Harith's son and comes from Lamu himself, and has known Ustadh Mau for many years. This contribution is part of a wider joint collaborative research project—one we seek to pursue further—on Swahili scholars, thinkers, and regional intellectual culture. Here, we draw in part from a joint paper on Ustadh Mau and other Swahili Muslim thinkers from the Lamu region presented at an international workshop on Islam in Africa in Berlin in October 2019; the workshop was organized by Benjamin Soares and Terje Ostebro (University of Florida, Gainesville), John Hanson and Ron Sela (Indiana University), and Ruediger Seesemann (Bayreuth University). Ustadh Mau himself read, checked, and commented on the text in April 2020.

2   On these two takes on the nickname, albeit with a somewhat different twist, see also Timammy Rayya, "Shaykh Mahmoud Abdulkadir 'Mau': A Reformist Preacher in Lamu," *Annual Review of Islam in Africa* 12, no. 2 (2015): 85–86.

© KAI KRESSE AND KADARA SWALEH, 2023 | DOI:10.1163/9789004525726_003

This is an open access chapter distributed under the terms of the CC BY-NC-ND 4.0 license.

human life and society—which was the central topic of my research then.[3] At the time, the poem was popular among Swahili speakers on the Kenyan coast and beyond not only because of its dramatic narrative and meaningful message, seeking to guard young women from downfall and treacherous temptations, but also because of its critique of society, and most of all for its beauty. It was popular as much for its verbal composition as for the particular vocal performance of the recording that was circulating at the time, that of Abdalla el-Shatry from 1996 (there is another recording, from 1977, by Muhammad Kadara).

While I focus on this poem in greater detail elsewhere[4] and intend to expand upon this study in the future, my portrayal of Ustadh Mahmoud Mau here draws from my own research biography for its narrative perspective. As an anthropologist interested in knowledge, reflection, critique, and debate in society, I have been in more or less regular, and at times frequent, contact with Ustadh Mau over the years since 1999 (both in person and via letter, email, and WhatsApp).[5] My personal narrative is complemented here with further detail and sociohistorical context courtesy of my colleague Kadara Swaleh, who has known Ustadh Mau for many years. Kadara is himself an insider to the Lamu community and son of one of Ustadh Mau's teachers, the recently deceased Ustadh Harith Swaleh (d. 2020). From such a vantage point, our account here intends to situate Ustadh Mau within the wider social field of intellectual practice in Lamu, and thus within the specific kind of historically grown and transregionally shaped urban Muslim trading environment that the Swahili coast constitutes. Our aim is to convey an understanding of Ustadh Mau as someone who, through the kinds of interactions he engages in both as an imam and as a poet, personally embodies a dedication and commitment to particular sets of ideas and values that are socially acknowledged as moral obligations, grounded and reflected in social interaction.[6] His commitment is visible in the ways by which he attends to the needs of the community and the specific individuals around him.

We understand Ustadh Mau as a specific case of a "teacher of (and for) society" (*mwalimu wa jamii*). This is a generic term for Swahili intellectuals in a communal context that we have taken over from our conversations with

---

3 Kresse, *Philosophising in Mombasa: Knowledge, Islam and Intellectual Practice on the Swahili Coast* (Edinburgh: Edinburgh University Press, 2007); "Enduring Relevance: Samples of Oral Poetry on the Swahili Coast," *Wasafiri* 66 (2011): 46–49.

4 Kresse, "Enduring Relevance."

5 On visits to Lamu in 1999; 2005; 2006; 2007; 2010; 2012; 2015; 2017; 2018; and 2019.

6 This builds on earlier work on the intertwined nature of knowledge and social obligation and the ongoing relevance of mutual acknowledgement of others in social interaction. See

the Mombasan scholar Sayyid Abdulrahman Alawy, known as Mwalimu Saggaf (d. 2017). We have found the term useful to work with, as it helps us to think through the intertwined spheres of knowledge, education, and mutual moral obligation recognized among members of society.[7] To this end, not only is the discursive sphere relevant; the sphere beyond discourse is crucial as well. The discursive dissemination of advice and insight is obviously a main concern for imams as well as poets, yet any such discursive communication is embedded in forms of social interaction both more widely and more specifically shaped and performed on an interpersonal level in everyday life. The fundamental sense underlying this—that social action (*kitendo*) and one's performance of self is (or should) underpin one's words (*maneno*)—corresponds to a long-established tradition of social expectation that is illustrated by proverbial expressions, for instance the saying *utu ni vitendo* ("goodness is action").[8] These expectations, linked to moral (and moralizing) mutual demands and obligations among community members, also (and particularly) apply to knowledgeable figures and intellectual leaders. Those who are truly successful in advising and directing their peers are regarded as "men/women of the people" (*mtu wa watu*). Their influence manifests itself in terms of what action to take and how to respond to certain pressing social, political, or economic challenges; they manage to do so through the ways they connect and "click" with the community. Acquiring a reputation as *mtu wa watu* is achieved by artful and persuasive ways of speaking, or by their interactive social performance, showing an embedded and integral (and thus potentially principled, flawless, and unassailable) position within the community. In this sense, Ustadh Mau is clearly and surely recognized in Lamu as a *mtu wa watu* in how he conducts himself, and works, as a *mwalimu wa jamii*. The expression *mtu wa watu* is also applied to popular local and regional leading figures in East Africa more widely, as well as to national and international ones, often politicians who are admired and the same time seen as 'one of us' (like Nyerere, Mandela, or Obama).

Kresse, "Knowledge and Intellectual Practice in a Swahili Context: 'Wisdom' and the Social Dimensions of Knowledge," in "Knowledge in Practice: Expertise and the Transmission of Knowledge," ed. K. Kresse and T. Marchand, special issue, *Africa* 79, no. 1 (2009): 148–167; Kresse, *Swahili Muslim Publics and Postcolonial Experience* (Bloomington: Indiana University Press, 2018), chapter 1.

7   Kai Kresse held formal interviews and informal conversations with Mwalimu Saggaf in Mombasa between 1998 and 2016.

8   Elsewhere, I have worked in depth on the social understanding of *utu*, and, in relation to that, on its philosophical interpretation as articulated by the poet Ahmad Nassir Juma Bhalo (d. 2019) in his poem *Utenzi wa mtu ni utu*; see Kresse, *Philosophising in Mombasa*, chapter 5.

Prominent Swahili scholars and public intellectuals in recent history can also be seen from this angle—though the ways and means of being embedded and appreciated socially may differ significantly. For instance, the three renowned East African ulama Sheikh Al-Amin Mazrui (d. 1947), Sheikh Abdalla Saleh Farsy (d. 1982), and especially Sayyid Omar Abdalla (d. 1988)—the former director of the Muslim Academy in Zanzibar, who was even known as Mwenye Baraka (the Blessed One)—are commonly referred to by this expression. They were admired for their respective agendas, their writings, speeches, and arguments, and how they managed to connect with ordinary Muslims and address their concerns.[9] But let us not overgeneralize and get ahead of ourselves; let us now turn back to Ustadh Mau and the details that matter to our understanding of his contributions.

2 Biographical Trajectories: Education and Scope of Social Engagement[10]

Born in Lamu in 1952, Ustadh Mahmoud Abdulkadir is a Muslim scholar, imam, and poet based in Lamu town, in the area near the old fort, Ngomeni. Since

---

9 On Sheikh Al-Amin Mazrui, see the foreword by Alamin & Kassim Mazrui in *Guidance* (Uwongozi) *by Sheikh Al-Amin Mazrui: Selections from the First Swahili Islamic Newspaper*, ed. Kai Kresse, trans. Kai Kresse and Hassan Mwakimako (Leiden: Brill, 2017); Nathaniel Matthews, "Imagining Arab Communities: Colonialism, Islamic Reform, and Arab Identity in Mombasa, 1897–1933," *Islamic Africa* 4, no. 2 (2013): 135–163; and R.L. Pouwels, "Sheikh al-Amin bin Ali Mazrui and Islamic Modernism in East Africa, 1875–1947," *International Journal of Middle Eastern Studies* 13, no. 3 (1981): 329–345.

On Sheikh Abdalla S. Farsy, see the obituary by Sheikh Abdilahi Nassir 1982 in *Sauti ya haki*, no. 8 (summarized in Kresse, *Swahili Muslim Publics*, 137); and sections in Justo Lacunza Balda, "Translations of the Qur'an into Swahili, and Contemporary Islamic Revival in East Africa," in *African Islam and Islam in Africa*, ed. D. Westerlund and E.E. Rosander (London: Hurst, 1997), 95–126, and R. Loimeier, *Between Social Skills and Marketable Skills: The Politics of Islamic Education in 20th Century Zanzibar* (Leiden: Brill, 2009).

On Sayyid Omar Abdallah, see M. Bakari, "Sayyid Omar Abdalla (1919–1988): The Forgotten Muslim Humanist and Public Intellectual," in *The Global Worlds of the Swahili: Interfaces of Islam, Identity and Space in 19th and 20th Century East Africa*, ed. Roman Loimeier and Rüdiger Seesemann (Berlin: Lit-Verlag, 2006), 363–388; M. Bakari, *The Sage of Moroni: The Intellectual Biography of Sayyid Omar Abdallah, A Forgotten Muslim Public Intellectual* (Nairobi: Kenya Literature Bureau, 2018); and a summary portrayal in Kai Kresse, "On the Skills to Navigate the World, and Religion, for Coastal Muslims in Kenya," in *Articulating Islam: Anthropological Approaches to Muslim Worlds*, ed. M. Marsden and K. Retsikas (Amsterdam: Springer Press, 2013), 77–99.

10 Our biographical sketch here is by no means meant to be comprehensive, leaving aside some important aspects of his family history, his experiences in becoming a poet, the

1985, he has been the imam of Pwani Mosque, which is Lamu's oldest mosque still in use, and the second of at least seven Friday mosques currently in Lamu town. At the time, Pwani Mosque was the first mosque in Lamu to switch to the use of Swahili for the Friday sermon, and Ustadh Mau played a crucial role in this heavily contested transition.[11] The dispute over the matter escalated and was even referred to the Lamu District Magistrate Court, which ruled in favor of Ustadh Mau's party in its arbitration. Notably, a main representative of the opponents was Sayyid Hassan Badawy (d. 2007), a former teacher and mentor of Ustadh Mau. Despite their disagreement, however, these two scholars subsequently maintained good relations of mutual respect.[12] Sayyid Hassan had been the main teacher, mentor, and role model for the young Mahmoudi. As the imam of Rodha Mosque, he was one of two grandsons of the famous Habib Saleh (d. 1935) who broke away from the Riyadha community that their grandfather had established.[13] Sayyid Hassan was nicknamed the "Socrates of Lamu" within the community, both because of his intellectual and critical stance and for his simple lifestyle. He intrigued Mahmoud Abdulkadir, who associated himself closely with him, becoming his student and follower. He felt intellectually inspired and politically sensitized by this highly learned man, who dressed in simple clothes and interacted with everyone without pretension, making a point of being accessible to all.

Beyond his ongoing role as imam, Ustadh Mau was long in charge of a family-owned bakery.[14] Baking and selling bread, however, were activities that he abandoned and passed on to family members after some economic struggles

---

specifics of his engagement in Muslim organizations, and other biographical details; for instance, he was also based in Dar es Salaam for two years as a petty trader before returning to Kenya and pursuing Islamic higher education. For fuller coverage and details, see e.g. Timammy, "A Reformist Preacher in Lamu," and Vierke, this volume.

11   Timammy, "A Reformist Preacher in Lamu," 87.

12   Communication by Kadara Swaleh and Ustadh Khattab Khalifa Abubakar, April 6, 2020. Khattab is a graduate of Riyadha Mosque College Lamu, and for some time assisted Ustadh Mahmoud in running the Friday ritual at Pwani Mosque.

13   The other one was Mzee Mwenye (Sayyid Alwy bin Sayyid Ahmad Badawy, d. 2008), who went on to found Swafaa Mosque in 1975, which from the 1980s onward became the main base for Shii Ithnashari Islam in the Lamu region, attracting a significantly growing constituency. Habib Saleh, i.e. Sayyid Saleh Alwy Jamalail (d. 1935) was the founder of Riyadha Mosque in around 1892; see Anne Bang, *Sufis and Scholars of the Sea: Family Networks in East Africa, 1860–1925* (London: Routledge, 2003), and A.H. el-Zein, *The Sacred Meadows: A Structural Analysis of Religious Symbolism in an East African Town* (Evanston, Ill.: Northwestern University Press, 1974).

14   Wade Huie, "This Fine Poet from Lamu Bakes Bread That Is Tamu," *Daily Nation* (February 8, 1980).

at the turn of the new millennium. His paternal grandfather, Abdulkadir Abdulatif (d. 1930), hailed from Kutch, specifically the port of Surat on the Malabar coast, while other branches of the family had already been based in Lamu for a longer time. Ustadh Mau, unlike many ulama in Lamu, lays no claim to *masharifu* descent.

After completing his general education and seeking further and higher Islamic education, Ustadh Mau sought to leave Lamu to attend a Salafi-oriented school of Islamic education, the Madrasatul Falah, in Mombasa in the late 1960s. From there, he moved on to a similarly oriented college in up-country Kenya, the Machakos Muslim Institute. There, he overlapped with an old acquaintance, Sheikh Ahmad Msallam (b. 1947) from Kizingitini in the Bajuni islands north of Lamu—who at the time was teaching some of the lower classes in Machakos before going to Omdurman Islamic University in Sudan for further studies. This opportunity had been provided to Sheikh Msallam through his former teacher in Kzingitini, the renowned reformist scholar Ustadh Harith Swaleh (d. 2020). Having studied in Omdurman, and before that at Al-Azhar University, Egypt, Ustadh Harith was a highly educated and intellectually superior Islamic scholar, and as an influential teacher became a key figure for reformism in Kenya. Moreover, he was also a highly sought-after healer (*mtabibu*). Ustadh Harith had styled himself in opposition to the regionally dominant and Lamu (and Riyadha) based Alawiyya *masharifu* as a young teacher in the Bajuni area.[15] When Mau's returned to Lamu from Machakos, Ustadh Harith, who was now based there too, temporarily became his mentor. He had warmed to his promising young peer, but is reported to have worried that Ustadh Mau was busying himself too much with politics and poetry. Thus Ustadh Harith took him under his tutelage to focus on religion, using him as a junior partner to teach his *tafsir* sessions at Bawazir Mosque (known as *msikiti was bandani*) in central Lamu. Ustadh Harith would begin the *tafsir* classes, pass on to Ustadh Mau midway through, and at the end they would take turns responding to questions raised by the congregation.

Between 1975 and 1978, Ustadh Mau was actively involved in local politics as a poet, taking sides in the election campaigns for the regional member of Parliament. Like Sheikh Ahmed Msallam—who is also a prominent poet-scholar in the region—he supported the local Bajuni candidate Mzamil Omar Mzamil (d. 1998), whom he saw as morally upright and a representative of justice, against an opponent whom he regarded as representing the darker forces of

---

15   Kadara Swaleh "Islamic Proselytising between Lamu and Mozambique: The Case of Kizingitini Village." *Social Dynamics* 38, no. 3 (2012): 398–348.

Kenyan power politics under KANU at the time. At this point, he composed a series of political poems under the title of *Kimwondo* ("Shooting Star"), praising his candidate and criticizing the opponent. These poems were publicly recited and performed, as well as recorded and circulated. They were composed as consecutive, dialogic responses to the rival party, in so-called *kujibizana*-style verse, consisting of mutual challenges between the two parties.[16] The poems became popular both within and beyond the Lamu area as its audio-cassette recordings were widely distributed and circulated. These compositions, in particular, established Ustadh Mau's reputation as a poet to a wider public.[17] It is notable that twenty years later, during my fieldwork in 1999, I was still able to acquire cassette recordings of *Kimwondo* in a local shop.

On the whole, poetry is a highly relevant and respected skill in Swahili society, as most occasions on the calendar and all special events are commonly marked with a poem. Moreover, poetry is said to acquire more social value when it is used for the public good. In this regard, poets who embody the combined expertise of Islamic knowledge and verbal artistry, as poet-sheikhs, are seen to wield particular influence in the community.[18] One can thus say that over the years, Ustadh Mau has been building and cultivating the potential to exert influence within society. In his dual position as both sheikh and poet, he can be seen as using his skills for the good of the community.

There is much more to write and discuss about Ustadh Mau's poetic career, as the present volume undoubtedly makes clear. The scholarly reception and recognition of his work are still only in its early stages,[19] while audio recordings and, to a lesser extent, printed versions (though no proper publications) of his poems have been circulating on the Kenyan coast and beyond. Remarkably, an excellent recent ethnography of Lamu includes three poems of his as illustrative windows onto society and representative discursive samples, presenting them as "interlude" texts between chapters.[20] Topic-wise, his poetry covers

---

16   Ann Biersteker, *Kujibizana: Questions of Language and Power in 19th- and 20th-Century Poetry in Kiswahili* (East Lansing: Michigan State University Press, 1996), and Ridder Samsom, "Tungo za kujibizana: 'Kuambizana ni sifa ya kupendana,'" *Swahili Forum* 3 (1996): 1–10.

17   Assibi A. Amidu, *Kimwondo: A Kiswahili Electoral Contest* (Vienna: Afro-Pub, 1990).

18   On this, with a particular view to such dualism of power in the Somali context, see Ahmed Jimale, "Of Poets and Shaykhs: Somali Literature," in *Faces of Islam in African Literature*, ed. Kenneth W. Harrow (London: James Currey, 1991), 279–309. On Sheikh Ahmad Msallam, see also Kadara Swaleh, "What Does Philosophy Want: A Swahili Poem by Sheikh Ahmad Msallam of Lamu, Kenya." *Annual Review of Islam in Africa* 12, no. 2 (2013/2014): 79–84. On the wealth of poetry in Swahili society and its relevance, there is abundant literature.

19   E.g., Kresse, "Enduring Relevance" and Timammy, "A Reformist Preacher in Lamu."

20   The three poems are *Mila yetu hufujika* ("Our Traditions Are Being Destroyed"), *Kiswahili*;

overarching sociopolitical issues and (often practical) matters of concern to the community. He seeks to educate, "wake up" (*kuamsha*), inform, and guide his peers through what he says, and how he says it. Thus he can be viewed as seeking to strengthen communal ties of solidarity and mutual support in society. Some of his poems reflect such concerns, such as those on the institution of marriage (*ndoa*), composed from both a male and a female perspective, or on the human rights of children, which must not be ignored (*Haki za watoto*).

His poetry also specifically addresses certain groups in society. For instance, he warns girls and young women of the dangers of sexual temptation and seduction, vividly illustrating how this can destroy the lives of individuals and families as established values and forms of respectful interaction are eroded, and Lamu society exposed and subjected to external Western influences and common challenges of the modern world (in the abovementioned *Wasiya wa mabanati*, composed in 1974). In a similarly engaged vein, his poems also discuss pressing problems like drug addiction, as well as hygiene and different types of illness, including AIDS (*Ukimwi ni zimwi*). His overall agenda consists of informing, sensitizing, and alerting the community on matters of religion and politics. As sources of inspiration, he points to his local teachers and Muslim scholars from the region (some mentioned above), as well as prominent members of the global *umma* who have combined intellectual and activist tendencies, religion, and politics, like Hassan al-Banna (1906–1949) and Seyid Qutub (1906–1966), both leading figures of the Muslim Brotherhood (interview, 2019).

Both as an imam and more generally as a town elder (*mzee wa mji*) representing the community, Ustadh Mau has been engaged in initiatives on the part of concerned citizens that seek to maintain the influence and control of Lamu residents over their own town. On this count, the "Save Lamu" initiative has been successful and effective for several years, and Ustadh Mau and others were invited to India in 2019 on its behalf. During several visits to Lamu, I witnessed Ustadh Mau's involvement as a respectable elder within certain consciousness-building initiatives, like the recommendation of the use of treated mosquito nets (against malaria) in homes during an event at the fort; or as a participant during a workshop celebrating the recent attainment of Lamu's status as a UNESCO World Heritage site. Over the years, such initiatives have often unified the urban community across religious and class divides. Their members have stood up and made cases against external interests and pressures in political decision-making on and about Lamu—whether originating from the national

---

and *Tupijeni makamama* ("Let's Embrace"); see Sarah Hillewaert, *Morality at the Margins: Youth, Language, and Islam in Coastal Kenya* (New York: Fordham University Press, 2020), 41–45, 114–120, and 187–190. The latter two poems are also found in this volume.

government or the external economic interests of Chinese, American, Canadian, or Japanese companies, namely with respect to potential economic projects (often envisaged as gigantic) concerning the natural resources (oil; gas) that have been discovered in the region. This also concerns the recent and now nearly complete Chinese-funded deep-sea port project, LAPPSET, which seeks to provide a new transport route to South Sudan.[21] Ustadh Mau, like a few other local elders, is a regular presence within these groups, providing respectability and Islamic education, and acting as an important and well-connected mediating figure disseminating information.

As an imam, he told me, he is careful not to focus on the ideological differences or partisan interests of Muslim subgroups during his sermons, so as not to accentuate divides within the community. This distinguishes him from many other preachers, who often seek and cultivate confrontation. He rather chooses topics of common concern to all Muslims,[22] such as: factors in maintaining one's health and well-being; how to properly manage domestic differences between spouses; what is the proper procedure for divorce; and other issues. These are the recent thematic strands that he has covered in his recent talks— topics that I have heard him speak about live or in recorded sermons. Such a range of topics reconnects us with the field of poetry—as a complementary, distinct, and different form of teaching—where he has made rather similar choices (as we can see above), and arguably for similar reasons. In both his poems as well as his sermons, he is concerned with focusing and reflecting on the general aspects of humanity that come to the fore in exemplary situations of need, plight, and distress (loss of love; loss of life; illness; etc.)—and, to a lesser extent, also situations of love and success. This was illustrated most recently— in April 2020, amid the early impact of the current global corona crisis—by a thematic Friday sermon and another educational poem of his; both explained, in different, genre-specific ways, important facts about the virus and specific precautions to be taken against it (I received recordings of both from him via WhatsApp that same week).[23]

---

21   Lotte Knote, "The Promise of the Lamu Port: An Island Facing Change at the Margins of the Kenyan Nation" (MA diss., Freie Universität Berlin, 2018).

22   Interview by Kai Kresse, Lamu, August 2019.

23   The sermon was delivered on April 3, 2020, in the near-empty Pwani Mosque, and shared via video link; this was already the third week that no congregational Friday prayers had been held there due to the situation. The sermon was filmed by the Lamu Youth Alliance and made available on their YouTube channel on April 6, 2020, under the title "Friday Preach on COVID19": https://www.youtube.com/watch?v=j7PpAmiU72E (accessed January 15, 2021).

While little or no research on the reception of his poetry has (yet) been conducted, we find it likely that his own success as a poet in Lamu (and beyond) rests, at least partly, upon the wide-ranging accessibility of the language of his poems, treating the big questions and fundamental issues of human life in a thoughtful and reflexive manner that is at the same time approachable and open to wider audiences of Swahili speakers—not just to members of the social and intellectual elite (who are often already "clued in" to more sophisticated and less accessible styles and codes). For this reason, some of Ustadh Mau's poems may strike those readers looking for complex wordplay or demanding riddles as relatively straightforward, employing rather simple narrative strategies to the best didactic purpose.

Another level of Ustadh Mau's social commitment as a poet is shown by the fact that he not only composes poems for other people upon request—which is common for courtship and occasions like weddings and anniversary events—but also declines any payment in return, which is less common.[24]

We have hardly been able to dwell upon specific examples of his poetry here. However, what can be said is that, just like his sermons that focus on human and all-too-human topics, his poems are also socially embedded, and linked to specific events within the dynamics of society. While commenting and reflecting on such specifics, the composer, through his poetic narrative, is actually reflecting upon humanity itself, inviting everyone in reach to be his audience and think along. And while poetry has different pathways of appealing to people and of reflecting upon being human, different poets are known for their respective individual styles and specific ways of making this happen. While the verbal art of the renowned Mombasan poet Ustadh Ahmad Nassir Juma Bhalo (d. 2019), for instance, has been qualified by one of our interlocutors as having an immediate existential effect of "piercing the hearts" of listeners (*maneno ya Ahmad Nassir huchofa kwenye moyo*), the poetry of Ustadh Mau is said to reflect his social engagement. His poems "live" in communal life, one could say, and may in turn be kept alive by it. Taking *Wasiya wa mabanati* as an illustration, we can observe that this poem is still very much alive in Lamu society, more than three decades after this epic advocating for women's rights and the safety of girls was composed.

Ustadh Mau has long championed women's rights. In the early 1980s, he established a kindergarten and, building on that, a school (*madrasa*) for girls

---

24   It is not uncommon among Swahili poets to find authors advocating a particular cause in their poetry, while in reality, the composer does not necessarily have a commitment to the subject he is treating. The whole composition process thus becomes a mere composition exercise, either for pay or for the sake of composition itself.

that included religious teaching as well as a secular education curriculum. Both were called *Thamaratul Jannah* (Fruits of Paradise) and operated in the same building owned by his family. The school offered free tuition, while he paid the monthly teachers' wages out of his own meager proceeds from the family bakery. The kindergarten operated for half the day, and in the afternoon became a literacy center for elderly women with a limited knowledge of Islam. When, over time, the bakery business began suffering, the parents were requested to pay school fees to secure the teachers' wages.[25] In the 1990s, Ustadh Mahmoud helped to establish a "community-based organization" (CBO) for women, named the Annaswiha Women Group, which took over the running of the school and also engaged in community matters, including civic education, public health, and women's empowerment. When the student numbers increased, this women's group organized a fundraiser to build a larger school complex (completed around 2015). Currently, this CBO is well grounded and well connected in Lamu society, having become a force to reckon with. It offers a rich calendar of events, including a "teenagers' week" where both male and female youth are inducted into becoming responsible adults.[26] The group runs the administration of the school and related programs, while Ustadh Mau plays an advisory role. This example, too, illustrates how Ustadh Mahmoud can be regarded as a *mtu wa watu* and *mwalimu wa jamii*.

3 *Mtu wa watu*: The Importance of Socializing

Overall, Ustadh Mau is known and can be observed to interact well, actively, and regularly with people of all kinds and backgrounds in Lamu's urban community. As he told me, during one of our conversations in August 2019, "Knowledge is important—but what is more important is to relate to and interact well with people" (*ujuzi ni muhimu, lakini muhimu zaidi ni maingiliano mazuri na watu*). Prioritizing matters so explicitly in this way, namely ranking sociability before and above knowledge, is remarkable—all the more so as it is done by a teacher and imam, someone dedicated to education and the dissemination of knowledge as their primary concern. While this statement says quite a lot about the specific dedication of Ustadh Mau, it also says much about the value of

---

25 Telephone interview with Mwalimu Zainab Abdala Bathawab (Kidege) by Kadara Swaleh, April 8, 2020. Kidege is a disciple of Ustadh Mahmoud Mau and was among the early teachers at the kindergarten until 2007.

26 Telephone interview with Sheikh Muhammad Abdallah Swaleh by Kadara Swaleh, April 8, 2020. Sheikh Muhammad is a disciple of Ustadh Mahmoud Mau, a student chaplain at the University of Nairobi, and also gives *darsa* (preaching sessions) at Jamia Mosque, Nairobi.

socializing in Swahili society itself; indeed, the proverb-like phrasing employed here seems itself to represent some kind of reference to a social consensus that can be taken for granted. Accordingly, to actively concern oneself with community life and the needs and worries of its members, as Ustadh Mau does, is seen by him as a kind of obligation to the community; this applies as much to highly educated and qualified people like himself as to anyone else, regardless of their social status. Yet such an opinion is not necessarily standard among local ulama, as others, due to differences in character, upbringing, wealth, or descent, might not seek to build an open and egalitarian kind of social interaction in the same way.

Ustadh Mau can be seen to live a simple life, as he cultivates social relations with others, amid everyday interactions, on the basis of equality in a community where ideologies of descent and status continue to have strong resonance. Like his former teacher and mentor, Sayyid Hassan, he dresses in simple clothes and is accessible to everyone who seeks his advice. Members of the urban community know, for instance, that he can be found in his library— a study space that is directly accessible, separate from his house and living quarters—during certain hours of the day, when he is willing to be approached and interrupted. In the form, manner, and phrasing of his communication, he takes care to represent and create an egalitarian communicative atmosphere, in which issues of status do not come between people and their interactions. A few years ago, he co-initiated an early morning fitness and swimming group for men, where participants train and socialize at the channel every morning by sunrise after *fajr* prayers. Thus, we would argue, by means of his soft-spoken and open-minded conduct, his relaxed and measured composure, and his simple self-presentation in everyday life, he presents and conducts himself as a role model for how common interaction among Muslim community members should be performed.

As we have seen sketched out here, and as this present volume is surely set to illustrate and illuminate in detail, an accessible, rich, and manifold set of sources exists on the discursive and artistic work that Ustadh Mau has produced, in his many and wide-ranging contributions to public discussion and communal debate in Lamu. Studying some of these further, with more attention to detail, more context, and more comparison (than could be included here) is on our collaborative agenda for the future, in conversation with other coastal intellectuals and residents. There is much to be explored in, and through, Ustadh Mau's compositions; there is a lot to be learned about the lifeworld of Lamu, and also about the wider world as it is seen and conceived in Lamu. His speeches and writings pursue different pathways in various genres, including religious sermons and educational talks on the one hand, and different kinds of poetry on the other. Textual resources of his to be worked on (besides the poetry mentioned) also include the Friday sermon recordings provided by Ustadh Mau himself. And while he acts as public speaker at Pwani Mosque every Friday, and has presented religious lectures and talks at prominent national and international venues (e.g. Jamia Mosque in Nairobi and a Sudanese Islamic TV channel), the most remarkable feature of his practice of social guidance still lies in the direct interaction that he seeks and cultivates with his social peers, on the ground. He engages and guides by example, in word and deed.

4 Conclusion

The aim of this brief portrayal has been to convey a sense of how Ustadh Mau pays emphatic attention to the needs, wishes, and desires of the people around him, and how his sensitivity is directed to specific human demands and expectations within the Lamu community. Such attention and sensitivity are at the same time informed and expressed by his writings as well as his social interactions, his words (*maneno*) and deeds (*vitendo*). Both are constituent aspects of who he is and how he is to be understood as a poet, imam, and teacher of/for society (*mwalimu wa jamii*), and thus on the whole as a true and well-meaning human being (*mtu*).

An important topic not sufficiently covered here is how to properly understand and situate Ustadh Mau within the wider religious demography of Lamu, with all its internal groups and sub-differentiations. For this, we would need to consider the whole range of sub-factions—in all its locally specific (and translocally shaped) internal diversity—which often exist in mutual tension with each other, due to their competing ideologies as much as to personal rivalries. This itself takes place amid a national Kenyan scenario of political marginalization of Muslims,[27] as well as within a wider framework of (partly *longue durée*) transregional connections between the global *umma*, e.g. with a view to Hadhrami sharif families having long become part of the urban elite[28] or to the presence of South Asian traders.[29] Most importantly, with a view to the

---

27   Kresse, *Swahili Muslim Publics*; Hassan Ndzovu, *Muslim in Kenyan Politics* (Evanston: Northwestern University Press, 2014).

28   Bang, *Sufis and Scholars of the Sea*; Hillewaert, *Morality at the Margins*; el-Zein, *The Sacred Meadows*.

29   C. Salvadori, *Through Open Doors: A View of Asian Cultures in Kenya* (Nairobi: Kenway Publications, 1989); *We Came in Dhows*, vol. 1 (Nairobi: Paperchase Kenya Limited, 1996).

specifics of the local Muslim community, the internal dynamics of Lamu's religious demography is (and continues to be) mapped—at least in part—onto descent, as well as onto ethnic and linguistic identities of subgroups that have historically established forms and layers of social hierarchies, ascribing certain groups higher or lesser social status in relation to their claims and criteria.[30] In public disputes about Muslim unity, however, the divisions between the strong Alawiyya Sufi faction, with Riyadha Mosque as the main base for their wide-ranging East African networks, and the Salafi-oriented reformists, calling themselves *ahlul-sunna* or *Answar Sunna* and called "Wahhabi" by their opponents, are the most apparent.[31] Such disputes are most commonly about ritual practices, the visitation of graves (*ziyara*), and especially the performance of Maulidi celebrations, but also about the social status of *masharifu* families. These have been ongoing and characteristic features of the internal contestations within Swahili Muslim communities for at least about a century now. On the matter of the contested annual Maulidi celebrations of the birth of Prophet Muhammad—which, in their al-Habshi variant from the Hadhramawt that had been implemented by Habib Saleh at the turn of the 19th to 20th century, have been so popular that they have been taken to characterize Lamu itself—the local Shiite community (based at Swafaa Mosque) that has been growing fast over the last decades has sided with the Alawiyya Sufis against reformist "Wahhabi" pressures.[32]

Somewhat in contrast to the Sufi Alawiyya stance that dominated Lamu through most of the 20th century and remains relevant, Ustadh Mau himself has long identified with a Sunni reformist position that is Salafi-inspired.

---

30   See e.g. Sarah Hillewaert, "'Whoever Leaves Their Tradition Is a Slave': Contemporary Notions of Servitude in an East African Town," *Africa* 86, no. 3 (2016): 425–446; Jasmin Mahazi, "An Anthropology of Vave—A Bajuni Farmers' Ritual on the Swahili Coast" (PhD diss., Freie Universität Berlin, 2018); Patricia Romero, *Lamu: History, Society, and Family in an East African Port City* (Princeton, NJ: Markus Wiener, 1997); and Kadara Swaleh, "Islamic Proselytising between Lamu and Mozambique: The Case of Kizingitini Village," *Social Dynamics* 38, no. 3 (2012): 398–348.

31   Elsewhere, I have written in more detail on the internal dynamics and transformations of the coastal Muslim community since the 1970s or so. This includes pointers to account for an initial rise of "Wahhabi" influence and a subsequent sense of solidarity between Sufis and Shiites in response. Kresse, "The Uses of History", in E. Simpson and K. Kresse (eds), *Struggling with History: Islam and Cosmopolitanism in the Western Indian Ocean* (New York: Columbia University Press, 2008).

32   On debates about and arguments for and against established ways of *maulidi* celeberations, see also Kresse, "Debating maulidi", in R. Loimeier and R. Seesemann (eds), *The Global Worlds of the Swahili* (Berlin Lit-Verlag, 2006), as well as Kresse, *Swahili Muslim Publics*.

perspective. However, unlike other Salafi-oriented reformist groups and activists, who are locally called "Wahhabi" and have commonly sought to dominate Muslim publics and impose their stance on others through combative ideology and sharp language (*lugha kali*), including even *takfir* (the pronouncement of opponents as nonbelievers)—as we can find in the spoken and written discourses by proponents of Saudi-sponsored scholars, like Sheikh Msallam—is Ustadh Mau has chosen to remain sober and soft-spoken in his speeches and public utterances. Thus he cultivates the stance of what we might call a "soft Wahhabi". This entails—as we have been able to observe over the years—cultivating a quiet and forbearing attitude in the face of Lamu's highly popular rituals and events during the Maulidi period, while these include practices that he deems inappropriate or wrong. Over the years, Ustadh Mau has shown patience and confidence in the conviction that the position he has chosen to take would ultimately prevail (as truthful and reasonable). I remember how Ustadh explained to me, back in 1999, that the common Maulidi celebrations in Lamu—that were then so popular that they were taken by many as an unquestionable feature of Lamu's urban community itself—were actually relatively recent, "only" about a hundred years old. Over time, he indicated, people in Lamu would again cease to perform them. And by then, in retrospect, those kinds of contested Maulidi practices will have simply been a phase within the longer trajectory of regional social history.

In conclusion, we suggest that Ustadh Mau is best understood as a socially sensitive, politically engaged, and practically oriented local intellectual, whose normative horizon is laid out by an interpretation of Islam that is persistent in its critique of society (in Islamic terms, from a particular Salafi-oriented reformist position). His agenda is insistent on social change, yet at the same time, his attitude in pursuing this is calm and patient, informed by a rich understanding of society from within, as a compassionate peer. Mau refrains from seeking to impose his position upon others and instead rather pursues pathways of personal role-modeling and persuasion through practice. Trust in truth and the ultimate prevalence of one's position, and a steadfast resilience to adhere to it in the face of the current situation—in which other positions dominate—characterize his stance.

Our impression is that a conscious sense of the social value of and need for interacting (*kuwasiliana*) properly underpins Mau's position, which further means that an emphasis on egalitarian interaction fundamentally informs and underpins his activities. It is in this sense that an understanding of him as *mtu wa watu*, a man of the people—someone who is defined by his qualities of socializing with people on an equal level, of being among them—is presented here.

For such a focus on active performance in social interaction as a lead criterion also in terms of the authority attributed to a sheikh, the Swahili terms *kitendo* and *maweko* reflect a crucial conceptual importance here. *Kitendo* (as explained) is an established term denoting an "act," "deed," or "performance" that has a strong ethical connotation—in that it is used to contrast "deeds" (*vitendo*), as illustrative and telling evidence of one's position, with "words" (*maneno*), which may often be empty declarations. *Maweko* (from -*jiweka*, "to put oneself in a position"; -*weka*, "to put something somewhere"), then, carries the meaning of "composure" or "self-presentation." How one's actions are being presented and carried out in public, before others and in relation to one's knowledge, verbal expressions, and other qualities, is what matters; this is what people emphasize when they point to the *maweko* of a person. In conceiving Ustadh Mau's self-understanding, and his emphasis on the importance of social relationships as a fundamental reference point for his engagement also as imam, we think this is crucial. Next to other dimensions often included or invoked in the assessment of authority, like knowledge and education (*ujuzi*; *elimu*) or descent, this term stands for a performative approach that (as such) re-emphasizes social equality and egalitarianism.

Looking at Ustadh Mau as a contemporary example of a locally influential Muslim reformer on the northern Swahili coast, and proceeding from the reflections presented here, one may be compelled to acknowledge that "character matters" as a source of (and for) authority and respect within the community. This captures an insight, or a fundamental principle, that also seems generally understandable and similarly applicable to other lifeworlds across the globe as well, including our own, respectively—whether in the global North or the global South.

Acknowledgements

We would like to thank, most of all, Ustadh Mau himself for his ongoing attention to and patience for our interests; he has graciously read and approved the finalized draft of this text. We also sincerely thank *marehemu* Ustadh Harith, and *marehemu* Ustadh Msallam, who are both sorely missed; and Ahmed Msallam, as well as all our other conversation partners in Lamu, Mombasa, Nairobi, and elsewhere. We thank Clarissa Vierke and Annachiara Raia for the invitation to contribute to this volume, and Jasmin Mahazi and Joy Adapon for their comments and critical questions, as well as the participants of the Islam in Africa workshop in Berlin. For funding various travels to Lamu and Kenya over the years, Kai Kresse acknowledges the support of the DAAD, SOAS, University of St Andrews, DFG, BMBF, Columbia University, Leibniz-Zentrum Moderner Orient, and Freie Universität Berlin.

References

Amidu, Assibi A. *Kimwondo: A Kiswahili Electoral Contest*. Vienna: Afro-Pub, 1990.

Bakari, M. "Sayyid Omar Abdalla (1919–1988): The Forgotten Muslim Humanist and Public Intellectual." In *The Global Worlds of the Swahili: Interfaces of Islam, Identity and Space in 19th and 20th Century East Africa*, edited by Roman Loimeier and Rüdiger Seesemann, 363–388. Berlin: Lit-Verlag, 2006.

Bakari, M. *The Sage of Moroni: The Intellectual Biography of Sayyid Omar Abdallah, A Forgotten Muslim Public Intellectual*. Nairobi: Kenya Literature Bureau, 2018.

Bang, Anne. *Sufis and Scholars of the Sea: Family Networks in East Africa, 1860–1925*. London: Routledge, 2003.

Biersteker, Ann. *Kujibizana: Questions of Language and Power in 19th- and 20th-Century Poetry in Kiswahili*. East Lansing: Michigan State University Press, 1996.

Hillewaert, Sarah. "'Whoever Leaves Their Tradition Is a Slave': Contemporary Notions of Servitude in an East African Town." *Africa* 86, no. 3 (2016): 425–446.

Hillewaert, Sarah. *Morality at the Margins: Youth, Language, and Islam in Coastal Kenya*. New York: Fordham University Press, 2020.

Huie, Wade. "This Fine Poet from Lamu Bakes Bread That Is Tamu." *Daily Nation* (February 8, 1980).

Jimale, Ahmed. "Of Poets and Shaykhs: Somali Literature." In *Faces of Islam in African Literature*, edited by Kenneth W. Harrow, 279–309. London: James Currey, 1991.

Knote, Lotte. "The Promise of the Lamu Port: An Island Facing Change at the Margins of the Kenyan Nation." MA diss., Freie Universität Berlin, 2018.

Kresse, Kai. "Debating maulidi", in R. Loimeier and R. Seesemann (eds), *The Global Worlds of the Swahili*. Berlin Lit-Verlag, 2006,

Kresse, Kai. *Philosophising in Mombasa: Knowledge, Islam and Intellectual Practice on the Swahili Coast*. Edinburgh: Edinburgh University Press, 2007.

Kresse, Kai. "The Uses of History", in E. Simpson and K. Kresse (eds), *Struggling with History: Islam and Cosmopolitanism in the Western Indian Ocean*. New York: Columbia University Press, 2008.

Kresse, Kai. "Knowledge and Intellectual Practice in a Swahili Context: 'Wisdom' and the Social Dimensions of Knowledge." In "Knowledge in Practice: Expertise and the Transmission of Knowledge," edited by K. Kresse and T. Marchand. Special issue, *Africa* 79, no. 1 (2009): 148–167.

Kresse, Kai. "Enduring Relevance: Samples of Oral Poetry on the Swahili Coast." *Wasafiri* 26, no. 2 (2011): 46–49.

Kresse, Kai. "On the Skills to Navigate the World, and Religion, for Coastal Muslims in Kenya." In *Articulating Islam: Anthropological Approaches to Muslim Worlds*, edited by M. Marsden and K. Retsikas, 77–99. Amsterdam: Springer Press, 2013.

Kresse, Kai, ed. *Guidance (Uwongozi) by Sheikh Al-Amin Mazrui: Selections from the First Swahili Islamic Newspaper.* Translated by Kai Kresse and Hassan Mwakimako. Leiden: Brill, 2017.

Kresse, Kai. *Swahili Muslim Publics and Postcolonial Experience.* Bloomington: Indiana University Press, 2018.

Alamin & Kassim Mazrui. "Foreword." In *Guidance* (Uwongozi) *by Sheikh Al-Amin Mazrui: Selections from the First Swahili Islamic Newspaper,* edited by Kai Kresse, translated by Kai Kresse and Hassan Mwakimako, IX–XII Leiden: Brill, 2017.

Lacunza Balda, Justo. "Translations of the Qur'an into Swahili, and Contemporary Islamic Revival in East Africa." In *African Islam and Islam in Africa,* edited by D. Westerlund and E.E. Rosander, 95–126. London: Hurst, 1997.

Lamu Youth Alliance. "Friday Preach on COVID19." April 6, 2020. YouTube clip, 19:09. https://www.youtube.com/watch?v=j7PpAmiU72E.

Loimeier, R. *Between Social Skills and Marketable Skills: The Politics of Islamic Education in 20th Century Zanzibar.* Leiden: Brill, 2009.

Mahazi, Jasmin. "An Anthropology of Vave—A Bajuni Farmers' Ritual on the Swahili Coast." PhD diss., Freie Universität Berlin, 2018.

Matthews, Nathaniel. "Imagining Arab Communities: Colonialism, Islamic Reform, and Arab Identity in Mombasa, 1897–1933." *Islamic Africa* 4, no. 2 (2013): 135–163.

Ndzovu, Hassan. *Muslim in Kenyan Politics.* Evanston: Northwestern University Press, 2014.

Pouwels, R.L. "Sheikh al-Amin bin Ali Mazrui and Islamic Modernism in East Africa, 1875–1947." *International Journal of Middle Eastern Studies* 13, no. 3 (1981): 329–345.

Romero, Patricia. *Lamu: History, Society, and Family in an East African Port City.* Princeton, NJ: Markus Wiener, 1997.

Salvadori, C. *Through Open Doors: A View of Asian Cultures in Kenya.* Nairobi: Kenway Publications, 1989.

Salvadori, C. *We Came in Dhows.* Vol. 1. Nairobi: Paperchase Kenya Limited, 1996.

Samsom, Ridder. "Tungo za kujibizana: 'Kuambizana ni sifa ya kupendana.'" *Swahili Forum* 3 (1996): 1–10.

Swaleh, Kadara. "Islamic Proselytising between Lamu and Mozambique: The Case of Kizingitini Village." *Social Dynamics* 38, no. 3 (2012): 398–348.

Swaleh, Kadara. "What Does Philosophy Want: A Swahili Poem by Sheikh Ahmad Msallam of Lamu, Kenya." *Annual Review of Islam in Africa* 12, no. 2 (2013/2014): 79–84.

Timammy, Rayya. "Shaykh Mahmoud Abdulkadir 'Mau': A Reformist Preacher in Lamu." *Annual Review of Islam in Africa* 12, no. 2 (2015): 85–90.

Zein, A.H. el-. *The Sacred Meadows: A Structural Analysis of Religious Symbolism in an East African Town.* Evanston, Ill.: Northwestern University Press, 1974.

FIGURE 4   The District Commissioner awards Ustadh Mahmoud Mau a medal for his outstanding commitment for education on the Kenyan Jamhuri Day

Shaping and Being Shaped by Lamu Society: Ustadh Mau's Poetry in the Context of Swahili Poetic Practice

Jasmin Mahazi

As a father, Qurʾānic schoolteacher, chairman of the Lamu Muslim Youth, and speaker of the Education Trust Committee; as an imam, preacher, and poet, Mahmoud A. Mau not only illuminates, teaches, and molds society, but is himself shaped by the particularities of the society into which he was born. This essay shall provide background information about the conventions of language use, textual production, and speaking conventions of Lamu society in which Ustadh Mau has lived and worked most of his lifetime.[1]

In Lamu society, poetic discourse is prevalent in everyday speech; moreover, proper conduct in Islamic life and one's manner of speaking are necessarily intertwined. *Utendi* poems such as Ustadh Mau's *Ramani ya ndoa* (2006) and *Wasiya wa mabanati* (1974), as well as those by other contemporary poets, and even older ones such as the nineteenth-century *Utendi wa Mwana Kupona*, were composed to be taught at home and/or in Qurʾānic schools to instruct adolescents on how to respectfully interact with one another in their upcoming adulthood, and especially how to verbally interact with their spouses in their future marital lives.[2] These poems, together with other verbal art forms such as songs, verses, and proverbs, are, however, not only a means of teaching proper

---

1   Acknowledgement: This essay is heavily based on my PhD project, which investigated the agricultural Vave oral literary genre through the anthropology of text and the Islamic discursive tradition; on these approaches, see, respectively, Karin Barber, *The Anthropology of Texts, Persons and Publics: Oral and Written Culture in Africa and Beyond* (Cambridge: Cambridge University Press, 2007) and Talal Asad, *The Idea of an Anthropology of Islam*, Occasional Paper Series (Washington, DC: Center for Contemporary Arab Studies, Georgetown University, 1986). The observations are based mainly on the research I conducted in the Lamu archipelago between 2011 and 2014. I owe thanks to the people of Lamu and the Lamu archipelago at large who opened my senses to perceiving and understanding oral texts. The analysis, perspectives, and errors in this essay, for which I take responsibility, are solely mine.

2   In a YouTube video clip, two former neighbors in Mtaamwini/Lamu play the role of husband and wife, demonstrating how couples in Lamu conversed with each other through poetry in former times: https://www.youtube.com/watch?v=TdSs-Ks4zms (accessed September 1, 2022).

© JASMIN MAHAZI, 2023 | DOI:10.1163/9789004525726_004

This is an open access chapter distributed under the terms of the CC BY-NC-ND 4.0 license.

parlance or verbal interaction, but are themselves the products of respectful and proper communication.[3]

Poetic discourse is prevalent in Lamu because two fundamental paradigms of social interaction form the basis of a particular style of poetic communicative behavior and language use. These paradigms are *sitara* (modesty/concealment/protection) and *heshima* (honor/respect). In addition to poetry's function of teaching practical wisdom for life, it also has a role in conveying conflictual sentiments that may not be voiced explicitly in ordinary speech. The Swahili have the notion that conflictual sentiments, discontent, and denial may only be conveyed implicitly, through poetic art forms, in order to maintain one's modesty (*sitara*) and respect (*heshima*) as a fellow Muslim.[4]

Several authors have commented on the paradigm of *sitara* and *heshima* among the Swahili.[5] These paradigms not only refer to women and clothing in Muslim societies, but concern all aspects of life.[6] In Swahili communities, "modest concealment" is likewise applied in communication or verbal social interaction.[7] The verb *kusitiri* means to conceal, to veil, or to safeguard from being judged as having done something shameful, i.e. to safeguard one's honor

---

3 Longer poems, such as the didactic poems of the *utendi* genre, are also preserved in writing; some of these were composed as long ago as the eighteenth and nineteenth centuries, but were still taught in Qurʾānic schools as little as twenty years ago, such as the abovementioned nineteenth-century didactic poem *Mwana Kupona*.

4 Ibrahim Noor Shariff, *Tungo zetu: Msingi wa mashairi na tungo nyinginezo* (Trenton, NJ: Red Sea Press, 1988), 81. In a similar way, Lila Abu-Lughod has outlined how Bedouin women use poetic speech to express sentiments such as vulnerability and weakness, which if expressed in ordinary (social life) discourse would be inappropriate, according to the people's ideology of social life (i.e., basic cultural notions about one's society, social relations, and the individual). See Lila Abu-Lughod, *Veiled Sentiments: Honor and Poetry in a Bedouin Society* (Los Angeles: University of California Press, 1986).

5 Kjersti Larsen, *Where Humans and Spirits Meet: The Politics of Rituals and Identified Spirits in Zanzibar* (New York: Berghahn Books, 2008); John Middleton, The World of the Swahili: An African Mercantile Civilization (London: Yale University Press, 1992); David Parkin, Continuity and Autonomy in Swahili Communities: Inland Influences and Strategies of Self-Determination (London: School of Oriental & African Studies, 1995); J. Marc Swartz, The Way the World is: Cultural Processes and Social Relations Among the Mombasa Swahili (Los Angeles: University of California Press, 1991).

6 See also Rose Marie Beck, *Zeigen ist Gold: Zur Definition einer kommunikativen Gattung in afrikanischen Gesellschaften, Working Papers on African Societies 41* (Berlin: Das Arabische Buch, 2000); Rose Marie Beck, *Texte auf Textilien in Ostafrika: Sprichwörtlichkeit als Eigenschaft ambiger Kommunikation* (Cologne: Rüdiger Köppe, 2001); Minou Fuglesang, Veils and Videos: Female Youth Culture on the Kenyan Coast (Stockholm: Stockholm Studies in Social Anthropology, 1994); and Paola Ivanov, Die Verkörperung der Welt: Ästhetik, Raum und Gesellschaft im islamischen Sansibar (Berlin: Reimer Verlag, 2020).

7 Beck, *Zeigen ist Gold* and *Texte auf Textilien*; Ivanov, *Die Verkörperung der Welt*.

and respect, or as Ivanov says, "das Wahren des sozialen Gesichts."[8] One means by which to achieve such veiling in language is indirectness and ambiguity,[9] which is accomplished through the aesthetic styling of language, i.e. through verbal art forms such as proverbs, preexisting texts, and metaphors. Indeed, the Swahili regard this "veiled language" (*verschleierte Sprache*) as the highest aesthetic ideal.[10] Using "veiled language" is a modest way of communicating immodest sentiments.[11] So why is denial, negation, disagreement, or contradiction considered immodest? This is because one of the central ethical principles of Muslim societies is to discipline the tongue by using a "good," "fine," or "pure speech" that does not annoy or hurt others. The virtue of utilizing the "purest of speeches" is concretely invoked in several *āyāt* of the Qur'ān (sura/*āyāt* 4:148, 17:53, 22:24). For instance, God ordered the Messenger[SAW] to teach all Muslims:

> Say to My servants that they should (only) say those things that are best: For Satan doth sow dissensions among them: for Satan is to Man an avowed enemy.
>
> Qur'ān 17:52

It is also proclaimed:

> For they have been guided (in this life) to the purest of speeches; they have been guided to the Path of Him who is Worthy of (all) Praise.
>
> Qur'ān 22:24

In this latter *āyah*, it is stated that those who, in this life, guard their speech by pronouncing only good things shall be among those who enter paradise. Among the predominantly oral Swahili, the virtue of "good speech" is regarded

---

8   Ivanov, *Die Verkörperung der Welt*. The translation of the German statement would be "the maintaining of one's social face." This means that things are considered shameful in particular contexts depending on who the judging audience is. Usually, separate judging audiences are gender- and generation-segregated, but also distinguished by other categories. The complexity of this issue is outlined in ibid.

9   Beck, *Texte auf Textilien*, 110.

10 Ivanov, *Die Verkörperung der Welt*.

11 Cf. Abu-Lughod, *Veiled Sentiments*, 240 and D.F. Reynolds, *Heroic Poets, Poetic Heroes: The Ethnography of Performance in an Arabic Oral Epic Tradition* (Ithaca, NY: Cornell University Press, 1995). Similarly, Reynolds (*Heroic Poets*, 149), in the context of Egypt, talks about the *shakwa* theme (rhetorically structured complaints), which represents a poetic discourse in which one may express feelings and emotions that would be dishonorable to express in action or in everyday speech; see also Abu-Lughod, *Veiled Sentiments*.

as one of the most important virtues; a virtue that is thus consistently cultivated. On the other hand, it is at the same time the responsibility and moral obligation of all Muslims to guide each other by "commanding right and forbidding wrong," i.e. to remind and correct one another in order to lead one another to the "right path."[12] By holding fast to a way of polite and poetic speech that veils criticism through diverse literary devices, a Muslim can accomplish these two apparently contradictory demands: namely, being responsible for another's moral condition, that is, criticizing someone (e.g., for one's loose moral behavior) while not actually voicing any complaints or negative words, but couching them in euphemisms, which fulfills her/his duty of maintaining accord, harmony, and unity among mankind.

In general, the Swahili are said to be famous for composing on-the-spot,[13] which is due to the fact that expressions of dislike and discontent can only be voiced through poetic speech, not through ordinary speech. This has resulted in two interdependent discourses: poetic discourse and the discourse of ordinary social life.[14] As sentiments of negation, denial, dislike, disagreement, discontent, or contradiction are inappropriate to express in the discourse of ordinary speech, but ultimately unavoidable in social interaction, the Swahili have found a way of expressing them without violating their notions, namely by embedding these negative sentiments in a more detached, impersonal, and euphemistic speech; and by conversing in metaphorically saturated, obscure or ambiguous, and improvised or preexisting text forms such as poems, song verses, and proverbs.[15] These kinds of figures of speech conceal the negative content of what is being said, and foster the speaker's detachment from what she or he says.[16]

Although the practice of spontaneous poetic composition is receding in Lamu, preexisting texts such as song verses, poems, and proverbs continue to be inserted into the discourse of ordinary social interaction when sentiments of dislike or denial have to be expressed. Using the negative form is still considered impolite; thus, one will say "yes," although she or he means "no." One who is

---

12 Michael Cook, *Commanding Right and Forbidding Wrong in Islamic Thought* (Cambridge: Cambridge University Press, 2000). See also Kai Kresse, "'Swahili Enlightenment'? East African Reformist Discourse at the Turning Point: The Example of Sheikh Muhammad Kasim Mazrui," *Journal of Religion in Africa* 33, no. 3 (2003): 296.

13 Shariff, *Tungo zetu*, 76.

14 Cf. Abu-Lughod, *Veiled Sentiments*.

15 Beck, *Texte auf Textilien*.

16 The rigid form of verse and its high degree of conventional structure, also in formulaic language, affords a certain level of protection to the individual who is expressing "deviant" sentiments of dishonor and immodesty (cf. Abu-Lughod, *Veiled Sentiments*, 239).

not accustomed to the interplay of these two distinct but interdependent discourses within the same speech act might easily accuse one's conversation partner of being mendacious or hypocritical.[17] According to Western values, this way of speaking is often condemned as hypocritical behavior. Many Swahili, on the other hand, think of Western speech and manners of expression as too direct, harsh, or rude. Spontaneously recited oral art forms in ordinary speech are there to veil "deviant" sentiments, and should therefore be recognized as a form of discourse well integrated into a people's social life.[18]

Among the Swahili, poetry is an immensely rich and important field of social discourse.[19] Communicating in verse is associated with good manners (*heshima na adabu*)—a notion most obviously influenced by Middle Eastern culture. In Arabic, the term *adab* is used not only for the concept of literature or oral literary art forms, but also for education and a person's good conduct, good manners, and discipline: that is, everything entailing how a person should be.[20] Speech is therefore seen as one of the most important fields of knowledge that a Swahili should acquire and cultivate in order to become a respectful member of his/her society (i.e., *muungwana/mstaarabu*).

The Swahili regard the use of "polite" language as a way of practicing Islam, and vice versa; if one uses more direct or even insulting language, it is regarded as violating the Islamic faith. Islam is not only a way of living or walking,[21] but also a way of talking. In Lamu society, conflicts are dealt with or resolved through verbal art forms. Since expressions of discomfort, disagreement, or contradiction usually derive from or generate conflict situations, verbal compositions—which are created in order to sustain the ideology of modesty—have the characteristics of a call-and-response speech act. Thus, criticism is not a

---

17   Steven C. Caton also states that "truth" is merely alluded to: "Although it is important to be truthful and reliable, it is not necessarily a virtue to be frank and outspoken. In fact, a premium is put on the ability to allude to the truth rather than state it baldly. At the same time, the auditor has to be able to read between the lines, as it were, or infer the speaker's intentions and references, for these are rarely spelled out." See Caton, *"Peaks of Yemen I Summon": Poetry as Cultural Practice in a North Yemeni Tribe* (Berkeley: University of California Press, 1990), 36.

18   Cf. Abu-Lughod, *Veiled Sentiments*, 28.

19   Kai Kresse, *Philosophising in Mombasa: Knowledge, Islam and Intellectual Practice on the Swahili Coast* (Edinburgh: Edinburgh University Press, 2007); "Enduring Relevance: Samples of Oral Poetry on the Swahili Coast," *Wasafiri* 26, no. 2 (2011): 46–49.

20   Zachary Wright, Living Knowledge in West African Islam. The Sufi Community of Ibrahim Niasse (Leiden: Brill, 2015), 14.

21   Michael Gilsenan comes to the conclusion that his kind of walking differed considerably from the kind of walking of his interlocutors and friends in Lebanon. See Gilsenan, *Recognizing Islam: Religion and Society in the Modern Middle East* (New York: I.B. Tauris, 1982).

one-sided assault, but invites argumentative exchange.[22] This argumentative exchange is called *kujibizana* (composing in a call-and-response dialogue), and is regarded as a much-valued rhetorical device (see also the poems *Mchezo wa kuigiza* and *Jilbabu* in this anthology, which are composed in dialogue form). Thus, whenever a song or poem is voiced, the Swahili listener automatically presumes two things: there is a conflict, and this composition must be either a provocation or a response to some foregoing incitement. In most cases, one has to know the context to understand a poetic composition.

Poems that emerge from a personal conflict are not transmitted directly between the two individuals involved. Although the conflict has already been rendered detached and impersonal, most of the time, a transmitter or middleman is needed to convey the poem from the composer to the accused. Personal conflicts are mostly resolved through short, improvised or preexisting verbal text forms, and communal conflicts mostly through longer poems or songs that are uttered in a more public sphere, such as at weddings, funerals, political rallies, and during cultural or religious festivities and rituals.

The idiom of on-the-spot improvised poetry has vanished over time, especially due to formal education among the younger generations. As Kresse, who works on intellectual practice among the Swahili, says, "(F)ew Swahili poems or poets seem to be known to those in their teens and twenties. This marks a great cultural decline from the times, still remembered by the elderly, when practically everyone knew how to compose poetry."[23]

Especially in a society in which, due to modern formal education, composing on the spot is in decline, yet the notions of "pure speech" and "commanding the right and forbidding the wrong" are still of utmost importance, creative and versatile people like Ustadh Mau are important figures. Ustadh Mau not only composes longer didactic poems, but also composes on commission for people who are not as creative and versatile as he is, but who still feel the need to express something in a more polite, pure, and poetic language. The composition of poetry is especially still prevalent in the field of social events, such as weddings, funerals, and birth or name-giving ceremonies, for which many approach people like Ustadh Mau to compose pieces for their personal needs (see the poems *Jilbabu* and *Mola zidisha Baraka* in this anthology).

Cultivating the virtue of "pure speech," which gave rise to the particularly Swahili way of conversing through oral poetic art forms, contains the characteristics of various verse forms and the call-and-response speech act. These oral art

---

22   See also Asad, *Anthropology of Islam*, 232.

23   Kresse, *Philosophising in Mombasa*, 71.

forms, which are discursive and negotiative, are mostly performed and voiced on different communal occasions such as celebrations and rituals. Mohamed H. Abdulaziz gives the example of *gungu*, a great oration dance held at weddings and other important social and political occasions in Lamu, at which "[t]he poets would meet and challenge one another in the art of composing *mashairi*. Almost the whole town would attend these dances. It was a suitable occasion for the poet-sages not only to entertain their audience, but also to exchange ideas, and seek advice from one another, as happened in this case."[24]

Any communal occasion is also a platform for voicing social, political, or religious criticism and/or negotiating about controversial issues in a manner that reflects the people's standard moral way of conversing, i.e. through poetry. *Nyimbo* (sung poems/songs) are used to communicate and negotiate political affairs and other matters, while the *mashairi* (recited poems) that Abdulaziz mentions and the *utendi* (didactic poetry) genre in which Ustadh Mau most often composes are used to elicit religious criticism or to provide a response to previous religious criticism; thus, these genres are more closely associated with theological debates.[25]

In particular, public speech must conform to *heshima* and *adabu*:[26]

> Allah loveth not the shouting of evil words in public speech, except by one who has been wronged, for Allah is He who heareth and knoweth all things.
>
> Qurʾān 4:148

In 1975, for the first time, Ustadh Mau composed poems for election campaigns and the selection of candidates for the parliamentary seat of Lamu East. Ustadh Mau's poem *Kimwondo* ("Shooting Star," 1975) is named after the genre in which it was composed. The genre of poetry called *kimwondo* was part of the political debate in Lamu at that time (Amidu 1993). Amidu describes the satirical genre as a genre that "leads to inner self-examination and questions about the propriety of one's social, religious and political order and conduct." The *kimwondo*

---

24   Mohamed H. Abdulaziz, *Muyaka: 19th Century Swahili Popular Poetry* (Nairobi: Kenya Literature Bureau, 1979), 118.

25   Ann Biersteker, *Kujibizana: Questions of Language and Power in 19th- and 20th-Century Poetry in Kiswahili* (East Lansing: Michigan University Press, 1996), 234.

26   Official occasions such as the inauguration of groups, societies, or the opening meetings of conferences and workshops also always include the recitation of a poem that was specifically composed for the respective occasion (see Ustadh Mau's poems *Tupigeni makamama, Bandari ina mawimbi, Mwalimu, Kilio huliya mwenye,* and *Za Washirazi athari* in this anthology).

genre was utilized as an effective means of participating in the electoral process of the country, by which members of Parliament are elected as leaders of the Lamu East Constituency/County.[27] As Amidu says of this genre, it is "a political, social and religious whip. It is used in both a satirical and serious manner to bring political, social and religious deviants down to earth where common sense prevails. The Kimondo is also a vein for deep political and philosophical thought about the world and the behaviour of its peoples."[28]

Beyond these kinds of political issues, Ustadh Mau's poems address pressing social issues, such as excessive *khat* chewing (*Mukhadirat*, 2009) and AIDS (*Ukimwi ni zimwi, Mwenye ukimwi si mwanga*, and *Tahadhari na ukimwi*, all composed in the 1990s). Ustadh Mau's poetic guidance also includes the condemnation of moral decay and the appeal to proper religious conduct, thought, and behavior. Considering his repertoire of poems of critique, guidance, and advice to be a form of poetic discourse, Ustadh Mau fulfills God's demand of negotiating and counseling among each other.

Ustadh Mau not only contributes as a poet to the Muslim social obligations of "commanding the right and forbidding the wrong" by utilizing "pure speech"; as an imam, he carries a double weight of responsibility, offering moral advice to his fellow Muslims through sermons and religious lectures. The Friday sermon (*khutba*) in particular is regarded as an institutionalized tradition of social criticism.[29] Morally corrective criticism or giving moral advice (*nasiha*) is a concept of central importance in Islamic moral theology.[30] According to Asad:

> *Nasiha* signifies advice that is given for someone's good, honestly and faithfully. It also has the meaning of sincerity, integrity, and doing justice to a situation. *Nasiha*, then, is much more than an expression of good intention on the part of the advice giver (*nasih*): since in this context it carries the sense of offering moral advice to an erring fellow Muslim (*mansuh*), it is at once an obligation to be fulfilled and a virtue to be cultivated by all Muslims. Thus, in the context of the sermons and religious lectures under discussion here, *nasiha* refers specifically to morally corrective criticism.[31]

---

27   Assibi Amidu, "Lessons from Kimondo: An Aspect of Kiswahili Culture," *Nordic Journal of African Studies* 2, no. 1 (1993): 35.

28   Ibid.

29   Talal Asad, *Genealogies of Religion* (Baltimore: Johns Hopkins University Press, 1993), 213.

30   Ibid., 214.

31   Ibid.

In contrast to the Enlightenment view, in which criticism is regarded as a *right, nasiha* directed at religious or political authorities is, among Muslims, regarded as the *duty* of every Muslim, ruler and subject alike.[32]

Ustadh Mau was the first imam in Lamu to deliver his Friday sermons in the Kiswahili language, with the aim that his listeners could fully understand and comprehend his advice; this fact only reflects Ustadh Mau's utmost sincerity, integrity, honesty, faithfulness, goodwill, and sense of justice when practicing his obligation of leading his fellow Muslims onto the "right path." Ustadh Mau is, indeed, a social philanthropist[33] who through his poetry shapes, and is himself shaped by, Lamu society.

References

Abdulaziz, Mohamed H. *Muyaka: 19th Century Swahili Popular Poetry.* Nairobi: Kenya Literature Bureau, 1979.

Abu-Lughod, Lila. *Veiled Sentiments: Honor and Poetry in a Bedouin Society.* Los Angeles: University of California Press, 1986.

Amidu, Assibi. "Lessons from Kimondo: An Aspect of Kiswahili Culture." *Nordic Journal of African Studies* no. 1 (1993): 34–55.

Asad, Talal. *The Idea of an Anthropology of Islam.* Occasional Paper Series. Washington, DC: Center for Contemporary Arab Studies, Georgetown University, 1986.

Asad, Talal. *Genealogies of Religion.* Baltimore: Johns Hopkins University Press, 1993.

Barber, Karin. *The Anthropology of Texts, Persons and Publics: Oral and Written Culture in Africa and Beyond.* Cambridge: Cambridge University Press, 2007.

Beck, Rose Marie. *... Zeigen ist Gold: Zur Definition einer kommunikativen Gattung in afrikanischen Gesellschaften. Working Papers on African Societies 41.* Berlin: Das Arabische Buch, 2000.

Beck, Rose Marie. *Texte auf Textilien in Ostafrika: Sprichwörtlichkeit als Eigenschaft ambiger Kommunikation.* Cologne: Rüdiger Köppe, 2001.

Biersteker, Ann. *Kujibizana: Questions of Language and Power in 19th- and 20th-Century Poetry in Kiswahili.* East Lansing: Michigan University Press, 1996.

Caton, Steven C. *"Peaks of Yemen I Summon": Poetry as Cultural Practice in a North Yemeni Tribe.* Berkeley: University of California Press, 1990.

Cook, Michael. *Commanding Right and Forbidding Wrong in Islamic Thought.* Cambridge: Cambridge University Press, 2000.

---

32   Ibid., 215.
33   See Raia, this volume, p. 72.

Fuglesang, Minou. *Veils and Videos: Female Youth Culture on the Kenyan Coast*. Stockholm: Stockholm Studies in Social Anthropology, 1994.

Gilsenan, Michael. *Recognizing Islam: Religion and Society in the Modern Middle East*. New York: I.B. Tauris, 1982.

General Presidency of Islamic Research and IFTA, eds. *The Holy Qurʾān: English Translation of the Meanings and Commentary*. Medina: King Fahd Complex for the Printing of the Holy Qurʾān, 1988.

Ivanov, Paola. *Die Verkörperung der Welt: Ästhetik, Raum und Gesellschaft im islamischen Sansibar*. Berlin: Reimer Verlag, 2020.

Kresse, Kai. "'Swahili Enlightenment'? East African Reformist Discourse at the Turning Point: The Example of Sheikh Muhammad Kasim Mazrui." *Journal of Religion in Africa* 33, no. 3 (2003): 279–309.

Kresse, Kai. *Philosophising in Mombasa: Knowledge, Islam and Intellectual Practice on the Swahili Coast*. Edinburgh: Edinburgh University Press, 2007.

Kresse, Kai. "Enduring Relevance: Samples of Oral Poetry on the Swahili Coast." *Wasafiri* 26, no. 2 (2011): 46–49.

Larsen, Kjersti. *Where Humans and Spirits Meet: The Politics of Rituals and Identified Spirits in Zanzibar*. New York: Berghahn Books, 2008.

Middleton, John. *The World of the Swahili: An African Mercantile Civilization*. London: Yale University Press, 1992.

Parkin, David. *Continuity and Autonomy in Swahili Communities: Inland Influences and Strategies of Self-Determination*. London: School of Oriental & African Studies, 1995.

Reynolds, D.F. *Heroic Poets, Poetic Heroes: The Ethnography of Performance in an Arabic Oral Epic Tradition*. Ithaca, NY: Cornell University Press, 1995.

Shariff, Ibrahim Noor. *Tungo zetu: Msingi wa mashairi na tungo nyinginezo*. Trenton, NJ: Red Sea Press, 1988.

Swartz, J. Marc. *The Way the World Is: Cultural Processes and Social Relations Among the Mombasa Swahili*. Los Angeles: University of California Press, 1991.

Wright, Zachary. *Living Knowledge in West African Islam. The Sufi Community of Ibrahim Niasse*. Leiden: Brill, 2015.

FIGURE 5   The poet at the entrance of his Asilia Bakery on Lamu in 2000

"Born on the Island": Situating Ustadh Mau's Poetic Practice in Context

Clarissa Vierke

Nimezawa kisiwani wala nde sikutoka
Masomo ni ya chuoni ndiyo niliyobahatika
Wala dufu siiyoni mbee ya wailimika

I was born on the island; never have I left it.
My education is that of the Qur'ānic school; that is what I have been
   blessed with.
I do not regard myself as worthless compared to those with a school
   education.

> *Kilio hulia mwenye*, "Change Begins at Home," stz. 21

1 The Context of Ustadh's Writing: The Island of Lamu and Its Challenges

Ustadh Maḥmoud Aḥmad Abdulkadir, more commonly known as Ustadh Mau, was born and grew up on the island of Lamu, around 250 kilometers north of Mombasa.[1] His life, works, and poetry are interwoven with the island, its grand intellectual history, and its complicated present in many ways, as this chapter is meant to show. Coming from one of the reputed ulama clans on Lamu, Ustadh ran a bakery there to earn his daily bread, but has also been an important teacher and preacher. He never left the island, as he proudly announces in the verse given above.[2] Born in February 1952,[3] when Kenya was still a British crown colony, Ustadh Mau was not allowed to attend a secular school, as

---

1   In the Kiamu dialect, Lamu is referred to as "Amu" (see also the poem of the same title). Due to a historical sound law, /l/ is dropped before a vowel.

2   There is one exception: He lived in Dar es Salaam for two years.

3   In his passport, his year of birth is printed as 1950. This is a (common) mistake, which occurred because he was only registered long after his birth, in 1967. In his poem *Haki za watoto*, he urges parents to register their children right after birth, which is part of the UN Convention on the Rights of the Child, but can also be considered a response to his own experience of struggling with bureaucracy when he was already a teenager.

© CLARISSA VIERKE, 2023 | DOI:10.1163/9789004525726_005

This is an open access chapter distributed under the terms of the CC BY-NC-ND 4.0 license.

his father was suspicious of them. Like many other *wanazuoni* (Islamic scholars), his father considered colonial schools with a strong Christian affinity a perfidious strategy to estrange children from Islam, with the ultimate goal of making them convert to Christianity. As the stanza in the chapter epigraph above also alludes, Ustadh Mau received all his education at the madrassa, from renowned scholars.[4] While he is conversant in Arabic and keeps many connections with scholars in the Arab world—in addition to reading Arabic books, which he collects in his library (see Annachiara Raia's contribution "Seeking *'ilm* on Lamu," in this volume)—he proudly identifies as Swahili, and more specifically as *mwamu*, a Lamuan: he was the first to deliver the Friday sermon in Swahili in order to reach a wider audience on the island. Believing in the importance of intellectual progress, educating people on the island is his chief priority. This has also prompted him to explore poetry as a means of reaching his own people, who come from a culture of recitation, where the chanted word in rhymed form counts more than prose texts in printed journals and books. All truly important matters need to be expressed poetry (see also Jasmin Mahazi's contribution in this volume).

In many ways, Ustadh Mau's practices, ambition, and outlook conflict with the present world, in which Lamu, which used to be an important hub in the Indian Ocean, a center of scholarship and trade, is a remote place at the margins of the Kenyan nation-state. Since independence, people have become increasingly poor. Recently, even the daily means of subsistence, like fish, have become scarce, and drop-out rates in schools are high. There is a longer, complicated history of tension, resentment, and suspicion between *bara*, the mainland, and *pwani*, the coast, which permeates much discourse on Lamu, a phenomenon that surfaces most conspicuously and morphs into different forms whenever there is a crisis. On the one hand, domination and marginalization are recurring topics: the mainland is accused of discriminating against Muslims; of deliberately neglecting to invest in infrastructure on the coast, like schools or hospitals; stealing land; and of letting job-seekers overrun the coast, so that no jobs are left for those from *pwani* (see the poem *Kiswahili*, stz. 8 and 9). For instance, the new deep-sea port that was supposed to link Kenya with Uganda and South Sudan—in which so much hope for new jobs was initially vested, and which led to a real-estate boom and enormous speculation—has caused heated debate. The poem *Bandari* ("Port") spells out these fears: it will not only destroy the environment, leave fishermen without subsistence, and disrupt local cultural habitats and traditions, but will also merely benefit

---

4   See also the contribution of Kai Kresse and Kadara Swaleh in this volume.

SITUATING USTADH MAU'S POETIC PRACTICE IN CONTEXT   43

the engineers and skilled workers from *bara* if islanders do not hasten to acquire the skills and diplomas necessary to compete.

Education has been in a crises. Many schoolteachers from *bara* come to teach on Lamu, not only because they are sent by the government, but also because not enough people on the island have a teaching diploma or have attended university. The nationalized curriculum has met with much disapproval; the schoolbooks are written by mainlanders, as Ustadh Mau complains in his poem *Kiswahili*.[5] Nowadays, pupils on the island, which considers itself a cradle of Swahili and is proud of its poetic tradition, are corrected if they use forms of Kiamu, the dialect of Lamu, in class—much to the dismay of their parents. But mainland influence is not only imposed by educators on the island, but also comes in through social media, radio programs, and increased mobility. Parents often frown on their children's use of Sheng, the urban vernacular of Nairobi, ubiquitous in popular music, as well as their habit of dressing in skirts, basketball shirts, and baseball caps and growing dreadlocks, which in their view is a sign of moral and cultural decay. Morality has become a matter of heated debate in the increasingly antagonistic culture of discourse.

The tension is not merely an intergenerational one; sometimes the older generation is even less dogmatic than the younger ones, who know exactly what falls under good Islamic practice and what does not. For instance, women of the younger generation on Lamu, whose education is of great concern for Ustadh, have not exchanged their veils for miniskirts; on the contrary, many younger women are encouraged or even pressured but are often also proud to wear the niqab, the face veil that leaves only the eyes exposed, as well as socks to cover their feet. They tend to shy away from handshakes and find that non-religious music should not be played in public, increasingly not allowing for any other ideas or practices. This development is also fostered by the growing strict Islamic reformist influence on the island, often referred to as Wahhabi, which has introduced strict notions of purity and seclusion compared to previous decades.[6] It is a global rhetoric that finds its application in a local context amid ever greater claims of superiority, seeking to silence other Islamic dis-

---

5   See stanza 9: Angaliya na zitabu zisomeshwao shuleni / hazandikwi na Rajabu si Sudi wala si Shani / Njoroge ndiyo katibu ashishiyeo sukani / Charo na wake wendani nao nyuma hufuwata ("Look at the textbooks that are studied at our schools. They are written neither by Rajabu, nor by Sudi, nor by Shani. The author is Njoroge; he is the helmsman. Charo and his colleagues follow").

6   On the growing aggressiveness and dogmatic nature of rhetoric and discussions on morally correct behavior, see Kai Kresse, *Philosophising in Mombasa: Knowledge, Islam and Intellectual Practice on the Swahili Coast* (Edinburgh: Edinburgh University Press, 2007), 101.

courses. It has been challenging the notions of unity based on inner-Islamic diversity that have been celebrated as a hallmark of Swahili Islam, and which Ustadh Mau also promotes.[7]

It goes without saying that the tensions on Lamu are not unrelated to the phenomenon of a wider world caught between fierce dichotomies, also resulting in terrorism, on the one hand, and discrimination against Islam and any kind of minority, on the other. In Lamuan public discourse, such tensions are often projected onto the abovementioned Kenyan dichotomy of *pwani* and *bara*, such that coastal Muslims are discredited as fanatics from a *bara* perspective, while the mainland and foremost center of power, Nairobi, is portrayed as economically and morally corrupt from a *pwani* perspective. Furthermore, many Lamuans also find confirmation of the dichotomy between the decadent West and "real Islam" with an increasing emphasis on purity in last decades, in the kind of tourism they are confronted with. Despite continued terror warnings due to attacks in neighboring Mokowe and Garissa some years ago—which still make Lamu part of a red zone to which many foreign ministries caution against travel—big hotel complexes on Lamu as well as Manda, the island opposite Lamu, attract upscale tourists in search of extraordinary luxury and, to a lesser extent, backpacker tourists who celebrate the world as a colorful playground meant for one's own self-experience. Both add to the fantasy of the rich and debauched West, which is constructed as antithetical to the downtrodden "rest." On the one hand, the tourism industry makes jobs such as waiter, watchman, beachboy, tourist guide, ice-cream seller, and reggae musician concrete and viable options for the youth of the island, where school education has ceased to hold the key to the future. On the other hand, hotels exploiting the island's natural resources while promoting drug abuse and promiscuity have been criticized by many, and have even stoked the hatred of some, who use a new vocabulary of disdain backed up with quotations from the Qur'ān.

These are just some of the contradictory tendencies and tensions on the island, which sometimes seem to be insurmountable and which find their echo in Ustadh Mau's writings and stances. The poet has been actively fighting against the decline of education. He is worried about Western media and consumer culture sweeping the island—a fear that is very pronounced in poems

---

7 For a critical discussion of the notion of Islamic unity, see the chapter "A Neighborhood of Thinkers" in Kai Kresse's book *Philosophising in Mombasa*. He shows that unity has also served as a leitmotif used to undermine longstanding historical differences. However, he also critically discusses the increasing dogmatism, which has reached a new peak in recent years, not allowing for divergence.

like *Kilio hulia mwenye* ("Change Begins at Home"), *Kiswahili*, and *Haki za watoto* ("Children's Rights"). When, in an interview in July 2019, Annachiara Raia asked the poet about his biggest fears, he answered that his worry is that one day, the Swahili will be a minority on Lamu and their culture and traditions will be lost forever. His position is a criticism of all-engulfing capitalism and neocolonial structures that no longer allow for cultural specifics, a morally decent lifestyle, or the beauty of local craftmanship.[8] Far from placing the blame solely on external influences, however, he also does not tire of blaming his own community for their lack of dedication to studying, vision for the future, and discipline. Relentlessly, he uses his sermons as well as his poetry to address all social ills, like HIV, drug abuse, child neglect, and teenage pregnancy, as well as the high rate of divorce on Lamu. His tone, however, is not one of moral superiority, anger, or punishment, but one of care, like a father worried about his children's well-being.[9] His voice is warm-hearted. His aim is not to establish a strict regime of morality, but rather to work toward a better future. It is his responsibility to try to do his best, as he says, since he has been privileged—not because he is rich, but because of his own skills and knowledge: "I feel that everybody has the right to be helped by me. For instance, through my knowledge, I can serve the community" (*Mimi nahisi kwamba kila mtu ana haki ya kufaidika na mimi, kwa mfano kwa maarifa yangu, huduma naweza kutoa*). His recognized social standing aids his efforts to intervene: "Lamu is a society where my voice can be heard and that it can reach" (*Lamu ni jamii ambapo sauti yangu inaweza kusikiwa na kufika*).

While Ustadh Mau's own poetic agenda is modernist in a number of respects, some of his practices—writing Swahili mostly in Arabic script, as well as keeping manuscript copies and books of Swahili poetry composed in other eras, when the island took great pride in its poets and institutions of learning—also have a nostalgic ring. Not many people are able to read Swahili in Arabic script any longer; many Swahili manuscripts are kept at libraries in Europe and the US rather than Lamu,[10] and, as Ustadh Mau laments in his poem *Kiswahili*,

---

8   It also has a slight ring of the dichotomies of "corrupt West versus good Islam" that figure in reformist writings of a less aggressive era, which have influenced Ustadh Mau, as we shall explore below.

9   On the prominence of his care and empathy, see also Clarissa Vierke's chapter "How Ought We to Live," in this volume.

10   See Clarissa Vierke, "Between the Lines: Life and Work of the Lamuan Artist and Cultural Broker Muhamadi Kijuma," in *Muhamadi Kijuma. Texts from the Dammann Papers and other Collections*, ed. Gudrun Miehe and Clarissa Vierke, Archiv afrikanistischer Manuskripte 9 (Cologne: Köppe, 2010), 41–62.

poetry is no longer undisputedly the most prestigious form of public speaking, in which the most respected members of society engage because they take pride in speaking eloquently. Ustadh Mau understands his poetic project, on the one hand, as an effort toward progress, but, on the other hand, also as a very conscious and deliberate "pursuit of an ongoing coherence"[11] with reference to discourse traditions and practices with a much longer history. I will consider some aspects of them in the following.

2 Ancestral Roots and Individual Routes: Situating Ustadh Mau's Engagement in Lamu's Intellectual History

Ustadh Mau's works place themselves in and pursue continuity with an intellectual tradition of poetry writing that was not introduced in state schools, but reached its height in the nineteenth century, before and partly parallel to the colonial era.[12] Lamu, now at the edge of the state's territory, used to be a thriving hub in the Indian Ocean, with flourishing scholarship, poetry, and trade. Assuming a predominant role in the region after defeating the neighboring city-state of Pate at the end of the eighteenth century, Lamu underwent a golden age. Growing under the tutelage of the Omani sultan, who had moved his throne to Zanzibar and with whom Lamu was allied, it proudly referred to itself as *Kiwandeo*, "The Island of Pride," until the beginning of the twentieth century.[13] It was renowned for its Islamic scholarship and its manuscript production, as well as for the beauty of its musical culture and the depth of its poetry.[14]

---

11   Samira Haj, Reconfiguring Islamic Tradition: Reform, Rationality and Modernity. Cultural Memory in the Present (Palo Alto (Calif.): Stanford University Press, 2009), 5; I owe the reference to Samira Haj to Kai Kresse, who underlines the importance of discourse traditions—which I also find so essential to grasping coastal intellectual histories—in the introduction to his book, *Swahili Muslim Publics and Postcolonial Experience:* Kai Kresse, *Swahili Muslim Publics and Postcolonial Experience* (Bloomington: Indiana University Press), 22.

12   Poetry is also taught at state schools, where, however, more often than not, it is an unpopular subject. It not only lacks prestige, but the strategies for approaching the subject are also mechanical from the point of view of many pupils.

13   For a history of Lamu at that time, see, for instance, Patricia Romero, *Lamu. History, Society and Family in an East African Port City* (Princeton, NJ: Princeton University Press, 1997).

14   See also Vierke, "Between the Lines" and "From across the Ocean: Considering Travelling Literary Figurations as Part of Swahili Intellectual History," *Journal of African Cultural Studies* 28, no. 2 (2016): 225–240.

The eighteenth and nineteenth century was also the time of an Islamic movement which made Swahili-language poetry the most prominent vehicle for spreading Islam, using it to express their religious zeal and attract new believers: Lamu thus became the center of a new kind of Islamic poetry, which did not merely supplant but rather added to preexisting, chiefly oral poetry.[15] Numerous new poems, many in *utendi* form, were committed to manuscripts, adapting a variety of Arabic hagiographic accounts for Swahili-speaking audiences.[16] In the eighteenth century, for instance, the *Utendi wa Tambuka* ("Poem of Tabuk"), which is often cited as the first Swahili *utendi*, depicted the battle of Tabuk, a legendary battle between early Muslims and the Byzantines, in a new form of Swahili prosody based on Arabic stanzaic forms.[17] At the end of the nineteenth century, the story of how the Prophet Yusuf was sold to the Egyptian pharaoh was adapted into Swahili, building on various Arabic sources,[18] and Mwana Kupona wrote her legendary didactic *utendi*, the *Utendi wa Mwana Kupona*,[19] to advise her daughter on married life—a poem Ustadh Mau frequently cites as a source of inspiration. It was in this context that on the proud island of Lamu, the most respected members of the ulama, well-versed in Arabic scholarship, also recited and wrote Swahili verse. Kiamu became a literary dialect used all along the coast, also by non-Kiamu speakers and as far south as Mozambique in an effort to buy into the glory and vividness of its poetic tradition.

The charismatic Sufi movement was spearheaded by the Alawiyya tariqa in Lamu and its networks, reaching from Southern Arabia, mostly the Hadhramawt, all throughout the Indian Ocean.[20] This widespread network connecting faraway communities on Indonesia, India, East Africa, and Arabia, which Ustadh Mau's ancestors were also part of, was based on and kept alive through kinship relations, trade, and scholarly exchange. Highly learned scholars of the

---

15 See also Vierke, "From across the Ocean."

16 On *utendi* form, see Jasmin Mahazi's contribution in this volume.

17 See e.g. Jan Knappert, "Het epos van Heraklios: Een proeve van Swahili poëzie. Tekst en vertaling, voorzien van inleiding, kritisch commentaar en aantekeningen" (PhD diss., Leiden University, 1958).

18 See Annachiara Raia, *Rewriting Yusuf. A Philological and Intertextual Study of a Swahili Islamic Manuscript Poem* (Cologne: Köppe, 2020). There is a lot of scholarly literature on Swahili poetry from Lamu. The best anthology of Swahili poetry from Lamu is still Ernst Dammann, *Dichtungen in der Lamu-Mundart des Suaheli: Gesammelt, herausgegeben und übersetzt von Ernst Dammann* (Hamburg: Friederichsen, De Gruyter & Co., 1940).

19 Alice Werner and William Hichens, *The Advice of Mwana Kupona upon the Wifely Duty*, The Azanian Classics 2 (Medstead: Azania Press, 1934).

20 Anne Bang, *Sufis and Scholars of the Sea: Family Networks in East Africa c. 1860–1925* (London: Routledge, 2003).

Alawiyya tariqa, whose heirs and their works would shape Ustadh Mau's own education and intellectual position, did not arrive on Lamu only in the eighteenth and nineteenth century, but earlier. However, it was at that time that migration from the Hadhramawt gained momentum and the most learned of them started an Islamic revival.[21] Their aim was to pass on Islamic knowledge to a broader part of society that had previously not had access to religious knowledge, since it was taught and discussed almost exclusively in Arabic—such that only a restricted community of learned scholars, who had traveled widely in pursuit of knowledge, could engage in it. The adherents of the Alawiyya tariqa, who were well read in Arabic and belonged to a social elite, explored Swahili poetic adaptations as a new means of reaching out to those without Arabic proficiency[22]—not unlike Ustadh Mau would later do.

Swahili had previously been used in teaching and commenting on Arabic texts, but from the eighteenth century onward, adapting Arabic texts into written Swahili poetry became an esteemed scholarly pursuit for sayyids of Hadhrami descent.[23] The first known translation is the *Hamziyya*, a translation of the Arabic poem *Umm al-Qurā* by the thirteenth-century Egyptian poet Muhammad ibn Saʿīd ul-Būsīrī into an archaic Swahili. The first manuscript of the Swahili translation is believed to have been written in 1749 by Sayyid ʿIdarusi bin Athman, a prominent theologian and scholar of Arabic from Pate, who made a line-by-line translation.[24] Other translations, like the *Maulidi Barzanji*[25] and the *Tabaraka*[26]—produced in the nineteenth century by the renowned *sharifu* Mwenye Mansab Al-Seyyid Abu Bakr bin Abdul Rahman al-Husseiny (1828–1922), who had studied in Mecca and the Hadhramawt—

---

21 Bang, *Sufis and Scholars*, 25.

22 See Bang, *Sufis and Scholars*, 31 and Bang, *Islamic Sufi Networks in the Western Indian Ocean (c. 1880–1940): Ripples of Reform* (Leiden: Brill, 2014), 111 ff.

23 Vierke, "From across the Ocean."

24 Lyndon Harries, "A Swahili Takhmis from the Swahili Arabic Text," *African Studies* 11, no. 2 (1952): 59–67. Hichens gives the date as 1792; see Jan Knappert, "The Hamziya Deciphered," *African Language Studies* 7 (1966): 53. Knappert even talks of a manuscript from 1652; see Knappert, "Swahili Literature in Arabic Script," *Manuscripts of the Middle East* 4 (1989): 74. For a published edition, see Knappert, "The Hamziya Deciphered." The oldest manuscript that has been traced was written by Athman bin al-Kadhi in 1792, and today forms part of the Hichens Collection in the SOAS archives.

25 Gustav Neuhaus, "Kitabu Mauludi. Buch der Geburt Muhammed's. Suaheli-Gedicht des Lamu-Mannes Scharifu Mansabu bin Scharifu Abdurrahmani al-Hussaini, Manuskript in arabischer Schrift, wiedergegeben in Autotypien, übersetzt und erläutert," *Mitteilungen des Seminars für Orientalische Sprachen* 38, no. 3 (1935): 145–201.

26 Ernst Dammann, "Die paränetische Suaheli-Dichtung Tabaraka," *Mitteilungen des Instituts für Orientforschung* 7, no. 3 (1960): 411–432.

became highly popular all along the East African coast.[27] Mwenye Mansab, whom Ustadh Mau's grandfather most probably met, composed a number of popular Swahili poems adapted from Arabic sources, like the mythological *Kishamia*,[28] which Ustadh Mau still greatly admires. Mwenye Mansab was an authority on classical Swahili poetry, "unrivalled in his knowledge of archaic Swahili";[29] he copied Swahili manuscripts and knew poems like the *Al-Inkishafi*, the masterful meditation on the downfall of Pate and the vanity of human life, by heart. The social prestige of figures like him bestowed further authority on the poems and made the composition of poetry a most virtuous activity. Poems from this era have become classics and common points of reference—a set of texts that are central to Swahili Muslim poetic practice and that Ustadh Mau looks to as a source of inspiration.[30]

Mwenye Mansab became the teacher of another important member of the Ba Alawi clan, who was venerated all along the East African coast for his intellectual and spiritual abilities: Salih bin Alawi Jamalil-Lail (1844–1935), commonly known as Habib Saleh, a close friend of Ustadh Mau's grandfather Abdulkadir Abdulatif. He was born on the Comoros, where intellectual, mercantile, and scholarly links to the Hadhramawt were strong. In his youth, he was sent to Lamu and began studying with Mwenye Mansab, who recognized his piety and intellect.[31] The critical student soon started questioning Islamic education, which, according to his view, was still too disproportionately run by and targeted to a social elite. He began a new reform movement around an institution he established in 1901, the famous Riyadha Mosque, which trained future qadis, "Quranic commentators and prayer leaders," just outside of town on Lamu.[32] The movement placed emphasis on the scriptural tradition, for which knowledge of Arabic and Islamic scholarship was a precondition.[33] While not revolutionary in tenets, canon, or topics, it challenged the established elite by valuing knowledge and granting teaching certification (*'ijaza*) even to those not belonging to a reputed clan, thereby promoting "social re-

---

27   Bang, *Islamic Sufi Networks*; Jan Knappert, *Swahili Islamic Poetry*, vol. 1 (Leiden: Brill, 1971).

28   Dammann, *Dichtungen in der Lamu-Mundart*.

29   William Hichens, *Al-Inkishafi: The Soul's Awakening* (London: Sheldon Press, 1939), 8.

30   For a reference to the *Al-Inkishafi* in one of Ustadh Mau's works, see, for instance, stz. 5 of *Kiswahili: Inkishafi ngaliya / Ukisome na kidani* ("Look at the *Al-Inkishafi*; read it attentively"). See also stz. 4 of the same poem for further reference to master poets.

31   See Kai Kresse, *Philosophising in Mombasa. Knowledge, Islam and Intellectual Practice at the Swahili Coast* (Edinburgh: Edinburgh University Press, 2007), 87 ff.

32   Bang, *Sufis and Scholars*, 146; see also 144 ff.

33   Ibid., 146.

stratification."[34] In a strongly hierarchical and partly feudal society, now even "slaves" (watumwa) and the underprivileged could become educated. Such a valuation of education and reading is also reflected in the figures of Ustadh Mau's forefathers and himself.

Ustadh Mau's grandfather, Abdulkadir Abdulatif—also of Yemeni ancestry, and whose life course largely followed Alawiyya networks of family links and scholarship—helped construct the Riyadha Mosque. He led a life that was shaped by and took its course along the lines of the far-reaching Yemeni connections described above: some of his forefathers "had probably gone to India on business and then married and settled there," as Ustadh Mau explains in an account of his Indian roots that Salvadori published in one of her compendia on the Indian diaspora of East Africa.[35] Abdulkadir Abdul Latif was born as part of the Surti community of Gujarat and grew up in Mohammed-Nagar[36] near Pune, already an important trade city in West India by the time India came under British rule.[37] Even before the Portuguese incursions, Sunni Merchants from the southern parts of the Arabian Peninsula (Hadhramawt and Oman) had settled all over the Indian Ocean area—in East India, parts of Kerala, Indonesia, Malaysia, and East Africa, including the Comoros.[38] They preserved their economic and social and religious ties with relatives, business partners, and scholars back in their home regions.[39] Religious networks, mostly concentrated on the Alawiyya brotherhood, and kinship ties added to or provided the basis for far-reaching trade connections from the Hadhramawt to India and East Africa. These networks also shaped the life of Ustadh Mau's grandfather: at the age of fourteen, he came to Zanzibar, the capital of the Omani Empire and the biggest trade hub in nineteenth-century East Africa. Following ties of kinship, he moved to Dar es Salaam, where he entered an arranged marriage with the daughter of a local Surti family. His new wife gave birth to a son named Abdurahman. After his wife passed away prematurely, he moved to Lamu, where he married his second wife, Hadija, Ustadh Mau's mother, whose

---

34 Ibid.

35 Cynthia Salvadori, *We Came in Dhows*, vol. 1 (Nairobi: Paperchase Kenya, 1996), 35.

36 Ibid.

37 The city of Surat, in southern Gujarat, has a long history as an important Muslim-dominated seaport in the Indian Ocean. Besides Ustadh Mau himself, Salvadori's work is a chief source of this account (*We Came in Dhows*, 35).

38 On the migration of high-ranking Hadhrami descendants of the Prophet to Gujarat, who then intermarried with local Indian families and occupied high positions in local Muslim communities, see also Ho Engseng, *The Graves of Tarim. Genealogy and Mobility across the Indian Ocean.* (Los Angeles: University of California, 2016), 167.

39 Bang, *Sufis and Scholars.*

father was of Indian descent and her mother of Comorian and Yemeni origin—like Habib Saleh, the charismatic leader of the Riyadha Mosque, who became a close friend of his grandfather.

Ustadh Mau's grandfather was a devout Muslim, helping to construct the Riyadha Mosque, for which he built the windows and brought lamps from India. His technical expertise as an engineer, his main profession, proved to be very helpful. Likewise, Ustadh Mau's father, Ahmad Abdulkadir Abdulatif (1915–1970), was not only a dedicated student of religion, but also became the local "engineer":[40] he maintained the district commissioner's boat and was the first to own a motorboat, which he used to transport people from the jetty in Mokowe, where the buses from Mombasa and Malindi stop nowadays, to the island of Lamu. Apart from that, he was a devout Muslim, who joined and supported Habib Saleh in teaching. Later on, Ustadh Mau's father and uncles played an important role in the mosque,[41] which also significantly influenced the poet's own socialization until he took a critical distance from it.

Apart from following the family tradition of becoming a learned Muslim, Ustadh Mau would likely have also become an engineer himself had he grown up in the household of his mother, Barka Aboud Mbarak (about 1938–2002), and father together with his five younger siblings. Instead, a young uncle who ran the Asilia bakery on Lamu adopted him, and also passed his profession on to him. His uncle's wife, Thinana bin Abdalla of Shela, had given birth to ten children, all of whom died at an early age. She took good care of the young Ustadh Mau at their house in the neighborhood of Mtamwini on Lamu. As in many Swahili houses, where the women are important teachers and pass on much essential knowledge, she taught him the Qurʾān before he even started attending madrassa. His uncle took him to the bakery as a child, giving him small tasks to do, like sweeping the floors or selling bread. Before inheriting Asilia bakery from his uncle, however, Ustadh Mau went to Dar es Salaam to work as a shopkeeper for two years, then spent time studying in up-country Kenya (see below) before finally returning to Lamu due to the untimely death of his father in the 1970s. He took over Asilia bakery at that time, which is still the only bakery on Lamu selling all kinds of pastry, bread, and cake. At the turn of the millennium, the bakery was no longer generating enough profit and almost went bankrupt—an economic crisis that he reflects on in the poem *Mlango*

---

40   See also Salvadori, *We Came in Dhows*, 35 and Ahmad Abdulkadir Mahmoud and Peter Frankl, "*Kiswahili*: A Poem by Mahmoud Ahmad Abdulkadir, to Which is Appended a List of the Poet's Compositions in Verse," *Swahili Forum* 20 (2013): 1.

41   Salvadori, *We Came in Dhows*, 35.

("The Door").[42] In the poem, he is still wondering whether closing the bakery would be an option, while in real life, he ultimately opted to shut it down for some time. When his first son, Fatih, came back from studying in Sudan, he managed to pay off his debts and reopened it before two of Fatih's brothers took it over. Nowadays, the bakery, which the whole family still depends on, is run by Ustadh Mau's son Yasri.

Early on, Ustadh Mau also became one of the most important Muslim leaders on the island. In 1985, at the age of 33, he was appointed imam of Pwani Mosque, Lamu's oldest mosque, dating back to the fourteenth century.[43] Ustadh Mau was the first to preach the Friday sermon in Swahili rather than in Arabic, as was common at that time, which not many people were able to understand. He still teaches at the madrassa and delivers lectures on Qur'ānic commentary and law (*fiqh*) during Ramadan. His engagement with the community has earned him much respect and recognition, and he has served on many boards and committees, like the Lamu District Education Board and the Lamu West Constituency AIDS Committee.[44]

With regard to his own education, as explained in greater detail in the contributions of Annachiara Raia and of Kai Kresse and Kadara Swaleh, Ustadh Mau did not attend the state school, but Al-Najah, the Islamic primary school. He briefly studied in Mombasa and at another reformist institute (*chuo*) in Machakos, in Kamba land, close to Nairobi, where three scholars from Saudi Arabia and Egypt taught Islamic studies. His hope was ultimately to study in the Middle East, like his intellectual role models and teachers.[45] However, after his father passed away suddenly, he lacked the means to continue studying.

On Lamu, one of his first and most important teachers was the renowned Sayyid Hassan Badawy, a grandson of Habib Saleh, who began his own learning and teaching career at Riyadha before ultimately also turning away from it, and was a close friend of Ustadh Mau's father.[46] Ustadh Mau is still a great admirer of his teacher, his humble character, and his manner of encouraging students as well as mediating conflicts. Thus, Ustadh Mau was also supposed to become part of the Riyadha tradition: "I was raised to become part of the tariqa of my teacher Sayyid Hassan" (*mimi niliinukiya nikiwa ni mtu wa tariqa ya mwalimu*

---

42 I also discuss the poem in my contribution "How Ought We to Live."

43 Mahmoud and Frankl, *Kiswahili*, 2.

44 See Mahmoud and Frankl, *Kiswahili*, 3.

45 See also his own account in speeches posted on YouTube: https://www.youtube.com/watch?v=5l8LhET8G0E (*Me on TV*).

46 See Kresse, *Philosophising in Mombasa*, 222.

wangu Sayyid Hassan). Ustadh Mau's father highlighted the agenda of Habib Saleh and earlier scholars of the tariqa, namely to acquire and spread a classical canon of knowledge to the whole *umma*, in the poem *Hapo zamani za yana* ("Once upon a Time"), which he wrote for his son.[47] One may also consider Ustadh Mau's own agenda—that of educating, reading, and teaching the Qur'ān and the established canon of scholarship, while at the same time making an effort to reach the whole community in a poetic language that speaks to it—to echo Habib Saleh's values of integration and unity.

Thus, one can scarcely understand Ustadh Mau's intellectual position, or his ideals for learning and teaching, not to mention the continuities and changes in his own poetic production and ideals, without taking the tariqa into perspective. Yet, tradition does not mean simply recapitulating previous beliefs, but rather offers a framework for constant reflection. Over the years, Ustadh Mau became more and more critical of the mystical Sufi tenets and practices, like saint cults and the visitation of graces, but also the elevation of a group of "holy men." These men were believed to have more *baraka* (literally "blessings"), could perform miracles, and offered teachings and exhortations;[48] in this context, knowledge was not abstractable from the person of the teacher, but depended on his *baraka* and the direct, sensory transmission of it. Scholars like Habib Saleh not only imparted knowledge but, being a descendant of the Prophet himself, also materialized part of his spiritual essence, which the students sought to buy into. Placing an emphasis on individual religious experience, the praise of the Prophet became a central part of new practices of religious worship, in which Habib Saleh played a central role. He became widely known all along the East African coast mostly for his Maulidi celebration, i.e. the celebration of the Prophet's birthday, featuring processions of Muslims chanting qasida in the streets of Lamu and often expanding into *ngoma* dance performances.[49] By reciting and singing of the Prophet's heroic life, the intention was not merely to teach about his life, but rather to immerse one's soul into his glory and earn his blessings.

---

47   The whole poem, replete with references to the Qur'ān, echoes the father's learnedness, also reminding the son not to draw a difference between "slaves" and "patricians", as for instance in stz. 42, where he tells his son: *Usihishimu mungwana / Ukadharau mtumwa* ("Do not respect the patrician / And despise the slave"). See also the poem of Ustadh Mau's father, *Hapo zamani ya yana*, in which he urges his son to treat the privileged and the downtrodden equally.

48   Bang, *Sufis and Scholars*.

49   Starting from the beginning of the twentieth century, Ustadh Mau's family still played an important role in decorating the mosque in the 1970s and 1980s (Salvadori, *We Came in Dhows*, 35).

Despite growing pressure from reformist factions, Maulidi still continues, largely also taking the form of a cultural festival that attracts Muslims from all over East Africa every year. Yet, already in the 1960s, the reformist scholar Harith Swaleh, whose modernist agenda advocated breaking away from established practices and canons, started to preach against the Maulidi, causing a heated debate, as Ustadh Mau himself remembers.[50] In contrast to the later aggressive and dogmatic tone of so-called Wahhabi rhetoric—supported both financially and ideologically by Saudi Arabia—the reformist influences on Lamu in the 1950s and 1960s, which had a huge influence on Ustadh Mau, had a more intellectual modernist agenda, believing in progress and striving to overcome what they considered backward superstitions, like belief in magic or the visitation of graves.[51] Although Ustadh Mau was heavily criticized by fellow Muslims on Lamu, he began to disapprove of the ostentatious Maulidi celebration, which by then had become a symbol of Swahili Sufi Islam. While the Maulidi celebrations started as part of a reform movement in the late 19th century in an effort to purify Islamic practice, they became criticized by many as unislamic and impure at that time, which also influenced Ustadh Mau.[52] The colorful celebration of the *miraji*, the Prophet's ascension to the heavens, which is only briefly mentioned in the Qur'ān, and the veneration of the graves of local theologians (*wanazuoni*), endowed with spiritual powers, were further elements that he came to consider *bid'a* ("heresy"), i.e. inappropriate innovations, not grounded in the Qur'ān or the Sunna and, in a sense, "pollution of pure Islamic ideas."

Still, the polarization of a local Swahili Islam grounded in local practices (*mila*) and concepts of religion (*dini*) and a reformist movement with an agenda of both modernization and strengthening Arabic orthodoxy—albeit one constructed as compatible with and even foreshadowed by the Qur'ān—

50　It was Ustadh Harith who introduced Ustadh Mau to more critical reformist works, and also helped him to begin teaching at the mosque of Bandani in the 1970s (see the contributions by Kai Kresse and Kadara Swaleh as well as Annachiara Raia in this volume).

51　As Annachiara Raia explores in detail in this volume, one book that Ustadh Mau found in his teacher's library, *Laisa min al Islam* ("Not from Islam"), by the reformist Egyptian Muslim Brother Mohammed al-Ghazali, would prove to be a reference work of enduring importance for him. His efforts to weed out all later, hypertrophic influences in Islam, including the Maulidi, made a huge impression on Ustadh Mau and changed a number of his views.

52　On the irony of considering the Maulidi, itself an effort of reform, as part of an "African" local and hence impure Islam, see Rüdiger Seesemann, "African Islam or Islam in Africa? Evidence from Kenya," in *The Global Worlds of the Swahili. Interfaces of Islam, Identity and Space in 19th and 20th Century East Africa*, ed. Roman Loimeier and Rüdiger Seesemann (Münster, Berlin: LIT, 2006), 240.

only started later, as Kai Kresse carefully argues.[53] This is important for situating Ustadh Mau's reformist, but tolerant intellectual position with its sensitivity to Swahili culture.[54] His position and attitude are reminiscent of Sheikh Al-Amin Mazrui's efforts toward a "Swahili enlightenment" in line with modern life, which had earlier also influenced Sheikh Muhammad Kasim Mazrui.[55] Kai Kresse shows how they prioritized Swahili-language education with a focus on current issues in modern life, but also on Islamic history, which in their view was not sufficiently taught. The Mombasan chief qadi Sheikh Muhammad Kasim Mazrui was "at the heart of the reformist movement at the Kenyan coast."[56] Educated outside of East Africa in the Middle East, Sheikh Muhammad Kasim came back to East Africa with a critical attitude toward the veneration of Sufi leaders and other cultural practices that lacked any foundation in the Qur'ān and did not help society to progress. Instead, he and his followers emphasized rational principles in line with modern education and an agenda of modernization, which, as they argued, can already be found in the Qur'ān.[57] They strove for the unity of modern science and the holy book[58]— a topic that also recurs in Ustadh Mau's poetry.[59] Their agenda foreshadows Ustadh Mau's emphasis on education of all kinds—given that it does not violate the moral framework—and his openness to modern technology. For Ustadh Mau, progress is essential, and *ilimu*, education, the sine qua non of a better future that, according to him, has been so long neglected on the coast: "We stopped making an effort to progress with regard to education" (*Tumeacha kujiendeleza kwa ilimu*). Coastal inhabitants need to make the effort to catch up in all kinds of fields (not only religion), as he repeatedly asserts.[60] In an

---

53   Kresse, *Philosophising in Mombasa*.

54   On Arabic orthodoxy as gradually increasing since Busaidi rule and the strong emphasis on literacy, see Bang, *Sufis and Scholars*, 132.

55   See Kai Kresse, "'Swahili Enlightenment'? East African Reformist Discourse at the Turning Point: The Example of Sheikh Muhammad Kasim Mazrui," *Journal of Religion in Africa* 33, no. 3 (2003): 279–309; "Introduction: Guidance and Social Critique: Mombasa through the Eyes of Sheikh Al-Amin Mazrui, 1930–1932," in *Guidance* (Uwongozi) *by Sheikh Al-Amin Mazrui: Selections from the First Swahili Islamic Newspaper*, ed. Kai Kresse (Leiden: Brill, 2017), 1–29.

56   Kresse, *Philosophising in Mombasa*, 94.

57   See also Kresse, *Philosophising in Mombasa*, 95.

58   See Kresse, *Philosophising in Mombasa*, 99 ff.

59   In a discussion of education in a YouTube interview, Ustadh Mau also strongly vouches for the compatibility of the Qur'ān and the natural sciences (*Me on TV*).

60   I am again quoting here from the interview with Annachiara Raia. *Ilimu* is not only a matter of conveying information and knowledge, but shapes the whole human being as a social and morally responsible person, as Annachiara Raia also outlines in her contri-

almost eclectic way, he himself relies on a variety of sources for his khutbah and poetry, and does not reject any kind of knowledge categorically. In *Haki za watoto*, for instance, he draws on developmental psychology, the Qurʾān, and the United Nations Convention on the Rights of the Child in addition to his own observations. However, he also finds it important to study a Swahili repertoire of "texts, procedures, arguments and practices," as Haj summarizes key aspects of Islamic traditions.[61]

Ustadh Mau's proud self-identification as Salafi, which nowadays conjures associations with dogmatism and aggression, needs to be considered against this background and also with regard to the very specific way it emerges from his intellectual biography and spells out in his own practices. He is a modernizer seeking progress for his own community, not wanting them to lag behind. He acknowledges the existence of globalization, modern technology, and the media, and he wants his community to make an effort to catch up by studying a broad range of subjects without leaving Islamic faith. Furthermore, he is critical of the "backward" local Sufi practice of venerating human beings as if they were godlike; he doubts all kinds of superstitions and, as a consequence, seeks to stick to what is mentioned in the Qurʾān, in approved historical accounts, and by science, which, similarly to Kassim Mazrui, for instance, is not a contradiction to him. Here one can see the influence of "classical" ideas of the 19th century Egyptian Salafiyya movement on him, seeking to create a bridge between modern education, progess as well as the Qurʾān and the Sunna.[62] In opposition to the growing emphasis on dogma and on Arabic as the only language of theological engagement, however, Ustadh Mau is also proud of the local tradition of learning, debating, and composing in Swahili as well as of Swahili as a language of interpretation and scholarship. An easy dichotomy of traditional Swahili Islam, on the one ahnd, and reformist thougth, on the other, would hardly do justice to the complexities of Ustadh's own intellectual practices and outlooks. As Rüdiger Seesemann highlights, the use of Swahili which might seem at odds with the reformist emphasis on Arabic as the only pure and sacred language is a wide-spread feature of reformist movements on

---

bution. Motivated by the importance he attributes to *ilimu*, he sent not only his children to school—some even to university—but also his second wife, who studied education. His broad and much more ambitious concept of *ilimu* hence comes closer to the German notion of *Bildung*, derived from the verb *bilden*, literally "to form"—in the sense of forming and developing a human being to his or her fullest intellectual and moral capacity—than the English word "education."

61   Haj, *Reconfiguring Islamic Tradition*, 5.

62   See the contribution by Annachiara Raia on *ʿilm*, where she refers to a number of thinkers who have influenced Ustadh Mau.

the Swahili coast: Both Sheikh Alamin Mazrui and also Sheikh Abdallah Saleh al-Farsi, who even translated the Qurʾān into Swahili, considered Swahili as the most efficient way to educate a broader audience.[63] Ustadh Mau is of the same opinion and also cherishes his own dialect, Kiamu, which permeates his poems. Emphasis on a progressive agenda of education compatible with the Qurʾān does not prevent him from being proud of the long tradition of poetry, which he collects in his library; and he encourages others to do the same. In effect, he has become a representative of Swahili culture, invited to speak or to deliver an opening poem wherever there is a cultural festival or conference on the coast that focuses on Swahili.[64] He has also become an expert and reference person for Swahili scholars in the West—such as the various authors in this volume— and takes account of works written by Western academics, including classic ones. The first Swahili dictionary, published by the German Basel missionary, Johann Ludwig Krapf, in 1882 and which he found in a dump site on Lamu (what a telling sign!), is a constant reference point for him; likewise, he regularly refers to the still unrivaled Swahili-French dictionary, published in 1939, by the Holy Ghost missionary Charles Sacleux.

With an argument reminiscent of postcolonial criticism, which argues for conceptual decolonization,[65] Ustadh Mau urges his fellow Lamuans not to blindly venerate and merely imitate the canon of English literature and cultural production, forgetting about Swahili literary giants like Muyaka bin Haji (see, for instance, his poem *Kiswahili*). In his poetry, he repeatedly refers to Japan, which he considers a role model in sticking to its own traditions—which he sees as a precondition for developing one's own intellectual position and thus avoiding becoming merely an easily manipulated puppet on a string— while at the same time being open to new technologies, skills, and ideas.[66] Like many scholars of the tariqa in earlier centuries, for Ustadh Mau, poetry composed and recited in local languages—in this case, Swahili—is the key to reaching a broader audience, and he believes in poetry's ability to captivate listeners as well as to influence their behavior. He sees himself as part of a particular Swahili Muslim discursive tradition that, while not unchanging,

---

63   Seesemann, "African Islam or Islam in Africa? Evidence from Kenya," 243.

64   For instance, he read his poem *Kilio hulia mwenye* ("Change Begins at Home") at the opening of a conference on popular culture held in Mombasa in 2006. He composed the poem *Za shirazi athari* ("Influence of the Persians") on the occasion of a conference dedicated to the interconnection between Persia and East Africa.

65   Kwasi Wiredu, *Conceptual Decolonization in African Philosophy: Four Essays* (Ibadan: Hope, 1995).

66   For reference to Japan, see, for instance, *Haki za watoto* ("Children's Rights," stz. 117) and *Tupijeni makamana* ("Let Us Embrace", stz. 8).

also implies reference to previous modes of thought. His own poetic practice, through which he continues a long tradition of poetry writing as a practice of intellectual argumentation and exchange, is a strong example of his search for continuity in a discursive tradition, while at the same time advocating the need for modern education.

It is not only Ustadh Mau's tolerance of and openness to bodies of knowledge of different origins, but also his sensitivity to and love for his language, the beauty of poetry, his care for his community, and his emphasis on progress and education also for women that make him differ so strongly from any puritan ideologist. Finding a moral stance is not a matter of sticking to dogma, but an inquiry guided by *huruma* ("compassion") (see the contribution "How Ought We to Live" in this volume). Rather than taking the role of a preacher of one truth that is beyond doubt or reasoning, Ustadh Mau weighs the options and positions and understands human fallibility (see also Annachiara Raia's contribution on the *Wasiya* in this volume). With a tone full of empathy, he is an introspective thinker, free in developing his own stance by not merely following previously established conventions, always weighing other possibilities, as is very much in accordance with the Swahili ideal of intellectual practice.[67]

3   Writing Poetry

Ustadh Mau began composing poetry already in his early twenties. In 1974, he wrote the *Wasiya wa mabanati* ("Advice to Young Women"), a long *utendi* on a teenage pregnancy, which became highly successful (see Annachiara Raia's contribution in this book). In 1975, he wrote the poem *Kimwondo*, in which he warns the Lamuans not to vote for a political candidate who did not have a proper political agenda, but, being rich, instead influenced people's votes with his wealth.[68] In the appendix to the edition of the poem *Kiswahili* (republished in this volume), Mahmoud and Frankl list ten *tendi*, from the aforementioned *Wasiya wa mabanati*, to *Ukimwi ni zimwi* ("Aids Is a Monster"), a poem on HIV/AIDS composed in 1990; *Haki za watoto*, composed in 2000 (also in this

---

67   See Kresse, *Philosophising in Mombasa*, 70 ff.

68   See the analyses in Assibi Amidu, "Lessons from Kimondo: An Aspect of Kiswahili Culture," *Nordic Journal of African Studies* 2, no. 1 (1993): 34–55; Amidu, "Political Poetry among the Swahili: The Kimondo Verses from Lamu," in *Swahili Modernities*, ed. Pat Caplan and Farouk Topan (Trenton, NJ: Africa World Press, 2004), 157–174; and Kimani Njogu, "Kimondo, Satire and Political Dialogue: Electioneering through Versification," *Research in African Literatures* 32, no. 1 (2001): 1–13.

volume); *Mukharati* ("Drugs") a warning against drug abuse, composed in 2004; and a long poem, *Ramani ya maisha ya ndowa* ("The Map of Married Life," composed in 2006), in two parts—one part for men, the other for women. Many of his shorter poems form part of this book: *Tunda*, composed in 1976 on the occasion of his son's birth; *Kipande cha ini* ("Part of My Liver"), composed for his daughter Azra in 1989; *Jahazi* ("Dhow"), composed in 2002, reflecting on an economic crisis; and *Mama msimlaumu* ("Don't Blame My Mother"), composed in 2006. Furthermore, besides these poems, Ustadh Mau also "serves the community" (*kutumikia jamii*), as he puts it, by writing mostly short prayer poems, *dua*, on commission, which are read or recited on special occasions such as weddings, embarking on a pilgrimage, or when a child is taking an exam, with the intention to invoke God's blessings.

For Ustadh Mau, poetry has been part of his life as long as he can remember. Both of Ustadh Mau's parents were poets (see also Mahmoud and Frankl 2013). Ustadh Mau himself attributes his own talent for and interest in poetry to his father, whose own poetry he used to read when he was a child. As mentioned above, upon his birth, his father composed a poem for him, a didactic poem (*wasiya*) called *Hapo zamani za yana* (included in this volume), with the same intention inherent in all *wasiya* poems—to become a lasting heritage by providing his son with advice on how to live. One can hear the warm tone his father adopts, making an effort to write a poem of enduring quality to serve his son well—as we also find in Ustadh Mau's own poems, particularly the shorter *wasiya* for his children, like *Tunda* ("Fruit") or *Kipande cha ini* ("Piece of My liver").

For Ustadh Mau, poetry is a primary vehicle for reaching the people, including marginalized groups like women and children. Their education has been a special concern to him, which, according to him, has become increasingly important in his life since his first marriage and the birth of his own children. In 1975, Ustadh Mau married his first wife, Aisha Ali Waleedi, whose ancestry hails partly from Siyu, partly from Lamu. Mama Fatih, as she is called, after her first son, gave birth to eight children: five girls and three boys. According to him, watching his children grow up made him understand how important education at an early age is. In 1985, Ustadh Mau married his second wife, Sauda Kasim Bwanamaka, although he had previously not planned to take a second wife. Mama Azra, as she is also called, had come from Faza on the neighboring island of Pate to attend Lamu Girls' School, a secondary school on Lamu. To go to school everyday, she rented a place at Ustadh Mau's mother's house; thus they became neighbors. Helping her out with school fees from time to time, he got to know her better, and liked her for her ambition to study. Because his first wife, who had severe arguments with the much younger "schoolgirl," did not approve of his marrying her, they got married in Faza after she finished school. For some time, Ustadh Mau went to Faza every Saturday to see her, while living on Lamu, where he worked and taught, for the rest of the week. Only in 1990 did she move to Lamu and become a teacher at the local school. Mama Azra was ambitious, and Ustadh Mau supported her: she studied education and graduated from Moi University, Eldoret, where she lived for two years. Her three children, one son and two daughters, grew up largely in other households: while her daughter Hannan was raised on Lamu by Fatuma, who had escaped from Somalia and earned some money as a babysitter, her son, Aboud, grew up mostly in the house of Ustadh Mau's first wife. Azra, his beloved daughter, was raised on Pate, and only came to Lamu from time to time, for instance during the Maulidi. The poem *Kipande cha ini* ("Piece of My Liver"), which Ustadh Mau composed in 1989, speaks of how much he missed his daughter. Her studies were a source of great pride for her father: she studied to become a medical doctor, first in Kenya and later in Sudan. She too takes an interest in his father's poetry.

To reach all the people on Lamu, both the khutbah and poetry need to make use of plain language, a "light language" (*lugha nyepesi*) that is comprehensible and flows well, as Ustadh Mau tends to underline. The khutbah, however, is easier to compose, since it does not need to stick to prosodic rules, but can argue and help people understand; the poem, meanwhile, is a form that people enjoy listening to much more. As he underlines in personal communication, poetry has more *masharti* ("rules"), in that it needs to have a musical and rhythmic form that pleases the ear; he believes in audio recordings as a more effective means of reaching people on Lamu, "who do not read" (*watu hawasomi*). Furthermore, poets, even more than preachers, have and need to have the capacity to touch people emotionally. Ustadh Mau feels for the characters he depicts in his poems, such as the desperate girl in the *Wasiya wa mabanati* (see the contribution by Annachiara Raia in this volume). He emphasizes that the poet has to touch people emotionally to make them think: "to (effectively) think about the situation of girls in the *Wasiya*, you have to feel it" (*Wasiya kufikiria hali ya wasichana ni jambo ambalo lazima uhisi*). It is the audience that is made to feel what would otherwise escape its attention. Thus, emotions stir reflection, and reflection depends on emotional involvement. Poetry is rooted in reality and people's experiences, but also exceeds or transcends them by creating a heightened emotionality, and thus opens up new perspectives.

Poetry can also change one's view of a reality that previously seemed to be without any alternatives. In this sense, many of Ustadh Mau's poems even have utopian potential: not only because they all believe in the power of making a change, but also because they do so through the very act of narrating a differ-

SITUATING USTADH MAU'S POETIC PRACTICE IN CONTEXT

ent reality and making people think more consciously about alternative ways of living. They spell out alternatives, for example where women are not merely punished for becoming prematurely pregnant (see *Mama msimlaumu*, "Don't Blame My Mother"), children are nurtured according to their nature (see *Haki za watoto*, "Children's Rights"), and a younger generation rediscovers the rich intellectual tradition "at home" (see *Kiswahili*). As T.S. Eliot underlines in his essay on the social function of poetry, poems, which come closer to people's sentiments than any prose ever could, not only allow people to experience something new, but also make them more conscious of something they already feel, but cannot express: "In expressing what other people feel [the poet] is changing the feeling by making it more conscious; he is making people more aware of what they feel already, and therefore teaching them something about themselves."[69] The thought-provoking quality is linked to the ability to bestow a concrete poetic form on experience.[70]

It is the concrete narrative of the mother in *Mama msimlaumu*, who felt compelled to abandon her child, and the baby defending her through which Ustadh Mau makes the audience feel for her and engage in reflecting on alternatives. The personification in the poem *Kiswahili*, where the language takes on the role of a mother, renders the relationship to language an intimate one. In *Jahazi* ("Dhow"), the dhow that does not move on a windless day "translates" the common atmosphere of crisis and stagnation into an image that people on Lamu can relate to and in which they can recognize themselves and their tiring efforts to "make the dhow move." By making use of concrete imagery, poetry speaks to the audience in an immediate way, makes them understand or rather feel their position, gives sense to their emotions, and provokes acts of reflection. For the philosopher Hans Blumenberg, whose aim it was to explore the knowledge-producing effect of metaphor (and not merely of argument) in intellectual history, figurative language comes with concrete imagery that gives form to something that cannot (yet) be adequately grasped in other terms. In this sense, the poem and its metaphorical language circumscribe a kind of understanding before there is understanding. In Blumenberg's words, the poetic depiction—in his estimation, the metaphor—gives form to complex

---

69   T.S. Eliot, "The Social Function of Poetry," in *On Poetry and Poets*, ed. T.S. Eliot (New York: Farrar, Straus and Giroux, 2009), 9.

70   Following another line of thought in Eliot's essay ("The Social Function of Poetry," 7, 8), which singles out poetry as the least translatable art form—one where everything gets lost if one tries to convey the gist of it, since this lies in its form—one can understand how and why Kiamu, the local dialect, which is close to people's everyday lives, as well as its poetry matters so much to Ustadh Mau.

experience while we are still grappling with it: "The further we move from the short distance of fulfillable intentionality and refer to total horizons that our experience can no longer grasp or delimit, the more pervasive becomes the use of metaphors."[71] *Jahazi* depicts the emerging crisis like a huge wave about to crash into individual existences, and thus makes both the present and future sensorially palpable. The metaphor does not illustrate, but rather opens a view onto a complex totality that typically gives form not to a long-past event that can be judged and evaluated, but to the incandescent and emergent concerns of the lifeworld. The metaphor "gives a structure to the world and represents the unfathomable, unobservable totality of reality"; it gives an "imaginative orientation"[72] as it offers specificity, but not unequivocal certainty.

For Ustadh, poetry has the capacity to render something palpable, so that a scene is placed before the listener's eyes. The enlightening, prophecy-like character often leaves the audience surprised. Each poem is akin to a miracle, a feature that Ustadh Mau points to as characteristic of poetry. According to him, people on Lamu wonder, "Why can a poet say things we are not able to say?" (*Kwa nini mshairi anaweza kusema mambo ambayo hatuwezi kuyasema*).[73] Similarly, for Blumenberg,[74] what he calls "aesthetic evidence" is based is on the idea that "everybody has seen it without being able to express it." It is the sudden apparition of an image or a story that hits the nail on the head, but cannot be distilled to any clear-cut argument, that seems to be the miracle.

As Ustadh Mau underlines in a conversation we had, on Lamu, it is "a common belief that spirits give a poet his ideas of what to say" (*Watu wana iktadi kwamba mshairi anapewa mawazo ya kusema kutoka sheitani*). This notion of the poet who does not control his words, but whose words rather find him in a miraculous way, is reminiscent of Eliot's notions of the obscure, untraceable roots of poetry.[75] The question of why a poet composes in a certain way is, for him, ultimately a question that cannot fully be answered. Before there is understanding, there is an obscure impulse that lacks any clear reason that can be rationally grasped—an idea expressed with the reference to *sheitani*, "spirits," on Lamu. There is a hollow "creative germ" (*ein dumpfer schöpferischer Kaum*),

---

71 Hans Blumenberg, *Schiffbruch mit Zuschauer. Paradigma einer Daseinsmetapher*, 5th ed. (Frankfurt am Main: Suhrkamp, 2012), 90; my translation.

72 Blumenberg, *Schiffbruch mit Zuschauer*, 93.

73 Again, I am quoting here and in the following from an interview Annachiara Raia conducted with the poet in July 2018.

74 Blumenberg, *Schiffbruch mit Zuschauer*, 93.

75 T.S. Eliot, "The Three Voices of Poetry," in *On Poetry and Poets*, ed. T.S. Eliot (New York: Farrar, Straus and Giroux, 2009), 96–112.

as Eliot points out, drawing on the concept of the German poet Gottfried Benn: "There is something germinating in him for which he must find words; but he cannot know what words he wants until he has found the words."[76] The poem only gradually acquires its form as the poet struggles to find the words for the "thing" growing in him. In a similar way, for Ustadh Mau, it is "the poet, who has a talent to imagine and to choose words [for his imagination]" (*Mshari ana kipawa cha ubunifu, pia uhodari wa kutegua maneno*). It is the word *kipawa* ("talent"), literally "the thing given," "the gift," that encapsulates the uncontrolled and unlearnable foundation of poetry, namely the capacity to imagine, which precedes and transcends intention.

Thus, in listening closely to Ustadh Mau's observations on poetry, one finds elements of a kind of poetics that seem to extend his more commonly voiced understanding of poetry as being born out of a concrete concern to teach and reach an audience with respect to a previously defined subject: the idea of the poem functioning as a vehicle for the message. In poems such as the *Haki za watoto*, it is an argument rather than a "hollow germ" that seems to lie at its base (for a more detailed consideration, see "How Ought We to Live," this volume). Yet for Ustadh Mau, the relation of a poem to its words and scenes is also often one of wonder and serendipity. The *shairi* poem *Jahazi*, for instance, reflecting on the economic crisis in terms of a dhow that does not move, developed out of words he overheard on the streets. Passing by, he heard a man selling *mishkaki*, grilled meat skewers, saying *tanga aliembete na mongoti* ("The sail is tied to the mast"), referring to that fact that he did not sell much on that day. It was this one sentence, giving form to a sentiment but uttered in a rather incidental way on the street, that caught Ustadh Mau's attention, stirred his imagination, and inspired him to compose a whole poem out of one line. In a similar way, the newspaper article about a stray dog saving an abandoned baby and people's harsh reactions to the story prompted him to explore the narrative further in his poem *Mama msimlaumu*. It is the poet to whom these surroundings, experiences, and the language speak, that follow him and urge him to create in poetic form—and the poet, in turn, answers through poetry. And this is also why the repertoire of texts, the existing poems and tradition of narratives and motifs are so important, as they invite to breathe new life into them, allowing them to present concerns and feelings: "The persistence of literary creativeness in any people, accordingly, consists in the maintenance of an unconscious balance between tradition in the larger sense—the collective personality, so to speak, realised in the literature of the past—and

---

76   Eliot, "The Three Voices of Poetry," 106.

the originality of the living generation."[77] Thus, there is a part of his poetry—the question of why and how it takes a particular form, and what speaks to him and has the power to transform into a line, imagery, musical lines, and metaphors—that he does not choose, but which rather seem to choose him. Here we observe his close connection with his surroundings—not only in the sense that its problems and worries concern him, but also that its narratives, characters, words, and poetic forms speak to his imagination and urge him to find words for it.

Thus, to conclude, to approach the question of what Ustadh Mau does when he writes his poetry, one both has to and does not have to consider his own life and context, the island of Lamu and his family's history. What does this seemingly contradictory statement mean? There is a paraphrasable and an unparaphrasable relationship between the poet, his life, and his context. As for the former, as Ustadh Mau himself continually reiterates, serving his community with the aim of improving it is a major motivation for his composing poetry.[78] Poetry is a means to teach and to make people aware. However, this also implies an unparaphrasable relationship between the poet and his context as well as the language, which stirs his imagination to paint a concrete picture and to make characters speak, act, cry, and argue. Hence, his often dramatic poetry transforms the intention or message into an "example" (*mfano*) that touches the audience much more than any law (sharia). One cannot merely paraphrase his poetry like one can summarize a sermon, and have the same effect. Furthermore, poetry—its rhymes, meters, lines, and imagery—grows out of a verbal tradition so firmly entangled in Indian Ocean influences, yet also deeply rooted on Lamu, as well as out of the dialect of Kiamu, a literary language, which has shaped poetry but has also been reshaped by it for centuries. In composing, Ustadh Mau does not merely find a form for his thoughts, but the form, for instance the pattern and tone of the didactic *wasiya* genre, also shapes his thinking and imagination. Thus, not only as a social context to react to, but also as a place with an intellectual and poetic history, as well as a place that speaks to the senses through its words, phrases, sounds, and the everyday experiences

---

77   T.S. Eliot, "What Is a Classic?" in *On Poetry and Poets*, ed. T.S. Eliot (New York: Farrar, Straus and Giroux, 2009), 58.

78   See also Kai Kresse, "Knowledge and Intellectual Practice in a Swahili Context: 'Wisdom' and the Social Dimensions of Knowledge," *Africa* 79, no. 1 (2009): 148–167; Annachiara Raia, "*Angaliya baharini, mai yaliyoko pwani*: The Presence of the Ocean in Mahmoud Ahmed Abdulkadir's Poetry," in *Lugha na fasihi. Scritti in onore e memoria di/Essays in Honour and Memory of Elena Bertoncini Zúbková*, ed. Flavia Aiello and Roberto Gaudioso (Naples: Università degli Studi di Napoli "L'Orientale"), 223–250; and Annachiara Raia's contribution in this volume.

of people, Lamu is an essential part of Ustadh Mau's poetic practice and his understanding of what poetry is and can do.

References

Amidu, Assibi. "Lessons from Kimondo: An Aspect of Kiswahili Culture." *Nordic Journal of African Studies* 2, no. 1 (1993): 34–55.

Amidu, Assibi. "Political Poetry among the Swahili: The Kimondo Verses from Lamu." In *Swahili Modernities*, edited by Pat Caplan and Farouk Topan, 157–174. Trenton, NJ: Africa World Press, 2004.

Bang, Anne. *Sufis and Scholars of the Sea: Family Networks in East Africa, 1860–1925.* London: Routledge, 2003.

Bang, Anne. *Islamic Sufi Networks in the Western Indian Ocean (c. 1880–1940): Ripples of Reform.* Leiden: Brill, 2014.

Blumenberg, Hans. *Schiffbruch mit Zuschauer. Paradigma einer Daseinsmetapher.* 5th ed. Frankfurt am Main: Suhrkamp, 2012. First published 1979.

Dammann, Ernst. *Dichtungen in der Lamu-Mundart des Suaheli: Gesammelt, herausgegeben und übersetzt von Ernst Dammann.* Hamburg: Friederichsen, De Gruyter & Co., 1940.

Dammann, Ernst. "Die paränetische Suaheli-Dichtung Tabaraka." *Mitteilungen des Instituts für Orientforschung* 7, no. 3 (1960): 411–432.

Eliot, T.S. "The Social Function of Poetry." In *On Poetry and Poets*, edited by T.S. Eliot, 3–16. New York: Farrar, Straus and Giroux, 2009. First published in *Adelphi* (July and September 1945).

Eliot, T.S. "The Three Voices of Poetry." In *On Poetry and Poets*, edited by T.S. Eliot, 96–112. New York: Farrar, Straus and Giroux, 2009. First published 1954 by Cambridge University Press.

Eliot, T.S. "What Is a Classic?" In *On Poetry and Poets*, edited by T.S. Eliot, 52–74. New York: Farrar, Straus and Giroux, 2009. First published 1944 by Faber and Faber.

Engseng, Ho. *The Graves of Tarim. Genealogy and Mobility across the Indian Ocean.* Los Angeles: University of California, 2016.

Haj, Samira. *Reconfiguring Islamic Tradition: Reform, Rationality and Modernity. Cultural Memory in the Present.* Palo Alto (Calif.): Stanford University Press, 2009.

Harries, Lyndon. "A Swahili Takhmis from the Swahili Arabic Text." *African Studies* 11, no. 2 (1952): 59–67.

Hichens, William. *Al-Inkishafi: The Soul's Awakening.* London: Sheldon Press, 1939.

Knappert, Jan. "Het epos van Heraklios: Een proeve van Swahili poëzie. Tekst en vertaling, voorzien van inleiding, kritisch commentaar en aantekeningen." PhD diss., Leiden University, 1958.

Knappert, Jan. "The Hamziya Deciphered." *African Language Studies* 7 (1966): 52–81.

Knappert, Jan. *Swahili Islamic Poetry*. Vol. 1. Leiden: Brill, 1971.

Knappert, Jan. "Swahili Literature in Arabic Script." *Manuscripts of the Middle East* 4 (1989): 74–84.

Kresse, Kai. "'Swahili Enlightenment'? East African Reformist Discourse at the Turning Point: The Example of Sheikh Muhammad Kasim Mazrui." *Journal of Religion in Africa* 33, no. 3 (2003): 279–309.

Kresse, Kai. *Philosophising in Mombasa. Knowledge, Islam and Intellectual Practice at the Swahili Coast*. Edinburgh: Edinburgh University Press, 2007.

Kresse, Kai. "Knowledge and Intellectual Practice in a Swahili Context: 'Wisdom' and the Social Dimensions of Knowledge." *Africa* 79, no. 1 (2009): 148–167.

Kresse, Kai. "Introduction: Guidance and Social Critique: Mombasa through the Eyes of Sheikh Al-Amin Mazrui, 1930–1932." In *Guidance* (Uwongozi) *by Sheikh Al-Amin Mazrui: Selections from the First Swahili Islamic Newspaper*, edited by Kai Kresse, 1–29. Leiden: Brill, 2017.

Kresse, Kai. *Swahili Muslim Publics and Postcolonial Experience*. Bloomington: Indiana University Press, 2018.

Mahmoud, Ahmad Abdulkadir and Peter Frankl. "*Kiswahili*: A Poem by Mahmoud Ahmad Abdulkadir, to Which is Appended a List of the Poet's Compositions in Verse." *Swahili Forum* 20 (2013): 1–18, https://nbn-resolving.org/urn:nbn:de:bsz:15-qucosa-137405.

Me on TV. "Mahmoud Mau 1." Posted September 18, 2016. YouTube clip, 23:41. https://www.youtube.com/watch?v=5l8LhET8GoE.

Neuhaus, Gustav. "Kitabu Mauludi. Buch der Geburt Muhammed's. Suaheli-Gedicht des Lamu-Mannes Scharifu Mansabu bin Scharifu Abdurrahmani al-Hussaini, Manuskript in arabischer Schrift, wiedergegeben in Autotypien, übersetzt und erläutert." *Mitteilungen des Seminars für Orientalische Sprachen* 38, no. 3 (1935): 145–201.

Njogu, Kimani. "Kimondo, Satire and Political Dialogue: Electioneering through Versification." *Research in African Literatures* 32, no. 1 (2001): 1–13.

Raia, Annachiara. "Angaliya baharini, mai yaliyoko pwani: The Presence of the Ocean in Mahmoud Ahmed Abdulkadir's Poetry." In *Lugha na fasihi. Scritti in onore e memoria di/Essays in Honour and Memory of Elena Bertoncini Zúbková*, edited by Flavia Aiello and Roberto Gaudioso, 223–250. Naples: Università degli Studi di Napoli "L'Orientale," 2019.

Raia, Annachiara. *Rewriting Yusuf. A Philological and Intertextual Study of a Swahili Islamic Manuscript Poem*. Cologne: Köppe, 2020.

Romero, Patricia. *Lamu. History, Society and Family in an East African Port City*. Princeton, NJ: Princeton University Press, 1997.

Salvadori, Cynthia. *We Came in Dhows*. Vol. 1. Nairobi: Paperchase Kenya, 1996.

Vierke, Clarissa. "Between the Lines: Life and Work of the Lamuan Artist and Cultural

Broker Muhamadi Kijuma." In *Muhamadi Kijuma. Texts from the Dammann Papers and other Collections*, edited by Gudrun Miehe and Clarissa Vierke, 41–62. Archiv afrikanistischer Manuskripte 9. Cologne: Köppe, 2010.

Vierke, Clarissa. "From across the Ocean: Considering Travelling Literary Figurations as Part of Swahili Intellectual History." *Journal of African Cultural Studies* 28, no. 2 (2016): 225–240.

Werner, Alice and William Hichens. *The Advice of Mwana Kupona upon the Wifely Duty.* The Azanian Classics 2. Medstead: Azania Press, 1934.

Wiredu, Kwasi. *Conceptual Decolonization in African Philosophy: Four Essays.* Ibadan: Hope, 1995.

FIGURE 6   Ustadh Mahmoud Mau at the beach on the island in 1967. Behind him the motorboat of the District Commissioner

Seeking *'ilm* on Lamu: Ustadh Mau's Library and Services for the Benefit of His Community

Annachiara Raia

The way in which Ustadh Mau urges people, parents and teachers both to educate children and not to neglect their customs and faith is intertwined with his poetic compositions, and also lies at the core of his educational and religious services as a teacher and imam. For a better understanding of Ustadh Mau's view on Muslim education and learning culture, it is worth delving deeper into a talk he once gave on the benefits of knowledge and language ("Faida ya elimu na lugha"). Before doing so, I shall discuss Ustadh Mau's Islamic upbringing and his thirst for knowledge. This latter quality becomes evident when one explores Ustadh Mau's library, a storehouse of wisdom that nurtures his soul. I shall use his library as my departure point, a "breathing home archive" that enables him to disseminate knowledge and education to his Lamuan community.

1 *Dibaji,* introduction

I had the opportunity to be welcomed at Ustadh Mau's library for the first time in August 2014, and once again in March 2018. During my meetings and interviews with him there, people would routinely drop by to ask for advice or to commission poems. To fulfill their requests, he would turn not only to the books and pamphlets stacked on his shelves, which in some cases he would give his visitors as gifts, but also to his own poetry, in order to pass its lessons on to his community and open their minds.

From these experiences, I gradually realized the value of Ustadh Mau's library as a dynamic archive and its relevance in the making of social and intellectual practices on the island of Lamu. Furthermore, as I will consider at greater length in what follows, the dynamics of island communities are important to understanding Africa's connected histories and intellectual practices.

This investigation into Ustadh Mau's library and his services to Lamu will also help shed light on a yet-neglected hub of Islam on the island. Indeed, whereas much attention has been paid to the Riyadha Mosque, built by Sayyid Swaleh, who migrated to Lamu from the Comoros in the 1880s, there are much older mosques on the island. Ustadh Mau has waged his reformist battle from

---

© ANNACHIARA RAIA, 2023 | DOI:10.1163/9789004525726_006

This is an open access chapter distributed under the terms of the CC BY-NC-ND 4.0 license.

within the Pwani Mosque, located in an area called Nyuma ya Gereza ("Behind the Prison," referring to Lamu Fort, the stone fort located in Lamu Old Town), where he currently gives his Friday sermon or *hotuba* (Ar. *khuṭubah*, Anglicized as khutbah). In the past, the madrassa where he first began studying was also located close to the mosque; his teacher's private library—an apartment that he rented and called the *Baytu Thaqafa* (the "House of Culture")—was located in the area called Kijitoni or Farasi. While it is difficult to trace the network and circulation of ideas among sites that are no longer in existence, it is surely time to reconsider the legacy of classical Islam on Lamu as a dynamic tradition, able to provide us with a sense of identity, continuity, and modernity and to tell us not only where Muslims have been, but also where Ustadh Mau wishes his own Lamuan people to be.

2 Ustadh Mau's Thirst for Knowledge

2.1 *Preparing* L'Adulte initié: *Ustadh Mau's Islamic Education and Background*

> La pédagogie coranique ne se limitait pas à l'apprentissage de la lecture [...] mais visait plutôt à la formation totale de l'individu, à la transmission d'un modèle d'homme adapté à son état de société [...] C'est une initiation vers un statut nouveau, celui d'adulte initié.[1]

In classical Islam, the Islamic education of a student begins with being taught by select individuals representing a specific religious authority. As Loimeier notes, in the case of Islamic education on Zanzibar, students studied in circles that could have been hosted at the madrassa, but also at the mosque or a scholar's home. The existence of libraries at the mosques themselves is also attested, but in general, it is known that any collection of library books—comprising books in any specialized field of art or science—was "the result of purely human sentiment and love of learning and knowledge in the extreme."[2]

Ustadh Mau's education was carried out under the influence of a close friend of his father, Ustadh Sayyid Hassan Badawy, who became his private

---

1 Renaud Santerre, *Pédagogie musulmane d'Afrique noire: L'École coranique peule du Cameroun* (Montreal: Presses de l'Université de Montréal, 1973), 346–347; quoted in Loimeier, *Between Social Skills and Marketable Skills*, 155.

2 Mustafa Siba'i, *Some Glittering Aspects of the Islamic Civilization* (Beirut: Holy Koran Publishing House, 1984), 213.

teacher. Since the arrival of Islam on the East African coast, Swahili pupils have received their formal education at Qur'ānic schools (in Swahili known as the *chuo*, pl. *vyuo*, as well as madrassa), where they become acquainted with Arabic, learn to recite the Qur'ān, imprint suras in their memory, and study how to compose qasidas, poetic odes. His closeness and companionship (Arabic *ṣuḥba*) with his teacher Badawy has influenced Ustadh Mau's Islamic education well into adulthood. Indeed, at that time, the selection of texts (not yet disciplines) each pupil would study was chosen by the precise scholar the pupil studied with.[3] In this sense, Ustadh Mau received what Loimeier describes as "an education judged not on *loci* but on *personae*,"[4] namely in the form of Ustadh Badawy.[5] As a schoolchild, Ustadh Mau was part of a community that strongly believed that the secular school system was haram; this is why he never followed the secular Kenyan school system and classes, something that he quietly regrets and has not prohibited his own children from doing.[6] However, Ustadh Mau himself has fond memories of the time he spent at the Qur'ānic schools; as a student, he remembers how much he enjoyed attending madrassa, always being the first to enter the class, never "wanting to arrive late" (*sikuweza kuchelewa*). He still keeps a so-called *kibati* with which the madrassa students used to be beaten. In 2013, Ustadh Mau sat an exam for a certificate to teach primary education, and passed the national examination—a distinction that resonates with public opinion of him; as Peter Frankl describes:

---

3   Such an strategy, however, has encountered difficulties at times, as we find recorded in the newspaper *Sauti ya haki*. Along the lines of thinkers like Muhammad Abduh and Rashid Rida, Sheikh Al-Amin Mazrui took to the newspaper to warn his coastal community, "[B]ecause there is a lack of religious expertise in our towns, and a lack of religious schools (madrasa) agreeable to all Muslims, our Islamic community has been entered by a disease of sheikhs who are not known for the degree of their education in religion. So much so that anyone having a shawl, a board and a piece of chalk can call himself 'sheikh' and pose to have religious knowledge." August 1972, 5–6; quoted in Kai Kresse, *Swahili Muslim Publics and Postcolonial Experience* (Bloomington: Indiana University Press, 2018), 112–113.

4   Jonathan Porter Berkey, *The Transmission of Knowledge in Medieval Cairo: A Social History of Islamic Education* (Princeton, NJ: Princeton University Press, 1992), 23; quoted in Roman Loimeier, *Between Social Skills and Marketable Skills: The Politics of Islamic Education in 20th-Century Zanzibar* (Leiden: Brill, 2009), 150.

5   Focusing on Cairo in the Middle Ages, Jonathan Porter Berkey analyzes how the transmission of religious knowledge was indeed a highly personal process, one dependent on the relationships between individual scholars and students (Berkey, *The Transmission of Knowledge*).

6   Azra, for instance—Ustadh Mau's so-called *kipande cha ini* ("piece of liver")—has attended formal schools, and as a father, Ustadh Mau has never been afraid to put her in a secular context in which Muslims were the exception. Azra is currently a doctor and a caring mother to her child Afnan.

In a booklet issued for the investiture at State House, Nairobi, on Jamhuri Day, Sunday 12th December 2004 one reads on page vii: "Mr. Abdulkadir [...] is a renowned Kiswahili poet [...] despite lack of formal education. He is a social philanthropist who has single-handedly mobilized resources for communal projects within Lamu District, including a school for the mentally handicapped. He is currently actively involved in spearheading advocacy and publicity on HIV/AIDS in Lamu District. He is awarded the Head of State's Commendation for his immense contribution towards national development."[7]

At this juncture, Frankl has the readers reflect on a specific passage acknowledging Ustadh Mau's merits. His reflections are as follows:

A renowned Kiswahili poet [...] despite lack of formal education" is an interesting observation. The perception seems to be that those who have acquired "formal education" have acquired a form of that education which was first introduced to East Africa by European-Christians in the 19th century. If so, it would follow, for example, that the author of the 18th century poem *Inkishafi* composed his masterpiece "despite lack of formal education.[8]

Adding to Frankl's example of a well-known poet who has produced masterpieces "despite lack of formal education," we can also mention the name Abdilatif Abdalla, a master poet from Mombasa, famously known for his poetic anthology *Sauti ya dhiki* ("The Voice of Agony"), composed on toilet paper during his time in jail.[9] During a brief talk that I had with Bwana Abdilatif—whose modesty makes him reject Swahili epithets such as *profesa* and *sheikh*—he told me how little he liked going to "formal school," precisely the same kind from which Ustadh Mau was prohibited. Everything Abdilatif Abdalla knows comes from his intimate relationship with books and his passion for poetry.[10] Ustadh Mau learned English and many other subjects through self-study; as

---

7   Ahmad Abdulkadir Mahmoud and Peter J.L. Frankl, *"Kiswahili*: A Poem by Mahmoud Ahmad Abdulkadir, to Which is Appended a List of the Poet's Compositions in Verse," *Swahili Forum* 20 (2013): 16.

8   Ibid.

9   Cf. Abdilatif Abdalla, *Sauti ya dhiki* (Nairobi: Oxford University Press, 1973).

10   As in the case of Ustadh Mau, the height of Abdilatif Abdalla's bookshelves in Hamburg are taller than he is, and are definitely another "island" that requires future investigation.

the excursus on his book collection will show further, he knows about history, literature, and religion, but is also interested in psychology and motivational literature of all sorts and from all the corners of the globe. Besides this, he knows the fragilities of his people; he is the best keeper of their secrets, and particularly of women's desperation and hope.

Peter Frankl's remark, stressing the journalist's account of Ustadh Mau's achievements "despite lack of formal education," is reminiscent of al-Zarnuji's concern with "whole education" versus "mere academic attainment" by highlighting and distinguishing between what is education and what is rather knowledge. Al-Zarnuji (d. 1223), who flourished in Turkistan, was among the first to write on the theory and practice of professional education. His work *Instructions for the Student* was used as a standard textbook for over six centuries, and was translated into Latin in 1838. It is as if al-Zarnuji seems to say, you can have a PhD and yet still be uneducated—a common sentiment in contemporary Muslim societies. What one learns from al-Zarnuji's work *Instructions for the Student* is indeed that education is acquired through effort, aspiration, pursuit, and persistence, whereas knowledge is about moral and ethical acumen.[11]

Returning to the didactic yet intimate way Ustadh Mau received his own Islamic education, it is well known that the major aim of memorizing the Qur'ān—as taught at madrassa with the use of the *loho* (Swahili *ubao* "tablet, chalkboard")—is "not to inculcate rigid discipline, but to provide skills and social knowledge that could be translated in meaningful ways into social competence, when quoting the Qur'ān in public debates, for instance, in order to strengthen, legitimize and sanctify a particular."[12] In this regard, we can see from Ustadh Mau's upbringing that he went well beyond the objectives of classical Islamic education; as he also preaches in his poem *Mwalimu*, he encourages the use of more than just the *ubao* in teaching one's children. He firmly believes in people as the source of transferring knowledge and imparting skills, as being models of the change they seek.

Ustadh Mau serves as such a model, reinforcing what classical scholars, philosophers, and thinkers have claimed as "what a good education ought to be": "a good education, they thought, is not simply about transmission of know-

---

11   See Burhān al-Dīn al- Zarnuji, *Instructions for the Student: The Method of Learning* (US: Starlatch Press, 2003), vii–x. For a complete list of further classical works, see the concise article "The List: Ten Key Texts on Islamic Education," *Critical Muslim* 15.1, July–September 2015, https://www.criticalmuslim.io/the-list-ten-key-texts-on-islamic-education/.

12   Loimeier, *Between Social Skills and Marketable Skills*, 155.

ledge but also includes emotional, social and physical well-being of the student. It is about creating a well-rounded moderate person with passion for thought and learning."[13]

Emotional, social, and physical well-being are all well balanced in the figure of Ustadh Mau, as a result of the successful way he has attained the knowledge he seeks and become the *adulte initié* so in vogue and so prominent in each society. In other words, acquiring a Qurʾānic education in classical Islam was meant to build what Santerre defines as "une formation totale tant religieuse, morale et sociale, technique et professionale, qu'intellectuelle et littéraire [...] La pédagogie coranique ne se limitait pas à l'apprentissage de la lecture [...] mais visait plutôt à la formation totale de l'individu, à la transmission d'un modèle d'homme adapté à son état de société [...] C'est une initiation vers un statut nouveau, celui d'adulte initié."[14] Ustadh Mau's *modèl d'homme* corresponds perfectly to the *société* represented by Lamu island, where he was born and has lived ever since, as he says in the final stanza of *Amu*: *Makazi ni hapa Amu / Na ndiko nilipozawa*, "My home is here in Lamu / This is also where I was born" (stz. 57).

This also explains my personal interest in investigating his home library, the cradle of his quest for *ʿilm* and the core of his daily social-philanthropic activities and responsibilities. Ustadh Mau's seasoned experience in the service of his people was already anticipated, in his own words, in the opening line of his *utendi* poem *Wasiya wa mabanati*, in which he utters: "Listen, my child, to the advice I shall give you. I understand the ways of the world; I have spent many years on this earth, and what I tell you now, you should bear in mind." In fact, in this early work, Ustadh Mau fictionalizes his experience by depicting himself as a mature man in his sixties—though he was not yet even married when he wrote the poem. To some extent, we can say that he became a mature thinker before his time, eager to have a say in how young minds should be nurtured, thanks to the incredible speed of his learning, his thirst for knowledge, and his great compassion for his fellow man, which he acquired from a very early stage of his youth.

---

13   "Ten Key Texts."
14   Renaud Santerre, *Pédagogie musulmane d'Afrique noire: L'École coranique peule du Came-roun* (Montreal: Presses de l'Université de Montréal, 1973), 346–347; quoted in Loimeier, *Between Social Skills and Marketable Skills*, 155.

2.2   *Ustadh Mau and His Breathing Library*[15]

This section will focus on the private "home" library of Ustadh Mau.[16] As Derrida would say, "Let us not begin at the beginning, nor even at the archive";[17] I shall rather proceed to highlight how Ustadh Mau's joy lies in his books, and how this joy permeates his library, turning it into a vital place. More precisely, the poet says, "Books are my joy. This is the reason why I have set this area [i.e., the library] apart for myself, so that I can be alone with my books."[18] Whether or not the Greek definition of *arkheion* as "a house, a domicile, an address, the residence of the superior magistrates, the archons, those who commanded"[19] can be applied to Ustadh Mau's private library, this is more than a mere "place for books" (*mahala pa vitabu*) to be stored, as this place exists through and because of the learned literary individual who spends day upon day there—hence the term "breathing" as most suitable for describing the living magic of his library.

Ustadh Mau's library, located on a first floor in the Langoni area, is indeed truly a living and lively space—one to which he returns after swimming early in the morning, where he rests, keeps and stores his material, reads, receives people in search of help, and teaches those who need some guidance. In other words—namely, his own—the two-room library, which also has a couch and toilet, is his refuge, a *kituo* ("station") where he spends many of his daily hours, and where people are sure to find him, unless he is out at the mosque or on related duties. All the texts stored there—books in Arabic, English, and Swahili, spanning varied subjects and genres—are interconnected with each other in that they all contribute to expressing the thirst for knowledge of a singular scholar and his commitment to his people.

It is interesting to recall that an important feature of an archive is the so-called "principle of provenance," according to which "all the records that belong to it are strongly interconnected. In the past, archivists liked to use organic

---

15   A concept Yun Lee Too also uses to describe how "the library needs not be a physical collection of texts, and it explores the phenomenon of the learned literary individual who becomes a virtual library." See Yun Lee Too, *The Idea of the Library in the Ancient World* (Oxford: Oxford University Press, 2010), 1–28.

16   For further criticism on the Riyadha manuscript collection, see Anne Bang, "Localising Islamic Knowledge: Acquisition and Copying of the Riyadha Mosque Manuscript Collection in Lamu, Kenya," in *From Dust to Digital: Ten Years of the Endangered Archives Programme*, ed. Maja Kominko (Cambridge: Open Book Publishers, 2015), 136–142.

17   Jacques Derrida and Eric Prenowitz, "Archive Fever: A Freudian Impression," *Diacritics* 25, no. 2 (1995): 11.

18   My translation, from Ustadh Mau's interview for the Kiswahili Bila Mipaka corpus, ELLAf, minutes 17:7–12: *Raha yangu iko kwenye zitabu. Ndio maana nimetengwa sehemu hii [makataba] niwe yangu, mimi peke yangu na vitabu vyangu.*

19   Derrida and Prenowitz, "Archive", 9.

metaphors to address this key point: an archive was not artificial, but 'natural.' They suggested that the 'organic unity' of the archive expressed the life of the organization or the organism which created it, in our case Ustadh Mau. Other metaphors used in the same context are 'body' and 'organic growth,' for instance"[20]—as if, indeed, this place can be regarded as the core of his service to the community.

In a speech on connected histories and their relevance to Africa, Shamil Jeppie stresses the importance of islands in the reconfiguration of continental history. In the following, I shall outline the significance of Ustadh Mau's personal efforts to build his own library on the island; similarly to Ahmad Bul'arāf, the erudite scholar from Sus, Morocco who migrated to and settled down in Timbuktu, Mali,[21] Ustadh Mau can be regarded as a true bibliophile in search of and hungry for knowledge. I shall consider both scholars in their role as bibliophiles: just as "Ahmad Bul'arāf accumulated works from great distances away from Timbuktu[,] bought works and commissioned copies,"[22] Ustadh Mau's own library houses books that were ordered and transported from Cairo and Mumbai.

When he was just twelve years old, Ustadh Mau began ordering books on his own from a bookshop in Cairo run by Muṣṭafā al-Bābī al-Ḥalabī and his brothers. This Cairene bookshop is a well-known printing house located near Al-Azhar University.[23] It has played an important role not only in Ustadh Mau's quest for knowledge, but also in the early printing history of other renowned Shafi'i thinkers from East Africa, such as Aḥmad b. Sumayṭ of Zanzibar.[24] Aḥmad b. Sumayṭ's early works were printed there—a link that contributes to mapping both the earlier as well as the current Islamic book network across East Africa, and more broadly across the continent. Cairo was, after all, a favored destination for pilgrims and students on the hajj, which explains why it became an important cosmopolitan center for West Africa and the Sudanic routes as well as East Africa.[25]

---

20   Dietmar Shenk, "Getrennte Welten? Über Literaturarchive und Archivwissenschaft," in *Archive für Literatur Der Nachlass und seine Ordnungen*, ed. Petra-Maria Dallinger, Georg Hofer, and Bernhard Judex, Literatur und Archiv 2 (Berlin: De Gruyter, 2018), 18.

21   Shamil Jeppie, "A Timbuktu Bibliophile between the Mediterranean and the Sahel: Ahmad Bul'arāf and the Circulation of Books in the First Half of the Twentieth Century," *Journal of North African Studies* 20, no. 1 (2015): 65–77.

22   Jeppie, "A Timbuktu Bibliophile," 69.

23   One of the brothers, Isa, was still in business up until a few years ago, but it seems that even this business may have closed (Scott Reese, personal communication).

24   Anne Bang, *Sufis and Scholars of the Sea. Family Networks in East Africa, 1860–1925* (London: Routledge, 2003), 93.

25   With regards to the trans-Saharan book trade, as Krätli and Lydon note, "books were

As Anne Bang writes, the great contribution of the Muṣṭafā al-Bābī al-Ḥalabī family was printing and distributing books on Islamic learning throughout the world.[26] As Reese describes, "it was a firm with a growing reputation for publishing a wide variety of Sufi-related texts and other works that were often implicitly, if not explicitly, opposed to the growing trends of literal-minded scripturalist reform."[27] They were active in disseminating Islamic religious works not only in Arabic and several African languages, but also in India and Southeast Asia. Indeed, they appeared to have been "the publisher of choice for Somalis as well as pro-Sufi, anti-scripturalist elements from East Africa and Aden to Southeast Asia."[28]

Muṣṭafā al-Bābī al-Ḥalabī—also known as Halabi & Sons—has played an important role in the "modernization" of African Islamic literary production in this period. The regular correspondence that Ustadh Mau has had with Cairo up to recent times shows how the trajectory of such modernization pointed not only toward Zanzibar, but also toward Lamu. In the following, I shall delve into some of the eye-opening books that have made an impact on Ustadh Mau's thought and compositions. Surprisingly, it is not only the printing house that established the connection between Lamu and Cairo, but also the works of scholars precisely from Cairo who have become transregionally influential in shaping Ustadh Mau's self-learning and understanding of Islam.

---

ordered by the Emperors, or else were brought back from the *hajj* by returning pilgrims. Meanwhile, West African students were sent to places like Fez and Cairo to study"; see Graziano Krätli and Ghislaine Lydon, *The Trans-Saharan Book Trade: Manuscript Culture, Arabic Literacy and Intellectual History in Muslim Africa* (Leiden: Brill, 2011), 21. Reese also points out the two major factors that increased Muslim mobility from the 1850s onwards: advances in steamship technology and the opening of the Suez Canal after 1869. "The number of Muslims traveling on the Hajj during the second half of the century, for instance, increased exponentially with more believers taking part in the pilgrimage to Mecca than at any other time in the history of the faith"; see Scott Reese, "Shaykh Abdullahi al-Qutbi and the Pious Believer's Dilemma: Local Moral Guidance in an Age of Global Islamic Reform," *Journal of Eastern African Studies* 9, no. 3 (2015): 489.

26 Anne Bang, "Authority and Piety, Writing and Print: A Preliminary Study of the Circulation of Islamic Texts in Late Nineteenth- and Early Twentieth-Century Zanzibar," in "Print Cultures, Nationalisms and Publics of the Indian Ocean," special issue, *Journal of the International African Institute* 81, no. 1 (2011): 103.

27 Reese, "Shaykh Abdullahi al-Qutbi," 497.

28 Reese, "Shaykh Abdullahi al-Qutbi," 497–498; see also Michael Laffan, "A Sufi Century: The Modern Spread of Sufi Orders in Southeast Asia," in *Global Muslims in the Age of Steam and Print*, ed. James L. Gelvin and Nile Green (Berkeley: University of California Press, 2014), 25–39.

2.2.1   Pockets of Knowledge: Ustadh Mau's Literature of Ideas

A tour of Ustadh Mau's books also tells us about the network and details of Islamic intellectual production on Lamu—in other words, how ideas circulated in the East African region, and through which texts. This research is situated against the backdrop of the discipline of the history of books, which flourished in the eighties and is known as the *histoire du livre* in France, *Geschichte des Buchwesens* in Germany, and "book history" or even "book arts" in English-speaking countries. It is indeed useful to know that this can teach us "how ideas were transmitted through print and how exposure to the printed word affected the thought and behaviour of mankind during the last five hundred years."[29] Secondly, this investigation shows the formation of a precise literary canon, the so-called "core curriculum"—which, little by little, Ustadh Mau has acquired over time. I am particularly interested in seeing how the library reflects the existence of his private canon of learning.

In total, his books now number around one thousand. Among the Arabic books, the works that have particularly influenced and expanded his knowledge have been not only those of older writers, but also those of contemporary ones writing about Islam, Sufism, Muslim brotherhoods, literature, philosophy, and theology. To begin with, it is possible to recognize a strong Cairene influence on Ustadh Mau's library, which should not come as a surprise if we take into account that, from the twentieth century, "Cairo was regarded as a capital of Arabic printing and book production"[30] while also becoming an increasingly important center for the training of East African scholars. This Cairene influence can also be regarded as a consequence of the vibrant intellectual era in which Egyptian writers of the nineteenth and first half of the twentieth century found themselves; indeed, at the turn of the century, many political and intellectual movements arose. These movements also mirrored the rapid changes that Egypt was undergoing in its relationship with the West as well as with the other Arab regions of the Ottoman Empire. As we also find in other regions, such as Ethiopia, Somalia, and Djibouti, Egyptian publishing houses—in particular, those that spawned from the activity of the Bābī al-Ḥalabī family—were instrumental both in printing the Arabic books of Muslim scholars and in diffusing Arabic Islamic literature in the Swahili coastal region. To cite but a few names, Rifāʿa Rāfiʿ al-Ṭahṭāwī (1801–1873), also known as "the father of Egyptian nationalism and of modern Islamic educational thought," actively contributed to the cultural renaissance (*naḥda*) of Egypt.[31]

---

29   Robert Darnton, "What Is the History of Books?" *Daedalus* 111, no. 3 (1982): 65.

30   Reese, "Shaykh Abdullahi al-Qutbi," 497.

31   For a comprehensive account of the life and works of this scholar and his stay in France,

2.2.2 Ustadh Mau's Cairene Network

One of the first scholars who, in the form of his printed works, traveled from Cairo to Lamu is ʿAbbās Maḥmūd al-ʿAqqād (1889–1964), whose modus vivendi and writings have had a strong influence on Ustadh Mau's own learning experience. Ustadh Mau admired this Cairene thinker so much that, when he was just sixteen years old, he took "al-ʿAqqād" as his nickname (before becoming "Mau"). This moniker became known among his network of scholars, who would eventually begin addressing him by precisely this name. For instance, in 1389 EG, when the Egyptian Islamic theologian Yūsuf al-Qaraḍāwī (1926–) sent Ustadh Mau the book *Al-Nās wa-al-ḥaqq*, the envelope of the book was addressed to "Ustadh Mahmud Ahmed al-ʿAqqād." His nickname in homage to ʿAbbās Maḥmūd al-ʿAqqād and his correspondence with Yūsuf al-Qaraḍāwī already reflect the influence of his Cairene network, comprised of Cairene role models, books, and writers.[32]

It is interesting to note that some details of al-ʿAqqād's life also apply to Ustadh Mau, as both writers can be regarded as the products of similar circumstances; it is attested, for instance, that al-ʿAqqād received little formal education, completing only elementary school, and that what he learned later on was thanks to the books that he bought and read on his own. As mentioned above, Ustadh Mau also enriched his knowledge by ordering and reading books on his own. Moreover, just as al-ʿAqqād's "ideas and activities aptly reflected the mainstream current within the intellectual community,"[33] Ustadh Mau's social and literary services—as a poet, teacher, and imam—also mirror the society he lives in and its cultural challenges. This is reminiscent of what Ngũgĩ wa

---

see Rifāʿa Rāfiʿ al- Ṭahṭawi, *An Imam in Paris. Account of a Stay in France by an Egyptian Cleric (1826–1831)*, trans. Daniel L. Newman (London: Saqi Books, 2011).

32   Another work of al-Qaradawi, which I was shown and given by Ustadh Mau, is the English-language *The Lawful and the Prohibited in Islam* (London: Al-Birr Foundation, 2003), first published in 1423 EG. As for the scholar ʿAbbās Mahmoud al-ʿAqqād (1889–1964), he was born in the town of Aswan. His father was a government clerk who died quickly after ʿAbbās's birth. His Kurdish origins mother, remained widow and devoted her life to the upbringing of her children. al-ʿAqqād received only primary education and through his own initiative he became well acquainted with English literature, also thanks to the newspapers available in Aswan through the years because of the presence of British army officers and engineers in the flourishing center of tourism of his home city. (For further criticism see Awad, Louis *The Literature of Ideas in Egypt*. Atlanta: Scholar Press, 1986):166–175.

33   Israel Gershoni, "Liberal Democratic Legacies in Modern Egypt: The Role of the Intellectuals, 1900–1950," *The Institute Letter Summer 2012*, https://www.ias.edu/ideas/2012/gershoni-democratic-legacies-egypt.

Thiong'o says with regard to the "social character" of literature, which "cannot elect to stand above or to transcend economics, politics, class, race or what Achebe calls 'the burning issues of the day' because those very burning issues with which it deals take place within an economic, political class and race context."[34] Two major works by al-'Aqqād are found in Ustadh Mau's library: *Muṭāla'āt fī al-Kutub wa-al-ḥayāh* ("The Readings on the Books and the Lives") and *Al-'Athar al-'Arab fī al-ḥadārah al-'Urubiyyah* ("The Arab's Impact on European Civilization"). This latter book was first published by Dar el-Maarif in 1960, followed by many reprint editions, which serves to indicate the wide popularity of this title. The last of these editions was published by the Hindawi Foundation in 2013; Ustadh Mau has the 1966 edition published by the Dar al-Kitab al-'Arabiyy in Beirut at his disposal.

Among the other eye-opening books that have influenced Ustadh Mau's learning, we must also mention the works of Abu Hamid al-Ghazali (1058–1111), regarded as "the St. Thomas of Islam,"[35] whom Ustadh Mau calls simply "Imam Ghazali." Among the works of this author, Ustadh Mau has commented particularly on *Iḥiyā' 'ulūm ad-dīn* ("The Revival of Religious Knowledge"), which is well known as a monument of theological knowledge from the Islamic Middle Ages. A concise description of the work describes it as follows:

> Peppered with hadith (not all particularly authentic it has to be said), aphorisms, and pearls of wisdoms from pious sages, The Book of Knowledge [the first book of the work] offers a discussion on the value of knowledge, the praiseworthy and objectionable branches of knowledge, the qualities needed in teachers and students and ends with a blistering praise of the "noble nature" of the intellect.[36]

---

34 Ngũgĩ wa Thiong'o, *Writers in Politics* (Nairobi: East African Educational Publishers, 1981), 6. This is further reminiscent of what is said of the role of the intellectual in West Africa: in a section titled "Islam et modernité, le rôle de l'intellectuel," Penda M'bow reminds her readers that "l'intellectuel musulman n'est pas né au XXᵉ siècle. L'exemple le plus intéressant reste celui d'Ahmad Baba de Tombouctou qui a beaucoup réfléchi sur les problèmes de son temps comme la question de l'esclavage." Penda M'bow, *Être intellectual, être Musulman en Afrique*, Série Conférences 24 (Rabat: Institut des Études Africaines, 2005), 23.

35 "Il san Tommaso dell'Islam"; see Massimo Campanini, *Il pensiero islamico contemporaneo* (Bologna: Il Mulino, 2005) and Campanini, ed., *Al-Ghazali, Le perle del Corano* (Milan: Rizzoli-BUR, 2005).

36 "Ten Key Texts."

What particularly attracted Ustadh Mau's interest to this book was, firstly, the different ways (*ndiya*) the author has addressed and commented on religious questions (*maswali ya kidini*), and secondly, his style (*mtindo*) of explaining things in a light and simple way (*ndiya pesi*), differently from other scholars of his era.

Among the Egyptian works that have influenced Ustadh Mau's thinking and knowledge, we must also mention *Laisa min al-Islam* ("Not From Islam"), by Muhammad al-Ghazali (1917–1996). At a time when Sufism was very much prevalent on the island of Lamu, this book opened Ustadh Mau's eyes (*kufungua macho*) and induced changes in his thinking (*mabadiliko kwenye fikra*) about the movement: "This was an eye opener book that considerably helped me and caused a change in my thoughts while Sufism was on Lamu." (*Kitabu ambacho kilinisaidia sana kufungua macho na kilicholeta mabadiliko kwenye fikra zangu wakati huko Lamu Sufism ilikuwapo.*)[37]

Indeed, whereas until 1968, Ustadh Mau was a follower of the Alawiyya tariqa, the discovery of al-Ghazali's book changed his thoughts on Islamic doctrine. This change of heart caused strain in his relationship with his teacher, reformist scholar Sheikh Harith Swaleh, to whom Ustadh Mau was particularly indebted; once he abandoned his teacher's order, he became a Salafi supporter (literally, a follower of the *salaf al-salih*, or the "pious ancestors"). Like other thinkers from Mombasa, such as Sheikh Alamin bin Ali na Sheikh Abdalla Swaleh al-Farsiy, as well as Sheikh Muhamad Rashid Ridhaa of Egypt,[38] Ustadh Mau too now defines himself as a Salafist: *Mimi ni mtu wa salafi* ("I am a Salafist man").[39] When he distanced himself from the Alawiyya tariqa, however, some of his madrassa teachers were so disappointed that they "started saying he had become a Wahabi."[40] However, in matters of *fiqh*, he follows the *fiqh* of Shafi'i, although his grandfather was a Hanafi, a common trend amid Swahili with fathers or grandfathers of Indian origins.[41]

---

37 Ustadh Mau, personal communication, March 2018.
38 As Reese notes, "by the early twentieth century, religious texts printed in Cairo and Bombay were readily available in the coastal towns of East Africa, as were reformist newspapers such as Rashid Rida's *al-Manar*" ("Shaykh Abdullahi al-Qutbi," 490).
39 Ustadh Mau, personal communication, May 2018.
40 Rayya Timammy, "Shaykh Mahmoud Abdulkadir 'Mau': A Reformist Preacher in Lamu," *Annual Review of Islam in Africa* 12, no. 2 (2015): 86.
41 A similar example is Sheikh Yassen, owner of the book shop Adam Traders—also known as Maktaba 'Alawiyya—in Mombasa. Whereas Sheikh Yassen and his brother are Shafi'i and were born in Mombasa, the father Haj Ali Muhammad who started their press in the 1964 was Hanafi, born in 1920 and originary from India.

Sheikh Yusuf al-Qaradawi (1926) is another one of the prominent Muslim thinkers who have had an impact on Ustadh Mau's education. The poet is particularly indebted to the work *Al-Nās wa-al-ḥaqq*, another eye-opener of a book, as he says,[42] that helped him to begin understanding and accepting difficult and controversial aspects of the law (*jambo la haki laweza kupingwa na wengi*).[43] As Ustadh Mau explains it, Qaradawi's way of writing was light and easy to understand for him. He highlights that the author intentionally wrote it with a broad readership in mind.

Unlike Qaradawi's writings, Ustadh Mau was not initially attracted to Sayyid Qutb's *Ma'alim fi al-Tariq* ("Milestones") when he read it for the first time, and indeed was not able to consider its interpretation. According to him, the author seemed to be addressing expert readers, whereas he was not yet mature enough in terms of age and thinking at the time (*kwa umri na kwa fikra*). Ultimately, by reading it again, he came to fully understand the image of Islam that the work conveyed and wished to impart it to every Muslim (*taswira ambayo yatakikana kila muisilamu awe nayo juu ya isilamu*).[44]

Beyond the Cairene network that has contributed to the forging of book history on Lamu, from the very beginning of his career as a poet, Ustadh Mau has also been inspired by Shaykh 'Alī al-Ṭanṭawi. Born in Damascus, 'Alī al-Ṭanṭawi (1909–1999) was an influential Mecca-based, Salafi-oriented reformist scholar, one of the most famous, prominent, and best writers and preachers of Islam in the modern era (Munir 2014, 251). In his memoirs, he gives a vivid description of his school days at the then-prestigious school of Maktab Anbar in Damascus. This provides an insight into the system of education that was available in the early twentieth century in Damascus. Ustadh Mau was inspired by 'Alī al-Ṭanṭawi's *Ya-bintī* ("Oh My Daughter"), a pamphlet in prose form composed in 1954. His reading of this pamphlet inspired him to compose his first poem, *Wasiya wa mabanati*.

2.3 Faida ya elimu: *Debating Muslim Education and Learning Culture in Kenya*

What is the value of books in Islamic culture? In his speech "Faida ya elimu na lugha" ("The Benefits of Knowledge and Language")—which this paragraph will mainly reflect upon—Ustadh Mau tells an anecdote: during the Abbasid caliphate, under the aegis of the caliph Abbas ibn Abd al-Muttalib, the caliph

---

42   *Kilinifunguwa mato mapema* (personal communication, May 2018)

43   Ibid.

44   Ustadh Mau, personal communication, April 2018.

used to remunerate the person in charge of translating Greek texts into Arabic with a quantity of gold equaling the weight of the book, thus showing the extent to which people valued science. Yet if one is looking for a bookshop on Lamu nowadays, will the search be successful? I came across only two bookshops on Lamu: the Mani bookshop, close to Lamu Fort, and the Faiz bookshop, in the Langoni area. Yet the main books sold are the compulsory readings that the government has mandated for primary- and secondary-school syllabi in Kenya, along with books on information technology and English for passing exams and acquiring skill certifications. The books available represent only the so-called educational publishing, but say nothing about Islamic education, let alone the reading culture of a region.[45] This is indeed a paradox, given that Muslim education is famously religious in nature.

To begin with, the Qur'ān is widely regarded as the first, holiest example of wise writing, which Muslims were instructed to learn by heart. The oral memorization and transmission of texts was one of the first and foremost means of acquiring knowledge, which was regarded as knowledge only when it was truly "incorporated" as a body of knowledge in the memory, without the physical need to resort to any texts as a support material.[46] Still, as Bloom notes with regard to the Abbasid caliphate in the middle of the eighth century, "book and book knowledge became the aim of Islamic society."[47]

Ustadh Mau also proudly highlights that in Islam, learning represents the key to knowledge (*kusoma ndio ni ufunguo wa hikma*), and that the first order given to the Prophet Muhammad and his followers was اِقْرَأ, "Read." To start out by learning "the signs of the Wise Book" (*āyāh* 10:1) means for Muslims to start reading the Holy Qur'ān in Arabic even before knowing the letters of the *'abjād*.[48] As Ustadh Mau points out in his own wise words:

---

45   This is in line with an observation on educational publishing in Africa, which, "though lucrative and safe," "says nothing about a region's culture. Besides it, fiction is hardly part of educational publishing and this does not help in a better understanding of a regional literature." Stanley Gazemba, "African Publishing Minefields and the Woes of the African Writer," *The Elephant*, December 13, 2019, https://www.theelephant.info/culture/2019/12/13/african-publishing-minefields-and-the-woes-of-the-african-writer/.

46   See Loimeier, *Between Social Skills and Marketable Skills*, 155.

47   Jonathan Bloom, *Paper before Print: The History and Impact of Paper in the Islamic World* (New Haven: Yale University Press, 2001), 111.

48   For other *'āyāt* referring to the "Wise Book," see also 31:1–2, "Those are the signs of the Wise Book for a guidance and a mercy to the good-doers who perform the prayer, and pay the alms, and have sure faith in the Hereafter. Those are upon guidance from their Lord; those are the prosperers," and 36:1, "By the Wise Koran, thou art truly among the Envoys on a straight path."

Na dini yetu yote msingi yake ni msingi ya ilmu, msingi wa kusoma; kwa hivo swali la ilmu katika uislamu ni zitu zile haziwezi kuziachana: Usilamu na ilmu ziko sambamba.

The foundations of all our religions are educational ones, the fundaments of learning; therefore, the question of knowledge in Islam represents two facets that cannot be separated from each other: Islam and knowledge run parallel. (My translation)

That said, Ustadh Mau problematizes and laments the presence or absence of knowledge and education in contemporary Islamic society, and urges individuals to study and to reacquire what one should not forget as his or her own right (*haki*). In the following, I will reflect on specific selections from his speeches and poems; this analysis will help in further understanding his passion for books and his engagement with knowledge production in his community.

2.4 *Contesting Knowledge*

Hikma, maarifa, ujuzi ni kitu cha muislamu kilichompotea.

Wisdom, expertise, knowledge—this is something that Islam has lost.
USTADH MAU (my translation)

It seems that he lives in a sort of "frustrating postcolonial present" exactly like the one perceived among coastal Kenyans in Mombasa and investigated by Kai Kresse.[49] By saying this, Ustadh Mau wishes to reconfigure the value of knowledge in his own Lamuan community.[50] In his speeches, he expresses a nostalgic longing for a past golden age of Islam, when knowing Arabic was a source of pride; a time in which Islam, passing through Greek culture and texts, returned home in a new form, both fortified and different from Western culture and customs.[51] As he says in his nostalgic excursus on travelling Islam and

---

49 Kai Kresse, *Swahili Muslim Publics and Postcolonial Experience* (Bloomington: Indiana University Press, 2018), 3.

50 The fear that their own customs will fade away is also expressed in a short *shairi* poem titled *Mila yetu hufujika* ("Our Traditions Are Being Destroyed"); see Sarah Hillewaert, *Morality at the Margins: Youth, Language, and Islam in Coastal Kenya* (New York: Fordham University Press), 2020.

51 On the impact of Greek philosophy on early Islamic thinkers, see the chapter on Greek

SEEKING 'ILM ON LAMU: USTADH MAU'S LIBRARY AND SERVICES   85

the edification of its own sciences, Ustadh Mau implicitly refers to the Christian religious propaganda used in proselytism, which has not characterized the spread of Islam. He also situates his narrative by making reference to Qur'ānic *āyāt* 12:65 (from the Sūrat Yūsuf) and 35:28 (from the Sūrat Fāṭir).[52]

Yet his complaint comes out loud and clear with regard to education, which is a facet of Islam that has deteriorated rather than improved; for this, he blames his own people, himself included:

> *Makosa yetu ni kwamba kuna kipindi hatukujiendeleza, walichotuatia wazazi wetu hatukukipeleka mbele; tukashughulika na mambo ya ugomvi wa kisiasa na kutaka kutawala na elimu ikazorota.*

> Our mistake is that there was a time/phase in which we did not improve; what we were given by our parents, we did not pass forth. Instead, we would deal with political disputes and governance, while education deteriorated.

In this complaint, we can see also the lack of responsibility that he ascribes to parents, as he also reminds us in the poem *Mwalimu*, where he pleads with relatives and teachers to set good examples for their own children and pupils. Education should not be at the whim of politics, as the above excerpt from his speech clearly shows, nor should madrassa classes be limited only to those skills taught through *ubao*, as he points out in the stanza that follows. It emerges

---

heritage in Carmela Baffioni, *I grandi pensatori dell'Islam* (Rome: Edizioni Lavoro, 1995): Baffioni shows, for instance, how Aristotle's *Poetics* was summarized by Muslim philosophers such as al-Kindī, and was also commented on by Avicenna and Averroes. To name but a few examples, the author further tells us that Khwārizmī, in his *Mafātīh al-ʿulūm* ("The Keys to Science"), describes poetics as the creation of works able to touch listeners. Al-Fārābī distinguished the technical part related to prosody, and introduced the concept of syllogism, based on which every poetic comparison implies a syllogism (Baffioni, *I grandi pensatori*, 25).

52   The Qur'ānic verses, in their entirety, read as follows, based on Arberry's translation: 12:65, "And when they opened their things, they found their merchandise, restored to them. 'Father,' they said, 'what more should we desire? See, our merchandise here is restored to us. We shall get provision for our family, and we shall be watching over our brother; we shall obtain an extra camel's load—that is an easy measure'"; 35:28, "[M]en too, and beasts and cattle—diverse are their hues. Even so only those of His servants fear God who have knowledge; surely God is All-mighty, All-forgiving." Arthur J. Arberry, *The Quran Interpreted* (Oxford: Oxford University Press, 1984), 233, 447.

clearly from the examples taken from his speeches and poetry how much Ustadh Mau stresses the value of teaching our children by guiding them in life:

> *Haitoshi kusomesha, kwa kwandika ubaoni*
> *Ni dharura kufundisha, kwa mwendo wa maishani*
> *Sura njema kuonesha, wanafunzi igizani.*

> It is not enough to teach by writing on the blackboard;
> It is important to teach them how to live in this world.
> The good example you provide, pupils will imiate it!
>> *Mwalimu* ("Teacher"), stz. 8

Still, the importance of preserving those good morals (*tabia njema*) that make Muslims pious and trustful people runs parallel with acquiring knowledge (*elimu*), as is reiterated in another excerpt from the poem *Mwalimu*:

> *Bila ya uwaminifu, na ucha Mungu moyoni*
> *Hatupati ufafanifu, si wa duniya si dini*
> *Natupange zetu swafu, kwa kite tusomesheni.*

> Without being faithful and pious at heart,
> We will never succeed, neither in secular nor in religious education.
> Let us join hands; let us educate them with empathy.
>> *Mwalimu* ("Teacher"), stz. 10

As the above excerpts show, the lyrical "I"—be it in his sermons or in his poems—is always a polyphonic "we," which includes himself to begin with. He also indeed acknowledges the impact that his Friday *hutba* has on people, as such sermons serve to enlighten Muslims to their own forgotten Islamic knowledge. He tells one anecdote about a man who used to be a teacher in a madrassa and was having hard time earning a living from this; however, he wrongly used to believe that taking a side job would be considered haram, i.e. not allowed in Islam. The revelation he experienced after Ustadh Mau's sermon on *kazi katika Uislamu* ("work in Islam") is told as follows:

> [...] *baada ya ile hutba, yeye akaamua kwamba 'kumbe si makosa yoyote mimi nikifanya kazi bora kazi iwe halal.' Akaanza kubadilisha mipango yake, akaanza kazi ya kuajiriwa, kibarua cha kujenga. Mungu akambarikia, akaweza kununua hayawani; baada ya miaka minne mitano alhamdulil-lahi [amekuwa] mutanaffiz (mtu mwenye nafasi ya pesa), ana maduka,*

SEEKING ʿILM ON LAMU: USTADH MAU'S LIBRARY AND SERVICES   87

hutoa zakat na kadhalika. Na chanzo cha mabadiliko yake ni alisikia hutba ya jumaa na watu wengine pia wameathirika. Kwa hivo hiyo ni jambo ambalo mimi naona ni muhimu: na la kuchangia katika kuweka mabadi-liko ya mujtamai.

After that Friday sermon, he was surprised to discover 'there is no prob-lem if I take a better job, as long as the job is allowed (halal).' He started changing his plans: he began employment as an assistant mason. God blessed him, and he was able to buy animals; after four or five years, thank God, he became a wealthy person; he runs shops, he gives money to the poor (*zakat*), and the like. The catalyst for his change was that he listened to the Friday sermon, and other people were also influenced. Therefore, this is something that I consider useful: to contribute in seeding change (*mabadiliko*) for the benefit of the community (*mujtamai*). (My transla-tion.)

The last opinion that Ustadh Mau shares here reflects the improvement and change he wishes to see in his community. A change, in my opinion, should aim for that fair balance between intelligence (*akili*) and soul (*roho*) that Islam is representative of, as Sheikh Abdilahi claims in his Ramadan lectures of 1998.[53] Ustadh Mau also clearly stresses his social commitment to attain-ing that change. What Ustadh Mau's *hutba* on *kazi katika Uislamu* triggered was not intended merely to prescribe norms, but also to make his people reflect.

Ustadh Mau's social engagement with his fellow Lamuans finds expression through the vehicle of his Friday sermons—as the abovementioned anecdote shows—as well as, and particularly, through poetry. As Ustadh Mau says:

Sisi mpaka sasa alhadulillahi utamaduni wetu unategemea mambo ya mashairi.

For us, up to now—thank God—our culture relies on poetic composition (My translation).

Ustadh Mau mentions all the diverse occasions for which people might need a poem to be composed and recited—funerals, weddings, graduations, and the

---

53   See Kai Kresse, *Philosophising in Mombasa. Knowledge, Islam and Intellectual Practice at the Swahili Coast* (Edinburgh: Edinburgh University Press, 2007), 195 ff.

like. He understands and fulfills a very basic need that his community is constantly seeking: to know about what he calls *mambo ya kimaisha*, "the things of life," which Chinua Achebe before him would call "the burning issues of the days."[54] Aside from his religious teaching at the madrassa and during Ramadan, he feels most at the service of his society—in Arabic, *mujtamai* and or *jamii*—through his writing and poetry:

> *Kwa hivo nahisi kwamba nasaidia kiasi fulani kutumikia jamii yangu kupitia upande wa uandishi wa mashairi, [...] alhamdulillahi nashukuru, nahisi kwamba nafanya kitu kwa ajili ya mujtamai wangu; natekeleza isipokuwa ni sehemu ndogo jukumu ambalo nahisi jukumu langu.*

> Therefore, I feel that I am helping, to some extent, in serving my society from the angle of writing and poetry [...] I am grateful to God; I feel I am doing something for the benefit of my community; I make an effort despite the fact that it is just a tiny portion; I can see it as my responsibility. (My translation).

2.4.1 The Knowledge We Seek

The pleas to Ustadh Mau's community—expressed in the plural *sisi* "us" or *tu* "we"—work like a refrain in his speeches and poetry: *tusione ... tusome ... tusomeshe ... tusifuate ... tufanye* ("we should not think ... we should read ... we should teach ... we should not follow ... we should do ...").

To begin with, he states the things that his community ought to know and learn:

> *Tusome ilmu, kila sampuli ya ilmu; hakuna makosa ya kusoma ilmu. Ilmu ni mali ya ulimwengu si mali ya nchi maalum. Ni kitu ambacho ni haki yetu na lazima tukikumbatie tukitie kwenye kitujo zile ambazo hazitufai, lakini yale maarifa na ujuzi na ilmu zenye faida tuzifuate popote zilipo.*

> We should study every kind of subject, because there is nothing wrong with learning. Knowledge is the universal good, not the good belonging to a powerful country; it is something that is our right, and we have to embrace it and use a sieve (*kitujo*) to sift out the things that are not good for us; but beneficial knowledge and skills, we should follow them wherever they are. (My translation).

---

54   Thiong'o, *Writers in Politics*, 6.

Ustadh Mau's belief in the right to education is quite clear in this speech, and also clearly stresses the importance of incorporating into one's own culture any sort of benefits derived from learning other epistemologies. He reminds listeners how such a universal good—knowledge—is not a pricey commodity far removed from themselves and their customs; he further points out that no matter how much you take from knowledge, it only continues to grow, whereas when you use your wealth, it becomes ever less—hence his motto, "knowledge is richness beyond wealth" (*elimu ni utajiri kuliko mali*).[55]

In *Tupijeni Makamama*, he compares his community to a ship and foresees that it will wreck unless customs are rediscovered and ignorance is replaced by cultural awareness:

…

Tusiyone ni dufu mila yetu tukapuza	We should not see ourselves as ignor-
Chombo chetu kitasoza	ant or neglect our customs,
	Otherwise our ship will sink.

     Tupijeni, stz 2

In comparison to the first excerpt, in this stanza we find a parallel to his plea for knowledge, namely in calling for the community to revisit their own customs.[56]

From this point of view, Ustadh Mau promotes a sort of rebuilding of confidence in and respect for Lamu's own customs. Such confidence should derive first and foremost from the local people, as he sees this as the only way that others may also respect and appreciate the local customs. His reference to the Swahili saying *kilio hulia mwenye na mtu mbali naye akalia* (see below) also adds to the idea that the change should begin at home, and serve as a model for those who are far:

> *Chetu kama hatukithamini sisi wenyewe na wangine piya hawawezi kuki-thamini; lazima mtu ajihishimu yeye ili wangine wamhishimu. Waswahili husema: "kilio hulia mwenye na mtu mbali naye akalia."*

> If we don't value our own things (or: knowledge/products), others can't value them either; a person must respect himself so that others may do the same. As the Swahili people say, 'Change begins at home.'[57]

---

55   Uttered by Ustadh Mau in a reply to my provocative question of whether "knowledge is richness" (*je, elimu ni utajiri?*) during our interview at his library in March 2018.

56   See also Ustadh Mau's poem *Mila yetu hufujika* ("Our Traditions Are Being Destroyed") in Hillewaert, *Morality at the Margins*, 44–45.

57   See the poem in this volume titled *Kulia hulia mwenye*, inspired by the saying *Kulia hulia*

It is interesting to note that change is a recurring theme in his didactic voice and agenda. While in the excerpt here it is represented by *kilio* ("the cry"), we may also notice the term *mabadiliko* ("change") mentioned above, which the Muslim devotee underwent by listening to Ustadh Mau's Friday sermon.

2.4.2 Ustadh Mau's *Art de vivre*

Ustadh Mau's speech "Faida ya elimu na lugha" closes on this impressive note, which Ustadh Mau himself considers his calling (*mwito*) and credo (*nashuhudiya*, lit. "I testify"); in Ustadh Mau's call to action, one can sense the emphasis on tirelessly inviting every Muslim to change things for the better, that "we should make an effort" (*tufanye bidii!*).

Doing one's own best is exactly what Ustadh Mau tries to pursue in his ordinary life. At every small step, wherever there is a need to reform something, Ustadh Mau feels a duty to be there and do his best. As the Gujarati people say, "'The son of the tailor will sew clothes so long as he is alive,' and if he is still with a needle in hand when his time arrives, he will have accomplished his masterpiece.'[58] I personally believe that the social-philanthropic responsibility that Ustadh Mau feels and indulges every single day will never abandon so long as he is alive. As he puts it, "You have to live in a community (*jamii*) where you are ready to help and care of the issues of the others"; *kuishi maisha yangu si maana ya maisha kwa maoni yangu* "living only for the sake of my own life it is not the meaning of how to live for me."[59]

Ustadh Mau concludes his call to action with the Arabic saying that he uses to prescribe to his Muslim community the basic steps for improving their state. How? Through education:

> *Kwa hivo huo ndo mwito wangu kwa wenzangu wote nashuhudiya tufany-eni bidii, tusione elimu ni ghali* [...] *elimu mwisho wake utapata faida, kuin-vest katika ilmu ndipo mahali bora zaidi. Na mtu ametuambia:* [switching to Arabic] *'ma naḥala walidun waladahu afḍalu bin 'adabin ḥasanin; Hak-una mzazi aliyempa mwanawe kitu bora kuliko ilm na maarifa* [Swahili translation of the Arabic passage].' *Kwa hivo sisi kama hatukupata fursa*

---

mwenye, na mtu mbali kalia, "If the affected one cries out, another will join in from afar," meaning that if you want to change something, you first have to do it yourself, so that others may then join in support.

58 Paraphrased in English from the Italian version in Alberto Bassoli and Davide Monda, *M.K. Gandhi: L'arte di vivere* (Milan: Mondadori, 1989), 72–73.

59 Ustadh Mau, personal communication, July 2019.

kusoma, tusomeshe watoto, watoto wasomeshe wasomesheke: hiyo ndia ya pekee ya kugeuza hali yetu ilivo.

Hence, this is my call to my peers, I testify: we should make an effort; we shouldn't think that knowledge is pricey. Investing in knowledge that rewards you with benefits is a better strategy [of investing] (*mahari*). We were indeed told [here Mau is referring to a hadith in Arabic by the Prophet Muhammad], *ma naḥala walidun waladahu afḍalu bin ʿadabin ḥasanin*, 'There is no better gift that parents can impart to their children than knowledge and science.' Therefore, if we do not have the chance to study, we should teach our children so they may be properly educated: this is the only way to change the state in which we are.

References

Abdalla, Abdilatif. *Sauti ya dhiki*. Nairobi: Oxford University Press, 1973.

ʿAqqād, ʿAbbās Mahmūd al-. *The Arab's Impact on European Civilisation*. Cairo: Supreme Council for Islamic Affairs, 1960.

Arberry, Arthur, J. *The Quran Interpreted*. Oxford: Oxford University Press, 1984.

Awad, Louis. *The Literature of Ideas in Egypt*. Part I. Arabic Writing Today 3; Studies in Near Eastern Culture and Society 6. Atlanta: Scholars Press, 1986.

Baffioni, Carmela. *I grandi pensatori dell'Islam*. Rome: Edizioni Lavoro, 1995.

Bang, Anne. *Sufis and Scholars of the Sea. Family Networks in East Africa, 1860–1925*. London: Routledge, 2003.

Bang, Anne. "Authority and Piety, Writing and Print: A Preliminary Study of the Circulation of Islamic Texts in Late Nineteenth- and Early Twentieth-Century Zanzibar." In "Print Cultures, Nationalisms and Publics of the Indian Ocean." Special issue, *Journal of the International African Institute* 81, no. 1 (2011): 89–107.

Bang, Anne. "Localising Islamic Knowledge: Acquisition and Copying of the Riyadha Mosque Manuscript Collection in Lamu, Kenya." In *From Dust to Digital: Ten Years of the Endangered Archives Programme*, edited by Maja Kominko. Cambridge: Open Book Publishers, 2015.

Berkey, Jonathan Porter. *The Transmission of Knowledge in Medieval Cairo: A Social History of Islamic Education*. Princeton, NJ: Princeton University Press, 1992.

Bloom, Jonathan. *Paper before Print: The History and Impact of Paper in the Islamic World*. New Haven, Conn.: Yale University Press, 2001.

Campanini, Massimo. *Il pensiero islamico contemporaneo*. Bologna: Il Mulino, 2005.

Campanini, Massimo, ed. *Al-Ghazali, Le perle del Corano*. Milan: Rizzoli-BUR, 2005.

Darnton, Robert. "What Is the History of Books?" *Daedalus* 111, no. 3 (1982): 65–83.

Derrida, Jacques, and Eric Prenowitz. "Archive Fever: A Freudian Impression." *Diacritics* 25, no. 2 (1995): 9–63.

Gazemba, Stanley. "African Publishing Minefields and the Woes of the African Writer." *The Elephant*, December 13, 2019. https://www.theelephant.info/culture/2019/12/13/african-publishing-minefields-and-the-woes-of-the-african-writer/.

Ghazali, Abu Hamid. *Iḥiyā' 'ulūm ad-dīn* Beirut: Dar al Jayl, 1985.

Ghazali, Muhammad. *Laysa min al Islām*. Beirut: Dar al-Kutub al-Islāmīyah, 1983.

Gershoni, Israel. "Liberal Democratic Legacies in Modern Egypt: The Role of the Intellectuals, 1900–1950." *The Institute Letter Summer 2012*. https://www.ias.edu/ideas/2012/gershoni-democratic-legacies-egypt.

Hillewaert, Sarah. *Morality at the Margins: Youth, Language, and Islam in Coastal Kenya*. New York: Fordham University Press, 2020.

Jeppie, Shamil. "A Timbuktu Bibliophile between the Mediterranean and the Sahel: Ahmad Bul'arāf and the Circulation of Books in the First Half of the Twentieth Century." *Journal of North African Studies* 20, no. 1 (2015): 65–77. doi: 10.1080/13629387.2014.983734.

Krätli, Graziano, and Ghislaine Lydon. *The Trans-Saharan Book Trade: Manuscript Culture, Arabic Literacy and Intellectual History in Muslim Africa*. Leiden: Brill, 2011.

Kresse, Kai. *Philosophising in Mombasa. Knowledge, Islam and Intellectual Practice at the Swahili Coast*. Edinburgh: Edinburgh University Press, 2007.

Kresse, Kai. *Swahili Muslim Publics and Postcolonial Experience*. Bloomington: Indiana University Press, 2018.

Laffan, Michael. "A Sufi Century: The Modern Spread of Sufi Orders in Southeast Asia." In *Global Muslims in the Age of Steam and Print*, edited by James L. Gelvin and Nile Green, 25–39. Berkeley: University of California Press, 2014.

Loimeier, Roman. *Between Social Skills and Marketable Skills: The Politics of Islamic Education in 20th-Century Zanzibar*. Leiden: Brill, 2009.

Mahmoud, Ahmad Abdulkadir and Frankl, Peter J.L. "*Kiswahili*: A Poem by Mahmoud Ahmad Abdulkadir, to Which is Appended a List of the Poet's Compositions in Verse." *Swahili Forum* 20 (2013): 1–18.

M'bow, Penda. *Être intellectual, être Musulman en Afrique*. Série Conférences 24. Rabat: Institut des Études Africaines, 2005.

Munir, Ahmad. "Sheikh Ali al-Tantāwi and His Educational and Literary Services." *Shaykh Zayed Islamic Centre: University of Peshawar* 29, no. 2 (2014): 254–272.

Qaradawi, Yusuf. *Al-Nās wa-al-ḥaqq*. Kuwait: Dar al-Manar, n.d.

Qaradawi, Yusuf. *The Lawful and the Prohibited in Islam*. London: Al-Birr Foundation, 2003.

Qutb, Sayyid. *Ma'alim fi al-Tariq*. n.d: n.d., 1964.

Reese, Scott. "Shaykh Abdullahi al-Qutbi and the Pious Believer's Dilemma: Local Moral Guidance in an Age of Global Islamic Reform." *Journal of Eastern African Studies* 9, no. 3 (2015): 488–504.

Santerre, Renaud. *Pédagogie musulmane d'Afrique noire: L'École coranique peule du Cameroun*. Montreal: Presses de l'Université de Montréal, 1973.

Shenk, Dietmar. "Getrennte Welten? Über Literaturarchive und Archivwissenschaft." In *Archive für Literatur Der Nachlass und seine Ordnungen*, edited by Petra-Maria Dallinger, Georg Hofer, and Bernhard Judex. Literatur und Archiv 2. Berlin: De Gruyter, 2018.

Siba'i, Mustafa. *Some Glittering Aspects of the Islamic Civilization*. Beirut: Holy Koran Publishing House, 1984.

Ṭahṭawi, Rifāʿa Rāfiʿ al-. *An Imam in Paris. Account of a Stay in France by an Egyptian Cleric (1826–1831)*. Translated by Daniel L. Newman. London: Saqi Books, 2011. First published 2004.

Tantawi, Sheikh Ali al-. *Ya-bintī*. Medina: Mujawharāt al-Maghribal, 1985.

"The List: Ten Key Texts on Islamic Education." *Critical Muslim* 15, no. 1 (July–September 2015): https://www.criticalmuslim.io/the-list-ten-key-texts-on-islamic-education/.

Thiong'o, Ngũgĩ. *Writers in Politics*. Nairobi: East African Educational Publishers, 1981.

Timammy, Rayya. "Shaykh Mahmoud Abdulkadir 'Mau': A Reformist Preacher in Lamu." *Annual Review of Islam in Africa* 12, no. 2 (2015): 85–90.

Too, Yun Lee. *The Idea of the Library in the Ancient World*. Oxford: Oxford University Press, 2010.

Zarnuji, Burhān al-Dīn al-. *Instructions for the Student: The Method of Learning*. US: Starlatch Press, 2003.

FIGURE 7   A book shelf in Ustadh Mahmoud Mau's private library

How Ought We to Live? The Ethical and the Poetic in Ustadh Mahmoud Mau's Poetry

Clarissa Vierke

Sharuti tuwe imara, kuunda twabiya bora
Tuimarishe fikira, za kutuonesha ndiya

We must be firm, and build good characters.
We should strengthen the thoughts that will guide us on the right path.

Bandari ina mawimbi ("The Port Makes Waves", stz. 9)

1   *Dibaji*: Ustadh Mau's Moral Concern

Many of Ustadh Mau's poems are replete with moral concerns: he judges, takes sides with the underprivileged, evaluates the past, criticizes the present, urges change for a better future, and gives advice on what to do best. In the poem *Bandari ina mawimbi* ("The Port Makes Waves"), he warns his audience to critically ponder the construction of a deep-sea port close to Lamu, since it might have positive, but also destructive effects on Lamuan society. In *Mama msimlaumu* ("Don't Blame My Mother"), it is a baby who speaks out against placing blame on the mother for abandoning it rather than considering the involvement of society at large. In *Haki za watoto* ("Children's Rights"), he gives advice on child care and defends the rights of children. In *Amu* ("Lamu"), he pleads with fellow Lamuans, who have lost family members in a shipwreck between Lamu and Pate, to be patient and to accept the catastrophe as part of human life, rather than advance conspiracy theories that are of no avail. Thus, much of his poetry centers around basic ethical questions: what is the right path? What is good or bad? How ought one to live? These add to the more general question, what is the human good?

In this chapter, I would like to reflect on the relationship between morality and poetry in Ustadh Mau's poetic practice. Drawing on Michael Lambek's notion of "ordinary ethics" and his emphasis on "doing ethics," I consider ethics or morality—I use the two terms interchangeably—not as existing in the form of a list of defined and unchangeable virtues, but rather as a continuous practice and a struggle toward the right path. In my reading, for Ustadh Mau, poetry is a major site of "doing ethics"—finding a language for it, weighing

---

© CLARISSA VIERKE, 2023 | DOI:10.1163/9789004525726_007

This is an open access chapter distributed under the terms of the CC BY-NC-ND 4.0 license.

arguments, and judging and criticizing in relation to life situations and occurrences.

2   "Doing Ethics"

The intention to do right and to decide what is right and what is wrong is essentially human and part of the human condition. As Lambek underscores, humans are essentially moral beings: they judge, condemn, evaluate, criticize, reason, and are driven by the question: "How ought I to live?" It is this basic human faculty, which does not merely find its expression in constitutions, laws, or philosophical treatise on ethics, but—and this is important for Lambek—is very much part of everyday life and comportment, constantly in the making and thus never complete:

> In this sense, ethics is far from the presumptions or moral codes and pre-scriptions and closer to irony, particularly in the sense of recognizing the limits of self-understanding [...] and that one cannot fully know that one means what one says or does.[1]

In everyday life, ethics are often not even voiced; they exist rather unnoticed in their "relatively tacit nature, grounded in agreement rather than rule,"[2] and become explicit only if breached and ethical problems occur. As the examples below and, more generally speaking, throughout this book show, these are also the typical moments when Ustadh Mau composes a poem: for instance, to speak out against the community's indecision to plan the island's future (see *Bandari ina mawimbi*, "The Port Makes Waves") or to intervene in their political intrigues (see *Amu*, "Lamu"). Occasionally, prophetic movements also seek to promote agendas, or such agendas are voiced by "priestly figures" whose role it is to offer guidance.[3] As an imam, Ustadh certainly belongs to the latter category: qua position, it is not only his choice to take sides, condemn social ills, and pronounce warnings, but also his obligation—which sometimes weighs heavily on him, but also earns him much respect in his community. He gives advice and educates the *umma*, for instance, in his Friday sermons.[4]

---

1   Michael Lambek, "Introduction," in *Ordinary Ethics. Anthropology, Language, and Action*, ed. Michael Lambek (New York: Fordham University Press, 2010), 9.
2   Lambek, "Introduction," 2.
3   Ibid.
4   As previously highlighted elsewhere, Ustadh was the first imam to give his sermons in Swahili

The concern for ethics is not limited to his sermons, but also extends to the advice he gives privately to individuals, like, for instance, quarreling couples who come to him for guidance and support. Furthermore—and this will be the focus here—a concern for ethics permeates his poetry, as Annachiara Raia outlines: "Finally, being a writer entails the formidable mission of guiding (*kuwalekeza*) and advising (*kuwashauri*) people on how to go about their lives (*jinsi yakwenda maishani*)."[5] His poetry ranges from practical advice (*shauri*) on what to do, to metaphorical lines that convey a message in a form that invites reflection. Occasionally, it also takes a more personal tone, reflecting upon his own life experience. His poems echo the human difficulty of deciding what is right or wrong in light of the rather fuzzy nature of ordinary life, full of ambivalences, which Lambek highlights as the "ever-present limits of criteria and paradoxes of the human condition."[6] *Mlango* ("The Door"), for instance, speaks of his own moment of crisis, when his bakery went bankrupt, but people would not believe that he was in a financially difficult position. Furthermore, feeling deeply for human weaknesses and inconsistencies in his own community, Ustadh Mau does not promote one set of values in the same way but, depending on the context and event, he argues in different ways, promotes even contradictory and conflicting judgments, and also uses different rhetorical and poetic techniques, which, as I would like to argue, are essential to the ethical argument. For instance, though emphasizing the virtue of chastity and virginity for girls in poems like *Ramani ya ndoa* ("A Map of Married Life"), he strongly takes sides with the "fallen women" in *Mama msimlaumu* ("Don't Blame My Mother") and *Wasiya wa mabanati* ("Advice to Young Women").[7]

My concern is how in his poetry and, importantly, through poetic form, he develops a stance on ethical issues that can more broadly be summarized as "how society ought to live." Considering ethics as a practice in which values are never fixed but need to be weighed, argued for, and negotiated in relation to specific situations, I look at his poetry as an important site of doing ethics. His poetry varies in the way it involves ethics: sometimes as part of proclamations, other times in less explicit modalities of doubt. More often than not,

---

with the intention to reach broader audiences on Lamu. See Ahmad Abdulkadir Mahmoud and Peter Frankl, "*Kiswahili*: A Poem by Mahmoud Ahmad Abdulkadir, to Which is Appended a List of the Poet's Compositions in Verse," *Swahili Forum* 20 (2013): 1–18.

5 Annachiara Raia, "*Angaliya baharini, mai yaliyoko pwani*: The Presence of the Ocean in Mahmoud Ahmed Abdulkadir's Poetry," in *Lugha na fasihi. Scritti in onore e memoria di/Essays in Honour and Memory of Elena Bertoncini Zúbková*, ed. Flavia Aiello and Roberto Gaudioso (Naples: Università degli Studi di Napoli "L'Orientale," 2019), 230.

6 Lambek, "Introduction," 4.

7 As for the *Wasiya wa mabanati*, see the contribution by Annachiara Raia in this volume.

even in those poems that proclaim values and prescribe what and what not to do—such as, for instance, the *Haki za watoto*—the moral framework is not just a given, but composing such works is an ethical thought process itself, a consideration of perspectives and a self-interrogation. Accordingly, given the importance of poetry in ethical thought, a consideration of how poetry—its specific means of expression and its ways of relating to the world—shapes the ethical becomes an important consideration as well: the poetic also permeates the ethical. I understand this perspective as a way of entering into and listening to Ustadh Mahmoud Mau's poetic voice.

3　The Ethical and the Poetic in the Swahili Context and with Respect to African-Language Literatures

A view on ethics and their connection with the poetic can broaden the exploration of Swahili poetics and knowledge production in the Swahili context, where the centrality of questions on how to live has recurrently been noted. Kai Kresse points out the practice-oriented and social dimension of knowledge production on the Swahili coast while focusing on *busara* ("wisdom") in his article "Knowledge and Intellectual Practice in a Swahili Context."[8] He defines *hekima* ("wisdom, knowledge, judgment") and *busara* ("good sense, wisdom, sagacity"), which are often used together, as "to endorse or commend the wisdom or good common sense of someone's action."[9] Here, he refers to wisdom as being not an abstract quality, but the quality of the one who *acts* in a *good* sense. Furthermore, acting also includes speaking: a wise person is someone who *speaks* with carefully chosen words at the right time for the benefit of his or her community. To be recognized as such, wisdom needs to be socially relevant, answering to pressing demands, and it needs to offer advice on how to act at times when there are either divergent opinions on what to do, or no idea on how to act or even the necessity of acting at all.[10]

This brings his elaborations on wisdom close to Lambek's emphasis on the aspect of doing ethics, which he grounds in his reading of Aristotle, for whom

---

8　Kresse, "Knowledge and Intellectual Practice in a Swahili Context: 'Wisdom' and the Social Dimensions of Knowledge," *Africa* 79, no. 1 (2009): 148–167.

9　Ibid., 152. Note also the notion of judgement entailed in *hekima*, which implies a notion of making a decision as to which road—the good or bad one—to take, as the late Ahmed Nabahany once explained to me.

10　It requires sustained attention, which I will come back to under the notion of care, below (see also Lambek, "Introduction," 11–12).

THE ETHICAL AND THE POETIC IN USTADH MAHMOUD MAU'S POETRY   99

ethics is related to action (and not abstract reason).[11] Even if there is a catalogue of virtues, there needs to be a constantly ongoing reinterpretation and negotiation of and for them. They demand application with respect to life and they demand careful reasoning. Kai Kresse describes the negotiations on the human good in the context of the *baraza*, where young people are inspired to emulate highly respected intellectuals and elders, making an effort to copy their manners of speaking and depth of reflection for their own intellectual and human development and as part of

> becoming a better person, of increasing one's moral status: of following the role model of Prophet Muhammad (and other prophets). An admirable example of good and decent behavior is copied and internalized, so as to make oneself a better person, and in terms of the application of one's knowledge to the particular setting in which one is situated, more wise.[12]

Thus, as this quotation shows, speaking ethically is part of *habitus*, a form of copied, and hence internalized, behavior. Furthermore, as Kai Kresse highlights, adding further evidence to my concern with the situated reaction of moral discourse, it is not transmission or the simple reiteration of moral knowledge per se that entails "wisdom." Rather, it is the intellectual's capacity to make an intervention at the right time, when it is needed. The explicit statement cuts through the implicit continuity of ethical agreement, creates awareness, and makes the cracks and ruptures, conflicting values, or alternative ways of acting visible in the immediate circumstances. It is the sensitivity to act and, as we may add, to speak and to strike the right balance that Aristotle highlights as the virtue of moral action.[13] And it is a virtue that comes only of action—and of speaking.[14]

Furthermore, it is not only the question of *when* to speak, but also *how* to speak that matters. The manner of putting the statement forward is not of secondary importance: ethical involvement is essentially tied to a consideration of the appropriate and most effective form to leave an impact "on the thinking of the others."[15] The wise person is someone who brings forward "convincing

---

11   Lambek, "Introduction," 14.
12   Kresse, "Knowledge and Intellectual Practice," 156.
13   Lambek, "Introduction," 19, 20.
14   On the moral dimension of *busara* "wisdom," which also implies speaking with the right words at the right time, see also Gerlind Scheckenbach, "*Busara*: Besonnenheit und Takt," in *Zwischen Bantu und Burkina. Festschrift für Gudrun Miehe zum 65. Geburtstag*, ed. Kerstin Winkelmann and Dymitr Ibriszimow (Cologne: Köppe, 2006), 207–234.
15   Kresse, "Knowledge and Intellectual Practice," 153.

arguments from unconventional and expected angles or positions [...] even (or perhaps specifically) when this runs against established modes of thinking."[16] It is the versatility of the rhetor's thought, his wit and intelligence—his drawing on a huge variety of sources from different, seemingly unrelated domains and flexibly adopting perspectives, as we find in Ustadh Mau's poetry—that is appreciated.

Considering the literary and the ethical as interwoven also seems to be nothing new for scholarly discourse on Swahili and other African-language literatures.[17] Rather, it has been one of its constant features. Social engagement or intervention, as it has been called, has been a primary criterion by which to measure African literature for many literary critics and authors since the 1960s, the formative period of scholarship and modern writing in African languages. As Simon Gikandi underlines in his article "Theory, Literature and Moral Considerations," the poets of the independence period and the early days of decolonization "believed that their works and word had an innate and functional capacity to intervene in everyday life and to transform the tenor and vehicle of political discourse."[18] Thus, the poets, the "self-appointed guardians of the public good,"[19] make up what Lambek has called a "priestly class," since it was primarily their role to spell out a vision for society in the era of independence. And it is not a coincidence that many state presidents of the independence era, like Léopold Sédar Senghor, Julius Nyerere, and Agostinho Neto, not only promoted poetry, but also wrote poetry themselves.

While the alliances between the political elite and the poet-scholar of the independence period were soon shattered and many poets imprisoned, the vision of poetry as a weapon for fighting for a better future became even stronger. In vocabulary echoing the Marxist approaches to literature of the 1960s and 1970s that have so thoroughly shaped discourse on Swahili literature, the Kenyan poet Abdilatif Abdalla spells out the poet's "responsibility" (*wajibu*) to be a "poet of the people" (*mshairi wa jamii*), a concept that, by his own admission, he borrowed from Jean-Paul Sartre.[20] While Sartre enthusiastically celebrated the liberating force of negritude that he found in African

---

16 Ibid.

17 See also Flora Veit-Wild and Clarissa Vierke, "Introduction: Digging into Language," in "Reading Closely: Investigating Textuality in Afrophones Literatures," ed. Flora Veit-Wild and Clarissa Vierke, special issue, *Research in African Literatures* 48, no. 1 (2017): ix–xviii.

18 Simon Gikandi, "Theory, Literature, and Moral Considerations," *Research in African Literatures* 32, no. 4 (2001), 1.

19 Ibid., 2.

20 Abdilatif Abdalla, "Wajibu wa mshairi katika jamii yake," in *Abdilatif Abdalla: Poet in Politics*, ed. Rose Marie Beck and Kai Kresse (Dar es Salaam: Mkuki na Nyota, 2016), 85.

poetry,[21] for Abdilatif Abdalla, "the poet of the people necessarily sides with the masses who have remained in misery, since they have been increasingly exploited and oppressed" (*mshairi wa jamii ni lazima aweko upande wa hao wengi wakabakia katika hali duni kwa kuzidi kunyonywa na kukandamizwa*).[22] According to the Marxist view of society as a dichotomy between the affluent in power and the subjugated masses, the poet is compelled to take sides, to become a mouthpiece of the downtrodden, fighting for their liberation in his or her own writings.[23] Thus, literature is primarily judged by the values it exposes and its call for action—in this case, against the oppressive postcolonial Kenyan government.[24] It is the daring author who brings forward an argument in line with his or her own convictions, not shying away from the risk of being imprisoned or killed, who earns the utmost respect in this context.

Until now, not only in East Africa, social engagement has remained the highest value that can be attributed to and analyzed in literature—often held up against a stereotypically evoked Western notion of art-for-art's sake.[25] For instance, Marxist views and African writers' rhetoric of liberation fell on fertile ground in the form of postcolonial theory, one of the most prominent fields of literary criticism in recent decades and most strongly concerned with the—essentially ethical—ability of literature "to speak back" to power. However, in contrast to postcolonial approaches—which, by imposing preconceived categories of race, class, and gender, have shown a growing insensitivity toward specific social and historical contexts and practices, as well as languages and genres[26]—there have also been attempts at honing in on situated practices, discourses, and texts; Kai Kresse's research is one example of this. Moreover,

---

21   Jean-Paul Sartre, *Qu'est-ce que la littérature?* (Paris: Gallimard, 1948).

22   Abdalla, "Wajibu wa mshairi katika jamii yake," 84.

23   In a similar way, King'ei, for instance, defines the "real poet" as someone who "sacrifices himself or herself to give a voice to those who have been oppressed. He urges his fellow citizens to join him in recognizing and unraveling all ills in society" (*mshairi akajitoa mhanga kuwa chombo cha kuwapa sauti walionyamazishwa. Anawahimiza wanajamii wenzake kuungana naye kutaumbua na kufichua maovu yote yaliyomo katika jamii*). Geoffrey Kitula King'ei, "Taswira za Ukosoaji na 'Utopia,'" in *Dunia Yao. Utopia/Dystopia in Swahili Fiction. In Honour of Said A.M. Khamis*, ed. Clarissa Vierke and Katharina Greven (Cologne: Köppe, 2016), 169.

24   While Ustadh Mau was never a political rebel, overtly protesting against the federal government, his nickname "Mau" speaks of a period when associating oneself with Mao Tse Tung and socialism broadly evoked a leftist stance and hence also a criticism of the neoliberal government in power. He was quick and clever enough to change the *o* of Mao into *u*, veiling any direct reference.

25   See also King'ei, "Taswira za Ukosoaji na 'Utopia,'" 2016.

26   See, for instance, Veit-Wild and Vierke, "Introduction."

in suggesting productive themes for an agenda for the comparative study of African-language literatures, Karin Barber and Graham Furniss highlight the study of the "purposive dimension" of texts, calling for an approach that involves the careful reading of texts and contexts.[27] For them, such a study "concerns the ways in which written texts are used to mobilize their constituencies for moral action"; this is further echoed in "the value placed upon particular writings and kinds of writing in the architecture of culture."[28] To me, this calls for a *descriptive* project, entailing the cautious observation of how notions of poetry and morality are interrelated; how poems speak to and seek to mobilize constituencies, i.e. by which means; which kind of effect they have; and how they are assessed by the community. It also involves paying attention to culturally specific notions, language-specific poetic strategies, and genres that frame the interpretation and the production of discourse.

It also implies reflecting more closely on the literary: treating poetry primarily as a tool to convey a socially relevant message has often meant downplaying its particular literary nature. It treats the purpose as more important than the literary form, which is merely a container for the message. This is not in line with local Swahili notions of the eminence of poetic form and the specific poetic force that can affect and effect audiences. It also entails not oversimplifying social life as a well-defined structure shaped by clear-cut antagonistic forces—for instance, racism or sexism—but rather looking at it, as mentioned before, as a vague, continuous, and individual experience of conflicting options and ideas, many of which even escape notice. In *Forms*, Levine argues against focusing on coherent systems and structures as the "truly powerful shapers of life" that literature reacts to and seeks to dismantle, drawing on the Brazilian legal theorist and politician Roberto Mangabeira Unger.[29] Rather than being shaped by "deep structural forces such as capitalism, nationalism and racism," as Levine puts it, social life is "composed of 'loosely and unevenly collected' arrangements."[30]

Accordingly, as I would like to add, echoing Levine, poetry's engagement is also more complex. Some of Ustadh's poems show the many perspectives one can assume with regard to the "social." And many lyrical poems do not provide the conclusive and final argument of a previous debate, but rather offer

---

27 Karin Barber and Graham Furniss, "African-Language Writing," *Research in African Literatures* 37, no. 3 (2006): 11.
28 Ibid., 12.
29 Caroline Levine, *Forms. Whole, Rhythm, Hierarchy, Network* (Princeton, NJ: Princeton University Press, 2015), 17.
30 Levine, *Forms*, 17.

THE ETHICAL AND THE POETIC IN USTADH MAHMOUD MAU'S POETRY   103

room for reflection, interrogation, and contemplation—also for the poet himself. Looking at the poetic as practice, the ethical and the poem are not a *fait accompli*. They are intertwined and come into being in the composition. Considering ethics as part of poetic practice accounts for a dynamic perspective that goes beyond a functional analysis of a literary text.[31] Thus, my twin focus on the poetic and the ethical represents an approach to investigating Ustadh's poetic search for "the good" by reading his poetry.

4   The Language and Poetry of Morality in the Swahili Context

"Ethics is intrinsically linked to speaking as much as it is to action," as Lambek contends.[32] On a very fundamental level, it is language, with its words and grammatical forms, that provides our categories of uttering or even thinking about what is good and what is bad:

> We may find the wellsprings of ethical insights deeply embedded in the categories and functions of language and ways of speaking, in the commonsense ways we distinguish among various kinds of actors or characters, kinds of acts and manners of acting; in specific nouns and adjectives, verbs and adverbs, or adverbial phrases, respectively; thus, in the shared criteria we use to make ourselves intelligible to one another, in 'When we say when.'[33]

In the Swahili context, both Alena Rettová's and Kai Kresse's studies on the notion of *utu*, commonly translated as "humanism," in the poetry of Swahili poets like Ahmad Nassir can be considered exemplary studies in this regard.[34] It is the meaning of the word *utu* that is constantly reshaped in reflections, discussions, proverbs, and poems. An example of the entanglement of ethical discourse and Swahili grammar is the study of the use of the Swahili *ki* class by Abel Mreta, Gerlind Scheckenback, and Thilo Schadeberg.[35] Though epi-

---

31   See also Lambek ("Introduction," 21), who places emphasis on practice and the means of acting rather than the end result.

32   Ibid., 5.

33   Ibid., 2.

34   Alena Rettová, "Lidství utu? Ubinadamu baina ya tamaduni," *Swahili Forum* 14 (2007): 89–134; Kai Kresse, *Philosophising in Mombasa. Knowledge, Islam and Intellectual Practice at the Swahili Coast* (Edinburgh: Edinburgh University Press, 2007), 139 ff.

35   Abel Mreta, Thilo Schadeberg, and Gerlind Scheckenbach, "Kiziwi, kipofu na kilema: Ubaguzi au heshima?" *Afrikanistische Arbeitspapiere* 51 (1997): 23–54.

stemologically and historically unfounded, as the three linguists show, the *ki* class, in which, for instance, many nouns referring to disabled people are found, has notoriously been considered to impart a derogatory meaning to nouns; it is a noun class that is believed to attribute moral value.[36] Apart from the affordances of Swahili words and grammatical items, communicative genres shape the forms of ethical perspectives.[37] Forms of giving advice, teaching, and preaching, each of whose dramaturgy follows culturally specific scripts, play a particularly important role in Ustadh's life.[38] Each utterance is voiced within a frame that creates a link to previous utterances and texts and raises expectations about the linguistic means, the topics raised, and the perspective on reality.[39]

One culturally specific way of judging behavior, as Jasmin Mahazi describes in this volume, is the use of veiled language, particularly common when addressing socially risky topics. It confronts the recipient with a riddle, which can mask harsh criticism. A number of studies have explored the use of *mafumbo*, literally "knots," as a face-saving strategy, since the sender can easily retreat behind the literal, "knotted" meaning, denying any other intention.[40] *Mafumbo* also find their way into short lyrical *mashairi* poems. As Nababany explains, *Mshairi hutunga shairi kwa lengo la kumfundisha mtu kitu fulani, kumfumba mtu (kama vile mshairi mwengine) au kwa kumwambia mtu jambo ambalo*

---

36   The argument hinges on the fact that one finds terms designating physically handicapped people, like *kilema* "cripple," *kibubu* "mute person," *kipofu* "blind person," and *kiziwi* "deaf person," only in the *ki* class, which seems to add a notion of deficiency to them. Thus, accordingly, activists have advocated for the use of *mlemavu* instead of *kilema* for handicapped persons, thereby moving the noun to the *m* class, reserved for human beings.

37   "Affordances" is a term borrowed from the field of design, which Levine (*Forms*) explores to think about the potentials and possibilities entrenched in the materiality of form, which allows for certain functions more than others.

38   Swahili's pragmatic frames have been studied particularly with reference to politeness. See, for instance, Nico Nassenstein, "Politeness in Kisangani Swahili: Speakers' Pragmatic Strategies at the Fringes of the Kiswahili Speaking World," *Afrikanistik/Ägyptologie Online* (2018): 1–18.

39   Barber and Furniss describe the genre as an orienting framework in which each poet/scholar inscribes himself/herself and which defines the discourse, also because it necessarily places the text within a line of tradition (Barber and Furniss, "African-Language Writing"); see also Furniss, *Orality: The Power of the Spoken Word* (Basingstoke: Palgrave Macmillan, 2004), 46. On specific speech acts and genres in everyday Swahili speech, see Reinhard Klein-Arendt, *Gesprächsstrategien im Swahili. Linguistisch-pragmatische Analysen von Dialogtexten einer Stehgreiftheatergruppe* (Cologne: Köppe, 1992).

40   E.g., Carl Velten, *Desturi za Wasuaheli na khabari za desturi za sheria za Wasuaheli* (Göttingen: Vandenhoeck & Ruprecht, 1903); Sauda Sheikh, "Yanayoudhi kuyaona. Mafumbo na vijembe vya Kiswahili," *Swahili Forum* 1 (1994): 7–11.

hawezi kumwambia usoni mwake moja kwa moja ("A poet composes a poem to teach something to someone, to make up a riddle for somebody [e.g., another poet], or to tell someone something that he cannot tell him/her directly to his or her face").[41] The decisive benefit of this strategy, as Beck argues—with reference to metaphorical communication via *kanga* textiles—is that critical points are addressed rather than neglected, and social cohesion created rather than threatened.[42] *Mafumbo* lie between muting an issue and speaking out about it, addressing and not addressing an issue, and thus both interrupt the unnoticed stream of speech and reveal something—since otherwise there would be no riddle—but also blur it, because its indexical reference first needs to be unveiled. Thus, the metaphor, through its very being, has a provocative effect and urges the recipient to ponder on it and answer.[43] *Mafumbo* are engrained in the poetic practice of *kujibizana*, dialogue poetry, because they demand a reaction.[44] It is the opponent's task to react immediately in an equally heightened and veiled speech to safeguard his or her moral integrity. Poetry is part of *habitus* (see also below): the social person is attacked, formed, and maintained in poetry. Arguments emerge and evolve as part of the ongoing verbal exchange, in line with the processual and dialogic perspective, which Lambek also favors: judgment reacts to, but also anticipates communication with others.[45]

However, *mafumbo* are not the only way of expressing judgment in the Swahili context. Poetry as such is the key way of voicing essential thoughts, which need to be advanced in "such an extraordinarily beautiful and memorable way that this now becomes a common expression or a new and relevant insight shines out of the creative and innovative use of language within a poem."[46] To rephrase it, poetic form is of the utmost relevance, since it "shines out" from the incessant flow of casual everyday speech, less carefully and thoughtfully constructed, and hence has the capacity to call the audience's attention. Besides practical considerations, there is also the idea that what is essential needs to find an adequate form that does not diminish its importance: there is thus a correlation between the "ethical good" and the "aesthetic good," i.e. a well-constructed and harmonious poetic form.

---

41 Ahmed Nabahany, "Uketo wa tungo za Kiswahili," *Lugha* 4 (1990): 5.

42 Rose Marie Beck, *Texte auf Textilien in Ostafrika: Sprichwörtlichkeit als Eigenschaft ambiger Kommunikation* (Cologne: Köppe, 2001).

43 A good example of Ustadh's use of *mafumbo* in poetry is *Jahazi*. In the last stanza, he asks his fellow poets to think about the "deeper" meaning of the sinking ship.

44 Ann Biersteker, *Kujibizana: Questions of Language and Power in Nineteenth- and Twentieth-Century Poetry in Kiswahili* (East Lansing: Michigan State Univ. Press, 1996).

45 Lambek, "Introduction," 24.

46 Kai Kresse, "Knowledge and Intellectual Practice," 157.

The genre most often associated with ethical discourse is the *utendi* (pl. *tendi*), because the genre as such has been ascribed a normative, authoritative tone and a "purposive dimension" of providing proper guidance on how to live a virtuous life.[47] Like the sermon (*khutba*), which Ustadh regularly delivers at the mosque,[48] the *utendi* is essentially a publicly voiced moral guideline often addressing the community at large.[49] Kresse characterizes the *utendi* as

> [...] usually *didactic* in nature, providing lengthy elaborations about *what to do, how to behave* and the like, in different kinds of life situations. In normative terms, Islamic references provide a guideline and the goal is, commonly, to pass on knowledge to the audience which may help them *to become better people, with stronger moral character*.[50] (Emphasis mine.)

The *utendi* plays an important role in Ustadh Mahmoud Mau's poetic oeuvre. For him, the most valuable aim of poetry is to teach and educate to prevent the community from taking the "wrong path" and to set good examples. Witty *mashairi*, which play with sounds and meanings, are rather a waste of time to him.[51] For him, the poet is a teacher (*mwalimu*) whose responsibility it is to educate (*kuelimisha*) society.[52] Poetry as a means of education, particularly in *utendi* form, has the advantage of being appealing to the audience. The *utendi*'s language has to be rhythmic and rhymed but also clear, so that everybody can understand and memorize it. For instance, both the *Haki za watoto* ("Children's Rights", see below) as well as the *Ramani ya maisha ya ndoa* ("The Map of

---

47 Its purpose is to treat a topic of utmost concern to the community. This, however, does not mean that a *utendi*, once composed, is essentially static and unchanging in text or standing. On the contrary, it invites reflection, criticism, and discussion, and thus also the composition of further *tendi*.

48 See also Raia, "*Angaliya baharini.*"

49 On Ustadh's own perception concerning the closeness of edifying poetry, like his *tendi*, and the *khutba*, "working together for the benefit of the community (*umma*)," see Raia, "*Angaliya baharini,*" 229.

50 Kresse, "Enduring Relevance: Samples of Oral Poetry on the Swahili Coast," *Wasafiri* 26, no. 2 (2011): 48. Besides the explicitly didactic *tendi* that expound values, narrative *tendi* also have the aim of teaching—by example—how to live an honorable and pious life. Ustadh Mau's compositions tend toward the former, but often involve narrative elements.

51 For Ustadh Mau, poetry as such is not morally good, as he once underlined in a lecture, since it can also be misleading. In particular, he notes that *mashairi* poems can often be of morally dubious character. The *utendi*, however, is meant to inspire others to strive for the better.

52 See also Kresse, "Knowledge and Intellectual Practice," and Raia, "*Angaliya baharini.*"

THE ETHICAL AND THE POETIC IN USTADH MAHMOUD MAU'S POETRY   107

Married Life"), a book of advice for a happy married life, provide extensive guidelines on how to act. In the *Ukimwi ni zimwi* ("AIDS Is a Monster"), he calls on people not to forget about the fatal epidemic and to abstain from promiscuity. According to him, educating through poetry has always been important, but has become even more urgent due to the decline of traditional institutions of learning, the high drop-out rate in local schools, and the manifold media influences negatively affecting young people, who no longer know what is right or wrong (see also his poem *Kiswahili*).

In contrast to the often fleeting nature of *mashairi, tendi* are meant to make a lasting statement. There is a tradition of composing didactic *tendi* for one's children: in the *Utendi wa Mwana Kupona* ("The Poem of Mwana Kupona"), composed around 1830, which became the most famous moral catalogue of the genre, a mother who is about to die provides advice to her daughter on how to be a good wife for her future husband.[53] In the *Siraji* ("The Lamp"), to give another prominent example, the poet Muhamadi Kijuma teaches his son how to correctly behave, running through all kinds of possible domestic and public contexts where he fears his son might fail to act properly, losing his dignity.[54] For generations, both *tendi* have been memorized, recorded, and copied again and again, becoming "an effective longer-term normative poetic reserve that is still tapped into, reiterated and regularly listened to."[55] For Ustadh, too, both of the abovementioned poems serve as models: he refers to them and even quotes whole lines. Moreover, Ustadh also wrote edifying *tendi* for his own children, as his own father had done for him, intending to show them "the proper path in life" (*njia bora kwenye maisha*). Furthermore, his own poetry has become part of the cultural "archive," as Kai Kresse highlights,[56] for instance, with regard to the "enduring relevance" of Ustadh's *Wasiya wa mabanati* (see also Annachiara Raia's contribution in this volume). *Wasiya*, a loanword from Arabic meaning "last will, legacy," and in pre-Islamic times referring particularly to the spiritual testament to the survivors, recurs in the titles of *tendi* and hints at the intention to compose a poem for future generations.[57] In this sense, it is also an ethical

---

53   Alice Werner, "The *Utendi wa Mwana Kupona*," in *Harvard Studies*. Vol. 1, *Varia Africana I*, ed. O. Bates (Cambridge, Mass.: Peabody Museum, 1917), 147–181; Alice Werner and William Hichens, *The Advice of Mwana Kupona upon the Wifely Duty*, Azanian Classics 2 (Medstead: Azania Press, 1934); J.W.T. Allen, ed., *Tendi: Six Examples of a Swahili Classical Verse Form with Translations & Notes* (New York: Africana Pub. Corp, 1971).

54   Gudrun Miehe and Clarissa Vierke, *Muhamadi Kijuma. Texts from the Dammann Collections and Other Papers* (Cologne: Köppe, 2010).

55   Kresse, "Enduring Relevance," 48.

56   Ibid.

57   See the *Encyclopedia of Islam* s.v. *waṣiyya*.

"investment" in the future, wisely recognizing both "human finitude but also hope."[58] The poem is meant to outlast the composer. At the end of the *Haki za watoto*, he dedicates the poem to his son, while referring to the fact that even his own father had composed a poem for him (see stz. 257).[59]

If the ethical is so closely linked with the poetic, the poet is also the ethical person par excellence. He or she is the one who speaks wisely—i.e., advising on what to do and how to do it—and well, i.e. with a careful choice of words and arguments. The impeccable external form, the rhyme and rhythm, and the careful choice of meaningful words need to corroborate the content. A "good" poem is one that is both "meaningful" (*lenye maana*) and well composed in "rhyme and verse" (*lenye vina na mizani*). A "good" poet is of good reputation (*mwenye heshima*) and intellect, showing refined manners, including first and foremost his or her poetic skill. The poet is a *mungwana*, often translated as "person of manners," concerned with keeping his or her *heshima* "dignity, respect," a central category of the social as well as moral persona (see also Jasmin Mahazi's contribution in this volume). Pouwels characterizes the *mungwana* not only in terms of his patterns of consumption, but also in terms of his distinguished manners in public, diligence in religious worship—and distinguished way of speaking. He refers to him as a person, who "dressed in a certain way, ate certain food, earned his livelihood in certain ways, attended to his prayers assiduously, lived in certain types of houses, behaves in certain ways in public, and above all, *spoke the vernacular Swahili well.*" (my emphasis)[60]

Many of the practices he mentions are unconscious and embodied, like the consumption of certain foodstuffs, which make them fall into Bourdieu's notion of the *habitus*, a notion linking individual practice and social values, referring to "systems of durable, transposable dispositions"[61] acquired through imitation that become manifest in habitual behavior.[62] Speech patterns are also part of the *habitus*, and so is the esteem and practice of poetic composition in the Swahili context. The composition of *tendi* characterizes the poet

---

58   Lambek, "Introduction," 4.
59   Ustadh's *tendi* also come with a rhetorical force and passion to forge an engaging discourse, not only by highlighting an indexical relationship between "you," the listener, and "I," the poet, but also by addressing and urging the audience, leaving no doubt about its intention as a call to action.
60   Randall Pouwels, *Horn and Crescent: Cultural Change and Traditional Islam on the East African Coast, 800–1900* (Cambridge: Cambridge University Press, 1987), 73; emphasis mine.
61   Pierre Bourdieu, *Outline of a Theory of Practice* (New York: Cambridge University Press, 1977), 72.
62   Ibid., 167.

as a *mungwana*, since it is elevated speech and above all the composition of poetry, a quasi-embodied practice acquired gradually in the form of imitation, that differentiates him or her from lower social classes. The *mungwana* is a poet and the poet is a *mungwana*. Furthermore, by their didactic nature, *tendi* are also concerned with guiding the *mungwana* to keep his or her *heshima*.

The link between "speaking in a refined way" (*kusema kwa ufasaha*), on the one hand, which finds its most virtuous expression in poetry, and moral dignity, on the other, as well as reputation and leadership, has a long history on the coast. From the ancient and mythical master poet Fumo Liyongo, fighting for his right to inherit the throne of Pate, to Muyaka bin Haji al-Ghassany, the nineteenth-century court poet of the Mazrui, and Bwana Zahidi Mngumi, the wordsmith who defeated the powerful city state of Pate on the battle-field, respect and authority are not merely reflected, but earned by swift poetic interventions. In the nineteenth century, when didactic *tendi*, like the ones described above, became the most important genre in a period of Islamic renewal, they also turned the composer into an essentially morally acting subject, who earned a heavenly reward through his or her compositions and turned the listener into a pious person.[63]

This might urge us also to reconsider the notion of poetry. Poetry is not a written text, even if written down later, but a practice carried out by a *mungwana* responding at the appropriate time and in the adequate form. I do not merely mean to question the centrality of the *written* text by highlighting practices of oral composition and recitation, including improvisation.[64] Rather, I would like to highlight the connection between poetry and the person of the poet. Poetry indeed refers less to the product, the result of speaking, than to the act of speaking and, accordingly, to the acting speaker, i.e. the poet. The change in meaning of the term *fasihi* in the twentieth century, from "one speaking well" to "literature" (increasingly valued in its printed book form), is telling in this respect. Traditionally, like in many other cultural and historical contexts, there is no overarching term for poetry or literature in Swahili that would group together the various genres, like the *tendi*, the *shairi* or, later, also the novel. While the term *fasihi* has generally been used since the 1970s to refer to what we call "literature" in English,[65] in his dictionary, Sacleux still reports

---

63   See Ibrahim Noor Shariff, "Islam and Secularity in Swahili Literature: An Overview," in *Faces of Islam in African Literature*, ed. Kenneth Harrow (Portsmouth, NH: Heinemann, 1991), 37–57.

64   Ustadh himself attributes more power to the spoken and recited word when it comes to his own poetry.

65   It was Ustadh who dated the term *fasihi* "literature" back to the 1970s in a conversa-

the meaning of *fasihi* as referring to an "eloquent person who speaks well and expresses him- or herself abundantly and in a lucid way" ("éloquent, qui parle bien, qui s'exprime avec abundance et lucidité").[66] Thus, *fasihi* did not refer to the literary product, but to the "lucid" rhetor, who did not fall short of words.[67] Poetry is thus not the sum of a poet's words, handed down and memorized, but primarily the poet's persona, his way of composing and speaking, as well as the knowledge he has acquired. This is similar to the German context of the sixteenth century where, mostly by analogy with French, literature was used with reference to the *literatus*, the well-read erudite, the *homme de lettre*, having a mastery of Latin.[68] It is thus the author's erudition and charisma that is in focus.[69]

As I have been trying to show, Ustadh is certainly a *homme de lettre*, conversant with the large cultural archive that he draws on. The poet is a mediator who—given his broad knowledge and overview of important debates that often comes from books that people do not have access to or cannot read (since the books are, for instance, written in Arabic)—has to make the effort to "translate" (*kutafsiri*) the most important moral guidelines into a language that is understandable and speaks to the people.[70] He is a *fasihi* in the old sense of *hodari ya kuzungumza*, "skillful in speaking" Swahili, which likewise confirms his role as a *mungwana*. The ethical, the social persona, and the poetic, coming together in the poet's *habitus*, are intertwined.—In the following, I will turn to the reading of a specific poetry.

---

tion we had. When I asked him about the use of the term on Lamu, he responded that *fasihi* was a recent coinage, dating from when literature courses were introduced at East African universities. The other Arabic term, *adabu*, which was also used for some time, was later abandoned. Interestingly, the latter also implies a whole range of "good manners" and "conduct," of which a refined way of speaking and composing is just one element.

66   Charles Sacleux, *Dictionnaire swahili-français* (Paris: Inst. d'Ethnologie, 1939), 217. The example Sacleux gives is *fulani ni fasihi wa kusema.*

67   Krapf glosses *fasihi* with the adjectives "clean, pure, correct, perspicuous," which imply the notion of a fine style of speaking as well as the idea of purity, i.e. veracity and truth. Johann Ludwig Krapf, *A Dictionary of the Suahili Language* (London: Trübner, 1882), 63.

68   See Weimar's informative article on "Literatur" and its diachronically changing meaning in the *Reallexikon der deutschen Literatur*, vol. 2, edited by Harald Fricke et al. (Berlin: De Gruyter, 2007), 443–448.

69   See also Frederic Ponten, "Cosmopolitanism and the Location of Literary Theory," paper presented at the Location of Theory symposium at the European University Viadrina Frankfurt (Oder), February 7, 2020.

70   Here, *kutafsiri* does not so much mean to translate from one book, but rather to draw on different sources and compile a coherent overview.

THE ETHICAL AND THE POETIC IN USTADH MAHMOUD MAU'S POETRY   111

5   Caring for and about the Children: *Haki za watoto*

Mwana umleavyo, ndivyo akuavyo

As you nurse your child, so it grows up.[71]

For Ustadh Mau, the *Haki za watoto* ("Children's Rights"), which he composed in 2000, is one of the most important poems he has ever composed. The *haki* "rights" in the title refers to the poem's far-reaching agenda. It is the same word as that found in the Swahili translation of the Universal Declaration of Human Rights: *haki za binadamu*. While there is a commonly shared body of knowledge on what a child needs as well as practical knowledge on how to raise a child on Lamu, which is usually not explicitly addressed and falls to the responsibility of women, Ustadh Mau deemed it necessary to write the poem after experiencing his own and other people's ignorance about children's needs. As he explained to us, he only gradually became aware of children's needs after he became a father. He saw many parents either abusing or neglecting children, which made him embark on the reflection that ultimately led to the composition of the poem.[72] Further, his discontent with his wives—who did not care enough, in his view—prompted him to read more and more about developmental psychology and child care in both English and Arabic.[73] His poem draws on a number of different sources. At the beginning of the poem (stanzas 7 and 8), he refers to the Qurʾān and hadith as major inspirations for his poem, but he also makes use of his own observations; he draws not only from the UN conventions, but also from literature on baby care.

In the poem, he underlines the importance of minding the children's age (stz. 237) and treating and guiding them accordingly. He starts by considering infants, then schoolchildren, and finally adolescents—in line with the *utendi*'s tendency to approach a topic systematically and coherently. As he explains at the end of the poem, his aim is to point out how to adequately handle and bring up children, so that they grow up to become responsible human beings. The poem thus moves chronologically from infants to adolescents, reflecting the *utendi*'s aim of an exhaustive treatment of the topic. Furthermore, its stanzas are structured thematically and topically, systematically

---

71   William Taylor, *African Aphorisms: Or, Saws from Swahili-Land* (London: Soc. for Promoting Christian Knowledge, 1891), proverb xxii, 6.

72   This is very much in line with Lambek's finding, described above, that is it the rupture with tacit moral values that triggers the need to make them explicit.

73   See also our introduction to the poem *Haki za watoto*.

addressing the different points that must be considered in child care, as well as the violations he has witnessed, like the severe corporal punishment of children.

Rather than providing a rigid list, he seeks to argue carefully to convince his audience of the particular needs of children as well as the value of a conscientious upbringing. In the poem, he makes himself an advocate of children in a society that, according to him, increasingly tends to disrespect, neglect, or abuse them and where, as a result, the children ever more frequently turn into uncontrollable tyrants. The poem includes practical advice as well, for instance in favor of breastfeeding and official registration after birth, but frequently also reads as a broader ethical consideration. In enumerating both what *is* good for a child and what *makes* a child a good person, his poem turns into a philosophical and anthropological consideration of the human good, a reflection on the human condition and strategies of making it better: what is, and what makes, a good person?

Above all, Ustadh Mau makes love and care central concerns, on which hinge not only the child's but also society's well-being. At the end of the poem, he describes himself as *mwenye kite na dhuriya* "someone who feels deeply for children" (stz. 255). *Kite* is one of the crucial concepts here, which firstly implies a deep, heartfelt affection and fondness for children that touch the narrator's heart.[74] *Kite* thus overlaps with *mapendi* "love," which he stresses over several stanzas: the right and need of the children "to be loved and to be brought up with love" (*ni haki yake kupendwa na kwa mapendi kuundwa*, stz. 36).[75] Love for the child is not a given; he critically adds *wazazi wengi hushindwa* "many parents fail" (stz. 35) to have or show it. But he highlights love as the most existential need of the child—more existential than even food (stz. 37)[76]—and hence the most important human good to be passed on, so that the child too becomes a "good person." *Ruhuma* "compassion, sympathy" is another relevant key word in relating to children with a loving heart and in a gentle manner (stz. 39). It evokes a sense of empathy, i.e. the capacity to put oneself in the position of the child to be able to understand its wishes and needs, but also to forgive its

---

74 Sacleux (*Dictionnaire swahili-français*, 411) glosses it as "passion, inner suffering" ("passion, souffrance intime"), which hints at the intensity of the feeling. In other contexts, *kite* can also stand for "bitterness" or "pain," referring to women in labor, or as for instance in the sentence *amekufa kwa kite* "il est mort de chagrin" (ibid., 411). *Kite* refers to a strong emotional involvement.

75 Literarily, the line is even stronger, since it uses the verb *kuundwa* "to be built." So the child should "be built" with love. Love thus becomes an ontological foundation of a good person.

76 To underline its importance, he uses the metaphor of a seedling in need of water (stz. 54).

THE ETHICAL AND THE POETIC IN USTADH MAHMOUD MAU'S POETRY   113

failures. *Ruhuma* is the same concept often evoked in referring to the Prophet's loving relationship toward mankind, for whom he is the intercessor, praying for God's mercy and forgiveness on the day of judgment despite all human failures and sins, which is the subject of many narrative *tendi*.[77] It is this "unconditional love" (stz. 45) that Ustadh demands from parents and that is, on the other hand, also the basis of all good relations.

Kite and *ruhuma* are hence more than individual feelings, but are ethical in that they call for, demand, and incite a whole spectrum of good actions, which I relate to the notion of care. This notion has increasingly received attention in the social sciences and philosophy in the past decades. "The central focus of care," as Held underlines in her book *The Ethics of Care*, "is on the compelling moral salience of attending to and meetings the needs of the particular others for whom we take responsibility."[78] Accordingly, it challenges the injustices entrenched in political thought, as well as political and social institutions that do not adequately value the care work that is typically part of the household and thus is excluded from any public recognition, yet most essential in recreating society—and thus also became an important concern of feminist theories.[79] Lambek defines care as an essentially moral action by referring to Hannah Arendt's notion of "labor," essentially a "labor of love and reproduction" (as opposed to "work" in the sense of industrial production) that relates to "looking after and looking out for the well-being of others."[80] It is particularly care for human beings who are dependent, like children, that has been in focus.[81] Care involves work, as also evident in Ustadh Mau's recommendations on child care, but it is more than merely utilitarian, since it involves and is based on emotions, like *kite* and *ruhuma*. They resemble Held's description of the basis and essence of care as "close attention to the feelings, needs,

---

77   See also Clarissa Vierke and Chapane Mutiua, "The Poem about the Prophet's Death in Mozambique—Swahili as a Transregional Language of Islamic Poetry," *Journal for Islamic Studies* 38/2 (2020), 44–74.

78   Virginia Held, *The Ethics of Care. Personal, Political and Global* (Oxford: Oxford University Press, 2006), 10.

79   See, for instance, Joan Tronto, *Moral Boundaries. A Political Argument for an Ethic of Care* (New York: Routledge, 1993) for one of the early agendas of the morality of care. For her, paying attention to care work as an essential part of "doing good" in society (hence as moral action) is a way to overcome the racism and sexism that normally prevent the recognition of these tasks, and to give a fuller account of morality: "We must honor what most people spend their lives doing: caring for themselves, for others and for the world" (ibid., x).

80   Lambek, "Introduction," 15.

81   Held, *The Ethics of Care*, 10.

desires and thoughts of those cared for, and a skill in understanding a situation from that person's point of view."[82]

In Ustadh Mau's poem, one finds several layers of care that he prescribes. At a minimal level, this firstly implies not hurting or abusing the child; he argues against verbal and psychological violence, such as ridiculing the child, for instance, by giving him or her a "bad name" (*ina ovu*), "which will remain like a scar" (*kwake itakuwa kovu*, stz. 28).[83] He is also against corporal punishment beyond "one lash of a whip" (*ngongo*, stz. 134), as well as against child labor: *Wana tusilazimishe wala tuskalifishe*, "Let us not force our children nor overburden them" (stz. 121). While it is good to send them on little errands, make them help in the household (stz. 124, 126), or sell some food in the street (stz. 125), hard work "destroys their character" (*huwavuruga tabia*, stz. 122). He recommends being indulgent, mild, and forgiving—all characteristics implied by *ruhuma*—toward the child. With regard to the question of how to *make* a good child, his poems argue for the right balance between rectifying mistakes, not leaving them unremarked, but also giving the child a second chance (see also stz. 246): "If a child misbehaves, it is necessary to discipline him, but in a careful way, and show him the right way" (stz. 245). He urges parents to carefully guide their children by talking to them (stz. 190 ff.). Parents should build a relationship of trust with the child, so that the child feels free to talk about his or her concerns. Trust is the seed of a good person later on. And, as he argues a few stanzas later, it is not only for the benefit of its parents, but it also makes the child a good and responsible member of society.[84]

Secondly, care also demands very practical measures: he underlines the child's right to have a proper name, under which the child will also be registered (stz. 31). Moreover, registering the child right after birth will save it from dif-

---

82   Ibid., 31; see also ibid., 10. On the particular commitment Ustadh feels toward caring about children and youth, see also Raia, "*Angaliya baharini*," 230.

83   In stanza 247, he urges his audience not to speak ill of the child all the time or constantly to compare it with others.

84   This view is crucially different from the account of Mwengo Bakari, for instance, published by Carl Velten in his *Mila na desturi*, and which also involves a lot of ethical guidelines. According to Bakari, parents are urged to teach their children "how to behave" (*kumfundisha adabu*) from the "age of six or seven" (*omri wa miaka sitta ao saba*), which means obeying the parents' "orders" (*amri*) without objection. Parents are supposed to punish their children physically for any kind of misbehaviour. The child is not supposed to make its own decisions or speak up in front of adults unless it is asked to do so (see particularly ibid., 52–54). On the whole, Bakari's *Mila na desturi* is an interestingly detailed guide on how to behave well, and deserves further study as a late nineteenth-century anthropological account.

THE ETHICAL AND THE POETIC IN USTADH MAHMOUD MAU'S POETRY 115

ficult bureaucratic steps later on (35). These two points seem to echo article 7.1 of the UNICEF Convention on the Rights of the Child: "The child shall be registered immediately after birth and shall have the right from birth to a name [...]."[85] Echoing advice on baby care, he reminds the audience that the child has the right to be properly nourished with a balanced diet—breastfed rather than bottle-fed in the early days (stz. 63–68)—given clean water (92–95), to be dressed, given a bed to sleep in (stz. 81), and have medical check-ups (stz. 78), vaccinations, and medical treatment if the child falls sick (stz. 96–100). He also includes the right to schooling as well as religious education.

Care in Ustadh's poem emphasizes the concrete and constant nature of ethical engagement: care, referring to sustained attention, is first of all part of ordinary life, carried out in the realm of the family.[86] And it is the habitual, which is part of everyday life, in which love needs to be enacted and parents have to show love and goodness, as he also highlights with the concept of *mazoweya*. Literally, this term means "habit," "practice," and in this context it refers to a constant, unflagging relation with children built by listening to them (*wana wakizungumza yataka kuwasikiza*, "when children address us, we should listen to them," stz. 41) or by playing with them (*na wana wetu tuteze*, "let us play with our children," stz. 44). This also implies showing one's love: recalling bonding theory, he stresses that expressing affection with kisses is equally important (stz. 48). As he underlines, these expressions have a lasting effect on the child's personality: "they do not go away, but remain" (*hayondoki hubakiya*, stz. 24). He underlines the relationship between the love and affection shown toward the child and "bright minds" and mental stability (stz. 51).[87] It is a lack of care and protection that turns children into a troublemakers, little "devils" (*iblisi*, stz. 58) "who will go astray" (*hunenda mapopo*, stz. 52).

The poem makes the parent a moral subject.[88] It is a guide on how to act as a good, caring parent and hence also a responsible, benevolent member of society, who is morally compelled to help the dependent infant (as failing to do so would make the parent an immoral person). Moreover, the parent also has to ensure that the child turns into a good, responsible person: it is the adult's responsibility to teach the child "to do only good": *yalo mema ayatende* (stz. 140). The two aspects, the caring adult and the morally good child, are interre-

---

85 See UN General Assembly, "Convention on the Rights of the Child," *Treaty Series* 1577 (November 1989): 3.
86 Lambek, "Introduction," 15.
87 A more literal translation would be, "the mind shines and it calms down mentally."
88 See also Held, *The Ethics of Care*, 45.

lated in the poem. Ustadh starts his poem by stressing the importance of the "good mother"—and in this sense, he also directly addresses his adult target audience. Care for children starts before conception, in thoughtfully choosing the right mother, "who is excellent not in appearance, but in character" (*aliyo mzuri mno / si kwa sura kwa tabiya*, stz. 10). As in other poetry, like in the *Wasiya wa mabanati* ("Advice to Young Women"), he warns the reader or listener, whom he addresses directly, not to be seduced by outward appearances, but to choose *mama bora* ("the best mother," stz. 16), who is religious and has a good conduct (stz. 16), who is *mtulivu* ("calm," stz. 19), *muyuzi alo mwerevu* ("knowledgeable and smart," stz. 19), and "who is not too busy but will truly look after the children" (*aso mengi mashughuli / tawatunga kwelikweli*, stz. 20). It is the good mother, just described, who is "a child's first most important teacher" (*mwalimu wa kwanda mno muhimu*, stz. 23). Shaping the child's behavior, the mother must first of all be a good role model (see stz. 141). The parent teaches the child good conduct and how to behave toward others through his or her own behavior. This also demands that the adult and teacher be sincere and act according to his or her words, which Ustadh Mau stresses as an important ethical tenet for humans as such: "And you also have to stick to your rules" (stz. 196; see also stz. 145, 209).

Stressing the importance of influence, he underlines the negative impact that friends and the media can have, which spreads like an infectious disease (stz. 153–168). He defines *zifaya za anasa* ("media of entertainment," stz. 169) as the source of much harm. TV programs destroy *mazuri mambo* "all morality," according to him. Being easily accessible, they are like *ulimbo* ("a bird trap," stz. 171) and mostly offer bad programs. The trope of "deceit," so common in Swahili Sufi poetry but also the reformist Islamic literature so important to him, is essential to reflecting upon the morally good which it endangers and seems to have found a new form in his poetry.[89] Here it is the TV and its colorful programs, full of all "types of perversions" (*nyendo za ulanisi*, stz. 177), that does "away with our sense of decency" (*na kuondosha ya haya*, stz. 178). The senses threaten to lead the human being astray—a recurring point in poetry. In earlier classical poems, such as the nineteenth-century *Inkishafi*, sensual pleasures, like food and the promise of erotic encounters lying in looks, gestures, scents, and textiles, take the senses hostage and prevent the soul from its spiritual ful-

---

89   See Clarissa Vierke, "Im Gebälk die Fledermäuse. Figurationen der Vergänglichkeit und der Täuschung in der klassischen Swahili-Dichtung," in *From the Tana River to Lake Chad. Research in African Oratures and Literatures. In Memoriam Thomas Geider*, ed. Lutz Diegner, Raimund Kastenholz, Uta Reuster-Jahn, and Hannelore Vögele, Mainzer Beiträge zur Afrikaforschung (Cologne: Köppe, 2014), 285–309.

fillment.[90] In the *Inkishafi*, the individual not able to refrain himself or herself cannot develop his or her fullest potential as a "good person" rewarded by paradise, but debases himself or herself and is punished in hell. In Ustadh Mau's poem, it is the consumption of TV as well as pornographic magazines (stz. 186) that make the individual lose all dignity, which also finds direct expression in dressing shamelessly, which he condemns (stz. 181–183). According to him, TV programs have a deliberate main agenda of destruction, set by the West (stz. 180), "to promote immorality and to spread it according to well-made plans worldwide" (*kuu ni tabiya jongo / kuzeneza kwa mipango / zitapakaze duniya*, stz. 176).

The topic of education occupies a large part of the poem. For Ustadh Mau, education is essential not only to the child's future, but also to society's, since the benefits of an educated child spread "so that we can also profit from them" (*Na kwetu husikili*, stz. 112). The poem reflects Ustadh Mau's constant worry— also expressed in other poems, such as *Kiswahili*[91] and *Bandari ina mawimbi* ("The Port Makes Waves")[92]—about the low level of education on Lamu, which has ranked high in the Kenyan statistics on school dropouts for decades. In this climate, where education has lost its value, he tries to urge the community—by the use of an inclusive "we"—to make sure that children go to school and make an effort to learn: "We will not see any good results, unless they work hard" (*faida hatutoona / illa wakisoma sana*, stz. 114). It is only *ilimu* "knowledge, education" that can lead to progress and development, as he argues by referring to the example of Japan and Western countries, where education has been the key to success (stz. 117–119). Thus, education essentially builds the foundation of a "good life," in the sense of both financial benefit as well as a broader understanding of things, which is a precondition for any judgment or decision-making.

It is independence in thought and action that Ustadh Mau highlights as important values toward the end of the poem, alongside generosity in giving, volunteering to take responsibility in the community, and the courage to confidently speak out on one's own behalf or to defend the rights of those who are weaker (stz. 222, 223). It is the relational aspect of caring about and for others, as well as independence in making decisions not "depending on others" (*mwenyewe asiajizi wangine kutegemeya*, stz. 228), that he stresses.[93]

---

90 William Hichens, ed., *Al-Inkishafi: The Soul's Awakening* (London: Sheldon Press, 1939); Vierke, "Im Gebälk die Fledermäuse."

91 See also Mahmoud and Frankl, "*Kiswahili.*"

92 See also Raia, "*Angaliya baharini.*"

93 Later in the poem, on the one hand, he reminds parents to watch over the child, not letting

What about the poet as a moral subject? In the poem, Ustadh Mau as the lyrical I takes on the role of the morally responsible and caring person. He formulates directives and imperatives for his audience and speaks up for their dependents, just as he wants parents to teach their children to do. The narrator is not only an ethical person in voicing imperatives and listing values, but rather in the sense that he intercedes by judging the unquestioned, habitual practices he has witnessed and by suggesting alternative ways of acting. The starting point is not values, but observations: he imposes judgment on observed practices, singling them out from the continuous, unquestioned flow of everyday action with the intention to change them. This echoes Lambek's understanding:

> It is precisely because practice is not mechanical, automatic, or fully determined that we have ethics. We must continuously exercise our judgment with respect to what we do or say. The criteria by which we do so are made relevant, brought into play, by means of performative acts, such acts themselves being conducted in consequence of practical judgment.[94]

The initial impulse to intervene is first of all not founded on unchangeable criteria, but on the emotional virtues of *ruhuma* and *kite*, on which his notion of care hinges.[95] They allow him to feel for the child and to put himself in the child's position, to be benevolent and forgiving, and they urge him to further his intention to "repair the 'world'" he lives in, to rephrase Joan Tronto and Berenice Fisher's notion of "to take care of."[96] In his arguments, Ustadh reflects upon criteria. However, while the values expounded in the poem are meant to be of enduring quality, they are also relative, as Ustadh is also aware. In stanza 253, he acknowledges his own fallibility and invites his fellow poets to correct him:

Hakuna mja kamili	There is no perfect human being.
Kutokosa nimuhali	It is impossible not to make mistakes.
Nawaomba tafadhali	I beg you, please
Nanyi kunisaidiya	Help me.

---

him or her do whatever s/he wants to do. On the other hand, he also encourages parents to give children the possibility to take over tasks, like selling food in the street (see above), and to give them money so that they can learn how to spend wisely (stz. 215 ff.).

94   Lambek, "Introduction," 29.

95   On emotion as an essential aspect of the ethics of care, see Held, *The Ethics of Care*.

96   Berenice Fisher and Joan Tronto, "Toward a Feminist Theory of Care," in *Circles of Care*, ed. E. Abel and M. Nelson (Albany: SUNY Press, 1990), 3.

As this stanza underlines, ethics means a communal, dialogic search for values and criteria to decide on a "better path," since the latter is anything but fixed: there are always alternative possibilities, and the decision requires a careful weighing of criteria. As described above, Ustadh makes use of various sources, from existing poetry to books on child development. He sketches scenes of everyday life and dialogues to make the practices he refers to palpable and concrete. In his poem, he stages dialogues between children and parents to show rather than tell about good and bad examples and to make everyday scenes come to life. In this sense, the ethical is not a claim of a fixed truth, but rather a constant search, which for Ustadh Mau takes place largely in his poetry. How much the ethical emerges in reference to lived experience becomes even clearer in some other poems, like the next one.

6 Demanding Social Responsibility: *Mama msimlaumu* ("Don't Blame My Mother")

Imenibidi kunena, kabla wangu wakati
Sababu nimewaona, mamangu humlaiti
Mamangu makosa hana, sipweke amezohiti
Kosa hili nda ummati

I have been compelled to talk prior to my time,
because I have seen you condemning my mother.
My mother is not the one to blame; it is not her fault alone.
It is society's fault.

> *Mama msimlaumu* ("Don't Blame My Mother", stz. 1)

In the poem *Mama msimlaumu*, which takes the shorter *shairi* form, Ustadh Mau talks about an abandoned baby that a dog found in the woods and saved. A newspaper article reporting the incident prompted him to write about it. While many around him condemned the mother for leaving the child to die, he defends the mother and rather places the blame on a society in which a mother is so desperate that she sees no other option but to abandon her own child. In seeking to challenge society's stereotypical blame of women, he takes the perspective of the abandoned baby in the poem, who outwardly defends its mother (see the lines given above).[97] The narrative perspective comes with

---

97   This narrative technique is not unusual: in his *Sauti ya dhiki*, Abdilatif Abdalla also makes

important effects linked to the moral intent of the poem, as I shall argue. First of all, however, I would like to take a look at the argument put forward by the child.

The child empathetically underlines the fallibility or weakness (*dhaifu*) of all human beings (not only the mother) who, despite a general consensus on what is right or wrong, fail to stick to it (which is exactly the reason why, for Lambert, "doing ethics," like judging, is a constant concern): "As all of you know, there are times of weakness, in which we fail to control ourselves" (stz. 3). Thus, the mother is not portrayed as the monster who callously abandoned the child, but as a fallible and thus normal human being. The "we" that Ustadh Mau uses in this stanza includes himself as well as the audience, and asks for their understanding, drawing attention to everyone's fallibility. Counter to society's tendency to socially marginalize pregnant single women, exempting men from any responsibility, the baby urges the audience to equally distribute the blame (stz. 5). The baby highlights the "share" of the man, who did not only "contribute," but might have even taken the mother against her will (stz. 4). In the following stanza, the poem rises in emotionality; the child defends the mother even more emphatically, putting the blame solely on the father, who "pushed her" to such an act, leaving her without a choice although she loved the child. The expression "putting shame on my mother" (*kumuaziri mamangu*; stz. 4) reflects the passive role of the woman, who might have seen no alternative and who also could not deny the illegitimate intercourse, as it was immediately revealed by the pregnancy. Moreover, this has a lasting effect: children born outside of marriage become marginalized and are called names. With the line "I feel so much bitterness if I hear people talking" (stz. 8), the baby narrator is referring to the humiliating practice of gossip, against which the poem seeks to speak out. It is the performative act of the poem that questions and redefines existing criteria and practices of shaming.

The poem continues by further elaborating on the mother's love (as opposed to the man's cold-heartedness), referring to *ruhuma* "mercy," the concept that was so central to the *Haki za watoto*, as the emotion that dominated her feelings (stz. 10). According to the baby's argument, the fact that the mother abandoned

---

the embryo, which the mother wants to abort, speak to ask her for mercy in a poem with the telling title *Usiniuwe!* "Don't Kill Me!"; see Abdilatif Abdalla, *Sauti ya dhiki* (Nairobi: Oxford University Press, 1973), 51–55. The translation is by Ken Walibora and Annmarie Drury, who have been working on a translation of the anthology *Sauti ya dhiki*; see Drury, "Lyric Presence in *Sauti ya dhiki*," paper presented at the Reading Poetry workshop, Johannes-Guttenberg University Mainz, October 9, 2016.

THE ETHICAL AND THE POETIC IN USTADH MAHMOUD MAU'S POETRY   121

the child was not an act of cruelty or despair (as depicted in the newspaper article), but an act of *wema wake*, i.e. her "goodness" or "kindness," since firstly she did not abort the child before giving birth (stz. 11 and 12), and she even put a cloth around it when leaving it in the forest (stz. 13). The child highlights the uniqueness of the mother with the rhetorical question, *Walimwengu naul-iza, tazawa mara ya pili?* ("I ask you human beings: Can I possibly be born a second time?", stz. 14). At the end, the baby thanks the dog and the people who saved it, who have become role models of altruism: "There are still people in the world who are altruistic" (*Wangaliko duniyani, waja wapendao kheri*,[98] stz. 15).

Again, judgment takes place here in relation to a specific incident that Ustadh felt compelled to comment on. While warning against and castigating pregnancies outside of marriage in other poems or stressing the utmost moral responsibility to love an infant in *Haki za watoto*, he does not merely impose the previously established criteria on the mother abandoning her baby, but adopts a different position through the lyrical I, who completely reverses the perspective. It is the baby who, again out of *ruhuma*, is able to forgive, to feel pity for the mother. It is even able to understand the mother's choice, or rather, it calls into question the mother's freedom to act according to her own will.

The narrative perspective and the lyric presence of the baby's voice here is not a byproduct of the poem, a kind of trickery to rivet the audience's attention, but necessary to the ethical statement. It is a role reversal: the fact that it is the baby itself—the victim, who cares for the mother—is what lends its voice so much weight and constructs the poem in antagonism to the hostile social environment. The newborn baby in its state of nature—it is even found in the woods by a dog—is not (yet) a member of society, and thus can speak outside of it and raise its voice against the practices of gossip and exclusion. Against society's fixed judgment, the baby shouts out its questions, which make the poem particularly touching and emotional.[99]

The poem shows the power of Ustadh's poetry in "performing ethics," since in contrast to a catalogue of values, it gives the audience the possibility to plunge into the baby's and mother's experience of pain and pity. It fleshes out real characters, makes them act and talk, so that the audience does not merely understand Ustadh Mau's argument in favor of the mother, but rather feels for the mother's plight and fear, sees her fallibility in a larger context, and wonders at the surviving baby, siding with her. The poem has a cathartic or

---

98   Literally, "there are (still) people who love the (human) good" or "who are benevolent."
99   When Ustadh recited the poem during the Jukwaani poetry festival at the Goethe-Institut Nairobi in 2009, the audience fell silent.

purifying effect: the poem stages human fallibility and vulnerability, such that it is not only the baby feeling *ruhuma* for the mother; *ruhuma* is also what the audience feels—a precondition, as the *Haki za watoto* had already shown, to care in a morally responsible way. *Kite* and *ruhuma* are staged to produce an effect on the audience and urge it to change its attitude—a phenomenon that recalls Aristotle's concept of the cathartic effect of tragedy. For Aristotle, pity and fear are the essential ingredients of tragedy, which, "employing the mode of enactment" throughout a unifying plot, accomplishes the "catharsis of such emotions":[100] "For the plot should be so structured that, even without seeing it performed, the person who hears the events that occur experiences horror and pity at what comes about."[101] The enactment of a tragic fate makes the audience fear for the protagonist as well as feel pity, while at the same time, it gives them the chance to live through these emotions communally as the story unfolds. For Aristotle, it is catharsis that changes the audience's attitude and thus lays the groundwork for future good deeds. In a similar way, in thinking about philosophical discourses of morality, the contemporary philosopher Martha Nussbaum also highlights the capacity of literature to sensitize others to human pain, vulnerability, experiences of loss, and fragility as a precondition for acting ethically.[102] Taking the example of Greek tragedy, she highlights its particular way of developing morality through an emotionally compelling staged drama, which involves the audience differently than a philosophical treatise on morality, which relies on abstract arguments. In *Mama msimlauma*, the narrative technique of telling the story through the eyes of the baby—by piercing the reality with questions—is linked to the ethical concern of the poet.

7   Poetry as a Site of Self-Interrogation: *Mlango*

While there are many other poems through which Ustadh seeks to make a public intervention, questioning existing practices, in what follows, I will turn to a more personal, reflective, and intimate poem—namely *Mlango* ("The Door")—to show the variability of his poetic and ethical voice. He composed the poem in 2003 or 2004 at a time when his bakery, with which he had always earned his living, was no longer making enough money to cover his family's

---

100   Aristotle, *Poetics*, trans. S. Halliwell. (Cambridge, Mass.: Harvard University Press, 2004), 48, 49 (1449b).
101   Aristotle, *Poetics*, 74, 75.
102   Martha Craven Nussbaum, *The Fragility of Goodness: Luck and Ethics in Greek Tragedy and Philosophy* (Cambridge: Cambridge University Press, 1986), 2.

needs, including his children's university fees, and his debts were increasing to the point that he was forced to think about closing the bakery.

It is a poem about loss, disappointment, and despair, and it struck me because of its deeply melancholic tone; the narrator here does not side with someone else, but cries out about his own fate, yet at the same time looks for ways to comfort himself. Differently from the other poems discussed here, this poem is a lyrical, interior self-exploration. It is a form of "self-care," if one wants to stick to the notion of "care" introduced above, but, more importantly to me, self-care is not merely the aim of the poem, but rather emerges through its lyrical voice. In line with Earl Miner's comparative exploration of the "lyrical" in the world's literatures, I understand the lyrical as a "radical presence" that suspends the flow of the narrative, enhances the palpability of the depicted scene, and plunges into emotional intensity in a well-conceived and pithy form.[103] In a similar way, Ustadh also acknowledges a lyrical quality in some of his poetry, where he explores his emotions (*hisia*) with regard to his own experience: "a poet also composes to talk about feelings that are his or her own, concerning things that happened to him or her personally."[104] In other words, the lyrical voice and intention—whose ethical core is "to do good to oneself" or "to care about oneself" and implies a strong element of self-reflection—are intertwined.

Self-interrogative poems, in turn, are an important part of Swahili poetic tradition.[105] In *Moyo iwe na subira* ("Be Patient My Heart"), the Kenyan poet Abdilatif Abdalla—who had been sentenced to solitary confinement by Kenya's first president, Kenyatta, because of his political activism against the government—argues with his own heart: *usijitie matungu, siliye 'tajiumiza* "don't hurt yourself by crying."[106] Addressing his heart, he explains to it, the fate of imprisonment is "a lesson for you—learn from it, heart, learn" (*haya ni mafunzo kwako, funzika moyo funzika*).[107] As in Ustadh Mau's poem, the lyrical voice in *Moyo iwe na subira* struggles with the discrepancy between his strong feelings of loss and sadness and his previous confidence—"it wasn't meant to be" (stz.

---

103   Earl Miner, *Comparative Poetics. An Intercultural Essay on Theories of Literature* (Princeton, NJ: Princeton University Press, 1990), 87 ff.

104   *Mshairi anatunga kwa ajili ya kuelezea hisia ambazo ni zake yeye mwenyewe kwa mambo ambayo yamemtokeya yeye binafsi.* Quoted from Raia, "Angaliya baharini," 231; my translation.

105   See also Ibrahim Noor Shariff, *Tungo zetu: Msingi wa mashairi na tungo nyinginezo* (Trenton, NJ: Red Sea Press, 1988).

106   Abdalla, *Sauti ya dhiki*, 48, stz. 1. This translation, like that of the following line, is by Ken Waliaula Walibora and Annmarie Drury (cf. Drury, "Lyric Presence").

107   Abdalla, *Sauti ya dhiki*, 49, stz. 12.

14)—and the situation as it is, which he cannot change.[108] While the narrator urges the heart to be patient, since *na yale ambayo huwa, huwa ni ya kuwa nayo* "whatever happens is usually what is meant to be,"[109] the self-interrogative form of the poem acknowledges the essential ambivalence of the human condition: despite *knowing* about the fickle nature of life, one still *hopes* for the contrary, struggling with feelings of loss, deprivation, and limitation. Above all, it is in poetry where the discrepancy between the hope for a better life, on the one hand, and coercive reality, on the other, is staged.[110]

Mlango also starts from the point of loss as a fait accompli, as the narrator struggles to make himself realize that there is nothing else to do but close the bakery. No matter how hard he tries to find a solution, the situation is getting worse and worse: *nimemaliza mipango, siyoni kurakibika*, "I have tried everything; I do not see any improvement" (stz. 1). In focusing on the moment when the narrator is struggling for final certainty about a major loss that represents a turning point in his life, the poem is similar to *Jahazi* ("The Dhow"), which stages a major economic crisis that struck Lamu as if it were the sinking of a ship, into which water keeps pouring despite the sailors' efforts to save it:[111]

> *Ngurudi imeshopoka, mai ngamani hujiri*
> *Haitaki kuzibika, na hata kwa misumari*
> *Kuyafua tumechoka, mikono hutuhairi*

> The stopper is out, and water is pouring into the bilge
> It doesn't want to be plugged, not even using nails
> We are tired of scooping out water; our hands hurt.
> > *Jahazi* ("The Dhow", stz. 2)

It is the moment of fatigue that is in focus in both poems, as neither situation changes for the better. *Mlango* speaks of the same weariness toward waiting as *Jahazi*, where, rather than a storm or the water rushing in, it is inertia that dries up all courage. In *Jahazi*, the narrator reaches the point where he would prefer the ship to "hit a coral reef than [confront] this nuisance" (*ni heri mwamba kupanda, kama hunu utiriri*, stz. 4). In *Mlango*, the narrator has just made the

---

108 The most famous poetic self-interrogation is certainly the poem *Inkishafi*, in which the poetic narrator struggles with his heart to make it understand that despite all worldly pleasures, death is inevitable and life ephemeral (Hichens, *Al-Inkishafi*).

109 Abdalla, *Sauti ya dhiki*, 50, stz. 14.

110 On poetry as a site of voicing loss, see Drury, "Lyric Presence."

111 See also Raia, "*Angaliya baharini*," 241 ff.

THE ETHICAL AND THE POETIC IN USTADH MAHMOUD MAU'S POETRY 125

unavoidable, "hard decision" (*uwamuzi thakili*, stz. 2) to close the bakery against his will, and is seeking to come to terms with it. The latter is not an easy task, since he has spent his whole life working in the bakery, which he inherited from his uncle, and the future is uncertain.

In contrast to *Jahazi*, where the lyrical I is a plural "we"—it is the whole community of Lamu that is suffering—the narrator of *Mlango* is alone. Over the course of the poem, it becomes clear that there is a bigger personal threat than the sheer economic one: the lyric narrator does not only fear losing his means of livelihood, but it is his very persona, defined through moral engagement—his *heshima*—that is at stake. The narrator also feels compelled to close the shop's door as a way of making the bankruptcy visible to everybody, since the people who used to beg or borrow from him and have relied on his generosity do not believe him to be in a difficult situation. They take his confessions about his miserable situation for a "joke" (*dhihaka*, stz. 4) or a sign of "arrogance" (*ujauri*, stz. 5), a lame excuse to "avoid all responsibility" (*jukumu kuepuka*, stz. 8)— and start slandering him behind his back. He is considered a liar and a miser who no longer lives up to his moral code and has become as unreliable and moody as the proverbial "*mkizi* fish" (stz. 7), which is hard to catch and whose behavior is difficult to predict. The sad voice of his poem contradicts the slanderous speech of the others, whom he quotes: "It has become his habit: when someone begs him, he says, 'Nowadays, things have gone wrong'" (*Imekuwa ndake kazi, mtu kitu akitaka / Humwambiya siku hizi, mambo yameharibika*, stz. 7). Not unlike in the other poems, the lyrical voice expresses great disapproval toward how they speak and act. However, this poem is not a public proclamation castigating wrongdoers, explaining his situation to everyone beyond doubt and reminding the audience of *kite* and *ruhuma*.[112] This would run counter to dignity (*heshima*) linked to the concept of *sitara*,[113] since it would mean publicly shaming himself. Rather, this poem is the outcry of the abandoned and mistrusted narrator against all the slander and cruelty around him. As he cannot rectify his mistakes through speaking publicly, he resorts to a monologue in which the lyrical I can lament his humiliation and find a place to console himself and consider what to do. The narrator starts wondering if closing the

---

112   In a situation where he can no longer afford to be generous or maintain his previous habits, which includes fulfilling the socially prescribed, superior role that comes with the obligation of giving, he has to rely on the *kite* and *ruhuma* of the others—who, however, "do not remember his previous favors" (*Ya nyuma yote mazuri, huwata kuyakumbuka*, stz. 5). The lyrical narrator himself turns into a suffering, dependent individual—like the child in *Haki za watoto* or the mother in *Mama msimlaumu*—depending on the mercy of others, who instead humiliate him.

113   See Jasmin Mahazi's contribution in this volume and the following footnote.

shop would be a possibility to prove the truth and veracity of his claims. Here too the conclusion about what to do has not yet been drawn, but the poem as such becomes a site of reflection, comparable to a diary, as is best reflected by the modality of possibility in stanza 9, which starts with "perhaps" (*huenda*) and turns into a conditional clause: he wonders if the "reproaches and provocations of those surrounding me will stop if I close the shop's door" (*zikapungua lawama, za wenye kunizunguka na utune ukakoma, mlango kiushindika*).

At the end of the poem, the narrator finally urges himself to be patient despite all the impatience that has taken hold of him, and not to be led astray by emotion, but to rather resort to God, the ultimate good above all human beings, who is able to "repair" the world even when it seems to be lost forever. In a similar way, he pleads for patience in *Jahazi* and *Amu:* in the latter poem, the catastrophe of an actual sunken ship brings the community of Lamu to the verge of emotional and social breakdown. On the one hand, patience (*subira*) means accepting misery as a challenge sent by God, but on the other hand, also believing that God will bring relief: *Ni yeye pweke Khallaki, atuwao na kutweka*, "It is only the Creator who can lift the burden or put it on our shoulders" (stz. 10). To appease his troubled heart, he—similarly to Abdilatif Abdalla— heeds the enlightening aspect of misery, since, as he argues in *Mlango*, it will tell him who his true friends are. Furthermore, he also reminds himself that *Mola amenisitiri tangu nalipoinuka*, "God has always safeguarded me since my childhood" (stz. 12).[114] In the end, he encourages himself with the phrase *afuwa haiko mbali*, "relief is not far" (stz. 13). As these last stanzas underscore, through their growing intensity in imploring God to change his fate, on the one hand, and their seeking to accept the situation *tel quel*, on the other, the poem is a site of struggle for hope—and not an expression of a previously gained certainty about what best to do.

The poem *Mlango* reminds us that not only in poems like the *Haki za watoto* or *Mama mslimlaumu*, which seek to intervene in public affairs, are the poetic and the ethical intertwined, but also in more introspective, lyrical forms, which can express dissent with the status quo and particularly common practices that hurt and objectify others. The lyrical form is not supplementary to, but a pre-

---

114   Tellingly, here he uses the verb *-sitiri*, literally "to conceal, to hide," related to the noun *sitara*. A person of integrity and dignity, *mwenye sitara*, is someone whose shameful side is hidden. The most concrete and obvious example, also included in Johnson's dictionary, is "to cover the private parts," but it also refers to concealing immoral deeds or what could cause them (cf. the practice of veiling women). Ustadh Mau also refers to *sitara* as his main reason for rejecting contemporary films and media, since they shamelessly show intimacy and nakedness, which are not supposed to be shown in public (see *Haki*, stz. 171 ff.).

THE ETHICAL AND THE POETIC IN USTADH MAHMOUD MAU'S POETRY 127

condition for its moral force: its questions, staged dialogues, and reflections pierce through the unquestioned and imposed practices and speech of society. However, more than *Haki za watoto* and *Mama msimlaumu*, where the poet intends to and believes in changing existing social conditions and advises on what to do, *Mlango*—like *Amu* and *Jahazi*, which essentially speak from a position where no longer can anything be done to avert misery—also struggles with the limitation of the human condition as such. There is nothing that can be done to avoid all suffering, which is a difficult conclusion for the suffering lyrical voice. In this context, the only and ultimate resolution is "to be patient" (*kuwa na subira*). This does not mean merely waiting and hoping for the better, but rather implies a form of "doing" as well, since it demands that the individual make a constant and painstaking effort to trust in God and His mercy (*ruhuma*). In this sense, *subira* is also a form of doing "good"—as the poems suggest, the ultimate one.

8 Conclusion: The Poetry of Care and the Care for Poetry

Boya hili la maisha, kattu halitozamisha / Ashikao tamvusha, bandari tasikiliya

This life buoy never sinks; it will rescue the one who holds onto it, so that s/he reaches the port.

> *Ramani ya maisha ya ndoa* ("The Map of Married Life", stz. 9)[115]

In seeking to explore Ustadh Mahmoud Mau's poetry, I have sought to explore the close connection between his care for poetry and his poetry of care. My major concern has been highlighting that the poetic is not secondary to the ethical, but rather an essential part of his ethical explorations. It is poetry that has the built-in authority and effective voice to cut through the unconscious continuation of life, to express dissent from the status quo, and to suggest or rather to carefully explore ways of doing things better. Furthermore, in his poetry, Ustadh Mau does not merely resort to rules or received codes of conduct; his process is not that of making general statements without taking into account the details of specific, recurring challenges that society confronts. It is through abstraction that ethical guidelines and rules lose their palpability and their capacity to involve people emotionally and to make them imagine con-

---

115 Taken from Raia, "*Angaliya baharini*," 247.

crete scenes and applications. In staging dialogues and incorporating scenes of, for instance, parent-child interaction before their eyes or a baby speaking out in defense of its mother, his poetry becomes compelling in that it urges the audience to put themselves in the place of the characters and hence to *care* for and about them. It is the *kite* that, for him, is the basic incentive of all morally good action and is ultimately grounded in God's own unconditional care for his creation, which Ustadh Mau does not preach but rather seeks to evoke through his poetry, turning the audience into a caring community. Thus, Ustadh Mau's poetry has a cathartic effect in that it has the power to transform the audience or even the self—as the last poem, *Mlango*, seeks to do, where patience as trust in the ultimate good is reached not *before* but *through* the poem.

In this sense, "educating people" (*kuwaelimisha watu*), which he considers a major goal of his poetry, does not mean merely to form their "intellect" (*akili*) or to increase their "knowledge" (*ujuzi*), but also to turn them into morally acting thinkers, or rather "carers," who intervene whenever they deem it to be necessary; not to impose strict rules, but rather to act on behalf of "dependents" who cannot speak for themselves or do not even recognize the wrong inflicted on them. Intellectual practice, closely intertwined with poetry, is primarily of ethical concern.

References

Abdalla, Abdilatif. *Sauti ya dhiki*. Nairobi: Oxford University Press, 1973.

Abdalla, Abdilatif. "Wajibu wa mshairi katika jamii yake." In *Abdilatif Abdalla: Poet in Politics*, edited by Rose Marie Beck and Kai Kresse, 81–86. Dar es Salaam: Mkuki na Nyota, 2016. First published 1977 in *Lugha Yetu* 30.

Allen, J.W.T., ed. *Tendi: Six Examples of a Swahili Classical Verse Form with Translations & Notes*. New York: Africana Pub. Corp, 1971.

Aristotle. *Poetics*. Translated by S. Halliwell. Cambridge, Mass.: Harvard University Press, 2004.

Barber, Karin, and Graham Furniss. "African-Language Writing." *Research in African Literatures* 37, no. 3 (2006): 1–14.

Beck, Rose Marie. *Texte auf Textilien in Ostafrika: Sprichwörtlichkeit als Eigenschaft ambiger Kommunikation*. Cologne: Köppe, 2001.

Biersteker, Ann. *Kujibizana: Questions of Language and Power in Nineteenth- and Twentieth-Century Poetry in Kiswahili*. East Lansing: Michigan State Univ. Press, 1996.

Bourdieu, Pierre. *Outline of a Theory of Practice*. New York: Cambridge University Press, 1977.

Büttner, Carl. *Anthologie aus der Suaheli-Litteratur (Gedichte und Geschichten der Suaheli)*. Berlin: Emil Felber, 1894.

Drury, Annmarie. "Lyric Presence in *Sauti ya dhiki*." Paper presented at the Reading Poetry workshop, Johannes-Guttenberg University Mainz, October 9, 2016.

Fisher, Berenice, and Joan Tronto. "Toward a Feminist Theory of Care." In *Circles of Care*, edited by E. Abel and M. Nelson, 35–62. Albany: SUNY Press, 1990.

Furniss, Graham. *Orality: The Power of the Spoken Word*. Basingstoke: Palgrave Macmillan, 2004.

Gikandi, Simon. "Theory, Literature, and Moral Considerations." *Research in African Literatures* 32, no. 4 (2001): 1–18.

Held, Virginia. *The Ethics of Care. Personal, Political and Global*. Oxford: Oxford University Press, 2006.

Hichens, William, ed. *Al-Inkishafi: The Soul's Awakening*. London: Sheldon Press, 1939.

King'ei, Geoffrey Kitula. "Taswira za Ukosoaji na 'Utopia.'" In *Dunia Yao. Utopia/Dystopia in Swahili Fiction. In Honour of Said A.M. Khamis*, edited by Clarissa Vierke and Katharina Greven, 167–184. Cologne: Köppe, 2016.

Klein-Arendt, Reinhard. *Gesprächsstrategien im Swahili. Linguistisch-pragmatische Analysen von Dialogtexten einer Stehgreiftheatergruppe*. Cologne: Köppe, 1992.

Krapf, Johann Ludwig. *A Dictionary of the Suahili Language*. London: Trübner, 1882.

Kresse, Kai. *Philosophising in Mombasa. Knowledge, Islam and Intellectual Practice at the Swahili Coast*. Edinburgh: Edinburgh University Press, 2007.

Kresse, Kai. "Knowledge and Intellectual Practice in a Swahili Context: 'Wisdom' and the Social Dimensions of Knowledge." *Africa* 79, no. 1 (2009): 148–167.

Kresse, Kai. "Enduring Relevance: Samples of Oral Poetry on the Swahili Coast." *Wasafiri* 26, no. 2 (2011): 46–49.

Lambek, Michael. "Introduction." In *Ordinary Ethics. Anthropology, Language, and Action*, edited by Michael Lambek, 1–36. New York: Fordham University Press, 2010.

Levine, Caroline. *Forms. Whole, Rhythm, Hierarchy, Network*. Princeton, NJ: Princeton University Press, 2015.

Mahmoud, Ahmad Abdulkadir, and Peter Frankl. "*Kiswahili*: A Poem by Mahmoud Ahmad Abdulkadir, to Which is Appended a List of the Poet's Compositions in Verse." *Swahili Forum* 20 (2013): 1–18. https://nbn-resolving.org/urn:nbn:de:bsz:15-qucosa-137405.

Miehe, Gudrun, and Clarissa Vierke. *Muhamadi Kijuma. Texts from the Dammann Collections and Other Papers*. Cologne: Köppe, 2010.

Miner, Earl. *Comparative Poetics. An Intercultural Essay on Theories of Literature*. Princeton, NJ: Princeton University Press, 1990.

Mreta, Abel, Thilo Schadeberg, and Gerlind Scheckenbach. "Kiziwi, kipofu na kilema: Ubaguzi au heshima?" *Afrikanistische Arbeitspapiere* 51 (1997): 23–54.

Nabahany, Ahmed. "Uketo wa tungo za Kiswahili." *Lugha* 4 (1990): 10–16.

Nassenstein, Nico. "Politeness in Kisangani Swahili: Speakers' Pragmatic Strategies at the Fringes of the Kiswahili Speaking World." *Afrikanistik/Ägyptologie Online* (2018): 1–18. https://www.afrikanistik-aegyptologie-online.de/archiv/2018/4654/politeness kis_pdf.pdf

Nussbaum, Martha Craven. *The Fragility of Goodness: Luck and Ethics in Greek Tragedy and Philosophy*. Cambridge: Cambridge University Press, 1986.

Ponten, Frederic. "Cosmopolitanism and the Location of Literary Theory." Paper presented at the Location of Theory symposium at the European University Viadrina Frankfurt (Oder), February 7, 2020.

Pouwels, Randall. *Horn and Crescent: Cultural Change and Traditional Islam on the East African Coast, 800–1900*. Cambridge: Cambridge University Press, 1987.

Raia, Annachiara. "Angaliya baharini, mai yaliyoko pwani: The Presence of the Ocean in Mahmoud Ahmed Abdulkadir's Poetry." In *Lugha na fasihi. Scritti in onore e memoria di/Essays in Honour and Memory of Elena Bertoncini Zúbková*, edited by Flavia Aiello and Roberto Gaudioso, 223–250. Naples: Università degli Studi di Napoli "L'Orientale," 2019.

Rettová, Alena. "Lidství utu? Ubinadamu baina ya tamaduni." *Swahili Forum* 14 (2007): 89–134. https://nbn-resolving.org/urn:nbn:de:bsz:15-qucosa-97671.

Sacleux, Charles. *Dictionnaire swahili-français*. Paris: Inst. d'Ethnologie, 1939.

Sartre, Jean-Paul. *Qu'est-ce que la littérature?* Paris: Gallimard, 1948.

Schacht, Joseph. "Waṣīya." In *Encyclopaedia of Islam, First Edition (1913–1936)*, edited by M.Th. Houtsma, T.W. Arnold, R. Basset, and R. Hartmann. http://dx.doi.org/10.1163/2214-871X_ei1_SIM_5969.

Scheckenbach, Gerlind. *"Busara*: Besonnenheit und Takt." In *Zwischen Bantu und Burkina. Festschrift für Gudrun Miehe zum 65. Geburtstag*, edited by Kerstin Winkelmann and Dymitr Ibriszimow, 207–234. Cologne: Köppe, 2006.

Shariff, Ibrahim Noor. *Tungo zetu: Msingi wa mashairi na tungo nyinginezo*. Trenton, NJ: Red Sea Press, 1988.

Shariff, Ibrahim Noor. "Islam and Secularity in Swahili Literature: An Overview." In *Faces of Islam in African Literature*, edited by Kenneth Harrow, 37–57. Portsmouth, NH: Heinemann, 1991.

Sheikh, Sauda. "Yanayoudhi kuyaona. Mafumbo na vijembe vya Kiswahili." *Swahili Forum* 1 (1994): 7–11.

Taylor, William. *African Aphorisms: Or, Saws from Swahili-Land*. London: Soc. for Promoting Christian Knowledge, 1891.

Tronto, Joan. *Moral Boundaries. A Political Argument for an Ethic of Care*. New York: Routledge, 1993.

UN General Assembly. "Convention on the Rights of the Child." *Treaty Series* 1577 (November 1989): 3. https://www.unicef.org/sites/default/files/2019-04/UN-Conven tion-Rights-Child-text.pdf.

Veit-Wild, Flora, and Clarissa Vierke. "Introduction: Digging into Language." In *Reading Closely: Investigating Textuality in Afrophones Literatures*, edited by Flora Veit-Wild and Clarissa Vierke. Special issue, *Research in African Literatures* 48, no. 1 (2017): ix–xviii.

Velten, Carl. *Desturi za Wasuaheli na khabari za desturi za sheria za Wasuaheli*. Göttingen: Vandenhoeck & Ruprecht, 1903.

Vierke, Clarissa. "Im Gebälk die Fledermäuse. Figurationen der Vergänglichkeit und der Täuschung in der klassischen Swahili-Dichtung." In *From the Tana River to Lake Chad. Research in African Oratures and Literatures. In Memoriam Thomas Geider*, edited by Lutz Diegner, Raimund Kastenholz, Uta Reuster-Jahn, and Hannelore Vögele, 285–309. Mainzer Beiträge zur Afrikaforschung. Cologne: Köppe, 2014.

Vierke, Clarissa, and Chapane Mutiua. *The Poem about the Prophet's Death in Mozambique—Swahili as a Transregional Language of Islamic Poetry*. Special issue, *Islamic Africa* 38, no. 2 (2020): 44–74

Weimar, Klaus. "Literatur." In *Reallexikon der deutschen Literatur*, vol. 2, edited by Harald Fricke et al., 443–448. Berlin: De Gruyter, 2007.

Werner, Alice. "The *Utendi wa Mwana Kupona*." In *Harvard Studies*. Vol. 1, *Varia Africana I*, edited by O. Bates, 147–181. Cambridge, Mass.: Peabody Museum, 1917.

Werner, Alice, and William Hichens. *The Advice of Mwana Kupona upon the Wifely Duty*. Azanian Classics 2. Medstead: Azania Press, 1934.

Yahya-Othman, Saida. "Covering One's Social Back: Politeness among the Swahili." *Text* 14, no. 1 (1994): 141–161.

FIGURE 8   Ustadh Mahmou Mau as a small boy in 1963, next to a *kiti cha enzi*, a prestigious, commonly shared Indian Ocean piece of furniture from the epoch of Portuguese rule

Mabanati in Search of an Author: Portable Reform Texts and Multimodal Narrative Media among Swahili Muslim Communities

Annachiara Raia

This chapter seeks to situate the poem *Wasiya wa mabanati* (hereafter "*Wasiya*"), its genre, media, and content in relation to modern Swahili Muslim publics in a postcolonial era characterized by reforms and opposition toward Western customs. The focus on its genre, media, and narrative reveals a plethora of aesthetic and performative experiences that help to explain the poem's social resonance and public reflexivity.[1]

Based on latest works on *al-Islam al-sawti* ("voiced Islam")[2] and Muslim media in coastal Kenya,[3] both the *Wasiya* and the Arabic prose pamphlet *Yābintī*, which inspired Ustadh Mau's work, provide instructive case studies for investigating the multimodal vehicles through which reform and didactic ideas may be spread and broadcast among Muslim communities in the twentieth and twenty-first centuries. In doing this, the present chapter will also draw from and contribute to the so-called "new media" (i.e., those new media that provide access to messages and voices that preexisting mass media "restrict or relegate to less public channels") in the Muslim world[4] by adding the scenarios of those Muslim communities of the Kenyan coastal belt, islands included, where solo

---

1 A first draft of this paper, titled "Reading Poetry—Listening to Advice," was presented in 2017 in occasion of the "Reading Poetry" workshop organized by Clarissa Vierke and Mark Verne at the University of Mainz. I am extremely grateful for the inspiring and fruitful exchange of thoughts and opinions that this paper has enjoyed at various stages along its path.

2 Annachiara Raia, "Texts, Voices and Tapes. Mediating Poetry on the Swahili Muslim Coast in the 21st Century," in "Power to the People?—Patronage, Intervention and Transformation in African Performative Arts," edited by Ricarda de Haas, Marie-Anne Kohl, Samuel Ndogo, and Christopher Odhiambo, special issue, *Matatu* 51 (2019): 139–168. I owe this concept (which I came across for the first time while reading Bang, "Authority and Piety") to Dale, F. Eickelman and Jon W. Anderson, who have applied this term to their analysis of new media in the Middle East; see Dale F. Eickelman and Jon W. Anderson, *New Media in the Muslim World: The Emerging Public Sphere*, 2nd ed, Bloomington: Indiana University Press, 2003. Subsequently, I began using it also in the context of Muslim coastal phenomena in Kenya.

3 Kai Kresse, "Enduring Relevance: Samples of Oral Poetry on the Swahili Coast," *Wasafiri* 26, no. 2 (2011): 46–49.

4 Eickelman and Anderson, *New Media in the Muslim World*, x.

© ANNACHIARA RAIA, 2023 | DOI:10.1163/9789004525726_008

This is an open access chapter distributed under the terms of the CC BY-NC-ND 4.0 license.

recordings of the poem have been disseminated, thus listened to, and used to direct consciousness and craft models of piety.

Yet it is within the *Wasiya*'s story, rooted in social drama, that the poem reveals its aesthetic power. To describe the *Wasiya* narratively, I refer to Michael Bakhtin's concept of polyphony as applied to Dostoyevsky's novels, as well as to an example of a dramatic play, Luigi Pirandello's *Six Characters in Search of an Author*, whose characters and their "masks," concealing real biographies and family dramas, have inspired both a comparison with the content of the *Wasiya* and the title of this contribution.

The title *Wasiya wa mabanati* translates to "Advice to Young Women," and it is the earliest attested written poem composed by Ustadh Mau, in 1974. Only two years later, in January 1976, the novice poet married his first wife, the mother of his firstborn, Tunda. Ustadh Mau was thus only in his twenties when he composed this poem, still living at his uncle's house, and yet, though just a young man, he shows a surprising empathy and sensitivity to the needs of young women.

When Ustadh Mau was asked to imagine being a painter depicting the *Wasiya*, he said:

> *Kuhusu rangi, ningetumiya rangi ya samawati na nyeupe na nyeusi kwa wasiya wamabanati. Rangi yasamawati niishara yabahari namaisha kwajumla nikama bahari yana mambo mengi yaaina tafauti nawatu aina mbali mbali wabaya nawema. Rangi nyeusi niishara yashida namatatizo namtu kuzumgukwa na majamga kila aina yakamtatiya kama giza lausiku; ama nyeupe nialama yakuwa mambo yanaweza kubadilika badali yadhiki nashida ikajsafuraha naraha; ama nyekundu piya niishara yakuwa duniyani wpo watu wasiojali kufuja nakuharibu maisha yawmngine kwa ajil yakutimiza raha na starehe zao.*

I would have used blue and white and black to paint *Wasiya wa mabanati*. The blue colour represents the sea, and life in general which is is like the sea: It is so diverse and full of different people, both bad and good. The black colour represents the problems and tribulations and a person surrounded by all sorts of tragedies like darkness at night. And white is a symbol of change, joy and happiness instead of trials and tribulations. And red is a sign that there are people in the world who do not care about ruining somebody else's life for the sake of their own joy and happiness.[5]

---

5   Translation by Abu Amirah, founding editor of Hekaya Initiative.

He would use blue, "the color of the sky" (*rangi ya samawati*), which symbolically refers to the ocean (*bahari*). The ocean means ambiguity: it implies various good and bad things and people. He would use the color black (*nyeusi*), symbolically indicating the problems and concerns (*shida na matatizo*) that envelop each individual; and finally, the color white (*nyeupe*) which is for him a sign that "things can change" (*mambo yanaweza kubadilika*). As is evident from this visual rendition of the poem, Ustadh Mau maintains the hope (*tumaini*) that rather than only agony and difficulties, things can change and there can be joy and happiness (*furaha na raha*) in the community. Nevertheless, he is realistic enough also to use red (*nyekundu*) as a color that symbolizes the cruelty of this world, in which there are people who spoil and sabotage the lives of others (*kufuja na kuharibu maisha ya wengine*) for the sake of their own interest and happiness.

As noted by previous scholars,[6] Ustadh Mau composed his poem for young women, whom he refers to (stz. 7) with the epithet *binti Hawaa* ("daughter of Eve"), drawing from an Arabic pamphlet in prose form titled *Ya-bintī* ("Oh My Daughter"), composed in 1954 by the Syrian ʿAlī al-Ṭanṭawi—"one of the most famous, prominent and best writers and preachers of Islam in the modern era."[7]

Ali al-Ṭanṭawi's text was meant to warn young ladies and his own daughter not to let themselves be deceived by men in matters of love. His thirty-page booklet, with an image of the famous Umayyad Mosque in Damascus on the cover, enjoyed great popularity and the text was reprinted at least forty-six times.[8] Ustadh Mau read this text in the '60s and was inspired by it; a decade later, in 1974, this inspiration prompted his decision to write a story adapted from that booklet in verse: his admonitory poem, the *Wasiya*.[9] In other words, Ustadh Mau turned al-Ṭanṭawi's ideas, conveyed through the medium of a pamphlet, into a didactic Swahili verse poem. Still, the Swahili poem is not a translation of the Arabic *Ya-bintī*; apart from several verses that have been

---

6 Kresse, "Enduring Relevance."

7 Ahmad Munir, "Sheikh Ali al-Tantāwi and His Educational and Literary Services," *Shaykh Zayed Islamic Centre: University of Peshawar* 29, no. 2 (2014): 254–272.

8 As Ustadh Mau explained to me, one of the printed versions of *Ya-bintī* ("Oh My Daughter") is part of Ali al-Ṭanṭawi's larger work, of 385 pages, titled *Ṣuwaru wa khawāṭir*. On the other hand, the *Ya-bintī* booklet version that he received was printed in Kuwait, and sadly we could not retrieve its publishing year.

9 Al-Ṭanṭawi is a Syrian writer whose grandfather was Egyptian; he first moved to Syria and then to Egypt. He died in Jeddah, Saudi Arabia, in 1999, at the age of 90. His *Ya-bintī* ("Oh My Daughter") has been published in Pakistan and translated into Urdu and Farsi. Another work composed by the author, titled *Ya-Ibnī* ("Oh My Son"), did not find the same success that *Ya-bintī* did.

adapted by the poet, the entire composition, its plot, characters, and the surprising metanarration framing the last part of the poem comes from Ustadh Mau's own pen, and marked his beginning as a talented storyteller and poet.

It is beyond the scope of this chapter to carry out a comparative reading of al-Ṭanṭawi's pamphlet versus the *Wasiya*. Rather, since narrative can be realized through many different media, in the following, I will use narrative and its related media (i.e. the media chosen to tell a story; in the context of this study, the *same* story, that of the *Wasiya wa mabanati*) as a conceptual frame for shaping social and religious discourse on coastal Kenya.[10]

More precisely, this chapter investigates the role of these so-called "reform and didactic texts" and their fictional power according to the context in which they have been produced, their authors, genres, and the media—intended as the channel of communication/entertainment and technical means of artistic expression—that Muslim audiences have become accustomed to and that allow stories to travel and be adapted.

1   Situating the *Wasiya* and *Ya-bintī* in Their Context of Knowledge Production

The *Wasiya wa mabanati* is a 140-stanza rhymed verse poem that was written at a time when the Ustadh Mau felt that local customs were under threat on Lamu: poets like Ustadh Mau would plead for the respect of Muslim customs and culture at a moment when, according to him, hippies came to the island, bringing cannabis and the habit of using drugs.[11] More broadly, the context of the *Wasiya*'s composition seems to reflect how Muslim reformers strove to resist the kind of European-style modernity emerging in various African societies in the shadow of Western influence. As Robert Loimeier puts it, "all Africans, including Muslims, had to learn to live with and within the boundaries of modern (European-style) nation states in this period [the nineteenth century]."[12]

Ustadh Mau's community was also experiencing what he considers a Western-style modernity, which he refers to with the epithet *shetwani wa sasa* ("the devil of modernity," stz. 5) or explicitly by the literal term *mila ya kizungu* ("Western customs," stz. 134). For him, the Westernization of customs was

---

10   For further criticism on narrative and media, see Marie-Laure Ryan, *Narrative across Media: The Languages of Storytelling* (Lincoln, Neb.: University of Nebraska Press, 2004).

11   Ustadh Mau, personal communication, July 2019.

12   Robert Loimeier, *Islamic Reform in Twentieth-Century Africa* (Edinburgh: Edinburgh University Press, 2016), 2.

MABANATI IN SEARCH OF AN AUTHOR: PORTABLE REFORM TEXTS

haunting the Swahili Muslim people, particularly the youth, and most of all the young ladies (Sw. *mabanati*, a term of Arabic origin, or Sw. *wanawake*), and this moved the poet Ustadh Mau to compose a poem offering advice and warnings to the younger generation in Lamu and beyond the archipelago, along the Swahili Muslim coastal belt (*pwani*). As a matter of fact, Ustadh Mau's main audience is his Muslim coastal community in Kenya.

Both al-Ṭanṭawi's booklet as well as Ustadh Mau's *Wasiya* can be regarded as reform texts—particularly intended to help and educate women—which, in their own style, touch on moral and ethical themes dear to their respective communities. Surprisingly, a similar text that al-Ṭanṭawi composed for his son, *Ya-'ibnī* ("Oh My Son") did not gain as much popularity as the *Ya-bintī*. At this point, one might wonder if, content-wise, addressing and delivering advice to the abovementioned "daughters of Eve," the young women, was a more pressing issue in the time of postcolonial reform time, and one that Muslim publics were accustomed hearing about; this would explain the writers' sense of responsibility to open people's minds and caution Muslim girls, who represented the most fragile and neglected side of Muslim society.

To start with, I shall delve into some of the main features of reformist and didactic poems.

2 Features of Didactic and Reformist Texts

It is commonly known that didactic poetry in ancient Greece or Rome was not regarded as a separate genre of literature; the term encompasses "a number of poetic works (usually in hexameters) which aim to instruct the reader in a particular subject-matter, be it science, philosophy, hunting, farming, love, or some other art or craft."[13] In Arabic literature, Arabic didactic verse (*shi'r ta'līmī*) is regarded as instructive, adding to one's knowledge and aiming at improving one's morals. Yet it has been conceived by some Arabic critics "not as true poetry since it is devoid of emotion and imagination, both of which are essential constituents of poetry, besides metre and rhyme."[14]

If one delves into modern African examples of didactic poetry, much of modern Hausa verse, for instance, can be either didactic in tone or is written in

---

13   Schiesaro, Alessandro, "Didactic Poetry," December 22, 2015, https://oxfordre.com/classic s/view/10.1093/acrefore/9780199381135.001.0001/acrefore-9780199381135-e-2153.

14   Ṣafā' Khulūṣī, "Didactic Verse," in *Religion, Learning and Science in the 'Abbasid Period*, ed. R.B. Serjeant, M.J.L. Young, and J.D. Latham (Cambridge: Cambridge University Press, 1990), 498.

praise of God, a person, or a political party.[15] West African Arabic poetry mainly follows the Arabic canon and can be split into two poetic genres: lyrical (*al-shiʿr al-ghināʾī*) and didactic (*al-shiʿr al-taʿlīmī*). Lyrical poetry represents the majority of poems, which range from panegyric to elegy. It is interesting to consider a feature that Abdul-Samad Abdullah highlights with regard to the register West African Arabic poets use in composing didactic poetry: "their didactic poetry is characterised by popular language understandable to the masses."[16]

Taking this last statement into account, I would like to investigate the language used in the *Wasiya* and the evocative power that resides in its "popular language." I will not make use of this notion of popular language as a depreciative one, as has been done in the past, to the point of neglecting and/or pushing aside didactic texts considered as devoid of lyricism. On the Kenyan coast, the dialects of Kiamu, spoken on Lamu, or Kimvita, spoken in Mombasa, were used for literary and public purposes up to postcolonial times. The use of these dialects was prominent in traditional, precolonial genres, such as the *utendi* meter, and they were also employed and strongly advocated by the Swahili Muslim editors of postcolonial local Swahili Muslim newspapers. Kiamu in particular became the literary language of the didactic genre both within and beyond the Lamu archipelago from the nineteenth century onwards.[17] More precisely, as Ustadh Mau himself describes the *Wasiya, ni utendi wa mafundisho, mfano wa utendi wa Mwana Kupona, si utendi wa masimulizi tu*; "it is a didactic poem like the *Utendi wa Mwana Kupona* [an admonitory poem on the wifely duty of the poet's daughter]; it is not merely a narrative poem."[18] The term *mafundisho* "teaching" that Ustadh Mau uses here derives from from the causative form *kufundisha*, meaning "to instruct someone, to teach someone." As his statement clearly highlights, the precise educational objective inherent in this genre differentiates it from purely epic or historical war narratives like the *Utendi wa Miqdadi na Mayasa* ("The Poem of Miqdad and Mayasa") or the *Utendi wa Vita*

---

15   Graham L. Furniss, "Aspects of Style and Meaning in the Analysis of a Hausa Poem," *Bulletin of the School of Oriental and African Studies* 45, no. 3 (1982): 546.

16   Abdullah Abdul-Samad, "Sheikh Ali al-Tantāwi and his Educational and Literary Services," in *al-Idah* 29, no. 2, (2004), 369.

17   See C.H. Stigand, *A Grammar of the Dialectic Changes in the Kiswahili Language. With an Introduction and a Recension and Poetical Translation of the Poem Inkishafi. A Swahili Speculum Mundi by the Rev. W.E. Taylor*, Cambridge: Cambridge University Press, 1915; Gudrun Miehe, "Die Perioden der Swahililiteratur und ihre sprachliche Form," Paideuma 36 (1990): 201–215; and Roy Mathieu, KIAMU, archipel de Lamu (Kenya): Analyse phonétique et morphologique d'un corpus linguistique et poétique, French ed. (Saarbrücken: PAF, 2013).

18   Ustadh Mau, personal communication, March 2020.

vya Uhd ("The Poem of the Battle of Uhd"), meant to be told without any concrete instructive precepts.[19]

Returning to the languages used in didactic poetry, on a more contemporary note, the newspaper *Sauti ya haki*, founded by Sheikh Muhammad Kasim in 1972, was another attempt to use a dialect of the coast, namely Kimvita, the dialect of Mombasa, to address his readers—as Kresse notes, the appropriate local variety for a journal published in Mombasa, "a more genuine Swahili idiom lending itself to Islamic discourse."[20] The abovementioned traditional literary examples, along with contemporary ones from news media, show that if the language used in the didactic genre is a so-called "popular language," this is done as a means of making Islamic discourse more accessible to ordinary local Swahili Muslim communities. It is also worth recalling that Ustadh Mau was the first imam on Lamu to make the reformist choice to deliver the Friday sermon in Swahili; this choice, as explained by Timammy, "put Mahmoud in a difficult position, as he now had to negotiate between the reformist ideas he shared with his fellow youth and the respect he owed to his teachers who opposed them."[21] Yet he considered this a challenge worth taking up, as he realized how his community, unable to understand Arabic, was at risk of allowing particularly the younger generation lose their own religious path.

From poetry to journals, passing through khutbah, it seems evident that across coastal Kenya, language is revealed to be the foremost medium used to convey ideas and precepts. The *Wasiya* is an experiment in line with the initiative, dear to Ngũgĩ wa Thiong'o, of decolonizing the minds of previously subjugated countries in order to avoid the self-colonization of language, as it is

---

19   In this category of historical poems—reflecting colonial times—Saavedra Casco includes the following examples of *tendi*: the *Utendi wa Vita vya Maji Maji*, composed by Abdul Karim Jamaliddini in 1908; the *Utenzi wa Swifa ya Nguvumali*, composed by Hasan bin Ismail around 1962; and the *Utenzi wa Vita vya Kagera*, composed by Henri Muhanika in 1980. See José Arturo Saavedra Casco, *Utenzi, War Poems, and the German Conquest of East Africa: Swahili Poetry as Historical Source* (Trenton, NJ: Africa World Press, 2007), 26. Contrary to what Saavedra Casco states but as Vierke asserts, one could argue that the classical epics were also meant to provide society with role models and moral teachings.

20   Mazrui 2007, 102, quoted in Kresse, *Swahili Muslim Publics and Postcolonial Experience* (Bloomington: Indiana University Press, 2018), 106. Along the same lines, it is worth referring to Ngũgĩ wa Thiong'o's efforts to establish the first journal in the Kikuyu language, despite the hesitations that Prof. Mazrui shared with him. See *Matata Leo*, "Ali Mazrui, Ngugi, Kiswahili, Kikikuyu (African Languages)," last accessed January 15, 2021, YouTube clip, https://www.youtube.com/watch?v=PrSc9OWpU3s.

21   Timammy Rayya, "Shaykh Mahmoud Abdulkadir 'Mau': A Reformist Preacher in Lamu," *Annual Review of Islam in Africa* 12, no. 2 (2015): 87.

not merely a medium of communication, but also a medium of culture.[22] This attention and care for local African languages comes out particularly clearly in Ustadh Mau's poem *Kiswahili*, where he depicts the Swahili language as a mother who has born bright sons, i.e., poets like Muyaka, Zahidi Mngumi, Nabahany, and Chiraghdin—all native speakers of their own Swahili dialects, which have since been forgotten, precisely when the standardization of the language began and the first dictionaries of standard Swahili came into being (see stanzas 4 to 6 of *Kiswahili*).

Besides the language—which must be regarded as an important vehicle for addressing the masses—one should consider that didactic poems, by definition, are normally addressed to a particular individual who is seen as the primary object of instruction and acts as a model for the reader.[23] It is striking to see how much both the *Wasiya* as well as the Arabic *Ya-bintī* enact and entwine in their texts with vivid characters, dialogues, and biographies mirroring social drama. This shows that for both writers, being reformist means not only adopting the language best understood by their people, mainly the youth representing the new generation, but also styling their texts as closely as possible to their lifeworlds, depicting realistic conversations and credible, everyday characters.

We shall explore this by focusing on some excerpts from both the Arabic pamphlet and the *Wasiya*.

Beginning from the end, al-Ṭanṭawi's pamphlet dedicated to his daughter concludes on the following lines:

> This is my advice, my daughter. And this is the truth; don't listen to any other. Mind that it is in your hands and not in ours, the men's, hands: in your hands lies the key to change. If you want, you will correct yourself, and by correcting yourself, you will correct the entire community.[24]

---

22 Ngũgĩ wa Thiong'o, *Decolonising the Mind: The Politics of Language in African Literature* (London: Currey, 1986).

23 Schiesaro, "Didactic Poetry."

24 Translation mine; adapted from the Swahili of Ustadh Mau: *Huu ndio ushairi wangu kwako, binti yangu. Na huu ndio ukweli usisikilize mengine. Na ujue kwamba ni katika mkono wako wewe na si katika mkono wetu wanaume: katika mkono wako pana ufunguo wa mlango wa marekebisho. Ukitaka utajirekebisha wewe na kwa kurakibika wewe utarakibisha umma wote.*

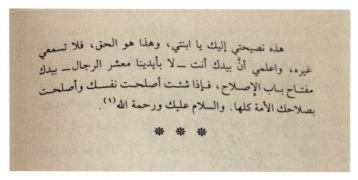

FIGURE 9   Excerpt from the Yā-bintī by al-Ṭanṭawi, EG 1406/AD 1985, 28

In his text, al-Ṭanṭawi is proclaiming his truth (*al-ḥaq*), admonishing his daughter (*ya-bintī*, lit. "oh my daughter") not to listen to anything else but his own sincere words. The final passage continues with an exhortation to be self-confident and know (Ar. imperative *'alamī*) that the key to any change lies in her hands (*bi-yadika* "in your hands"); more precisely, al-Ṭanṭawi stresses that she holds in her hand "the key to the door of change" (*al-miftāḥa bāb al-'iṣlāḥ*). The nominal derivative *iṣlāḥ* used here plays a crucial role in this final moral message. The author concludes by solemnly claiming that the changes one makes on his own consequently affect the whole community (*al-'ummat kulluhā*).

It is certainly far from the strain of Islamic feminist thought interested in transformation and engagement within society, as encouraged by prominent Islamic woman such as Huda Sharawi and Nawal Sadawi, who stimulated the feminist movement via printed pamphlets, articles, and debates on authority, relationships, and sexual abuse in the '70s, an epoch when the feminist movement was growing in the Islamic world.[25] What does emerge from this message, however, is that al-Tantawi's pamphlet was aligned with the author's own agenda of the '50s, calling for good morals, righteousness, and virtue, as the collection of pamphlets *Fi sabil al-Iṣlāḥ* ("Along the Path of Reform"), composed in 1347 EG/1928 AD, amply illustrate.[26]

---

25   Fatima Mernissi, "Women's Song: Destination Freedom," in *Islam and Democracy* (New York: Perseus Books Group and Basic Books, 2002), 189.

26   Another example of printed didactic and cautionary texts from West Africa can be identified in *The Life Story of Me, Seligola*, which began being published as series of letters in Yoruba (July 1929 to March 1930), allegedly ascribed to an old prostitute, Segilola, who was recounting her life story from her deathbed. The series—published in the *Akede Eko* ("The Lagos Herald")—greatly resonated with Yoruba readers and was collected and repub-

From this excerpt alone, one can hardly avoid drawing comparisons with the reform ideas that drove Ustadh Mau to plead for change (*mabadiliko*) in his own community (*jamii* or *mujatamai*), as he does in stanza 131, where he equates the potential for progress with the girls' ability to refrain from harmful customs and continue progressing on a Muslim path.

> 131. *Ni sisi banati*   *wazi tawambiya*
> *Tujengao nti*   *na kuvunda piya*
> *Tukijidhibiti*   *nakujiziwiya*
> *Ni hono wakati*   *wakuendeleya*

It is we, the girls, I am openly telling you,
Who build the country, and we destroy it too.
If we are firm and restrain ourselves,
Only then, we can progress

> 142. *Hapa nimekoma*   *kuwapa wasiya*
> *Kwa hini nudhuma*   *nilowandikiya*
> *Ilahi karima*   *tatuonya ndiya*
> *Yakuiyandama*   *ilo sawasiya*

Here I conclude, giving you advice
Through this composition I have written for you.
God the Most Gracious will show us the way,
The one that is straight and must be followed.

---

lished as a small, ninety-page book, with copies distributed among newspaper editors. As Barber says, "Segilola's letters looked real [...] They overflowed with emotion, mixing pious exhortations with knowing and nostalgic allusions to the shared popular culture of Lagos, past and present"; Karin Barber, *Print Culture and the First Yoruba Novel: I.B. Thomas's Life Story of Me, Segilola and Other Texts* (Leiden: Brill, 2012, 5). And as the fictional author expresses in the preface to the stories, "My prayer is that God in his infinite mercy will go with this story of my life all over the world, and that book will be able to change many people for the better." The editor, Isaac Babalola Thomas, who concealed his authorial role, also used to say: "To sum up, our prayer is that this little book may do blessed work of redemption among those of our people, male and female, who rejoice in promiscuity and prostitution in their lives. Anyone who has ears to hear warnings, let them hear" (Barber, *Print Culture*, 79, 83). This extraordinary Yoruba experiment with genre and addressivity and the editor's capacity to write dramatic speech in the voice of an imagined character can be regarded similarly to what Ustadh Mau as an author has done with his imagined character in the *Wasiya*.

In the penultimate stanza (stz. 142), the poet announces that he has finished giving advice (*wasiya*), the same way al-Ṭanṭawi explicitly wraps up his work by uttering "this is my advice, my daughter." In this stanza, Ustadh Mau seems to pass the last word to God, the Most Generous, who is the only one with the power to show them all the right path (*ndiya*), the poet included. The concept of the "path" echoes al-Ṭanṭawi's emphasis on truth (*al-ḥaq*), access to which is possible only with the right keys (*al-miftāḥa*), and how one must begin with oneself and not rely on anybody else. Each conclusion highlights the evident dialogism between the writer, a fatherly figure and dispenser of advice, and the unnamed daughters of Eve, whom each author is addressing. In this way, anyone listening to or reading the text can immediately identify herself in its plea for change and progress, as if its advice, warnings, and story were precisely for and about the would-be reader.

On the other hand, the *Wasiya*, composed two decades later than the *Ya-bintī*, builds on a tradition of admonitory Swahili Islamic didactic poetry. Roughly a century earlier, another admonition in the form a didactic poem, namely the *Utendi wa Mwana Kupona*—which later became one of the most venerated of all classical Swahili *utendi* compositions—was composed and addressed to the daughter of the author, Mwana Kupona. The poetess Mwana Kupona, who was born in Siu but spent her adulthood in Lamu,[27] her mother's hometown,[28] used the *Utendi wa Mwana Kupona*[29] to impart advice on wifely duties and social behavior with the aim of preserving moral values such as those Ustadh Mau recalls in the *Wasiya*.

However, the *Wasiya* is also said to be inspired by a tragic incident leading to further calamity: a young woman from his own island had lost her honor "after being seduced by a male companion who befriended her but turned out not to care about her as a person. Having lost all hope of parental and social support and belonging after giving birth to a little baby—her parents die of shock upon the news—her attempt at suicide (and infanticide) fails as an alert fisherman saves her and the baby after she throws herself into the sea."[30] This

---

27   The plaque affixed outside her house, in in the Mta Muini area of Lamu, reads as follows: "Above here, in about 1880, Mwana Kupona wrote her *utendi*." Ustadh Mau kindly provided me with a photo of the plaque, which allowed me to reread it and to quote it here.

28   Patricia W. Romero, Lamu. History, Society, and Family in an East African Port City (Princeton, NJ: Wiener, 1997), 32.

29   Alice Werner and William Hichens, *The Advice of Mwana Kupona upon the Wifely Duty*, The Azanian Classics 2 (Medstead: Azania Press, 1934); J.W.T. Allen, *Tendi. Six Examples of a Swahili Classical Verse Form with Translations & Notes* (New York: Africana Publishing, 1971).

30   Kresse, "Enduring Relevance," 157.

specific and dramatic event illustrates an important element of Ustadh Mau's approach to poetry: the event supplies the inspiring and meaningful catalyst that drives the poet to compose a poem in order to immortalize it and as a way to spell the drama out for others. Hence, one could wonder if the poet should be considered a liar? In reply to this question, which I addressed to Ustadh Mau in July 2019, he smiled and said, *Wasiya, kufikiria hali ya wasichana, ni jambo ambalo lazima uhisi moyoni*, "Wayisa (implies) reflecting on the situation of girls. This is something one has to feel in his heart." He continued, "The problem of a lie (*uwongo*) is that it can hurt someone else, but if the main aim is a good purpose, there is nothing wrong; you can invent things."[31] The *Wasiya* indeed shows Ustadh Mau's capacity to creatively experiment in a genre that was new to him, the *utendi*, and to write dramatic speech in the voice of an imagined character and based on imagined events.

3   How to Make Advice Spread: Mediated Poetry

> Even if only a minority of the population read books, a much larger number hear them spoken about.[32]

Ustadh Mau's *Wasiya* further differs from al-Ṭanṭawi's booklet when it comes to the medium through which these similar didactic texts have traveled so widely. Whereas the text of al-Ṭanṭawi's printed booklet in Arabic script was very popular—to the point of having been reprinted several times, and now being freely available on the Internet—for the *Wasiya*, it is as if print media was never the most popular vehicle through which the poem reached nor resonated with its Swahili Muslim audience. When I visited Ustadh Mau's library in 2018, he showed me the tiny corner where his poems were piled up, collec-

---

31   See also Vierke's contribution "Born on The Island" in this volume. In this respect, Ustadh Mau also highlights the Swahili saying *mashairi matamu ni yale yenye uwongo zahidi*, which relates to the Arabic saying كدب ا الشعر ا اعدب (*adabu ushiri akdabu*). His reflections on lying find some echos in the thought of Dostoyevsky, who once argued: "In Russia, truth almost always assumes an entirely fantastic character. In fact people have finally succeeded in converting all that the human mind may lie about and belie into something more comprehensible than truth, and such a view prevails all over the world" (*Dostoyevsky, "Something about Lying," in Diary of a Writer 1873* (Northwestern University Press: Evanston, Illinois 1994), 119; quoted in Malcom V. Jones, *Dostoyevsky after Bakhtin: Readings in Dostoyevsky's Fantastic Realism* (Cambridge: Cambridge University Press, 2009), 2). Such makes me think of Plato: "all poets lie."

32   Eickelman and Anderson, *New Media*, 35.

ted in dusty A3 envelopes. The majority of his poems are written in his own handwriting, with a ballpoint pen on loose sheets of paper. When these poems were typed in Roman letters with a standard keyboard, it was not done by the poet himself, but by a local typist. Ustadh Mau himself uses Arabic script for writing, because this is the script he has been used to since he was a pupil at the madrassa. Yet his first poem, the *Wasiya*, is an exception, as it was first composed in Roman script, differently from all his other compositions, which were first composed in Arabic script. Furthermore, the *Wasiya* also differs from the poems he composed later in his life because, within this poem, Kiamu features are not as abundant as in his other compositions. The poet surely meant to address this poem to a wider Swahili Muslim audience, not exclusively the Lamuan community, hence the reason for adopting a more widely known script and a more standard Swahili than the local variety. This further explains why, rather than a plethora of Kiamu forms, the poem features a mosaic of Swahili dialects (like Kimvita words, e.g. *jiaswiya*, stz. 3), while also including words from both Arabic (*kalbi* "heart," *ummu* "mother") and standard Swahili (e.g., *miyaka* rather than Kiamu *nyaka*; *michinjo* rather than Kiamu *mitindo*).

The ad-hoc writing process through which the *Wasiya* was crafted already clearly points to a unique feature of the new adaptation: the *Wasiya*—a poem handwritten in Arabic script, inspired by a preexisting Arabic prose booklet, has bypassed print media straight to oral: why?

In his speech on the benefits of knowledge,[33] Ustadh Mau shares an interesting reflection on the reason he has never decided to publish his own poetry:

> *Na mimi tendi zangu ama tungo zangu nyingi hazikuandikwa kwenye vitabu na sababu moja nilofanya nisitie bidii kwenye kitabu ni kwa kuwa kwa bahati mbaya jamii yetu si jamii ya kusoma na ni jambo la sikitisha sana; sisi ni watu tukitaka tuwe misitari mbele kabisa kwa sabau dini yetu msingi yake ni misingi ya kusoma, misingi ya elimu lakini kwa bahati mbaya jamii yetu hivi sasa imekuwa hatuwajulikani ni kwamba ni watu hatuna kile kitu wazungu wanakiita "reading culture." Sisi zaidi twapendele kusikiliza kuliko kusoma, kwa hivo tungo zangu zimewekwa katika CDs, katika santuri hizi, zamani zilikuwa zile cassetti sasa hivi ni mambo za cd; hii insahilisha ule ujumbe kufika kwa watu wengi, kwa sababu kusikiliza haina kazi na CD moja kwa wakati mmoja za kusikiliza watu kadhaa kuliko kitabu; kitabu ingekuwa wakati moja husikiliza mtu mmoja lakini cd waweza kusikiliza watu tanu kumi zaidi kwa wakati moja kwa hiyo ujumbe wangu hupitisha*

---

33   Discussed at length in the article "Seeking *'ilm*" in this volume.

kupitia zombo kama hizo za CDs *na hivi sasa nina kama cd sita ambazo zinagumzia mada tofauti tofauti za kimaisha.*[34]

As for myself, the majority of my own compositions, they have never been printed in books. One of the reasons I have not made any efforts in (publishing) a book is because unfortunately, our society is not a reading society, and this is something very sad. If we wanted to, we could be much more advanced, since the foundation of our religion is based on reading, the pillar of education, but unfortunately, our society nowadays is not well known for this. People do not have what Westerners call a "reading culture." We prefer listening rather than reading, which is why my compositions have been recorded on CD. With regard to recordings, in the past, there were those tapes, but now it is CDs. This makes it easy for the message to reach many people, because listening does not require any effort, and a single CD can be consumed by more people at the same time than a book. If it were a book, only a single person could consume it at a time, but a CD can be listened to by five, ten, or even more people at once. Therefore, my message can arrive through such media, like CDs. And as of now, I have six CDs in which I speak of various life topics.

It is worth citing Ustadh Mau's reflections in this regard, as they supply us with a good entry point into the notion of multimodality involving his message (*ujumbe*) and the medium chosen to deliver it, called *zombo* in Kiamu (Sw. *vyombo*, sg. *chombo*), which literally denotes the "media, vehicles, tools."

The practice of recording his poetry on CD—the digital technology that replaced the cassette tape (Sw. *kanda or kaseti*) from the late 1990s and even earlier—deserves attention, as it should not be seen as a stand-alone practice; on the contrary, it is quite popular among Muslim publics. To begin with, his first compositions (as he says, *tungo zangu*), which began by being recorded on tape, was the poetic trilogy *Kimwondo*, which was issued as a series consisting of *Kimwondo I, Kimwondo II*, and *Kimwondo III*. The *Kimwondo* songs, a term coined by Ustadh Mau, meaning "Shooting Star"/"The Devil's Torch,"[35] were poems in *shairi* form meant to deliver political propaganda in support of his favorite political candidate, Mzamil, versus Aboubakar Madhbuti, whom he considered a less able and even corrupt ruler.[36]

---

34 *Me on* TV, "Mahmoud Mau 1," posted September 18, 2016, YouTube clip, 23:41, https://www.youtube.com/watch?v=5l8LhET8GoE.

35 Assibi Amidu, *Kimwondo: A Kiswahili Electoral Contest*, Beiträge zur Afrikanistik 39 (Vienna: Afro-Pub, 1990).

36 Amidu, *Kimwondo*, 83. See also Kresse in this volume.

In 1975, at the time of the elections in Kenya, Ustadh Mau composed these poems in Arabic script, and they were recorded by Muhamad Abdalla Bakathir (henceforth "Kadara"). In these poems, he combines politics and ethics by reminding his community (*umma*) of the significance of the duty of voting (*kupiga kura*) and its importance to the democractic rule of their own country (*nchi ya Demokrasi/kama hini yetu sisi*, "a democratic country like ours here," stz. 9).[37] These *Kimwondo* poems migrated to audio cassettes soon after the written composition came into being, and they began being distributed by Bwana Radio Station, located in the Kibokoni area of Mombasa.[38] From there, people would listen to these tapes everywhere, as Ustadh Mau recalls: *migahawani, madukani, majumbani; hata magarini* "in restaurants, stores, houses; even in buses."[39]

After the *Kimwondo* poems, the *Wasiya* was the first poem produced as several solo recordings, as it is worth shortly recounting here. During my research on the *Wasiya*, which began in 2017 and was followed by a field trip in 2018, the poem had already been recorded by Abdallah el-Shatry of Mombasa— who died prematurely of HIV—and by Kadara, the same singer who recorded *Kimwondo* and many other poems by Ustadh Mau. As noted elsewhere,[40] the request to have the *Wasiya* recorded was not made by the poet himself, but rather by a man from Lamu named Swaleh Aredy, who wanted his children to listen to it, and thus he asked Kadara to record the poem. Afterward, this recording began being shared and copied among the community, and in this way it spread widely and started becoming known. The second singer, Abdallah el-Shatry, was also not contacted by Ustadh Mau personally, but rather by the owner of a CD kiosk, Ghalib Muhadhari, who asked el-Shatry to sing it. Kadara's audio recording is available in shops in Lamu (Al-Hussein Original Shop) and Mombasa (Mbwana Radio Station) to this day. Since 2017, el-Shatry's vocal recording can also be found on SoundCloud, split in three parts ("Wasiya #1," "Wasiya #2," "Wasiya #3"), and easy to access and to listen to.[41]

---

37 Amidu, *Kimwondo*, 83.
38 For some biographical info on Kadara and his role as singer of Ustadh Mau's poems, see Raia, "Texts, Voices and Tapes." For some excerpts from my interview with him on his role of reenacting, by "giving voice" to, even classical *utendi* poems, see Raia, "A Network of Copies. The *Utendi wa Yusuf* Manuscript Traditions from the J.W.T. Allen Collection (Dar es Salaam)," in "One Text: Many Copies," edited by Clarissa Vierke & Ridder Samsom, special issue, *Journal of Manuscript Cultures* (forthcoming): 69–98. The shop owner of Bwana Radio Station has sadly passed away on the 5th of August 2022. Ustadh Mau attened his funeral in Mombasa.
39 Ustadh Mau, personal communication, April 2020.
40 Raia, "Texts, Voices and Tapes."
41 "Wasiya #1" is 59:59 in duration; "Wasiya #2," 22:33; "Wasiya #3" is 24:56. See Mashairi,

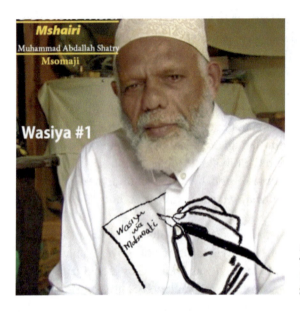

FIGURE 10
The cover art for the three *Wasiya* tracks available on SoundCloud

Besides the poetic examples, like the *Kimwondo*, *Wasiya*, and many other compositions recorded on CD, the message, guidelines, and warnings that Ustadh Mau delivers to his community via his sermons (*hotuba*, or khutbah) are recorded and sent off through external hard drives across his online network. This listening practice—be it for poetry (*mashairi*) or sermons (*khutba*)—is similar to that of sermon tapes among the Cairene Muslim public. Within this distant yet similar context, Charles Hirschkind has noticed what follows:

> [S]ermons are listened to as a disciplinary practice geared to ethical self-improvement: a technique for the cultivation and training of certain forms of will, desire, emotion, and reason, conceived of as intellectual and bodily aptitudes or virtues that enable Muslims to act correctly as Muslims in accord with orthodox standards of Islamic piety.[42]

What is shown here and can be viewed in parallel between the Arabic pamphlet *Ya-bintī* and the recording of the *Wasiya* is that prescriptions on how to "act

---

"Wasiya wa mabanati," SoundCloud, last accessed April 4, 2020, https://soundcloud.com/user-157462073/wasiya-wa-mabanati. Superimposed on the portrait on the cover, we find the name of the poet ("Mshairi") together with the name of the reciter ("Msomaji"). The illustration of a hand holding a pen seems to refer to the written composition and reveals the work's entire title, namely *Wasiya wa mabanati*.

42 Charles Hirschkind, *The Ethical Soundscape: Cassette Sermons and Islamic Counterpublics* (New York: Columbia University Press, 2006), 36.

correctly as Muslim" (ibid.) have, in the digital era, found more and more new broadcasting channels, which are less expensive and easy to access, share with friends and acquaintances, and travel with; hence, they are "portable media." This holds true for the tiny booklet of al-Ṭanṭawi, which was reprinted several times, as well as for the unbound sheets of the *Wasiya*, which have found their success and popularity through vocal recordings.

It is indeed known how well booklets and pamphlets lend themselves to allowing ideas to spread widely, being more portable and also more durable across time; in Isabel Hofmeyr's words, for instance, "Periodicals are not tied to one place and are driven by the temporality of circulation."[43] To add an example of this genre from East Africa, in Anne Bang's preliminary remarks on the circulation of Islamic texts in Zanzibar, she mentions a short treatise by Aḥmad b. Zayn al-Ḥibshī on how to live a Muslim life, titled *Risālat al-Jāmiyya*, which traveled widely and was repeatedly reprinted for *daʿwa* purposes on opposite sides of the Indian Ocean for Malay and Swahili pupils who needed to be instructed in Muslim piety.[44] Bang's case study further illustrates how specific media—oral and/or print media—can be chosen to craft certain models of civility and piety.

Along these lines of how to circulate ideas more widely and easily and have them reprinted repeatedly, the role of audio media also occupies a relevant place among Muslim publics. As pointed out by Dale Eickelman, print media were first replaced with audio cassettes, which offer some advantages: "inexpensive, easy to smuggle, and readily reproduced, they may be played in the home, automobile, mosques, or other meeting places."[45] As noted elsewhere, the term "voiced Islam," coined by Dale F. Eickelmann vis-à-vis "print Islam,"[46] is an emergent topic that has not yet been adequately researched amid the contemporary literary landscape of the Swahili Muslim coast.

As a matter of fact, broadcast media and cassettes/CDs have become an important medium of mass communication amid the daily activities of Swahili Muslims. Kai Kresse, for instance, recalls how much he was struck by the *Wasiya*'s sound "in passing, when walking through the narrow streets of Mombasa's Old Town, as it was emanating from one of the houses on the side."[47]

---

43 See Isabel Hofmeyr, *Gandhi's Printing Press Experiments in Slow Reading* (Cambridge, Mass.: Harvard University Press, 2013), 14.

44 Anne Bang, "Authority and Piety, Writing and Print. A Preliminary Study of the Circulation of Islamic Texts in Late Nineteenth- and Early Twentieth-Century Zanzibar," *Journal of the International African Institute* 81, no. 1 (2011): 97.

45 Eickelman, and Anderson, *New Media*, 40.

46 Ibid.

47 Kresse, "Enduring Relevance," 47.

Brian Larkin talks of the mediality of loudspeaker as it more widely spreads the call to prayer in Jos, northern Nigeria;[48] Debora Kapchan describes "how sound and practices of listening can become vehicles for Sufis to create a sacred place in a secular country such as France [...] and how the practitioners become transmitters not just of sound but of knowledge as well."[49] Taken together, this shows the changing nature of religious and political discourse, as well as how voice has an extreme impact on people's psychology and reflexivity, with the ultimate effect of either deep understanding or distortion based on the clarity of the voiced message; furthermore, and more generally, the spread of new media also shows how much technology reinforces and reconnects plural Islamic transnational networks, because they enact what Andrew Eisenberg calls "public reflexivity" and what Eickelman is also referring to when he says that "small media make it easier for Muslims to keep abreast of developments elsewhere in the Muslim world and to feel as if they participate in them."[50]

Indeed, it has been shown the transit and impact of a pamphlet like *Ya-bintī* by an author like al-Ṭanṭawi—who was born in Damascus and spent almost 40 years of his life in Jeddah, Saudi Arabia—which managed to reach all the way to the shores of Lamu in Kenya.[51] The act of reading inspired the new writing which, in turn, was recorded CDs and is also now broadcast on Internet now.[52]

To conclude, returning to Ustadh Mau's statement about his people not belonging to a reading culture, but rather eager to listen, I can thus assume that all his poems—which have now mostly been collected in this first comprehensive volume on his poetry—were written down by him only as an aid to memory and oral delivery. It indeed seems as if his texts have been composed for being read aloud and shared among his community. This recalls what Robinson succinctly points out with regard to oral knowledge and transmission in the Muslim world: as already expressed in Ibn Khaldun's *Muqaddima*,

---

48 Brian Larkin, "Techniques of Inattention: The Mediality of Loudspeakers in Nigeria," *Anthropological Quarterly* 87, no. 4 (2014): 989–1015.

49 Deborah Kapchan, "Listening Acts, Secular and Sacred: Sound Knowledge among Sufi Muslims in Secular France," in *Islam and Popular Culture*, edited by Karin van Nieuwkerk, Mark Levine, and Martine Stokes (Austin: University of Texas Press, 2016), 21.

50 Andrew J. Eisenberg, "The Swahili Art of Indian Taarab: A Poetics of Vocality and Ethnicity on the Kenyan Coast," *Comparative Studies of South Asia, Africa and the Middle East* 37, no. 2 (2017): 40.

51 Adil Salahi, "Scholar of Renown Sheikh Ali Al-Tantawi," *Arab News*, June 19, 2001, https://www.arabnews.com/node/212775.

52 More precisely, Ustadh Mau has at his disposal two copies of the *Ya-bintī*, the first one published in Kuwait, and the second, which was sent to him, published in Jeddah, Saudi Arabia.

MABANATI IN SEARCH OF AN AUTHOR: PORTABLE REFORM TEXTS

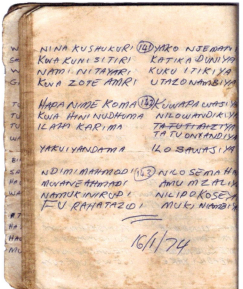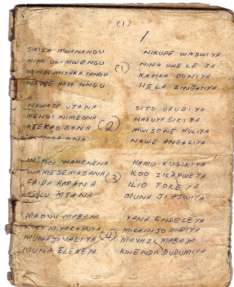

FIGURE 11   Original first (right) and last (left) page of Ustadh Mau's *Wasiya wa mabanati*, composed and handwritten in Roman script in a notebook

Robinson explains that the skepticism toward and distance from "the academic printed book" vs. the spoken word in the Muslim world are due to the fact that "person to person transmission was at the heart of the transmission of Islamic knowledge. The best way of getting at the truth was to listen to the author himself."[53] Thus, in this contemporary case of the audio recording of the *Wasiya*, it seems that through the voice (*sauti*) of the author (*mtungaji* "the composer" or *mshairi* "the poet")—who assumes the role of an imagined character—or that of the reader (*msomaji*) who rereads the dramatic story aloud, Swahili Muslim people can imbibe the truth, the advice, and the admonition contained in the poems, as they are *listening* to these words instead of passively reading them line by line.[54]

I shall now delve into the vocality and polyphonic threads weaving together the content of this beautiful *Wasiya*, with the support of the Tony melody transcription program and while drawing from Dostoyevsky's and Pirandello's works.

---

53   Francis Robinson, "Technology and Religious Change: Islam and the Impact of Print," *Modern Asian Studies* 27, no. 1 (1993): 237.

54   The request that people listen to Ustadh Mau's advice comes out clearly from the very first verse of the *Wasiya*, where the lyrical "I" uses the imperative form (*sikiza*) to invite the listener: *sikiza mwanangu*, "listen, my daughter."

4 Listening to Advice

Musicality and empathy: These can be considered the two major features that have made the poem *Wasiya* so extremely popular. The first feature, namely the poem's musicality (*muziki*), draws from Ustadh Mau's own idea of poetry, which to him "is made of words that are written are uttered in a syllabic meter in a specific prosodic pattern, and the reader or listener is affected by the words because of the music deriving from that structure."[55] Thus, Ustadh Mau gives the reason why the *Wasiya* has enjoyed such great popularity on Lamu and, beyond the archipelago, in Mombasa:

> *Wasiya wa mabanati husikitisha wengi na watu hupenda kusikiza kwa kuwa ni kiswa cha kusisimuwa na ni mambo yameshawapata baadhi ya watu.* (Mau, 2017)

> The *Wasiya na mabanati* makes many people sad, and people like to listen to it because it is a exciting/touching/moving story, and these are things that some people have already experienced.

That said, it becomes clear that the joy of listening to the *Wasiya* comes precisely from the deep sadness imbued in its verse, while its popularity comes from the shared experience of the common—but concealed—drama of neglected women. This brings us squarely back to the idea of empathy: if a young girl has gone through a calamity that others will also face, this encourages solidarity and makes the Muslim women feel less lonely in their own family dramas.

Where does the musicality stem from? When Ustadh Mau composed the *Wasiya*, he didn't know anything about the so-called *sheria za kutunga mashairi* ("rules for composing poems"[56]).

When he began composing the poem, he followed a prosodic pattern that resembles the *dhura al-mandhuma* meter, based on four bicolons (*mishororo*), each of which features a variable internal rhyme, and with six syllables (*mizani*) per verse (*kipande*). The rhyme form for the true line ends is retained; in

---

55   *Ushairi ni maneno yalio andikwa au kusemwa kwa mizani na mpangiliyo maalum—na msomaji au msikilizaji huathirika kwa maneno hayo kwa sababu ya muziki unao tokana na mpangilio wake* (Ustadh Mau, personal communication, 2017).

56   See K. Amri Abedi, *Sheria za kutunga mashairi na diwani ya Amri. The Poems of Amri with an Essay on Swahili Poetry and the Rules of Versification* (Nairobi: Kenya Literature Bureau, 1954).

the *Wasiya*, this is always -ya.[57] Hence, the *Wasiya* is cast in a meter that can be represented as follows, where – represents un unaccented and ' an accented syllable:

Scansion

First stanza

	First 6-syllable verse (*kipande*)						Second 6-syllable verse (*kipande*)					
1st 12-syllable	–	'	–	–	'	–	–	'	–	'	–	'
mshororo	Si	ki	za	mwa	na	ngu	Ni	ku	pe	wa	si	ya
	1	2	3	4	5	6	1	2	3	4	5	6
2nd 12-syllable	–	'	–	–	'	–	–	'	–	'	–	'
mshororo	mi	mi	u	li	mwe	ngu	ni	na	u	e	le	ya
	1	2	3	4	5	6	1	2	3	4	5	6
3rd 12-syllable	–	'	–	–	'	–	–	'	–	'	–	'
mshororo	ni	ngi	nya	ka	ya	ngu	ka	ti	ka	du	ni	ya
	1	2	3	4	5	6	1	2	3	4	5	6
4th 12-syllable	–	'	–	–	'	–	–	'	–	'	–	'
mshororo	na	we	ha	ya	ya	ngu	he	la	zin	ga	ti	ya
	1	2	3	4	5	6	1	2	3	4	5	6

As the chart shows, whereas the first internal rhyme, *-ngu*, is always unaccented, the final rhyme of each line ends is indeed accented, and also lengthened to be more salient to the ear. When Ustadh Mau's mother, Barka Aboud, heard the poem for her first time, she did not believe that it was a poem written by her son, since up to that time, she was unaware of his son's poetic talent.

---

57   According to Ibrahim Noor Shariff (*Tungo zetu*, 45), thirteen metrical patterns exist in Swahili poetry: 1. *wimbo*, 2. *shairi*, 3. *zivindo*, 4. *utenzi* of *utendi*, 5. *utumbuizo*, 6. *hamziya*, 7. *dura mandhuma/inkishafi*, 8. *ukawafi*, 9. *wajiwaji*, 10. *tiyani fatiha*, 11. *wawe*, 12. *kimai*, and 13. *sama*, *mahadhi* or *sauti*. *Dhura al-mandhuma*, which is الدرة المنظومة in Arabic and translates to "the composed pearl," is also and better known by the name of one of the most famous compositions in this meter, namely the *Inkishafi*.

Other people may share in Ustadh Mau's mother's surprise, as the *Wasiya* features a very complex prosodic pattern. At that time, the poet would have paid lot of attention to arranging the poem so that it would always contain the same number of syllables in each stanza: as mentioned above, six *mizani* in each *kipande*. If the *Wasiya* had not stuck to this pattern, the line would have been considered *guni* "defective," and besides that, the poem would not have fit the tune and could not have been sung correctly. This shows the dependence of the music on the text (or the text on the prosody), as stressed by Beverly Parker in an analysis of *tendi* meter as sung in performance.[58]

Based on these parameters, Ustadh Mau claims that "giving voice" to a poem is definitely an art (*fani*), and this is the reason while not all poets are also able to chant their own poems: you must have the *sauti ya mahadhi* ("melodic voice") for it. Conversely, good singers may not be able to compose a single poetic line because they don't possess the poet's talent or art.

In almost all the solo vocal recordings available on CD or as MP3 files nowadays, the intro includes details about the composer of the poem and the process of how the poem is sung and voiced, called *kuimbwa* and *kutiwa sauti*; the soloist can be referred to as *mwimbaji* ("the singer") or *msomaji* ("the reader"), and the recording and selling activities are known as *kurecordiwa* and *kuuzwa*.

One fact that the *Wasiya* meter has in common with the *utendi* is that like with *tendi*, the *Wasiya* can be read (*kusoma*) or voiced (*kutia sauti*), but has never been sung in a Western style.

The *Wasiya* has been sung three times by three different African Muslim soloists: Kadara and el-Shatry from the Riadah area, both singers from Lamu, and Mrs. Ridhai, a soloist from Siu. One spoken rendition, read by Ustadh Mau himself, has also been made available to me for comparison. Each time, the *Wasiya* has been infused with a *sauti ya mahadhi* "melodic voice," and it has been performed only in the form of a solo vocal recording, without any musical accompaniment. What causes this single dynamic to vary is when a singer stresses and lengthens a single syllable that would normally be stressed in a speech as well. What J.W.T. Allen has stated with regard to the very exaggerated accentuation of *tendi* in performance—namely, "it sounds to me exactly like the speech of a person desperately anxious to convince me of a story—probably untrue"[59]—can be paraphrased for the *Wasiya* by saying that each of its solo renditions sounds to me exactly like a sad and mournful conversation between an elderly man and a young lady.

---

58 Allen, *Tendi*, 29 ff.

59 Allen, *Tendi*, 35.

5   The Polyphonic Narrative of the *Wasiya*

Granted that this is a fantastic tale, but when all is said and done the fantastic in art has its own limits and rules. The fantastic must be contiguous with the real to the point that you must almost believe in it.[60]

They call me a psychologist: this is not true. I am just a realist in a higher sense, i.e., I depict all the depths of the human soul.[61]

The *Wasiya* contains a powerful polyphony that expresses itself not only through its melodic voices (*sauti za mahadhi*), but also via its narrative voices. Generally, polyphony is a concept found in literary theory, speech act theory, and linguistics to refer to the simultaneity of points of view, perspectives, and voices on a particular narrative plane. The concept was introduced by Mikhail Bakhtin and applied to Dostoyevsky's dramatic novels, where, according to the Russian scholar, conflicting views and characters are left to develop unevenly.[62] In an in-depth analysis of Abdilatif Abdalla's poetic anthology *Sauti ya dhiki* ("Voice of Agony"), Ken Walibora also makes use of the term polyphony to describe how "[The poet Abdilatif Abdalla's] *sauti*, or voice, is hence a synthesis of many voices—not a cacophony, but a polyphony through which we vicariously hear the unspoken agonies of the silent fellow sufferers or unspeaking others."[63] Just as the Kenyan poet Abdalla uses his *Sauti* to speak for the downtrodden in post-independence Africa, Ustadh Mau's *Wasiya* speaks to young ladies and uses several characters' voices to tell us about how the drama experienced by the main protagonist also affected her loved ones and the entire community. One should also keep in mind that the poet Ustadh Mau has clearly

---

60   Dostoyevsky's letter to Yu. Abaza, 15 June *1880, A.* 30(i) (pp. 191–192) p. 192. Quoted in Malcom V. Jones, *Dostoyevsky after Bakhtin: Readings in Dostoyevsky's Fantastic Realism* (Cambridge: Cambridge University Press, 2009), 2, 201.

61   Dostoyewsky's Notebooks for 1880–1881, A 27, p. 65. Quoted in ibid.

62   See Mikhail M. Bakhtin, *The Dialogic Imagination: Four Essays* (Austin: University of Texas Press, 1981). Speaking of Dostoyevsky's fantastic realism, Malcom V. Jones rightly points out something that also holds true for Ustadh Mau: "The author of the polyphonic novel does not fix and define his characters once and for all but himself enters into dialogue with them. The hero, then, interests Dostoyevsky not as a fixed character that can be defined, finalized and closed off from without, but as a point-of view on the world [...] The truth about the world is inseparable from the truth about the personality and, according to Dostoyevsky, an idea can and must be not only understood but also 'felt'" (Jones, *Dostoyevsky's Fantastic Realism*, 13).

63   K. Waliaula Walibora, "Prison, Poetry, and Polyphony in Abdilatif Abdalla's 'Sauti ya Dhiki,'" *Research in African Literatures* 40, no. 3 (2009): 132.

expressed how committed he feels, as a poet, to speak not merely to the Swahili community, but more precisely to his own Lamuan community: *Lamu ni jamii ambapo sauti yangu inaweza kusikiwa na kufika*, "Lamu is a community within which my voice can be heard and where it arrives."[64] The *Wasiya* reflects a microcosm consisting of a poet and his community facing familiar dramas that speak of bigger societal issues.

The *Wasiya* is not a poem where we will find a monologue in the voice of a young girl recounting her experiences, but is very much dialogic and mimetically powerful. Furthermore, its plot does not consist of just one thread, but many, entangled with each other and brought together by the poet in a single night.

The poem unfolds along the lines of a mimetic conversation between an elderly man and an ingenuous young girl, and digresses into subscenes where other characters perform, such as the girl's relatives and the careless boy who abandoned the girl. The *fil rouge* running through the whole poem is the tragedy, called *mswiba* "mourning," that is depicted in all its facets through the wisdom of the poet-narrator, who zooms in and out of several scenarios focusing on the girl, her pregnancy, and her desperation, as well as on the girl's mother and her great sorrow, on the "good" or "evil" boys who either abandoned the girl or came to propose marriage and console her, on neighbors and passersby who consoled the girl's mother, and eventually on the figure of a mysterious old man who rescued the girl from committing suicide. Intentionally or not, the poet has not named his characters, likely as a tool to allow his readers and listeners—be they victims or perpetrators—to relate to and imagine themselves in that story and character.

The narrative and its human dynamism shape the stanzas, which are linked by verbs such as *kwenda kumwangaliya* ("go and look after him/her"), depicting a sort of back-and-forth visit to every single character's inward drama, to which the reader is conducted by the poet's guidance. To name but a few examples, in stanza 51, the narrator announcing he will stop (*koma*) with his account of the pregnant girl in order to return (*kurudi*) to some new narratives about the girl's mother—implying that he had already spent some stanzas on them.

Furthermore, the presence of reported speech contributes to showing that it is not simply a young girl recounting her story. In stanza 67, for instance, the mother is talking to a man who has asked to marry her daughter. The scene is full of interjections like *hebu*, which contributes to making the stanza as dialogical as possible. Interrogative particles like *wapi* ("where?") and *lini* ("when?")

---

64   Ustadh Mau, personal communication, Mombasa, July 2019.

MABANATI IN SEARCH OF AN AUTHOR: PORTABLE REFORM TEXTS   157

are also used to reenact a realistic dialogue between the characters, and also evokes a sense of confusion, as the mother simply utters *sijakueleya* ("I have not understood") and wants things to be explained to her *nelezeya* ("explain to me").

> *Mama katamka*   *Akamuambiya*
> *Wewe ulofika*   *sijakueleya*
> *Wapi umetoka*   *hebu nelezeya*
> *Lini ulitaka*   *mambo kama haya*

> The mother spoke, asking him,
> "You who have just arrived; I don't understand.
> Where are you from? Please explain to me,
> When did you make this request?"

6   Zooming Into the Drama

The choice to begin his poem using the verb *-sikiza* shows that Ustadh Mau, rather than suggesting that his audience read his guidelines, is inviting them to listen to his advice as if his own daughter(s), drawing "physically close to him."[65] This plea to come close to pay attention recalls the incipit of the *Utendi wa Mwana Kupona*, the admonitory poem representing one of the first gems of classical Swahili *utendi* compositions, which reads as follows: *negema mwanangu binti*, "come closer my daughter," where the verb *-egema* means precisely "to come closer."[66] By uttering, "Come closer" (*egema*) and "listen" (*sikiza*), the poet instructs, as the composition unfurls from its beginning, enacting a scenario in which the characters seem as if they are on stage and the audience (in this case personified in the daughter) is in attendance to draw near and pay attention (*hela zingatiya*). Differently from the *Utendi wa Mwana Kupona*, however, where the recipient of the advice is never invited to speak or interact within the poem, as already noted above, *Wasiya* unfolds like a polyphonic narration in which even the young girl who is invited to listen (*sikiza*

---

65   As the poet himself declares, at that time he already had the feeling that he would have had more daughters than sons. As it happened in reality, Ustadh Mau has seven daughters, four sons, and thirty-four grandchildren.

66   In Werner and Hichens's translation, the first line of the *Mwana Kupona* poem—*negema, wangu binti*—is translated as follows: "attend to me, my daughter" (Werner and Hichens, *The Advice of Mwana Kupona*, 36–37).

mwanangu)—as well as other characters, like the girl's mother—will also take the narrative stage at some point in the poem.

Although the identity of the young girl's family is not revealed, the poet is said to have composed this poem inspired by an actual event that occurred in Mombasa. Soon after the poem had spread all along the coast, curious people began betting on who was the young man to be blamed. Thus it seems that in this poem, enacted like a play, rather than having characters without an author and looking for one—as in Pirandello's famous play *Six Characters in Search of an Author*[67]—in the *Wasiya*, the author, in the guise of an elderly man who has weathered the injustices of the world, creates characters whose stories want to be voiced, as if they need to be put on stage for show. Still, the poet thought up and searched for the invented characters (*wahusika wa kibuni*) whom he wanted to perform this drama by observing his own lifeworld and the people around him. Indeed, the poet's talent is evident in the way he has made his story and characters come alive as realistic characters. In other words, he achieved the poetic aim—unconsciously, in only his 20s—to make this poem more than just feasible, but credible: listeners considered the characters to be part of the real world, to the point of sparking their curiosity to meet the victim and the antagonist of the poetic drama in the streets of Mombasa. In other words, it was as if the realism had overcome the fiction.

The story starts by considering rumors told by people from Mombasa to Lamu, which is depicted still as a protected island, different from the coast, where bad and cruel things continue to happen (*maovu mabaya yanaendeleya*, stz. 4). The first ten stanzas indeed echo a lament over and reproach for the decay of the Muslim customs on the coast. A feeling of nostalgia for the past can be perceived through images of books that are no longer read and mothers who are worried about their daughters.

The topic of teenage pregnancy, outside marriage, is straightforwardly addressed from the beginning. The poet, in a very cynical way, mimicks what the "evil" boy falsely promised to the ingenuous girl: "Don't worry, we will be together/When you have the baby, I will be there to help" (stz. 9). The boy is compared to a *nyoka* "snake" (see stz. 32), but is also described in the poem as *fahali*, which metaphorically alludes to a man who does not care about others; in a stricter sense, it symbolizes strength, male sexual prowess, and unchecked masculinity. The story proceeds to show how the so-called *fahali* has gone off

---

67   In Pirandello's *Six Characters in Search of an Author*, the characters are also not named, but simply called the Father, the Mother, and four children; see Domenico Vittorini, "Pirandello's Sei personaggi in cerca d'autore," *The Modern Language Journal* 7, no. 6 (1923): 347–349.

to find new girls to sleep with, and the poet intervenes with some dialogue between the disappointed and desperate lady and the brute and arrogant guy. The dialogue does not refrain from either rude or quite elusive expressions, alluding to the brutal masculinity of the boy and the rather passive status of the girl—who is blamed by the boy as the one who, in fact, enjoyed having sexual intercourse with him and who had had other affairs prior to theirs.[68]

However, as things are more complicated in reality than they might appear from the harsh perspective of the boy—who refuses to admit his role and take on fatherly responsibilities—the poet delves into the girl's subsequent psychological and physical problems, after being fooled and abandoned with her own pregnancy. The plot zeros in on the inner world of the girl once she is alone and pregnant. In stanza 48, she is depicted in her room with a vivid realism evoked through descriptive scenes:

> Uko kitandani   mzazi huliya
> Zilo matumboni   zampa udhiya
> Mwake akilini   hayajamngiya
> Msiba nyumbani   uliotokeya

> The mother-to-be was on the bed, crying;
> What was retained in the uterus was causing her harm
> She had yet to comprehend in her mind
> The sad events that had befallen their home.

In this stanza, the poet-narrator shows a certain sensitivity in expressing the state of the pregnant woman, called *mzazi*, which means "parent" as well as "fertile woman, woman in childbirth." He writes and describes realistic feelings and scenes by zooming into private psychological realms, already highlighted by the locative classes -*ni*, -*ko*, and *mw*-: *kitandani*, *matumboni*, *mwake akilini*, *nyumbani*. The drama imbued in the stanza is reflected in a plethora of elements: the image of the future mother weeping, expressed by the verb -*liya*; the noun *udhiya*, which in itself already entails the negative feelings of being disturbed,

---

68   Female characters whose lives are ruined by cunning and careless man and who have to face their past are quite a frequent trope in Swahili narrative. Compare, for instance, some similarities with Kajubi D. Mukajanga's *Kitanda cha Mauti* ("Death's Bed") (1982), which is regarded as an educational story framed as a thriller: like Kezilahabi's *Rosa Mistika* almost ten years earlier, it is a moving account of the consequences of an overly rigid upbringing. See E. Bertoncini-Zúbková *Vamps and Victims: Women in Modern Swahili Literature* (Cologne: Köppe, 1996), 93–105.

vexed, annoyed. These feelings become even more "disturbing" when considering the notion of them occurring in one's own stomach, belly. In addition to the verb *-liya* and the noun *udhiya*, the noun *msiba*, meaning "bereavement, misfortune, sorrow," is certainly a term that encapsulates the entire tragedy borne by the girl.[69] In this specific line, *msiba* is referring to the death of her father, who dies of shock on hearing the news of his daughter's pregnancy. Broadly speaking, *msiba* captures the tragedy of the whole event: the boy abandoning the young girl after she gave birth, the girl's beloved parents dying of shock or becoming deeply upset, and ultimately, the miserable girl's lonely and sobering decision to commit suicide and infanticide because of the fatherless child, namely *mja haramu*, she had carried in her womb and then given birth.

The palpable tone of sadness throughout this tragedy is expressed through the unhappiness experienced by the woman. How can one make the feeling of depression palpable and commit this form of self-harassment to verse? As the following excerpt from the *Wasiya* shows, the poet sheds light on the girl's behavior and how she began treating and mistreating herself. This becomes evident in stanza 78, with the use of the reflexive pronoun *-ji-* infixed in causative and applicative verbs such as *hajifurahishi*, *hajilishi*, *akijishibiya*, and *amejitatiya*.

> *Ingawa aishi*   *hataki duniya*
> *Hajifurahishi*   *hata siku moya*
> *Wala hajilishi*   *akajishibiya*
> *Kama kifurushi*   amejitatiya

Even while she is alive, she rejects the world.
She doesn't enjoy herself, not even for a day.
Nor does she eat to satisfaction;
Like a bundle, she has tied herself.

The poet's choice of verbs sheds light on the mood and behavior of the girl and the lack of care she is exhibiting toward herself. Her decision to attempt suicide may already be hinted at in the first line of the stanza, where the verb *kuisihi* "to live," used in the first *kipande*, stands in contrast to her lack of will to live, as expressed by *hataki duniya*, where *duniya*, a recurrent word in this poem, stands for "life, world." The stanza ends with the metonymy of the lady compared to an object, a *kifurushi* "bundle" that is falling apart.

---

69   The noun *Msiba* also refers to a tragedy such as people dying (see, for instance, the poem "Amu," where the *msiba* the poet is recalling to concerns woman and children who passed away on the sea).

In addition to mimetic scenes, the poem is also replete with an abundance of metaphors (*mafumbo*), particularly linked to the woman's pregnancy (*mimba*) and her loss of virginity (*hali yakupoteza usichana*).[70] If we look at the very beginning of the poem, the poet is referring to the baby in the lady's womb with term *mzigo* (stanza 10), which literally means "burden, heavy load, bag." It is via *sitiari/isitiara* ("metaphor") that the poet stresses the girl's state of desperation and regret; the most recurrent metaphor concerns the woman's virginity, symbolized by her hymen, which is referred to firstly in stanza 26, *kipai cha jaha kimekupoteya* ("You have lost your sense of worth"), and as *ukuta* "wall" in the stanza 27 that follows.

> *Kipai cha jaha*   *kimekupoteya*
> *Huna la furaha*   *katika duniya*
> *Na mambo ya raha*   *hutaki sikiya*
> *Kwa mola ilaha*   *sasa wajutiya*

> You have lost your sense of worth.
> You are unhappy in this world.
> And have lost interest in all joyful things.
> You now direct your regrets to the Lord.

> *Sana unajuta*   *na kuzingatiya*
> *Umekwishapita*   *wakati wa haya*
> *Na wako ukuta*   *ulijivundiya*
> *Ni mwezi wa sita*   *sasa yatimiya*

> You now regret and continue to ponder;
> The time for this is now long gone,
> You tore down your own wall.
> It is now completing its sixth month.

Ukuta, which literally means "wall," is the woman's qualification as a good candidate for marriage, which, in the girl's case, has now been invalidated as she enters her seventh month of pregnancy. In the last stanza of this narrative analysis, the female protagonist of the drama will make the decision to tell her mother about her loss of virginity. Again, the poet has the girl speak up about having infringed the Islamic injunction that Muslim women remain virgins (*bikira*) through metaphors (stz. 32):

---

70   See also Mahazi's and Vierke's contributions in this volume.

Mama nipulika	*nitalo kwambiya*
Yai *uloweka*	*ukaniusiya*
Amekuja nyoka	*amenidomeya*
Limebaki **kaka**	*sasa laoleya*

"Mom, please pay attention to what I am about to tell you:
The egg that you bestowed upon me to protect,
A snake came and bit it.
All that is left now is an empty floating shell."

As the stanza shows, new terms are used to allude to the woman's virginity here: *yai*, which literally means "egg," and its exterior, namely *kaka*, which is used in the meaning of "eggshell," symbolizing the emptiness of the woman's "egg" once her walls have been breached.

7 **_Dulcis in fundo_: The Metanarration within the Muslim Drama**

Kamwambia Babu	*ukitaka haya*
Kiswa ukutubu	*kipate eneya*
Tafuta kitabu	*na kalamu piya*
Kisije wasibu	*wano inukiya*

She told him, "Oh grandfather, if you are interested in this,
Go find a book and a pen.
Then write the story so that it may spread,
So that the same thing doesn't befall those who are still growing up".

This is stanza 92 of the *Wasiya*, and the reader might wonder, who is speaking here and what is the girl doing? Clearly, she is asking the elderly man to grab a pen and a book and to write down her story. She is thus asking that the spoken mode be turned into a written mode that may circulate further.

Despite the tragic events related in the *Wasiya*, in the second part of the poem, hints of hope and positivity slowly emerge. A first clue of hope and acceptance can be already found in stanza 53, when the concerned voice of a friend tells the girl's mother: *kamwambiya nana | ndio kidunya watu hupambana | na zaidi haya*, "I told her, 'Lady, such is life. People are faced with tougher challenges than these.'" Here and there, the poet-narrator inserts verses meant to instruct the girl on her destiny (*mambo ya kadari*, stz. 62) and thus relieve her

MABANATI IN SEARCH OF AN AUTHOR: PORTABLE REFORM TEXTS 163

from the heavy load (*mzigo*) of feeling responsible for her father's death and her mother's mourning and sorrow (*mswiba*). This reflection becomes even more evident in stanza 75, when uttered by a good man who was supposed to marry the girl, and who tries to console the girl by reminding her that death is part of life: *hini ndiyo hali ya hini duniya / mauti ni kweli meumba Jaliya / wake na rijali watakafikia*, "This is the way of this world / death is a reality created by God / it will befall both men and women." The turning point that opens a window of hope onto the drama is related in stanza 83, which can be regarded as the most vividly dramatic scene, depicting the major protagonist's act of committing suicide and infanticide, as the narrator says, with the support of the devil (*shetwani*). Soon afterward, the poem introduces an elderly man (*kuhuli*, stz. 86) who, while walking, sees something floating in the sea; he jumps into the water with his clothes on and witnesses, with his own eyes, that there is a person about to die: *ruhu muhotoka / kuwaga daunia*, "Her soul was about to leave her and abandon this world" (stz. 87). Indeed, from stanza 91, a metastory begins: the elderly man asks the girl about her sorrows, and the girl invites him to take a pen and a book and start writing her own story so that it may be disseminated.

From stanza 93 on, a flashback begins telling us about the life of the young girl before the tragedy. The girl herself thus becomes the narrator of her own childhood and youth, and the elderly man becomes like her grandfather, namely *Babu*. From this stanza, the girl becomes both the "speaking subject," i.e. the narrator, and the "subject of speech" of her own life experience. "Life experiences" (*mambo ya kidunya*) are indeed at the core of many of Ustadh Mau's other written compositions, as previous contributions in this volume have also shown.

In the *Wasiya*, the girl recounts her story from the time she was born: how she was brought up by her parents, her father's refusal to let her study, and the temptations of the world she experienced through bad friends; at that point, her biography reaches precisely the occasion when she falls in love with the wrong boy and is seduced. This is a very creative section, embedding a flashback within the poem while switching the narrator and focus of the narrative. Furthermore, it lends veracity to the entire story, as if that very same victim of tragedy then finds the courage to speak out about what happened—as if she is taking the microphone and coming on the stage. The figure of the grandfather, in turn, becomes that of the listener and the writer who will record and rewrite her story. Again, returning to Pirandello's characters in search of an author, here it seems that the girl is rather in search of a poet-narrator, as she wants her drama to be written—as the verb *kutubu* and the reference to writing tools, like a pen and book, in the above-quoted stanza show—told, and spread—actions implied in terms like *kiswa* and the related verb *enea* "to spread"—among her peers, along the lines of what Pirandello's characters do when they "appear before troupe of players and insist on performing their drama."[71]

To conclude, when we read this part of the poem together with Ustadh Mau, I dared to ask him who was this old man who rescued the lady from committing suicide, and if we could even imagine it was Ustadh Mau in person. Interestingly, the narrator and this savior figure are indeed the same character, depicted as an elderly man. So the poet-narrator, the giver of advice, as the *Wasiya* incipit relates, also becomes the rescuer who by giving the lady the chance to speak about her own story, becomes her first listener and the storyteller of her drama for a wider audience. Eventually, he will enable this story to spread and help the girl go on with her life by offering her a place to stay from that moment on. His house thus signals a fresh start for both her child and herself.

The beauty of the poem indeed resides in the unexpected happy ending that the entire tragedy finally reaches, in which the reader can perceive the poet's own hopes for the progress and improvement of every human life. The *Wasiya wa mabanati* is a great example of Eric Bentley, in his work "The Play of the Century," describes: "a fantasy based on the notion that characters are not created by an author but preternatural people who seek an author to write their biographies or at least their family drama."[72]

References

Abedi, K. Amri. *Sheria za kutunga mashairi na diwani ya Amri. The Poems of Amri with an Essay on Swahili Poetry and the Rules of Versification.* Nairobi: Kenya Literature Bureau, 1954.

Allen, J.W.T. *Tendi. Six Examples of a Swahili Classical Verse Form with Translations & Notes.* New York: Africana Publishing, 1971.

Tantawi, Sheikh Ali al-. *Ya-bintī.* Medina: Mujawharāt al-Maghribal, 1985.

Abdul-Samad, Abdullah. "Sheikh Ali al-Tantāwi and his Educational and Literary Services." *al-Idah* 29, no. 2, (2014): 254–272.

Amidu, Assibi. *Kimwondo: A Kiswahili Electoral Contest.* Beiträge zur Afrikanistik 39. Vienna: Afro-Pub, 1990.

---

71   Vittorini, "Pirandello's Sei personaggi," 348.

72   Eric Bentley, "The Play of the Century," *The Yale Review* 86, no. 3 (1998): 72.

Bakhtin, Mikhail M. *The Dialogic Imagination: Four Essays*. Austin: University of Texas Press, 1981.

Bang, Anne. "Authority and Piety, Writing and Print. A Preliminary Study of the Circulation of Islamic Texts in Late Nineteenth- and Early Twentieth-Century Zanzibar." *Journal of the International African Institute* 81, no. 1 (2011): 89–107.

Barber, Karin. *Print Culture and the First Yoruba Novel: I.B. Thomas's Life Story of Me, Segilola and Other Texts*. Leiden: Brill, 2012.

Bentley, Eric. "The Play of the Century." *The Yale Review* 86, no. 3 (1998): 71–81.

Bertoncini-Zúbková, E. *Vamps and Victims: Women in Modern Swahili Literature*. Cologne: Köppe, 1996.

Eickelman, Dale F., and Jon W. Anderson. *New Media in the Muslim World: The Emerging Public Sphere*. 2nd ed. Bloomington: Indiana University Press, 2003. First published 1999.

Eisenberg, Andrew J. "The Swahili Art of Indian Taarab: A Poetics of Vocality and Ethnicity on the Kenyan Coast." *Comparative Studies of South Asia, Africa and the Middle East* 37, no. 2 (2017): 336–354.

Furniss, Graham L. "Aspects of Style and Meaning in the Analysis of a Hausa Poem." *Bulletin of the School of Oriental and African Studies* 45, no. 3 (1982): 546–570.

Hillewaert, Sarah. *Morality at the Margins: Youth, Language, and Islam in Coastal Kenya*. New York: Fordham University Press, 2020.

Hirschkind, Charles. *The Ethical Soundscape: Cassette Sermons and Islamic Counterpublics*. New York: Columbia University Press, 2006.

Hofmeyr, Isabel. *Gandhi's Printing Press Experiments in Slow Reading*. Cambridge, Mass.: Harvard University Press, 2013.

Kapchan, Deborah. "Listening Acts, Secular and Sacred: Sound Knowledge among Sufi Muslims in Secular France." In *Islam and Popular Culture*, edited by Karin van Nieuwkerk, Mark Levine, and Martine Stokes. Austin: University of Texas Press, 2016.

Jones, Malcom V. *Dostoyevsky after Bakhtin: Readings in Dostoyevsky's Fantastic Realism*. Cambridge: Cambridge University Press, 2009. First published 1990.

Khulūṣī, Ṣafāʾ. "Didactic Verse." In *Religion, Learning and Science in the ʿAbbasid Period*, edited by R.B. Serjeant, M.J.L. Young, and J.D. Latham, 498–509. Cambridge: Cambridge University Press, 1990.

Kresse, Kai. *Philosophising in Mombasa: Knowledge, Islam and Intellectual Practice on the Swahili Coast*. Edinburgh: Edinburgh University Press, 2007.

Kresse, Kai. "Enduring Relevance: Samples of Oral Poetry on the Swahili Coast." *Wasafiri* 26, no. 2 (2011): 46–49.

Kresse, Kai. *Swahili Muslim Publics and Postcolonial Experience*. Bloomington: Indiana University Press, 2018.

Larkin, Brian. "Techniques of Inattention: The Mediality of Loudspeakers in Nigeria." *Anthropological Quarterly* 87, no. 4 (2014): 989–1015.

Loimeier, Robert. *Islamic Reform in Twentieth-Century Africa*. Edinburgh: Edinburgh University Press, 2016.

Mathieu, Roy. *KIAMU, archipel de Lamu (Kenya): Analyse phonétique et morphologique d'un corpus linguistique et poétique*. French ed. Saarbrücken: PAF, 2013.

Me on TV. "Mahmoud Mau 1." Posted September 18, 2016. YouTube clip, 23:41. https://www.youtube.com/watch?v=5l8LhET8G0E.

Mernissi, Fatima. "Women's Song: Destination Freedom." In *Islam and Democracy* (New York: Perseus Books Group and Basic Books, 2002), 149–171.

Miehe, Gudrun. "Die Perioden der Swahililiteratur und ihre sprachliche Form." *Paideuma* 36 (1990): 201–215.

Mohamed, Mohamed Abdulla. *Comprehensive Swahili-English Dictionary*. Nairobi: East African Educational Publishers, 2011.

Munir, Ahmad. "Sheikh Ali al-Tantāwi and His Educational and Literary Services." *Shaykh Zayed Islamic Centre: University of Peshawar* 29, no. 2 (2014): 254–272.

Mukajanga, Kajubi, D. *Kitanda cha Mauti*. Dar es Salaam: Grand Arts Promotion, 1982.

Pirandello, Luigi. *Six Characters in Search of an Author*. Translated by Edward Storer. Mineola, NY: Dover Thrift Editions, 1998.

Raia, Annachiara. "Texts, Voices and Tapes. Mediating Poetry on the Swahili Muslim Coast in the 21st Century." In "Power to the People?—Patronage, Intervention and Transformation in African Performative Arts," edited by Ricarda de Haas, Marie-Anne Kohl, Samuel Ndogo, and Christopher Odhiambo. Special issue, *Matatu* 51 (2019): 139–168.

Raia, Annachiara. "A Network of Copies. The *Utendi wa Yusuf* Manuscript Traditions from the J.W.T. Allen Collection (Dar es Salaam)." In "One Text: Many Copies," edited by Clarissa Vierke & Ridder Samsom. Special issue, *Journal of Manuscript Cultures* (2021): 65–86.

Robinson, Francis. "Technology and Religious Change: Islam and the Impact of Print." *Modern Asian Studies* 27, no. 1 (1993): 229–251.

Romero, Patricia W. *Lamu. History, Society, and Family in an East African Port City*. Princeton, NJ: Wiener, 1997.

Ryan, Marie-Laure. *Narrative across Media: The Languages of Storytelling*. Lincoln, Neb.: University of Nebraska Press, 2004.

Saavedra Casco, José Arturo. *Utenzi, War Poems, and the German Conquest of East Africa: Swahili Poetry as Historical Source*. Trenton, NJ: Africa World Press, 2007.

Schiesaro, Alessandro. "Didactic Poetry." December 22, 2015. https://oxfordre.com/classics/view/10.1093/acrefore/9780199381135.001.0001/acrefore-9780199381135-e-2153.

Shariff, Ibrahim Noor. *Tungo zetu: Msingi wa mashairi na tungo nyinginezo*. Trenton, NJ: Red Sea Press, 1988.

Stigand, C.H. *A Grammar of the Dialectic Changes in the Kiswahili Language. With an Introduction and a Recension and Poetical Translation of the Poem Inkishafi. A*

Swahili Speculum Mundi by the Rev. W.E. Taylor. Cambridge: Cambridge University Press, 1915.

Vittorini, Domenico. "Pirandello's Sei personaggi in cerca d'autore." *The Modern Language Journal* 7, no. 6 (1923): 347–349.

wa Thiong'o, Ngũgĩ. *Decolonising the Mind: The Politics of Language in African Literature.* London: Currey, 1986.

Walibora, K. Waliaula. "Prison, Poetry, and Polyphony in Abdilatif Abdalla's "Sauti ya Dhiki"." *Research in African Literatures* 40, no. 3 (2009): 129–148.

Werner, Alice and William Hichens. *The Advice of Mwana Kupona upon the Wifely Duty.* The Azanian Classics 2. Medstead: Azania Press, 1934.

FIGURE 12   Barka Aboud, Ustadh Mahmoud Mau's mother, in 1968

PART 2

Poems by Ustadh Mau

∵

Introduction to Part 2

FIGURE 13   Ustadh Mahmoud Mau and his photo album

This section features twenty selected poems. Nineteen are by Ustadh Mau himself; one, *Hapo zamani za yana* ("Once upon a Time"), was composed by his father—a poet, most of whose poetry has been lost—with the intention of guiding his son on how best to live a decent life in the typical style of the *wasiya* genre, an admonitory poetic genre that Ustadh Mau himself would later frequently explore. With the exception of the poem *Kiswahili*, the poems are published here for the first time in Swahili, with English translations.

The poems that Ustadh Mau has selected for this publication are ones that the poet himself considers important compositions, also representing the different facets of his varied poetic practice; accordingly, they have been grouped in five thematic fields: 1. *jamii* ("society"), critical poetry about topical events on Lamu; 2. *ilimu* ("education"), poems that place emphasis on education; 3. *huruma* ("empathy"), poetry that reflects this signature ethical quality, defending the rights of the downtrodden; 4. *matukio* ("events"), poems with the function of a diary in which the poet reflects on his own experiences; and 5. *maombi* ("prayers/wishes") conveyed in poetry, either didactic or devotional, seeking

God's blessings. The categorization is not meant to be rigid, but to offer the reader a rough guide to the variety of his compositions.

The edited poems are not only different in topic but also in tone. Many were composed in response to burning societal questions, which Ustadh Mau, as a respected member of society and an imam, is supposed to address, thereby also addressing the *umma* at large and seeking to make lasting statements. Some were also composed on the occasion of meetings or conferences, like the *Za Washirazi athari* ("The Influence of the Persians") or *Kilio huliya mwenye* ("Change Begins at Home"), addressing the specific audience of the conference. As elaborated further in Part 1, most poems come with some advice (in those poems referred to as *wasiya*, *shauri*, or *nasaha*), warning, or call to action in the first-person plural; for instance, in *Mola zidisha baraka* ("God Increase Your Blessings"), stz. 12: *tufundisheni kwa ghera* "Let us work harder." They create a sense of community by focusing on the common obstacles and weaknesses humans confront in life,[1] but also by sharing knowledge on overcoming these difficulties.[2] Other poems have a much more personal, self-reflexive tone, like the melancholic *Mlango* ("The Door"), or the poems dedicated to his own children, which overflow with fatherly pride and emotion. Much of his poetry is narrative in style, whereby the narrative perspectives vary greatly: while some poems employ dialogue as a major dramatic device, like *Mchezo wa kuigiza* ("Play") or *Jilbabu* ("Veil"), other poems play with changes in narrative perspective, such as the *Wasiya wa mabanati* ("Advice to Young Girls"), where character dialogue complements an external narrator, or *Mama msimlaumu* ("Don't Blame My Mother"), in which the narrative perspective is that of the unborn child.

The poems also belong to different poetic genres, from the shorter *shairi* and *wimbo*, to the long narrative or didactic *utendi*—like *Haki za watoto* ("Children's Rights"), the longest poem—or even less common forms, like the long meter found in the *Wasiya wa mabanati*, which are part of the cultural history of the Swahili coast and have traditionally framed local discourse. How much Ustadh Mau's own poetic and intellectual practice is shaped by local genres and discourse, as discussed in the contributions in Part 1, is also reflected, for instance, in his use of metaphors and metaphorical poetry. In *Jahazi* ("The Dhow"), he

---

1 See *Mama Musimlaumu* ("Don't Blame My Mother"), stz. 3: *Na nyuteni mwafahamu, kuna dhaifu wakati/ Hushindwa kuidhibiti* "As all of you know, there are times of weakness in which we fail to control ourselves." See also *Wasiya Wa Mabanati*, stz. 17 *Kuwa insani mwana Adamiya* "Be Human, son of Adam!"

2 See *Kilio Huliya Mwenye* ("Change Begins at Home"), stz. 7: *Ilimu si ya fulani wala haina mipaka* "Knowledge does not belong just to one people, nor does it have limits."

INTRODUCTION TO PART 2   173

follows the typical model of dialogic riddle poetry, hiding the meaning behind a well-chosen metaphor (*mafumbo*) that he urges his audience to decode at the end of the poem, telling them: *Suwali si la jahazi, hili katika shairi* "The theme of the poem is not the dhow" (see *Jahazi*, stz. 6). Ustadh Mau learned how to compose Swahili poetry in Arabic script and the prosodic rules entirely on his own, thanks to his father's poetry, the madrassa, and self-practice, and he is among the few on Lamu still using the Arabic script to compose. Some samples of his handwritten Arabic manuscripts are included here.

The poems make ample intertextual references. Some characters, lines, and expressions in Ustadh Mau's compositions are taken from the Qur'ān; for instance, the figure of the rich tyrant Qarun, who appears in sura 28:76–84 (referred to in *Mchezo wa kuigiza*) or Ḥawqala, a verse commonly recited in the case of calamity (in *Amu*, stz. 18). We have included cross-references to specific *āyāt* in the majority of such cases. Unless otherwise specified, the English translations of the Qur'ān provided here are those of Arthur John Arberry.[3] The Arabic books that Ustadh Mau keeps at his home library have also been sources of inspiration for his poetry. This is the case of the *Wasiya wa mabanati*, inspired by 'Alī al-Ṭanṭawi's Arabic booklet *Ya-bintī* ("Oh My Daughter"), and *Mchezo wa kuigiza*, inspired by a prose version of the same story that the poet read in an Arabic textbook for class six in Saudi Arabia, where the story bore the title *Bayna al-ghanī na al-faqīr* ("Between the Rich and the Poor"). Furthermore, his poetry is full of references to Swahili proverbs and oral traditions, like the woman Mwantau from Siu, mentioned in his father's poem *Hapo zamani za yana*.

The language of Ustadh Mau's poetry reflects the mosaic of Swahili cultural interaction and maritime connections. Besides terms like *achari* ("chutney") and rupiya ("rupee") which create obvious links with Indian Ocean material culture, the ocean and its maritime vocabulary permeate his verse: the port and the waves (*bandari, mawimbi*), the sail (*t'anga*), the mast (*mongoti*), and above all—certainly the Lamuan maritime symbol par excellence—the jahazi ("dhow"). Metaphors involving the dhow and the sea are abundant, as in the poem Jahazi "Dhow." Arabic terms are abundant, but also terms taken from the so-called northern Swahili dialects. Besides Kiamu, the poet's own variant of Swahili, we also find terms from Kibajuni (e.g. the verb *kutoma* "to fish")— which the poet mostly knows from his second wife, who was born in Faza— or Kimvita (e.g., the negative relative construction asiye instead of aso). We

---

3   Arthur J. Arberry, *The Quran Interpreted* (Oxford: Oxford University Press, 2006). First published 1984.

give Standard Swahili equivalents for many unusual dialectal forms and lexical items in the commentary.

There are some structural features that recur in many other Swahili compositions. A number of Ustadh Mau's poems start with the Islamic eulogistic formula *Bismillahi ar-raḥmān ar-raḥīm*, addressing God. In the concluding stanzas, the poet often "signs" the poem by providing his name and address (as in the last stanza of *Amu*). In poems composed on commission for someone else, the poet concludes the poem by mentioning the name of the individual on whose behalf he composed it—in case of *Mola zidisha baraka* ("God Increase Your Blessings"), for example, his daughter Hannan—a phenomenon that is not unusual in poetry on commission. In shorter compositions, he often uses the widespread rhetorical formula of underlining the beauty of a short text, namely that it is easier to keep in mind (see *Bandari ina mawimbi*, last stanza).

Each poem in this part is preceded by a short introduction, and many verses are followed by comments drafted by the editors through ongoing conversation with Ustadh Mau and occasionally also his daughter Azra.

Jamii: Topical Issues on Lamu

FIGURE 14 Ustadh Mahmoud Mau giving a speech to motivate adults to have their children vaccinated against polio during the time of the *maulidi* celebrations in around 2010

1   *Amu* ("Lamu")

Ustadh Mau composed this poem on July 24, 1979, making it one of his first poetic works. The poem was in response to a calamity that hit Lamu hard: in Ramadan of that year, there was a shipwreck in which almost thirty-seven people, mostly women and children, lost their lives. July is generally a dangerous month for traveling—the wind can be strong, and the ocean rough—but this had been the worst accident in years. The first person to type out this poem was Derek Nurse, who was interested in deciphering and analyzing the Kiamu dialect. We obtained his copy from Ustadh Mau, went through it, and retyped it. It is a mere coincidence that we started translating this poem, during the last part of our research with him in 2019, exactly on the same days (July 23 to 24) that the incident had taken place forty years ago. May the souls of all victims rest in peace!

© USTADH MAU, ANNACHIARA RAIA AND CLARISSA VIERKE, 2023 | DOI:10.1163/9789004525726_010
This is an open access chapter distributed under the terms of the CC BY-NC-ND 4.0 license.

Ustadh Mau was driven to write this poem to calm the souls of all those who lost their wives, children, or other close friends or relatives. He expresses his empathy and his own sadness in solidarity with the community. The major theme stressed in this poem is that only God knows and plans life; human beings do not have His power, nor are they immortal. He furthermore tries to console people by hinting at the heavenly reward awaiting those who have died before their time: anyone who dies in an accident acquires high status as a martyr. Thus, his aim was to help his community accept fate. The belief in God and his provision is one that the poet seeks to impart to his audience stanza after stanza. In doing so, he also speaks out against all the rumors and conspiracy theories circulating after the tragedy, which occurred at exactly the same time as an election campaign in Lamu. According to the most widespread rumor, jinns had been sent to cause the accident in order to influence the election: the majority of the passengers were supporters of Madhubuti's right-wing party. Thus, according to this conviction, supporters of the left-wing politician al-Manzil had incited the jinns to make the boat sink.

The poet tempers these rumors, which were born from and added to already existing tensions, by suggesting a different perspective, namely a religious one. The ultimate reason for the accident is known only to God, and human beings have to accept it, however bitter it might be in the beginning. He shows understanding, but also pleads with his audience not to lose themselves in their emotions of sadness, grief, and anger to the point of nurturing evil thoughts. Furthermore, he stresses a sense of unity and communally shared tragedy, which can only be overcome by common religious belief: *tushikamane na dini* (stz. 55).

It is remarkable that Ustadh Mau composed this poem when he was only in his twenties. He was already married by that time, and had already fathered three children. Thus, one can read the empathy in his words, reflecting how he, the young husband and father, was able to put himself in the shoes of those who had just lost their families. However, in the poem, it is not (merely) the young husband and father talking, but a leader addressing his community, Amu,[1] with a firm voice, taking on the role of guiding "his" people. The poem already reflects his concern and care for the community; he assumes the role of guide, consciously countering other narratives and beliefs.

Prosodically, the utendi is composed in a -*wa* rhyme, which is less common and more difficult than the common -*ya* rhyme. Structurally, the poem features a considerable number of stanzas framing the *dibaji* (1–10) and *tamati* (43–57).

---

1 Amu in the Kiamu variant of Swahili is sometimes used to refer to the whole island of Lamu. More commonly, it only refers to Lamu town on the island.

JAMII: TOPICAL ISSUES ON LAMU

In both the preface and epilogue, the poet praises and thanks God. In the *dibaji*, he highlights His endless power and stresses how our lives are in fact decided according to His plan. In its conclusion, the poem becomes a devotional composition: the poet prays to God, the Almighty, to give people the strength to understand and accept His will, but also begs Him to spare them from further misery. In three stanzas of the *tamati*, the first *kipande*, invoking God and imploring him to put an end to the suffering, is repeated successively, which heightens the emotion of the verse (see *Ya Rabi iwe ni basi*, stz. 50; *Rabi yatie kikomo*, stz. 51; or *Rabi Mola yamalize*, stz. 52).

As in most of Ustadh Mau's *tendi* and *mashairi*, the last stanza reveals the author. Here it creates a link to the title of the composition, "Amu"—referring to the city/island of Amu—which is also the place where the author was born and lives. The connection between Ustadh Mau and his island is a motif recurring in several contexts, not only in his poetry but also in his everyday duties—which mainly concern his community in Amu—and the Friday sermons that he always delivers to the Lamuan public.

1.   *Yallahi ya Karimu*   Oh God, the Generous,
      Mwenye ezi ya kudumu   Having endless power,
      Upitishao kalamu   You are the one who has the power
      Kwandika yambo likawa   To write what will happen.

2.   *Yallahi sub'hana*   Almighty, you are perfect,
      Uso mke wala mwana   Without wife or child—
      Lolote ukilinena   Whatever you say
      Huwa pasi kuchelewa   Comes true without delay.

3.   *Yailahi ya Mannani*   O God, the Giver,
      Mola uso na kifani   God, you have no equal.
      Wambiapo yambo kuni   Whatever you say comes into being;[i]
      Haliinui khatua   It happens immediately.[ii]

i This is a reference to Qur. 36: 82, which reads as follows: "His command, when He desires a thing, is to say to it 'Be,' and it is" (Abr. 455). | ii More literally: "it does not take a further step."

4.   *Ndiwe muumba kadari*   You are the one who causes destiny.
      Ya kheri na yalo shari   Good and bad events,
      Ni wajibu tuyakiri   We are obliged to accept them;
      Twandame majaaliwa   Let us follow what was determined for us.

5.	*Hatu hili wala hili*
	Upitishalo Jalali
	Sisi mbwa kulikubali
	Tukaridhika Moliwa

We own neither this nor that;
His Majesty is the one who makes it come true.
We are the ones who accept;
We have to be satisfied with what God gives us.

6.	*Hakuna mwenye uweza*
	Upendalo kuziwiza
	Ndiwe muondoa kiza[I]
	Rabi kwa kueta yua[II]

There is no one with the power
To reject your will;
You, Lord, are the one who can ward off the darkness
By bringing sunshine.

I *kiza* Am. "dark, darkness" (Std. *giza*)| II *yua* (Std. *jua*) "sun, sunshine". (Std. *jua*)

7.	*Lolote likitupata*
	Ni lazima kufuata
	Tena pasina[I] kusita
	Wala kufurisha pua

Whatever happens to us,
We have to accept it.
We should not hesitate,
Nor be angry about it.[III]

I *pasina* Am. "there is not, without" (Std. *bila ya*) | II lit. "to snort with anger"

8.	*Twaamini kwa yakini*
	Akhira na duniani
	Insi hata majini
	Wote mbwa kuamriwa

We truly believe,
In the afterlife and in this world,
That human beings and even jinns
All receive orders.

9.	*Wote hutwii amri*
	Yako Ilahi Jabari
	Ulo na nguvu kahari
	Za kuhui na kuua

They all obey your order,
You, God the Restorer,
You, who has the strength and power
To give and to take lives.

10.	*Tumeamini kwa dhati*
	Lolote halitupati
	Tulo hai na mayiti
	Illa kwa kukadiriwa

We truly believe
Nothing ever happens to us,
To the living or the dead,
If it is not ordered by you.

11.	*Na sisi tumesalimu[I]*
	Amri kwako Rahimu

And we have given in
To your command, Merciful One

JAMII: TOPICAL ISSUES ON LAMU

Wala hatukulaumu	Nor do we complain
Kwa haya yamezokuwa	about what happens.

I -*salimu* < Ar. *salim amri* "to surrender."

12. *Tumewakosa ghafula* — We have lost them unexpectedly,
    Watu wengi kwa jumla — Plenty of people all at once,
    Kwa amri yako Mola — At your order, God—
    Utwekao[I] na kutua[II] — You who lift people up (to heaven) or send them down (to earth).

I *kutweka yuu* Am. "to lift sth. up" (Std. *kuweka juu*) | II *kutua* "to put sth. down". These verbs are often found in marine vocabulary, usually referring to the loading or unloading of a *jahazi* "dhow."

13. *Ndimi zetu kutamka* — Our tongues cannot speak
    Kuyanena yalotoka — To express what has occurred;
    Hazitoweza hakika — Certainly, they cannot—
    Kwa namna yalikuwa — Because of how it happened.

14. *Ni mambo mazito sana* — It is very tough
    Hayo kuweza kunena — To find some way to speak about it.
    Lakini budi hatuna — Still, we have no choice
    Yalo ndani[I] kuyatoa — But to speak our minds.

I *ndani*, lit. "inside," refers by extension here to the heart, the seat of our emotions, innermost part of the body.

15. *Yalo ndani ya mitima* — What is in our hearts
    Hututeketeza nyama — Burns our skin;
    Ndio haya kaatama — This is why I open my mouth—
    Asa yakapungua — To reduce the pain.

This stanza clearly shows the rationale behind this composition; as with the other texts Ustadh Mau has composed, e.g. *Mama msimlaumu*, *Hafi asiyetimiwa*, or *Mlango*, there is always a burning issue that triggers him to write the poem.

16. *Ni mambo sana mazito* — These are very heavy issues,
    Huwasha hushinda moto — Burning greater than fire,
    Si wakubwa si watoto — Easy neither for adults nor for children;
    Kwa wote ni sawa sawa — It is equally tough on all of them.

180   JAMII: TOPICAL ISSUES ON LAMU

17. *Ni kilio kilokwamba[1]*   It is a cry of grief that echoes everywhere:
    Kikaenea majumba   It spreads to all the houses.
    Hakuna ambao kwamba   There is not even
    Mmoya kilomvua   One who has been exempted.

1 *-wamba* Am., syn.: *-enea* "to spread out."

18. *Kimetutanganya sute*   It has affected us all,
    Pasi kutenga yoyote   Without exception.
    Lahaula[1] na tuete   "Lahaula"—let's say it!
    Tumshukuru Moliwa   Let us thank God.

1 This is the Ḥawqala (Ar. الحوقلة), a portmanteau of the Arabic words *ḥawla* ("might") and
quwwata ("power"). The full Ḥawqala is recited as follows: *lā ḥawla wa lā quwwata illā bil-
lāh* (لا حول ولا قوة إلا بالله), usually translated as "There is no might nor power except in
Allah." This expression is used by a Muslim whenever seized by calamity or in a situation
beyond their control. When uttered, it means that a person confesses his inability to do
anything except with God's help and facilitation.

19. *Hili si langu si lako*   This is not mine or yours personally,
    Ndetu sute sikitiko   But a grief shared by all of us.
    Cha mui[1] kibabaiko   It is the shock of the whole city,
    Na wangine huzidiwa   And for some all the more.

1 *mui* Am. "city" (Std. *mji*)

20. *Mtu mezokosa mke*   Someone who has lost his wife
    Huenga zijana zake   Looks at his children
    Kiwaza mwendani wake   And remembers his partner,
    Wa pili aliokuwa   His other half, who once was alive.

21. *Hangaliya mayatima*   He looks after the orphans,
    Wanuna[1] waso na mama   Infants without a mother,
    Kisongoyeka mtima   Whose hearts are in distress,
    Mato matozi kitoa   Tears falling from their eyes.

1 *wanuna* Baj. "the small ones" (Std. *wadogo*). On Lamu, the word appears only in literary
works and is part of an elevated style.

22. *Mama alokosa mwana*   Or the mother who lost her child
    Alokimpenda sana   Whom she loved so much—

JAMII: TOPICAL ISSUES ON LAMU

	Dharubu mno huona	For her it is a catastrophe
	Za kushindwa kutukua	That she cannot bear.
23.	*Walokosa akhawati*	People who lost their sisters—
	Huzuni haziwawati	Sadness will not leave them.
	Kula muda na wakati	Every single moment,
	Mswiba huwasumbua	Grief will trouble them.
24.	*Marafiki walokosa*	For those who lost their friends,
	Jaraha halitoisa	The wound will never heal.
	Takuwa huanda sasa	It will bleed anew
	Kikumbuka yalokuwa	Whenever they recall what has happened.
25.	*Walokosa majirani*	Those who lost their neighbors—
	Watakuwa hali gani	How will they feel
	Wakikumbuka hisani	When they start remembering their kind-ness
	Na mambo yalozowewa	And all they used to do?
26.	*Nao waliotanganya*	For those who have lost several family mem-bers,
	Wake zao na zijana	
	Wangine wakiwaona	Their wives and their children,
	Nyonyoni hulia ngoa	When they see [the wives and children] of others,
		Their hearts will be full of jealousy.
27.	*Na watu mui mzima*	For all the people of the city,
	Huzuni hazitokoma	The grief will never end.
	Watakumbuka daima	They will always remember it,
	Kulla wakihadithiwa	Every time they hear this story.
28.	*Milele yatasalia*	What has happened
	Haya yamezotokea	Will last forever,
	Nyaka toka nyaka ngia	Year in, year out.
	Kwelezwa wasiozawa	It will be told about for generations to come.
29.	*Kwandika mangi siwezi*	I can't write much about it,
	Kwa kunizidi simazi	For it makes me even sadder.

	Hutetateta matozi	I am fighting back tears;
	Mato siwezi kuvua	I can't open my eyes.

30.
Kabla siyamaliza — Before finishing,
Naomba Mola Muweza — I beg God the Mighty:
Atujazi njema jaza — May He reward us,
Na khaswa waliofiliwa — Especially those who have been bereaved.

31.
Tupe nyoyo[I] za subira — Give us the stamina to be patient,
Tupate malipwa bora[II] — So that we may obtain the best reward.
Tusitanganye khasara — Let us not get carried away with loss,
Ya funguni[III] kutolewa — Lest we be denied our share.

I *nyoyo* Am. "heart" (Std. *moyo*) | II Ustadh Mau is referring to Qur. 39:10, which urges human beings to be patient, not harboring other thoughts inside their hearts: "He knows the thoughts within the breasts" (Abr., 472). | III *fungu* "share," referring acc. to Mau to the heavenly "reward granted to those who are patient (*fungu la lile la wenye subira*).

32.
Fungu ni la wanosubiri — That share is for those who are patient,
Wapatapo maathuri — Even if they are bereaved
Kama haya yalojiri — By a catastrophe, like the one that happened,
Zipendi kuondolea — Where their loved ones are taken away from them.

33.
Utupe nguvu Jalali — Give us strength, Majestic One,
Tuweze kutahamali[I] — So that we can bear it.
Mswiba hunu thakili[II] — This sorrow is heavy;
Nyoyo[III] zimezoatua[IV] — Our hearts are broken.

I *kutahamali* Ar. "to bear," "to tolerate" (Std. *kuvumilia*) | II *thakili* Ar. "heavy" (Std. *nzito*) | III *nyoyo* Baj. "hearts" (Std. *mioyo*) | IV *-atua* Baj. "to be broken," "to split" (Std. *pasua*)

34.
Yailahi ya Mannani — Oh God, oh Generous One,
Tupe nyoyo ya imani — Fill our hearts with faith.
Tusingie makosani — Let us make no mistakes,
Kwa mambo kuyapotoa — Lest we spoil things.

35.
Nao wote marhumu[I] — And all those who died,
Marahamu yarahimu — Give them your mercy.

JAMII: TOPICAL ISSUES ON LAMU 183

Kwenye janati naimu[II]	To marvelous paradise
Wafuze[III] *ndani kutua*	May they go straight away.

I *marhumu* < Ar. "the deceased" | II *janati naimu* < Ar. "marvelous eden" | III *fuza*—Mau paraphrases this as *kwenda moja kwa moja* "to go directly."

36.	*Wanali na kusuudi*[I]	May they be lucky and obtain
	Daraja za mashahidi[II]	The status of martyrs;
	Wawe nae Muhamadi	May they be with Muhammad,
	Kipendi chetu rasua	Our beloved Prophet.

I *-suudi* < *sa'ada* Ar. "fortune" (Std. *bahati*). See the proverb *hasidi hasudi* "The jeaolous one does not succeed." | II According to Mau, "The one who drowns in the sea receives the status of martyr" (*mtu anayekufa baharini ana daraja ya shahidi*). They go directly to heaven in reward for their suffering. According to the hadith by Abu Huraira, there are five types of martyrs: the one who dies of a plague, the one who dies of stomach disease, the one who drowns, the one who dies under debris, and the one who dies in the way of Allah the Almighty.

37.	*Maini waloghariki*	Those who have drowned at sea
	Mewatukuza Khalaki	Have been rewarded by the Creator
	Kwa kuwapa cheo hiki	By receiving this status,
	Kikubwa cha kuzengewa	A great one that everyone desires.

38.	*Hakuna la kuwaswibu*[I]	Nothing will happen to them,
	Kabisa lenye taabu	Nothing at all bad;
	Kwa uwezo wa Wahabu	By the power of the Giver,
	Dhambi wameghufiriwa	All their sins have been washed away.

I *kumswibu mtu* "to happen to sb." (Std. *kumpata mtu*)

39.	*Rabi mewapa daraja*	The Lord has given them the high status
	Waitamanio waja	That humans long for,
	Na kwetu sute ni haja	And for us, it is our common desire
	Daraja hio kupoa	To be given this status.

40.	*Mola amewakhitari*	God has selected them
	Kuwavika lenye nuri	To award them a crown of light,
	Koja lao abrari[I]	The crown of the righteous people,
	Watu waloteuliwa	The chosen ones.

I *abrari* < Ar. "righteous" (Std. *barabara*)

184   JAMII: TOPICAL ISSUES ON LAMU

41. *Hili nalitatuliwaze* Let this be our relief,
    Na nyoyo litupumbaze And let this comfort our hearts,
    Kwa kuyua darajaze Being assured of the position
    Wao walotunikiwa That they have been awarded.

42. *Natusituse mipaka* Let us not cross boundaries
    Katika kuhuzunika In our sadness;
    Tuketi tukikumbuka Let us take our time and remember
    Mambo yamekadiriwa What was destined to be.

43. *Nimekoma wasalamu* I have reached the end,
    Naimaliza nudhumu And I complete my composition
    Kwa kumuomba Karimu By asking the most Generous One,
    Atupe yake afua May He grant us well-being.

44. *Tuafu Rabi tuafu* Protect us God, protect us;
    Utwepulie machafu Keep us away from improprieties
    Na kulla ya uvundifu And everything that is destructive.
    Ndiwe mwenye kuyepuwa You are the one who can prevent it.

45. *Ulotupija kibati* The punishment that you imposed
    Kwa makosa twalohiti For the sins we committed—
    Yallahi Jabaruti Oh God, the most Powerful One,
    Taabani tumekuwa We have been miserable.

46. *Ya Rabi haya mateso* Oh God, let these troubles
    Yawe basi ndio mwiso Finally be our last.
    Zing'arishe zetu nyuso Make our faces shine,
    Na nyoyo kuzikatua And purify our hearts.

47. *Twepulie kulla dhiki* Take away from us every agony
    Tulizo nazo Khalaki We are suffering from, Creator.
    Tupe kundufu¹ riziki Provide for us abundantly
    Matata kuyatatua To assuage our concerns.

   1 *kundufu* "abundant" (cf. *moyo mkundufu* lit. "an open heart," referring to "someone who
   is happy").

48. *Twepulie kulla baa* Keep away from us all misfortune;
    Utupe ya manufaa Give us what is of benefit to us.

Na hiki kizazaa[1]	And this huge sorrow,
Ukikomeshe Moliwa	Put an end to it, oh God!

1 *kizazaa*, syn.: *mswiba*. Mau paraphrases it as *ule mswiba uliotokea* "the grief that occurred."

49.
Rabi situonde tena	Lord, don't test us again
Kwa haya tumezoona	With what we have experienced,
Kwani ni mazito sana	Because it is very hard;
Na sute tumeemewa	We are all in shock.

50.
Ya Rabi iwe ni basi	Oh God, let it come to an end;
Mola turahamu nasi	God, have mercy on us.
Ziwaswiike[1] *nafusi*	May our souls rejoice,
Na miswiba kuyondoa	And take all our sorrow away.

1 *kuwaswika* "to rejoice" (Std. *kufurahika*)

51.
Rabi yatie kikomo	Lord, put an end to it.
Yafusie kwenye shimo	Cover it in a pit;
Yasalie momo homo	May the sorrows remain there,
Miini kutoetewa	And not be brought to the cities again.

52.
Rabi Mola yamalize	God, Lord, finish it;
Mazito usitwengeze	Don't put any more burdens on our
Na haya utuweleze	shoulders,
Kuweza kuyatukua	And enable us
	To carry the ones we have.

53.
Ya Rabi zako neema	Oh Lord, Your blessings—
Utuete daima	Bestow them on us forever.
Utwepulie nakama	Keep all suffering away from us;
Zisitubakie toa	May no scars remain on us.

54.
Tuswafishe tuswafike	Purify us and we will be pure.
Waume na wanawake	Men and women,
Amrizo tuzishike	Let us submit to Your orders
Zote tuloamriwa	To all Your commands.

55.
Ya Rabi tupe auni	Oh God, help us:
Tushikamane na dini	Let us embrace faith

	Na kumshinda shetwani	And defeat the devil
	Na kulla mlaaniwa	And every evil person.

56. *Amina Rabi Amina*   Amen, oh Lord, amen.
    Tuafikie¹ Rabana   Let us agree, our God,
    Haya tumezoyanena   On what we have said,
    Kabuli kupitishiwa   On what should happen in the future.

1 -*afikia* Ar., syn.: -*himiza.*

57. *Na mtu alonudhumu*   The person who composed this poem
    Ni Mahmudu isimu   Is called Mahmoud.
    Makazi ni hapa Amu   My home is here in Lamu;
    Na ndiko nilipozawa   This is also where I was born.

2   *Bandari ina mawimbi* ("The Port Makes Waves")

Ustadh Mau composed this poem on November 27, 2010, on the occasion of
a workshop held to inform the people of Lamu about the deep-water port
that had begun being constructed. The people of Lamu had complained that
although there was an initial meeting under Minister Ali Makwere, they had
not been properly informed about the construction plans, nor about any fin-
ancial compensation for those who owned the land on which the port would
be built. Furthermore, they also wanted to know more about the potential jobs
that the community could benefit from. The international company construct-
ing the port reacted to the complaints by sending a group of representatives
to provide the community of Lamu with more information. The deep-water
port—the biggest of its kind from Eritrea to South Africa, and a trinational
project involving Kenya, South Sudan, and Ethiopia—had caused a lot of spec-
ulation and rumors in the Lamu archipelago. Up to that point, the community
had often discussed the port, and was generally divided between those who saw
the port as a major opportunity to provide new jobs, and others—fishermen
and Islamic leaders, for instance—who worried about what the port would
bring. For the fishermen, the port would mean the loss of their fishing grounds;
Islamic leaders, meanwhile, recognized that the port would bring many for-
eigners, from both up-country and outside the country, with different cultural
values.

Ustadh Mau reacted to these heated debates by composing a poem. He
encourages people to prepare themselves for the port, which will need skilled

JAMII: TOPICAL ISSUES ON LAMU

workers. To underline the disruptive effect of the port, he compares it to a tsunami (stz. 7).

1. *Bismillahi awwali, kwa ina lake Jalali*
   Twaanda yetu kauli, ya karibu kuwambiya

   In the name of God first, in the name of the Almighty,
   We start our speech by welcoming you.

2. *Twawambiya karibuni, wenyeji piya wageni*
   Karibiyani ngomeni, muhadhara kusikiya

   We say *karibuni* to the hosts and guests.
   Come to the fort[1] to listen to the lecture.

   1 *ngomeni*, from *ngome* "fort"; refers to the fort in Lamu's old town, which nowadays hosts important meetings and workshops, like the one this poem is referring to.

3. *Muhadhara mufahamu, madda yake ni muhimu*
   Khususwa kwetu Waamu, dharura kuzingatiya

   Be aware, the subject of the meeting is important.
   Especially for us Lamu people, it is important to ponder it.

4. *Tupulike kwa makini, tuyatiye akilini*
   Na kisa twangaliyeni, ipi ya kwandama ndiya

   Let us listen carefully and reflect upon it,
   So that we can ultimately decide which way to go.

5. *Muhadhara mbwa bandari, yaweza kuwa ni kheri*
   Pangine ikawa shari, balaya ikatweteya

   The meeting concerns the port, which might bring good fortune,
   But can also bring destruction and ruin to us.

6. *Sharuti tuiyandaye, tangu sasa tuangaliye*
   Tusineneni niiye, mbona yamekuwa haya

   We must be prepared; from now on we should have a plan,
   Lest we wonder: why did it turn out this way?

7. *Bandari ina sunami, mawimbiye hayakomi*
   Chochote hakisimami, kwa kifuwa kuziwiya

   The port causes a tsunami, bringing endless waves.
   Nothing can resist them, no matter how hard one tries.

8. *Sunami hiyo ni kali, itazowa ma'adili*
   Ni sharuti yambo hili, akilini kulitiya

   The tsunami is so strong, it will wash away our moral standards.
   It is important for us to consider this.

9. *Sharuti tuwe imara, kuunda twabiya bora*
   Tuimarishe fikira, za kutuonesha ndiya

   We must stand firm and build good characters.
   We should strengthen the thoughts that will guide us on the right
   path.

10. *Tuipindeni mapema, kwa masomo kuyasoma*
    Tukitaka wetu umma, nao funguni kungiya

    We should quickly make an effort to study the relevant disciplines,
    If we want our community to get its share.

11. *Au tutamiza mate, na chochote tusipate*
    Watavuna tangu tete, kwa yuu wamezokuya

    Otherwise, we will remain longing for it, without getting anything,
    While others will profit already from the first harvest.

12. *Na tuwe wakakamavu, tukitaka kula mbivu*
    Tukibaki na uzivu, patupu taambuliya

    Let us be steadfast, so that we may eat ripe fruit.[1]
    If we remain lazy, we will have nothing to bite.

    1 See the proverb *Mvumilivu hula mbivu* "The one who is patient eats ripe fruits."

13. *Na hakuna cha bwerere, tusiitezeni shere*
    Ni sharuti tuikere, haki yetu kuteteya

JAMII: TOPICAL ISSUES ON LAMU   189

Nothing comes without effort. Let us not deceive ourselves.
We have to struggle if we want to fight for our rights.

14. *Ni kinyang'anyiro¹ hiki, kiwa ziwawa hutaki*
    Ng'o! Kitu hushiki, wendo watanyang'anyiya

    The winner is the one who is faster than the others. If you do not like
    to compete,
    You will never get it, but your opponents will snatch it away from you.

    1 *kinyang'anyiro* "a kind of competition or game, which depends on who is quicker or
    cleverer than the others" <*nyang'anya* "to take sth. away from somebody by force" (Scl. 695:
    "ravir qqch. à qqn., se rendre maître par violence"); see also *-nyang'anyiya* in the second
    verse.

15. *Tukisaliya na pwaji, na kwingi kuipa miji*
    Na hayazoleki maji, fahamu tukiyamwaya

    If we remain idle, speaking ill and boasting—
    Remember, once spilled, water cannot be gathered up again.

16. *Maneno tupunguzeni, na zitendo tutendeni*
    Ng'ombe hangii zizini, kwa tupuu domo kaya

    Let us stop talking and act instead.
    You do not get cows to enter the stable only by idle talk.

17. *Hapa tailazimisha, maneno kuyakomesha*
    Na ingawa huniwasha, mengi yaloyosaliya

    I will force myself to stop my words here,
    Although the words yet unsaid keep urging me to talk.

18. *Kauli yangu tammati, kwa hizi chache baiti*
    Huwa ni tamu katiti¹, wa nyuma walitwambiya

    With these few verses, I end my talk.
    Short is sweet; that is what our ancestors told us.

    1 *katiti* Am. "a bit" (Std. *kidogo*); see the proverb *Katiti tamu, kingi kuembeza* "Short is sweet;
    a lot makes you feel sick."

190 JAMII: TOPICAL ISSUES ON LAMU

3   *Jahazi* ("The Dhow")

Ustadh Mau uses the Lamuan maritime symbol of the *jahazi* ("dhow") to dis-
cuss the state of his island's economy, which gradually declined in the 1990s.
He particularly intends to portray the situation of economic statis: "I was refer-
ring to the economic situation on Lamu, when the economy was in a bad state"
(*Nalikusudiya hali ya uchumi wa Lamu ulikuwa uchumi umeharibika sana*, stz.
42). His inspiration came from the idiomatic expression *tanga liembete na mon-
goti* ("The sail is attached to the mast"), which he had overheard in the street,
uttered by a vendor of skewered meat (*mishikaki*). The street vendor used the
expression to complain about the bad economy. The saying is meant to describe
a calm moment, without any wind (*shwari*), when the ship does not move
(*jahazi haitembei*) and the sail (*t'anga*) is attached to the mast of the sailing
vessel (*mlingoti*; Am. *mongoti*). Ustadh Mau uses this image to depict a moment
when there is no economic hustle and bustle (*harakati za biashara*). Hearing it
by chance, he had the idea to write this poem.[2]

1.   *Liembete na mongoti[I], tanga kwa lingi shuwari*
      Hautukuti ukuti, imetuwama bahari
      Hata mai[II] hayavuti, tutapatae bandari

      The sail is attached to the mast in the intense calm.
      Not even a twig is moving, the sea is so settled.
      There is not even a current; how will we reach the harbor?

      I *mongoti* Am. "mast" (Std. *mlingoti*), a term Ahmed Sheikh Nabhany explains as: *mti mrefu
      unaosimamishwa katika chombo ili kuweza kuzuwiliya tanga ambalo limefungwa katika
      foromani* ("a tall mast that is put on the boat to support the sail, which is attached to the
      yard of the ship") (Nab. 35). | II *mai* Am. "water" (Std. *maji*)

2.   *Ngurudi[I] imeshopoka, mai ngamani[II] hujiri*
      Haitaki kuzibika, na hata kwa misumari
      Kuyafua[III] tumechoka, mikono hutuhairi[IV]

      The stopper is out, and water is pouring into the bilge;
      It doesn't want to be plugged, not even with nails.
      We are too tired to scoop the water out; our hands hurt.

---

2   For further criticism on this poem and the imagery of the ocean, animating the poet's mem-
     oirs and oeuvre and providing him with a means to reflect upon his lifeworld, see also Anna-

I *ngurudi* "special openings on the sides of the ship to allow the water to run off the deck" (Std. *nguruzi*). | II *ngama "bilge,"* a term explained by Nabahany as: *mahala nyuma ya jahazi au tezi ambapo maji yanoyoingiya hushukiya hapo, ikiwa yamengiya kwa omo au kwa tezi* ("The part at the end of the dhow or the stern where the water that enters the dhow from starboard or port side collects") (Nab. 36). | III *-fua*—According to Mau, *ku-yachota (maji) na kumwaga nje* ("to scoop up the water and pour it out of the boat"). | IV *-hairi* Ar. "to hurt" (Std. *-uma*)

3. *Tumekosa taratibu, hatuna tena shauri*
   Na bandari si karibu, hakupiti manuwari
   Zimetutanda dharubu, metuzunguka khatari

   We have lost our way; we don't have any plans,
   And the harbor is not even nearby; no ship is passing by.
   Difficulty has engulfed us and danger surrounds us.

4. *Hatuisi la kutenda, tumeshindwa kufikiri*
   Kiza kingi kimetanda, kote kimepija dori
   Ni heri mwamba kupanda, kama hunu utiriri

   We don't know what to do; we have run out of ideas.
   Total darkness is engulfing us.
   It is better to hit a coral reef than [confront] this nuisance.

5. *Hatuna ila Manani, wa kumuomba Jabari*
   Atwegeshe nasi pwani, yapokuwa kwa kihori
   Tuokowe Rahamani, waja wako tusitiri

   We have no one to pray to except God the Almighty.
   May he take us to the shore, even by canoe.
   Save us, most Merciful one; protect us, your servants.

6. *Suwali si la jahazi, hili katika shairi*
   Litambuweni wayuzi, mafundi mulo hodari
   Wa mtoni wendambizi, muzizamiayo duri[I]

---

chiara Raia "Angaliya baharini, mai yaliyoko pwani: The Presence of the Ocean in Mahmoud Ahmed Abdulkadir's Poetry." In *Lugha na fasihi. Scritti in onore e memoria di/Essays in Honour and Memory of Elena Bertoncini Zúbková*, edited by Flavia Aiello and Roberto Gaudioso (Naples: Università degli Studi di Napoli "L'Orientale," 2019), 223–250.

192   JAMII: TOPICAL ISSUES ON LAMU

The theme of the poem is not the *dhow*.
May the discerning and talented artists understand;
Let the deep-sea divers dive in pursuit of pearls.

1 *duri* syn.: *lulu* "pearl" (Mau).

4   *Tupijeni makamama* ("Let Us Embrace")

This is a twelve-stanza *shairi* poem that Ustadh Mau composed in 2010 for a
conference dedicated to the culture of the Swahili people, organized by the
Research Institute of Swahili Studies of Eastern Africa. In a similar tone as
Za Washirazi athari, the poet feels compelled to say a few words, and prom-
ises not to be too verbose. The major issue he is concerned with and begs his
people hear him on concerns their own culture and customs, which he feels to
be threatened (see also *Kilio huliya mwenye* and *Kiswahili*). Again, he borrows
the ship metaphor: he compares Swahili culture to a ship that, if abandoned
or forgotten, will sink (see stz. 2). *Tupijeni makamama* is thus an exhortation
addressed to the Swahili community. In stanza 3, he explicitly states the risk
at hand: becoming merely a shadow of oneself. He speaks out against the
dichotomous conceptualization of traditional heritage and progress as mutu-
ally exclusive of one another. Culture is not a barrier to progress or anathema
to modern education or technology: after all, does the taste of tea come from its
color, or from the way it is prepared and the ingredients it is made of? Instead
of waiting passively without taking any action, Ustadh Mau urges the audience
to study modern technology and to acquire as much knowledge and skill as
possible, while at the same time not relinquishing their moral standards. The
role model for him is Japan (see also *Kiswahili*), since the country has become
a world economic and technological leader without investing in destructive
technology, like bombs, in his opinion. At the end of the poem, Ustadh Mau
thanks the organizers of the conference by referring to them as captains guid-
ing the boats in the direction of a new era, toward change.

1.   *Muliyopo hadhirani waume na wanawake*
      Masikizi funguwani maozi musiyawike
      Nina machache moyoni napenda niyatapike
      Naomba munipulike

      All of you present in the audience, men and women—
      Open your ears; do not lower your gaze.

I have a few thoughts on my mind that I would like to express:
I beg you to listen.

2. *Sitoyafanya marefu nitakayowaeleza*
    Machache tawaarifu kusudi kutowembeza
    Tusiiyone ni dufu mila yetu tukapuza
    Chombo chetu kitasoza

It will not take much time to explain it to you;
Just a few things I will inform you about, with the intention not to bore you.
We should not see ourselves as ignorant or neglect our customs,
Otherwise our ship will sink.

3. *Tupijeni makamama mila yetu ya aswili*
    Kwani hatukuwa nyuma twali mbee Waswahili
    Mila tukiisukuma hatutoshika mahali
    Tutasaliya zivuli

Let us embrace our original customs,
For we did not lag behind: we Swahili were advanced.
If we brush aside our customs, we will have nothing to hold onto;
We shall remain shadows.

4. *Mila yetu si kikwazo kwenda mbee haipingi*
    Tusome tuhitajizo na ilimu nyingi nyingi
    Tuepuke ya muwozo yasokuwa na misingi
    Tamu ya chai si rangi

Our customs are not a hindrance; they do not hinder progress.
We should study what we need: diverse disciplines.
We should avoid matters that lead to decay, that lack any serious foundation:
The sweetness of tea is not in its color.

5. *Zama za utandawazi mipaka imeondoka*
    Aswilani hatuwezi pweke yetu kutengeka
    Zilizopita zizazi mno zalihifadhika
    Mambo sasa megeuka

In the era of globalization, the boundaries are gone;
We absolutely cannot isolate ourselves.
Previous generations were very well protected;
Now things have changed.

6. *Natuweni na hadhari twangaliye kwa makini*
Tutenge yaso mazuri hayo tusipokeeni
Na tufanyeni shauri kuzama tusingojeni
Tutangia lawamani

We should be cautious, watching out carefully:
We need to avoid what is no good; this is what we should not adopt.
Let us make a plan, so that we are not merely waiting to drown;
Otherwise, the blame is on us.

7. *Kutumiya si makosa za sasa ala na zombo*
Wa lakini yatupasa tuifunde na mitambo
Tusibaki kubebesa likitokeya la kombo
Si mambo hayo si mambo

It is not a mistake to use modern tools and equipment;
Rather, it is a must to teach ourselves new technology
If only just not to be dumbfounded when something goes wrong.
This is certainly not the way—not the way.

8. *Tuifunde kwa undani na mambo tuyafahamu*
Twangaliye Majapani hawayaundi mabomu
Lakini ulimwenguni Japani ni maimamu
Waendemwe na kaumu

We should thoroughly study modern subjects, so that we understand them.
Let us consider the Japanese; they do not construct bombs,
But in this world, the Japanese are leaders—
They are followed by the masses.

9. *Ulimwengu haukiri umma uliyo dhaifu*
Na tufanyeni shauri tukitaka utukufu
Zilizopita fakhari sasa hazifui dafu[1]
Yatakiwa ubunifu

JAMII: TOPICAL ISSUES ON LAMU

The world does not indulge a weak nation.
We should reach a consensus if we want excellence;
What caused pride in the past is of no avail now.
Creativity is needed.

1 -*fua dafu* "to be capable of doing something," lit. "to strike the unripe coconut."

10. *Na tubuni yetu sasa kwa misinji ya zamani*
    Maadili kutotusa mipaka tusiukeni
    Tuyapijeni msasa¹ ya kae tufufuweni
    Na usasa tutakeni

Let us now create our own culture on the foundations of the past.
We should not transgress morality; let us not trespass boundaries.
Let us smoothen what remains from our past,
And let us embrace modernity.

1 *msasa* "a kind of sandpaper used to make the surface of wood smooth." Here the narrator urges the audience not merely to take over Western technology without further reflection or without adapting it to the local context, which in his view would endanger local morality. Thus, one needs to "use sandpaper" to get rid of the unwanted aspects of modernity.

11. *Usasa twauhitaji katika yetu maisha*
    Kutuwama kama maji mwiso kutatunukisha
    Kwa ndoto mambo hayaji mwenye kulinda hukesha
    Havuni asiyonosha

Modernity is what we need in our lives.
Stagnating like water will make us stink in the end.
Things do not come true by dreaming about them; the watchman stays awake.
The one who does not irrigate, will not harvest.

12. *Tamati sitoongeza narudisha shukurani*
    Nashukuru manahuza wapeka mashua hini
    Inshallah hatutosoza tutapata bandarini
    Kipenda Mola Mannani

This is the end; I will continue no more. I offer my gratitude:
I thank the captains who sail these boats.
God willing, we will not drown; we will reach the port.
If the Almighty wills it.

Ilimu: The Importance of Education

FIGURE 15   Ustadh Mahmoud Mau visiting a school in the village of Barigoni on the mainland

1   *Mwalimu* ("Teacher")

Ustadh Mau composed this *shairi* in 2005, when the Kenya National Union of Teachers, the national association of teachers, invited him to contribute a sermon (*khutba*) for their assembly. Instead of inviting him to deliver the sermon, they asked him for a written sermon. Ustadh Mau objected; he said that he preferred not to submit a written sermon, because a written sermon loses all its flavor: it is like *bario* "leftover food" (*ni kama bario yaani chakula kilicholala*). He proposed to write and send a *shairi* instead. The poem echoes Mahmoud's own concern with education, which for him is an utmost priority. It is a precondition for the development not only of every individual, but also for society as a whole. In the poem, he highlights the importance of the teacher, who is "number one," i.e. of utmost importance, doing the most important job in and for society. It is studying that makes an individual a productive member of society. He reminds teachers, who often lack respect in a society where value is increasingly measured by the amount of money one earns at their job, to esteem their work and take pride in it. He also encourages teachers to make the effort to con-

ILIMU: THE IMPORTANCE OF EDUCATION   197

stantly increase their knowledge and not stop studying. Furthermore, for him, teaching does not just imply conveying knowledge, but being a moral guide and role model to the students. The poem has previously been translated by Mohamed Karama, whose translation we have revised here.

1. *Mabibi piya mabwana, mulioka hadhirani*
   Ni furaha nyingi sana, kuwa na nyinyi wendani
   Mimi ninavowaona, nyinyi ndio namba wani

   Ladies and gentlemen at this gathering today,
   I am very happy to be with you, my fellows.
   The way I see you, you are number one.

2. *Ni namba wani nasema, popote ulimwenguni*
   Tokea zama za nyuma, na za sasa za angani
   Mtu bila ya kusoma, ni nani hebu semeni

   I am telling you, you have been number one all over the world,
   From the most ancient times until the current era.
   Tell me, what is a human being without education?

3. *Mtu ende aendako, hata apae hewani*
   Ni chuoni hapo kwako, alipitia yakini
   Ni tunda la kazi yako, basi nawe jithamini

   No matter where one goes, even if one flies through the air,
   One must certainly have first passed through your school.
   This is the fruit of your labor, so teacher, take pride in yourself.

4. *Jithamini jihishimu, siwe na shaka moyoni*
   Juwa wewe ni muhimu, ni kuu yako thamani
   Bila ya wewe mwalimu, hakuna la kumkini

   Respect and value yourself; don't harbor doubt in your heart.
   Know that you are important; you are of great value.
   Without you, teacher, nothing is possible.

5. *Mwalimu bila ya wewe, unaeshinda shuleni*
   Nyumbani usipumuwe, ukakesha vitabuni
   Hatupati uelewe, wakuishika sukani

Oh teacher, without you who spends the day at school—
At home, you don't rest, but pass the night buried in books—
Understand, without you we wouldn't have someone to hold the steering wheel.

6. *Mwalimu wako uwezo, ni mkuu kwa yakini*
   Siufanyiye matezo, usiuwone ni duni
   Siketi kwenye pambizo, ngiya ndani wandani[1]

Teacher, you certainly have great abilities.
Don't underestimate yourself; don't think you are worthless.
Don't shy away, but get into full swing.

1 *wandani* = *uwandani* (Std. *uwanjani*) "dance floor."

7. *Ndani uwandani ngiya, usiketi pambizoni*
   Wazazi wamekweteya, zipande zao za ini
   Musaidane kuleya, pamoja muwaudeni

Go for it—do not shy away.
The parents have sent their precious children to you.
Help each other; assist each other in bringing the child up together.

8. *Haitoshi kusomesha, kwa kwandika ubaoni*
   Ni dharura kufundisha, kwa mwendo wa maishani
   Sura njema kuonesha, wanafunzi igizani

It is not enough to teach by writing on the blackboard;
It is important to teach them how to live in this world.
The good example you provide, pupils will imitate it!

9. *Wewe kwao kiigizo, wakutizama makini*
   Wawapa wengi mafunzo, hata kwa mwendo ndiyani
   Hiyo kazi si mchezo, kufundisha fahamuni

You are a role model for the children to carefully observe.
You teach them a lot, even how to behave in the streets.
The job of teaching is not a joke—consider it.

ILIMU: THE IMPORTANCE OF EDUCATION

10. *Bila ya uwaminifu, na ucha Mungu moyoni*
    Hatupati ufafanifu, si wa duniya si dini
    Natupange zetu swafu, kwa kite tusomesheni

    Without being faithful and pious at heart,
    We will never succeed, neither in secular nor in religious education.
    Let us join hands; let us educate them with empathy.

11. *Twapokeya mshahara, twalipwa kwa kazi hini*
    Natufanye kazi bora, ili halali tuleni
    Tufundisheni kwa ghera, wanafunzi tusikhini

    We receive a salary; we are paid for this job.
    Let's do our best so that we achieve virtuous results.
    Let's make an effort at teaching; let us not let the pupils down.

12. *Tusiwache watafiti, na wakubwa hafisini*
    Tumche kula wakati, Mola aliye mbinguni
    Tufanye kazi kwa dhati, tungakosa shukurani

    Let us not be afraid of the inspectors and senior officers,
    But let us always fear God, who is in heaven.
    Let us work harder, even though people might not be grateful for it.

13. *Tufanye mbwetu wajibu, tumeitweka shingoni*
    Tutarajiye thawabu, kutoka kwake Mannani
    Tatulipa kwa taabu, ni Mwelewa si khaini

    This is our responsibility; we have taken it on our shoulders.
    Let us expect a heavenly reward from him, the Giver.
    God will reward us for our efforts; He is the one who understands—He
    will not let us down.

14. *Na mwisho nawahimiza, nduzangu natusomeni*
    Tusomeni kwa kufuza, wala tusikhitimuni
    Maarifa kuongeza, kula siku sichokeni

    I finally encourage you, my brothers: let us also study.
    Let us study continuously and let it not come to an end.
    Let us not tire of increasing our knowledge every day.

15. *Tusome tena tusome, dhihaka tuziwateni*
Wenzetu tuwatizame, walivojaa zuwoni
Nasi tufanye shime, kushindwa tusikirini

Let us study, really study; let us stop playing games.
My fellow teachers, let us consider how many have joined the institutes,
So let us also make an effort, and let us not accept defeat.

16. *Kauli yangu tammati, hapa ndipo kikomoni*
Wageni nanyi wanati, nawaomba samahani
Kwa lolote nilohiti, niko kwenu maguuni

This is the end of my talk; this is where I will stop.
Guests and hosts, I apologize
For any mistake; I pay you obeisance.

2 *Kilio huliya mwenye* ("Change Begins at Home")

The saying *Kulia huliya mwenye, na mtu mbali kalia*, "If the affected one cries out, another will join in from afar," means that if you want to change something, you first have to do it yourself, so that others may then join in support.

Ustadh Mau wrote this poem in 2006 to inaugurate an international conference on popular culture in East Africa that had been organized in Mombasa by Andrew Eisenberg and Ann Biersteker. An international audience was present at the conference. This poem is reminiscent of his poem *Kiswahili*, in which he complains about the Swahili people deliberately abandoning their culture. In this poem, he laments the loss of values as well as pride in one's own culture, but the addressee is rather the West, which he believes to impose its values on all other cultures. As he says, many people on Lamu generally agree with him that their culture is under threat and should be protected, but, as he also notes, many do nothing to protect it. He gives the example of the Lamu Museum, meant to protect the local culture, but where the museum staff wears jeans—which, for him, is a contradiction.

1. *Naanda kwa shukurani kwa wote walohusika*
Wazo waliolibuni ni muhiumu kwa hakika
Mbali mbali tamaduni hapa zimejumuika

ILIMU: THE IMPORTANCE OF EDUCATION

I start by expressing my gratitude to all the organizers.
The idea they came up with is certainly important;
People of different cultures have gathered here.

2. *Wa hapa wa uzunguni wa Asia kadhalika*
    Walotoka zisiwani na bara la Afrika
    Mafundi wa nyingi fani na wasomi wasifika

People from here, from the West as well as from Asia,
Those who came from the islands and from the African mainland,
Experts in many fields and reputed scholars.

3. *Ni kubwa dalili hini ulimwengu mekutika[1]*
    Tumo katika sahani tukiiza tukitaka
    Hakuna tena ugeni milango imefunguka

This is a true sign that the world has shrunk:
We are in the same boat, whether we agree with it or not.
Foreignness is no more; the doors have opened.

1 -*kutika* "to shrink" (Std. -*kunjika*)

4. *Hata ngiya kipembeni hutoweza kutengeka*
    Funga mlango chumbani na madirisha shindika
    Yatakuingilia ndani bila hodi kutamka

Even retreating to the farthest corner, you will not be able to isolate
yourself.
Close the door of your room and keep the windows shut;
Things from outside will still reach you without even knocking at the
door.

5. *Yanayotoka tezini na omo kutiririka*
    Yadirikeni ngamani si kwa hiyari kumbuka
    Ni hukumu ya kanuni ya mambo kubadilika

The water that comes from the stern and flows from the bow,
Both reach the sinkhole; remember, there is no other option.
It is an inert principle that things change.

6. *Tusikirini wendani gozi letu kutwauka[1]*
   Kwenye yetu tubakini kwa mila tumetosheka
   Tusitwae ya wageni ila tunapodhikika

   My companions, let us not acquiesce to shedding our skin:
   Let us remain in our own, for our customs are rich enough.
   Let us not adopt foreign customs, except when we need them.

   1 *-twauka* "to shed the skin."

7. *Masomo tutapieni[1] ilimu kuilimbika*
   Tupije mbizi za ndani na lulu tupate zuka
   Ilimu si ya fulani wala haina mipaka

   Let us strive for better education and accumulate knowledge.
   Let us dive deeply, so that we may come back with pearls.
   Knowledge does not belong just to one people nor does it have limits.

   1 *-tapia* Mau: "to be eager to do sth. or to find sth. quickly" (*-fuata harakaharaka*).

8. *Sindano na tutieni kinga ipate inuka*
   Kwa yetu tutoshekeni ndipo tutasalimika
   Majinzi na tuvueni turudi tulikotoka

   Let us be vaccinated, so that we may build up resistance,
   And let us be satisfied with our culture; this is the way to thrive.
   Let us get rid of the jeans, and let us go back to where we come from.

9. *Hambaga tusileni tusiizowee koka*
   Hatuwi na punguwani hizo tukiziepuka
   Kwa zetu tutoshekeni ni mafundi wa kupika

   Let us not eat hamburgers, and not get used to Coca-Cola;
   We won't miss anything if we avoid these things.
   Let us be satisfied with our culinary arts, as we ourselves are cooking experts.

ILIMU: THE IMPORTANCE OF EDUCATION

10. *Tubaki Uswahilini na tusiweni mateka*
    Kwa dharura tuazimeni ikiwa yahitajika
    Kama samli tuweni maini kutodeuka[1]

    [1] *-deuka* "to melt" (Std. *-yeyuka*)

    Let us remain in our Swahiliness, and not become prisoners.
    Let us borrow only when necessary and when really needed.
    Let us be like clarified butter, which does not dissolve in water.

11. *Kama ziwa tusiweni mayini likimwaika*
    Mara huwa hulioni mayi yamelifinika
    Samli haiwi tini huwa yuu hutekeka

    Let us not be like milk that is poured into water,
    Disappearing suddenly as it mingles with the water.
    Clarified butter floats on the surface, and can be scooped from the
    top.

12. *Harufu tuangalieni yaani hizi za kuandika*
    Zilioko nda latini nyingine humunaika[1]
    Ziwapi za Kurani Mfano hono zunduka

    [1] *munaika* "to get lost, to disappear" (Std. *-potea*)

    Let us take a look at the letters, the ones used for writing:
    The ones that are in use now are those of the Roman alphabet; others
    are disappearing.
    Where is the Arabic script? Reflect upon this example.

13. *Yetu na tuyathamini wangine watayataka*
    Kilio huliya nyani Na mgine kaitika[1]
    Suali tulijibuni wasomi mulotukuka

    If we value our culture, others will aspire to it as well.
    Who is the one who cries so that the other will join in?
    Let us try to answer this question; would you, dignified scholars?

    [1] Literally, "If we do not cry out ourselves, who will be there to respond?" The phrase refers
    to the same proverb as the title, underlining the importance of taking one's own initiat-
    ive.

14. *Hatuizi asilani tamaduni kuangika[1]*
Zipo tu duniani toto na zilopanuka
Kwa pamoya tuishini kama zilopita nyaka

We don't deny that there are numerous cultures.
There are many of them in the world, small ones and those that have spread.
Let us live together in mutual respect as we did before.

1 *-angika.* Am. (Std. *-hesabika*). See *-wanga* "to count, to find the total of sth."

15. *Wenye nguvu hishimuni nanyi mutahishimika*
Mnyonge sidharauni mukatuona ni taka
Yetu nanyi yakirini bila ya kunung'unika

You, the powerful ones, respect others and you will be respected.
Do not despise the weak and treat us like scum.
You should also respect our ways without complaint.

16. *Hatuneni andamani kwa lazima kuyashika*
Nanyi nasi tuateni tuandame tuloridhika
Mashuga situvueni nanyi hatutowawika

We don't demand that you follow us, nor do we force you,
And you should also allow us to live as we like.
Don't force us to take off the veil, and we will not impose it on you either.

17. *Shakespeare Landani na kwetu tuna Muyaka*
Khayami Uwajemini Joji Thiri[1] Amerika
Kojiki ni Wajapani nao wote hutaika

Shakespeare worked in London, and here we have Muyaka;
Khayami in Persia, and George Thoreau in America;
Kojiki is for the Japanese, and all of them are well known.

1 *Joji Thiri*—Ustadh Mau might have meant to write George Thoreau, possibly referring to Henry David Thoreau, but he himself no longer knows whom he wanted to refer to. In this stanza, the poet wanted to mention the literary giants of various nations. He asked the people around him for big names; someone mentioned the name Joji Thiri (George Thoreau), probably misremembering the first name.

ILIMU: THE IMPORTANCE OF EDUCATION

18. *Twakiri mambo fulani[1] ni mamoya bila shaka*
    Yakiwa nda Uzunguni au Japani yatoka
    Asili hayagongani na yale ya Afrika

    We share certain values, which mean the same to all of us, for sure:
    No matter if they come from the West or from Japan,
    They never contradict the ones from Africa.

    [1] *mambo fulani* "certain things": according to Ustadh Mau, it was his intention to refer to shared moral values, like the rights of human beings, democracy, and the rights of workers.

19. *Hayo twataka suteni yawe yatandazika*
    Yasiwe kaskazini na kusini kutofika
    Ni watu nasi jamani maisha bora twataka

    These are the values that we all want to spread;
    They should not remain only in the north without reaching the south.
    Oh people, we are also human beings striving for a better life.

20. *Hapa ndipo kikomoni nakhitimisha waraka*
    Nawaomba samahani ikiwa nimetamka
    La kuwaudhi wendani maguuni napomoka

    This is the end; I am completing this composition.
    I beg your forgiveness if I have uttered any word
    That annoys you, my friends; I am falling at your feet.

21. *Nimezawa kisiwani wala nde sikutoka*
    Masomo ni ya chuoni ndiyo nilobahatika
    Wala dufu siiyoni mbee ya wailimika

    I was born on the island; never have I left it.
    My education is that of the Qurʾānic school; this is what I have been blessed with.
    I do not regard myself as worthless compared to those with a school education.

22. *Hini ndiyo anuwani ina piya taliweka*
    Aruba wa khamsini ni jaluba langu nyaka
    Amu ni kwetu nyumbani Mau ina hutumika

Now I put my address, together with my name:
"54" has been my postbox number for many years.
Amu is my hometown; people call me Mau.

3 *Kiswahili* ("Swahili")

Ustadh Mau composed this poem in 2003. A decade later, an edition of the poem, including its manuscript in Arabic script, was published by British Swahili scholar Peter Frankl, in cooperation with Ustadh Mau, in the journal *Swahili Forum*.[1] Peter Frankl, a lover of Swahili language and poetry who lived part of his life in Mombasa, passed away in 2020, but *Swahili Forum* kindly gave us permission to reprint the poem in this collection. A transliteration of the Arabic script also appeared in the introduction to Mathieu Roy's unpublished doctoral dissertation, together with a French translation (2013).[2] It is worth mentioning that apart from Ustadh Mau, many Swahili poets, like, for instance, Shaaban Robert, have written poetry in praise of the language.

In the poem, it is the Kiswahili language itself that takes on the role of narrator, lamenting her deplorable state: the children of Mother Swahili no longer care about her. She is looking back on her glorious poetic past on the northern coast, where, for instance, Muyaka bin Haji, the famous poet from Mombasa, or Ali Koti from Pate wrote "verses of enduring worth." Here, Ustadh Mau refers to examples of the written tradition of nineteenth-century classical poetry, as well as important scholars of Swahili from the twentieth century, namely Shihabdhin Chiraghdin and Ahmed Sheikh Nabahany, who put great effort into preserving Swahili manuscript traditions. At present, as Kiswahili laments, the grand intellectual tradition of the coast is no longer a source of pride for coastal inhabitants, who hardly cherish their respective dialects and take little interest in their own traditions and culture. Rather, as she cries, evoking the controversial dichotomy of the mainland and the coast, nowadays, Swahili is mastered by mainlanders, imposing a "dry," standardized language "without any flavor" or a "free verse" poetry void of the prosodic rules, which Ustahd Mau so much cherishes. Here one finds an echo of

---

1 Peter, J.L. Frankl & Ahmad Abdulkadir Mahmoud. "Kiswahili: a poem by Mahmoud Ahmad Abdulkadir, to which is appended a list of the poet's compositions in verse." *Swahili Forum* 20 (2013): 1–18.

2 Mathieu Roy, "Mathias E. Mnyampala 1917–1969: Poésie d'expression swahilie et construction nationale tanzanienne" (PhD diss., Institut National des Langues et Civilisations Orientales, 2013), http://tel.archives-ouvertes.fr/tel-00778667/

ILIMU: THE IMPORTANCE OF EDUCATION

Ustadh Mau's concern over the decline in education and his worries about increasing dropout rates on Lamu and the coast more generally, where a culture of learning and reading is missing. Both the translation and the notes are by Peter Frankl and Ustadh Mau. They differentiate between alveolar /t/ and /d/ and dental /t̲/ and /d̲/, which we have kept in this poem as well; in the other poems, we do not, since Kiamu speakers can hear this difference clearly but do not mark it in writing. We have also kept the bibliographical references given in footnotes as found in the previous article by Peter Frankl and Ustadh Mau.

1. *Kunyamaa nimechoka*   *t'anyamaa hata lini*
    wanangu huniepuka   *kuwaona natamani*
    walobaki kunishika   *si wangu ni wa wendani*
    Mimi nimewatendani   *mbona mwanipija zita*

    I am weary of staying silent. For how much longer am I to remain dumb?
    My own children avoid me, though I long to see them.
    And those who remain to embrace me are not my own, but the offspring of others.
    What have I done to you? Why do you wage war on me?

2. *Wanangu mimi wa d̲amu*   *wana wa Uswahilini*
    asili hawana hamu   *ya kuniyuwa ni nani*
    wamenat̲iya kaumu   *na wana wa majirani*
    kosa langu kosa gani   *mbona hunipija zita*

    My own flesh and blood, the children of Swahililand,
    origin(ally) are uninterested in knowing who I am,
    and have left me to other peoples, and to the children of neighbors.
    What kind of fault is my fault? [O my children] why do you continue waging war on me?

3. *Mimi mamenu si t̲asa*   *wala sina punguwani*
    nimezaawa Mambasa   *na kungine zisiwani*
    nizee wanasiyasa   *na ziyongozi wa d̲ini*
    mafundi wa kula fani   *na mashujaa wa zita*

I am your mother and am not yet infertile, nor has my ability to reproduce diminished.

I have given birth to children in Mombasa and on the other islands [of the Swahili],

to politicians as well as to religious leaders,

to craftsmen in every discipline (field), and to heroes of war.

4. *Ndimi mamake Muyaka* *piya Mwengo Athumani*
   na Zahidi kadhalika *na wengi wake wendani*
   Ali Koti na Mataka *wot'e mbwa moya karini*
   walitoka mtumboni *wa kawaa kama nyota*

I am the mother of Bwana Muyaka,[I] and also of Mwengo Athmani,[II] also,

and of Zahidi[III] too, and many of his companions (contemporaries),

Ali Koti[IV] and Mataka,[V] all from just one the same century,

they emerged from my womb, and shone like stars.

I Bwana Muyaka was the most outstanding Swahili poet of nineteenth-century Mombasa. After his death, many of his verses were recalled by Mu'allim Sikujua Abdallah al-Batawi (died 1890) and transcribed with annotations by W.E. Taylor (1856–1927). After Taylor's death, his papers were acquired by the library of the School of Oriental and African Studies (SOAS), London. | II Mwengo Athmani: this eighteenth-century poet from Pate composed the *Utendi wa Tambuka* ("The Epic of Heraklios"). | III Zahidi[3] | IV Ali Koti of Pate[4] | IV Bwana Mataka's full name is Muhammad bin Shee Mataka al-Famau (1825–1868). He was ruler of Siyu, as was his father. His mother was Mwana Kupona, famous for the poem of advice written to her daughter. Bwana Mataka died in Mombasa's fort while imprisoned by the Busa'idi.

5. *Inkishafi ngaliya* *ukisome na kidani*
   ndipo takapo kweleya *nikwambiyao mwendani*
   ni t'ungo zimesaliya *na hazifi asilani*
   walozitunga ni nyani *ni wanangu walopita*

Look at the *Al-Inkishafi*.[I] Read it attentively

and then, my dear friend, you will understand what I am telling you.

---

3 See Ali El-Maawy. *The Lamu Hero: The Story of Bwana Zahidi Mgumi* [1760–1832]. (Unpublished book manuscript, 2008 (1973).)

4 See Chiraghdin, Shihabdin. *Malenga wa Karne Moja*. Utangulizi na Ahmed Sheikh Nabahany. (Nairobi: Longman, 1987), 31–37

ILIMU: THE IMPORTANCE OF EDUCATION   209

These verses are of enduring worth and will never die.
Who were those who composed them? They were my children who
have passed on.

I The *Al-Inkishafi*, according to W.E. Taylor[5] is "a great, if not the greatest, religious classic of [the Swahili-speaking peoples]." The poem, concerned with the decay of Pate (formerly a flourishing town in northern Swahililand), may remind some readers of Thomas Gray's "Elegy Written in an English Churchyard"[6]

6.   *Na Malenga wa Mvita*   *na piya Chiraghudini*
     nyayo walizifuwata   *hawakukiri uduni*
     n-Nabahani huteta   *lakini hufaliyani*
     ndiye pweke uwandani   *inga(w)a ameikita*

And the Bard of Mambasa,[I] and Chiraghdin too,[II]
they followed the footsteps, they did not submit to lower standards.
Al-Nabhany[III] reproves, but to what effect?
He remains alone in the field, yet he stays strong.

I The "Bard of Mambasa" refers to Ustadh Ahmad Nassir Juma Bhalo.[7] | II Shihabdin Chiraghdin 1934–1976.[8] | III In an unpublished commendation from June 12, 1974, J.W.T. Allen writes of Ahmad Sheikh Nabahany, "... I am privileged to have a wide circle of friends and acquaintants among Swahili scholars of Swahili. I have some knowledge of their rating of themselves and I can name perhaps half a dozen (still living) who are always referred to as the most learned. To me they are walking dictionaries and mines of information and Ahmed is unquestionably one of them. He comes of a family of scholars whose discipline is as tough as any degree course in the world. They have no time for false scholarship or dilettantism. That this profound learning is almost wholly disregarded by those who have been highly educated in the Western tradition affects almost everything written today in or about Swahili. When I want to know some word or something about Swahili, I do not go to professors, but to one of the *bingwa* known to me. One of these could give a much greater detail of assessment, but of course his opinion would not carry the weight of one who can put some totally irrelevant letters after his name."[9]

5   Charles Stigand, A Grammar of the Dialectic Changes in the Kiswahili Language: with an Introduction and a Recension and Poetical Translation of the Poem Inkishafi, A Swahili Speculum Mundi by the Rev. W.E. Taylor, M.A. (Cambridge: at the University Press, 1915), 96–105.
6   Thomas Gray. *An Elegy Written at a Country Church Yard*. (London, Dodsley, 1751).
7   See Chiraghdin, Shihabdin. Malenga wa Mvita: Diwani ya Ustadh Bhalo. (Nairobi: Oxford University Press, 1971.)
8   See the biography by his daughter which came out in 2012. Latifa Chiraghdin, *Shihabuddin Chiraghdin. Life journey of a Swahili Scholar* (Mombasa: Jor's Publishers, 2012).
9   For a biography, see Said, Amira Msellem. *Wasifu wa Ahmed Sheikh Nabhany*. (Mombasa: JC Press, 2012).

7. *Bado kuzaa naweza* *siyakoma ukingoni*
    lakini mumenipuuza *mumeitowa fuwoni*
    wangine meitokeza *kunipangiya kanuni*
    musamiyati kubuni *nyinyi muliponiwata*

I am still able to give birth. I have not yet reached the limit,
but you have all despised me. You have left me high and dry,
now others have come forward to regulate me,
compiling standardized dictionaries, while you have deserted
me.[1]

1 For almost a century, Oxford University Press (OUP) has been the principal publisher
of standardized Swahili dictionaries. Clearly OUP has to be profitable, and profitable is
exactly what their Swahili dictionaries have been over the years. However, if one considers
excellence in research and scholarship, not one of OUP's Swahili lexicons can begin to
compare with the *Oxford English Dictionary* ("more than 600,000 words over a thousand
years"). Fortunately for Swahili and for Swahili studies, there exists the monumental *Dic-
tionnaire swahili-français* (Paris, 1939), compiled by Charles Sacleux—the greatest Swahili
lexicographer. Sacleux's chef d'œuvre ("unprecedented in historical depth, dialectological
detail and philological knowledge") can now be accessed electronically, courtesy of the
Swahili Forum. Heartfelt thanks for this labor of love are due to Thilo Schadeberg and Rid-
der Samson.

8. *Huliya kisikitika* *Changaliya jaridani*
    wengi wanaoandika *si wanangu ni wageni*
    idhaani kadhalika *wapeka t'ungo ni nyani*
    wengi hawatoki p'wani *licha kuwa mbwa Mvita*

I weep and lament when I look at the learned journals,
for many of those who contribute are not my children, they are
strangers [to me].
It is much the same with the media. Who are the ones who send in
their compositions?
Although they may have a Mombasa address, many do not come from
the coast.

9. *Angaliya na zitabu* *zisomeshwao shuleni*
    hazandikwi na Rajabu *si Sudi wala si Shani*
    Njoroge ndiyo katibu *ashishiyeo sukani*
    Charo na wake wendani *nao nyuma hufuwata*

ILIMU: THE IMPORTANCE OF EDUCATION

Look at the textbooks which are studied at our schools.
They are written neither by Rajabu, nor by Sudi nor by Shani.
The author is Njoroge[I], he is the helmsman.
Charo[II] and his colleagues follow.

I *Njoroge*: A [Gikuyu] name representing those who have their origins in the East African interior (the *bara*). | II *Charo*: A [Giriama] name representing those who have their origins in the coastal hinterland.

10.   *Hualikwa kongamano*   *Chenda hurudi ndiyani*
      huona utungu mno   *kuwa nyinyi siwaoni*
      na huziuma zitano [I]   *Lakini nitende nini*
      Wanangu mumeikhini   *mamenu mumeniwata*

When I am invited to conferences, I turn back before I arrive.
I feel exceedingly bitter that I do not see you all there.
I bite my fingers in frustration, but what can I do?
My children, you have missed your opportunity. You have abandoned your own mother.

I *Nahuziuma zitano*: these words echo the words of the *Inkishafi*, "*wakauma zanda na kuiyuta*."[10]

11.   *Na huliya kwa matozi*   *changaliya mitihani*
      wanafundi wa Kibwezi   *na wa Kisumu ziwani*
      ndiwo wanao barizi   *waliyoko kileleni*
      mulotoka kwetu p'wani   *muko t̲'ini hukokota*

And I shed tears when I look at the results of the school exams.
Students from Kibwezi [I], and from Kisumu by the lake,[II]
they are the ones who are ahead, who are at the top;
and you, students from the coast, you lag far behind.[III]

I *Kibwezi ... Kisumu*: places in the East African interior. | II The lake is Lake Nyanza, also known as Lake Victoria. | III *muko t̲'ini hukokota*: Over the years, young people on Lamu Island (and indeed elsewhere in northern Swahililand) have received a raw deal in their primary and secondary education. They have "lagged far behind" their counterparts from the interior, and so Mother Swahili grieves for her marginalized children.

---

10   On this Swahili gesture of regret, see Carol Eastman, & Yahya Ali Omar. "Swahili Gestures." *Bulletin of the School of Oriental and African Studies* 48, no. 2 (1985): 321–332.

12. *Wafanyao utafiti*   *wa uzamili zuwoni*
    Waswahili ni katiti   *au hawapatikani*
    ni nyani nimlaiti   *mwenye makosa ni nyani*
    mimi hamuni thamini   *mngine hamukupata*

Among those who are researching for degrees at the universities,
Swahili students are few—or non-existent.
Who is to be blamed? Whose fault is it?
You esteem me not at all, yet you have not replaced me by another.

13. *Kiwasikiya hunena*   *huniungonga moyoni*
    sarufi hakuna tena   *nahau naitamani*
    na hata ladha hayana   *kama mashapu kanwani*
    sielewi hunenani   *huimba au huteta*

When I hear those who are not mother-tongue speakers speaking, I
feel sick at heart.
Inflection is no longer employed, while grammatical [Swahili] is what
I desire!
Even [their speech] is wanting in flavor, like a plug of tobacco in one's
mouth.
I do not understand what they are saying. Are they singing? Are they
complaining?

14. *Lau Muyaka tarudi*   *ae tena duniyani*
    mwanangu itambidi   *kwenenda mahakamani*
    aete na mashahidi   *waniyuwao yakini*
    nyut'e mwenda gerezani   *kwa hatiya kuwapata*

Were Bwana Muyaka to return, were he to come back to the world,
it would be necessary, my child, for him to go to a court of law,
and he would need to call witnesses who know me well,
and all of you would go to prison for the offense that you have commit-
ted against me.

15. *Wallahi hamuna ghera*   *wala hamuna imani*
    hamuna la kuwakera   *kuwa hamuni thamini*
    mimi ni kama mpwira   *hutezewa uwandani*
    hupijwa teke ndiyani   *na kula anaepita*

ILIMU: THE IMPORTANCE OF EDUCATION   213

Truly you have neither zeal nor self-confidence.
It irritates you not at all that you do not esteem me.
I am just like a ball in the play-ground,
whoever passes me by in the street gives me a kick.

16.   *Haṯa kwenye ushairi*   *waso wangu wamebuni*
       zilizo huru bahari   *kwa kuoleza wageni*
       mimi hayo siyakiri   *si mashairi kifani*
       hayo yoṯ'e ni kwa nini   *hizo ni mbinu za zita*

Even in the field of Swahili prosody, those who are not mine have invented
free verse, imitating foreigners.
For myself, I cannot accept that. That is not worthy poetry.
What is the point of it all? These are the methods of war.

17.   *Hambiwa mwenyewe sina*   *hini ni ajabu gani*
       huwae kakosa shina   *kawa na tandu yangani*
       nyani alonipa ina   *alonandika ni nyani*
       kiwa si Uswahilini   *ni wapi nilipopata*

I am told that I belong to nobody in particular. How extraordinary!
How can I be rootless below ground and yet have branches abovc?
Who gave me my name? And who are they who wrote me down?
If I do not hail from Swahililand, then whence did I come?

18.   *Kuwa wengi huninena*   *si ḏalili aswilani*
       yakuwa wenyewe sina   *Kingereza hamuoni*
       hunenwa na wengi sana   *p'embe zoṯ'e ḏuniyani*
       kina na kwao shinani   *miziye haikuk'ata*

That many speak me, [Swahili], is not of itself proof of origins,
or of ownership. What of the English language?
It is spoken by very many, in all corners of the world,
yet the language remains firmly established in its homeland, its roots
have not been severed.

214 ILIMU: THE IMPORTANCE OF EDUCATION

4 *Za Washirazi athari* ("The Influence of the Persians")

Ustadh Mau composed this poem on March 1, 2011, on the occasion of a conference commemorating the Persian (Shirazi) heritage of the coast. This is a short poem in *utendi* meter in which Ustadh Mau invites his audience to remember the ancient Shirazi influence on the Swahili coast. He mentions places such as Kilwa and Zanzibar that are renowned for their Shirazi influence. He refers to words of Shirazi origin in Swahili, like *barafu* ("ice"), *bandari* ("port"), and *achari* ("chutney"), and refers to forms of craftsmanship—like styles of door carving, cuisine, and masonry—of Persian origin. In a way, the poem urges the audience not to forget the coast's history and its many cultural influences, which are also reflected in the language. The poet wants the audience to take pride in the history of the coast. Many visible traces still attest this history (*tarikhi hutwelezeya*, stz. 4). The poet urges the audience to keep watch for such evidence by looking up loanwords in the dictionary (*kamusini angaliya*, stz. 17) and studying patterns that are obvious to the careful observer (*kwa mato twashuhudiya*, stz. 14; *Mwenye mato huiyona/Katiti achangaliya*, stz. 11). The poem ends with the poet restraining himself from talking too much, so that those few reminders may be carefully considered by the audience. This poem was previously translated by Mohamed Karama.

1.	*Bismillahi awwali*	In the name of Allah,
	Naanda hii kauli	I begin my message.
	Kwenye kongamano hili	To this conference
	Karibuni twawambiya	We welcome you.
2.	*Twawambiya karibuni*	We bid you welcome,
	Wenyeji piya wageni	Hosts as well as guests
	Katika warsha hini	Of this workshop,
	Shirazi kuhadithiya	To talk about the Shirazi.
3.	*Lengo lake kongamano*	The objective of this conference
	Ni kuonesha mfano	Is to show examples
	La shirazi tangamano	Of past interactions with the Shirazi,
	Athari walotwatiya	And how they have affected us.
4.	*Washirazi wa zamani*	The ancient Shirazi
	Walikuya huku pwani	Came to the coast
	Kabula nyingi karini	Many centuries ago;
	Tarikhi hutwelezeya	That's what history tells us.

ILIMU: THE IMPORTANCE OF EDUCATION

5. *Kilwa ndipo walokita* Kilwa is where they settled;
   Unguja ikafwata Then Zanzibar followed,
   Na kungine walipata And somewhere else
   Tatuko kutatukiya They found a place to live.

6. *Washirazi na Warabu* The Shirazi and the Arabs,
   Waliambiwa karibu They were welcomed;
   Wakapata matulubu They got what they wanted—
   Makao ya kushukiya A place to settle.

7. *Athari za Washirazi* The influence of the Shirazi,
   Kuzikana hatuwezi We cannot deny it,
   Kwani ziko wazi wazi Because the impact is clear
   Kwa mwenye kuzangaliya To anyone who looks at it.

8. *Za Washirazi athari* The Shirazi influence
   Huitokeza dhahiri Is clearly visible
   Katika kazi nzuri In fine works
   Za mbao uwashi piya Of wood and masonry.

9. *Athari kwenye uwashi* One finds their influence in masonry,
   Mavazi piya upishi Attire and cuisine,
   Na milango ya nakishi And carved doors—
   Zitele zimesaliya Many have remained.

10. *Na athari za ufundi* And their influence on artisanship
    Ni moya katika kandi Is one of the treasures
    Washirazi na Wahindi That the Shirazi and Indians
    Amabazo wametwatiya Have left to us.

11. *Wametwatiya hazina* They have left a treasure,
    Kuu mno ya maana A huge one, of great importance;
    Mwenye mato huiyona Anyone who has eyes can see it
    Katiti achangaliya If he or she looks around just a bit.

12. *Na zombo za usafiri* And vessels of transportation,
    Yani hizi za bahari I mean those of the sea—
    Athari ni mashuhuri The influence is well known
    Shirazi walozitiya That the Shirazi contributed.

216   ILIMU: THE IMPORTANCE OF EDUCATION

13.   *Twalina wetu uyuzi*   We had our knowledge
      Kwenye za asili kazi   In our traditional works;
      Wangine na Washirazi   The Shirazi and others,
      Yao walitwengezeya   They added theirs for us.

14.   *Kuazima maarifa*   Borrowing techniques,
      Hiyo sisi ndetu sifa   That is our habit,
      Yetu kae haiyafa   An ancient one; it has not died.
      Kwa mato twashuhudiya   We can witness it with our own eyes.

15.   *Kwenye lugha kadhalika*   Also in the language,
      Athari ipo hakika   There is an influence, for sure.
      Kiswahili kupanuka   To expanding Kiswahili
      Shirazi walichangiya   The Shirazi contributed.

16.   *Ni tumbindima zilima*   There are many words
      Waswahili huzisema   That the Swahili speak, and
      Aswili ukitazama   When you consider their origin,
      Ni lugha ya Farisiya   It is the Persian language.

17.   *Neno barafu bandari*   The words *barafu*[i], *bandari*[ii],
      Kadhalika achari   And also *achari*[iii]
      Ni Kiajemi dhwahiri   Are clearly Persian;
      Kamusini angaliya   Take a look in the dictionary.

i *barafu* "ice" | ii *bandari* "port" | iii *achari* "chutney."

18.   *Zilima za kiajemi*   The Persian words
      Kwenye zetu sisi ndimi   In our tongue,
      Nikiziwanga sikomi   Were I to count them, I could not stop—
      Ni mno zimeeneya   There are too many.

19.   *Hapa tafunga shairi*   Here I will end my poem;
      Zaidi sitokariri   I will not go on any further.
      Hutosha niloashiri   This is enough, what I have already shown—
      Mifano niloashiriya   The examples I have given.

ILIMU: THE IMPORTANCE OF EDUCATION

20. *Ni za kitambo alaka* It is an ancient relation
    Kwa nguvu zimejengeka Built on a strong foundation;
    Haziwezi kuondoka It cannot be destroyed,
    Mitaimbo wangatiya Even if they use dynamite.

21. *Zalialaka imara* These are strong bonds
    Za dini na biashara Of religion and trade;
    Mno zalitiya fora[1] They flourished greatly
    Mreno kabla kuya Before the Portuguese came.

1 *-tia fora* "to prosper," "to flourish," "to be successful."

22. *Kauli yetu tammati* We cease our words
    Kwa hizi chache baiti After these few verses,
    Huwa ni tamu katiti Because short is sweet,
    Na huchoki kusikiya And you don't tire of listening.

Huruma: Social Roles and Responsibility

FIGURE 16   Ustadh Mahmoud Mau reading *Mama msimlaumu* at the Jukwaani Feistval in Nairobi in 2009; in his hand the newspaper report which inspired his composition

1   *Mama msimlaumu* ("Don't Blame My Mother")

Ustadh Mau wrote this poem in 2006 after finding an article in the *Taifa* newspaper about a dog rescuing an abandoned baby girl who had been left in the Ngong forest. The dog carried the baby to its owner, who at first thought that the baby was dead. Ustadh Mau reads the newspaper every day; touched by the baby's story, he decided to write a poem about it to defend the rights of women, who are commonly blamed for such acts. He has performed the poem twice for audiences. Before reading the poem, he reads them the newspaper article and asks the audience, whom do you blame for such an act? Normally, he says, the audience blames the mother. His intention is to change people's perspectives and to place the deed in a broader social context: not only the mother, but also society is to be held responsible.[1]

---

1   On the occasion of the first conference on Swahili literature at the University of Naples, organ-

HURUMA: SOCIAL ROLES AND RESPONSIBILITY

1.   *Imenibidi kunena, kabla wangu wakati*
      Sababu nimewaona, mamangu humlaiti
      Mamangu makosa hana, sipweke amezohiti[1]
      Kosa hili nda ummati

      I have been compelled to speak prior to my time
      Because I have seen you condemning my mother.
      My mother is not the one to blame; it is not her fault alone.
      It is society's fault.

      1 *-hiti* < Ar. syn.: *-fanya makosa* "make a mistake."

2.   *Nda ummati hili kosa, na ziyongozi wa nti*
      Kosa nda wana siyasa, na mahakimu wa koti
      Kosa nda wenye mapesa, na wasiyo na senti
      Kosa hili nda ummati

      It is the fault of society, and the leaders of the country.
      It is the fault of the politicians and the judges in the court.
      It is the fault of those who have money and those without a cent.
      It is society's fault.

3.   *Mamangu si Mariyamu, wa Imrani binti*
      Mama ni mwanaadamu, meishi hapa tiyati
      Na nyuteni mwafahamu, kuna dhaifu wakati
      Hushindwa kuidhibiti

      My mother is not Maryam, the daughter of Imran.
      My mother is a human being, living here on earth.
      As all of you know, there are times of weakness
      In which we fail to control ourselves.

4.   *Mama hakutenda pweke, na labda hakukiri*
      Ali na mwendani wake, aloifanya jasiri
      Ndipo mimi niumbike, mamangu kumuaziri[1]
      Pasi na yangu khiari

---

      ized by Flavia Aiello and Roberto Gaudioso in 2016, this poem was also read aloud, with a translation into Italian by Annachiara Raia under the title "Non incolpate la madre."

My mother did not do it alone, and probably not voluntarily.
She had a partner who feigned adventurousness.
That is how I came into being, putting shame on her—
Against my own will.

1 *kumuaziri*—Mau: *kumtia katika aibu* ("to put shame on s.o.").

5. *Ikiwa kuna lawama, lawama na zitanganye*
   Mukimlaumu mama, naye baba mumkanye
   ¹ Ndipo hapo yatakoma, ubaguzi musifanye
   Wanawake musifinye

If there is someone to be blamed, this blame should be distributed equally.
If you accuse the mother, the father also should be blamed.
Only then can this be prevented; don't be biased
And place the blame on women alone.

1 In this third line, he is referring to extramarital pregnancy. From his point of view, one can only stop men from dallying with women by making them legally responsible for their acts and not placing the blame solely on women, who thus become socially marginalized.

6. *Mimi kattu sikubali, mamangu kumlaumu*
   Na pweke kumkejeli, huwa ni kumdhulumu
   Kwaye pweke yambo hili, aswilani halitimu
   Hilo nyute mwafahamu

I do not agree if you blame my mother
And ridiculize only her, because this is an injustice.
She could never have done this by herself.
You all know that.

7. *Kitendo ni cha wawili, alipowa kapokeya*
   Haitokuwa adili, mama pweke kumwemeya
   Halihitaji dalili, wala huja kuzengeya
   Ayuwa kulla mmoya

HURUMA: SOCIAL ROLES AND RESPONSIBILITY 221

This can only be done by two people: the one who received [the offer],
also accepted it.
It's unfair to place the onus only on my mother.
No evidence is necessary nor need any proof be found.
Everybody knows it.

8. *Mno huwona utungu, kiwasikiya hunena*
Humlaumu mamangu, kwa kuwa mkosa sana
Mimi na wendani wangu, hatupati hata ina
Ni Sina au Sibina

I feel so much bitterness if I hear people talking,
Blaming my mother as the only wrongdoer.
My fellow sufferers and I, we are not even named—
Only Sina or Sibina.[1]

1 These two names are telling: Sina, "I don't have [sc. a father]," and Sibina, "it is not surprising," i.e. "it is not a surprise that these things happen." These are female names given to children who are born outside of wedlock.

9. *Menitupa wangu mama, si kwa kuwa hanipendi*
Ni baba memsukuma, kisa kumwawika landi[1]
Naye kwa kucha lawama, za wenye ndimi na tundi
Menitupa yake kandi

My mother threw me away, but not because she had no love for me.
It was the father who pushed her, putting the hangman's noose around
her neck.
It was just from fear of being accused by scandalmongers and chatter-
boxes
That she threw me, her treasure, away.

1 *landi* "noose"; *wenye tundi* (< *-tunda* "to find out") "chatterboxes."

10. *Naamini anipenda, mama hakunitukiya*
Ni lipi lilomshinda, pumzi kuniziwiya
Tokeya siku ya kwanda, duniani mimi kuya
Ni ruhuma kunoneya

I believe she loved me. My mother did not hate me.
What else would have prevented her from suffocating me right away?
From the first day I came into the world,
She felt compassion for me.

11. *Natamani natamani, wangu mama kumpata*
Nimwambiye shukurani, nimpe ahasanta
Kwa kunilicha tumboni, hata siku zikapita
Ndiya nami kafuwata

I wish, I wish, to find my mother,
So that I can thank her and show her my gratitude
For keeping me in her womb, until the time was due for me
To find my way out.

12. *Humpijiya siloti[1], mamangu kwa wake wema*
Wakuniwata niketi, matumboni kwa salama
Na wala simlaiti, kwa alilolifanya mama
Alitenda kwa lazima

I salute my mother for her kindness
To let me stay safely in her womb.
And I do not blame my mother for what she did.
She was forced to do so.

[1] *siloti* < Eng. "salute."

13. *Menitatiya tambara, kusudi kunidhibiti*
Nisipate la madhara, kiniweka kavu nti
Baridi ingenikera, nikakutwa ni maiti
Alofanya si katiti

She wrapped me in a piece of cloth to protect me
So that I would not be harmed when she placed me on the bare ground.
For if the cold had struck me, I would have been found dead.
What she did was not trifling.

HURUMA: SOCIAL ROLES AND RESPONSIBILITY 223

14. *Kabla ya kumaliza, kufunga yangu kauli*
   Walimwengu nauliza, tazawa mara ya pili
   Hakuna takaoweza, kuwa wa mama badali
   Nashukuru wafadhili

   Before I finish and conclude my speech,
   I ask you human beings: can I possibly be born a second time?
   There is no one to replace my mother.
   Still, I thank all my saviors.

15. *Wema wenu siukani, na wa mbwa mashuhuri*
   Mumenitenda hisani, mumenifanya mazuri
   Wangaliko duniyani, waja wapendao kheri
   Tammati hapa shairi

   I cannot deny your kindness, nor that of the famous dog.
   You have done me a favor and you have done good to me.
   There are still people in the world who are altruistic.
   Here my poem ends.

2   *Jilbabu* ("Veil")

Ustadh Mau composed this poem in the 1980s, when a group of women was campaigning for the proper veiling of Muslim women. They were of the opinion that women were not properly veiled, and they propagated the use of a (typically black) veil called the *jilbabu*, made of two parts: one piece wrapped around the hips, and another around the shoulders. This was supposed to replace the so-called *buibui ya Kiswahili*, which is one piece of cloth, sewn into a loop, and which women typically wore in a loose way. The "Annaswiha" movement was started mostly by women from Lamu who had studied in Nairobi, where they met other (mostly Somali) women and returned to Lamu with new ideas about proper clothing. Mama Azra, Ustadh Mau's wife, was the chairperson of the group. The poem was also performed at Mkomani Primary School, where Ustadh Mau has given lectures on moral conduct (*maadili*) every Thursday (in the Islamic Pastoral Program) for decades, ever since the 8-4-4 school system was introduced. This is one of the poems in this collection that has a dialogical structure, based on a conversation between a young girl, called only *binti* ("daughter"), and her father, *baba*. As the poem unfolds, the reader can see that while the girl is curious and feels

HURUMA: SOCIAL ROLES AND RESPONSIBILITY

ready to start wearing her veil, the father expresses his hesitation toward his daughter's wish.

1.	*Binti:*		Daughter:
	Babangu tangu kitambo		My father, for a while now
	Kwako nalitaka yambo		I have wanted something from you.
	Imekuwa kama nyimbo		It plays on repeat in my head
	Kula siku nakwambiya		Every day, I tell you.

2. *Baba:* — Father:
   Ewe binti sikiza — My daughter, listen—
   Mimi hilo sitoweza — I can't do that.
   Haja yako kutimiza — I can't satisfy your need.
   Siwezi kukutendeya — I can't do it for you.

3. *Binti:* — Daughter:
   Baba kituche[1] si ghali — Father, this thing is not expensive;
   Wala si cha mengi mali — It is not a lot of money.
   Alifu na mia mbili — One thousand two hundred—
   Hazizidi hata moja — It is no more than that.

   1 *kituche = kitu hicho*

4. *Baba:* — Father:
   Mwanangu hukufahamu — My daughter, you haven't understood me.
   Mimi sioni ugumu — I don't see any problem
   Wa kutowa tas'limu — In paying;
   Si bakhili kwa rupiya — I am not a miser when it comes to money.

5. *Binti:* — Daughter:
   Basi baba ni kwa nini — So, father, why then?
   Kwamba haiwezekani — Why is it not possible
   Ikiwa yake thamani — If its price
   Siyo ilokulemeya — Is not the thing that prevents you?

6. *Baba:* — Father:
   Mwanangu mimi naona — My daughter, I see
   Hilo halina maana — That this is not meaningful.
   Wewe ungali kijana — You are still a child;
   Ni mwando kuinukiya — You have only just begun growing up.

HURUMA: SOCIAL ROLES AND RESPONSIBILITY

7. *Binti:* — Daughter:
    Baba hela pulikiza — Father, listen
    Suali nakuuliza — To the question I am asking you:
    Wewe litakupendeza — Would you want me,
    Mimi mwano kipoteya — Your daughter, to go astray?

8. *Baba:* — Father:
    Utapoteya kwa nini — Why should you go astray?
    Wewe hapa si mgeni — You are not a foreigner here.
    Hata usiku kizani — Even on the darkest night,
    Ndiya zote zakweleya — You know all the roads.

9. *Binti:* — Daughter:
    Si kupoteya ndiyani — I do not mean getting lost on the road,
    Ni kumwandama shetani — But following Satan.
    Ni kungiya madhambini — It means to sin—
    Kutenda yaso na ndiya — To do what is not right.

10. *Baba:* — Father:
    Hilo mimi silitaki — I don't want that.
    Na kabisa siridhiki — And I do not agree at all with
    Mambo yaso alaiki — These things that do not befit us,
    Kwetu hatukuzoeya — That we are not used to.

11. *Binti:* — Daughter:
    Kama hayo wayaona — If you think
    Ni mambo yaso maana — That these concerns are meaningless,
    Nipa ningali kijana — Expose me to them while I am still young,
    Nipate kulizoeya — So that I may get used to them.

12. *Waswahili twalinena* — We, the Swahili, used to say
    Uwongo[I] hupatikana — The clay
    Ulimai[II] na mwenana[III] — Needs to be wet and soft
    Uweze kusinyangiya — So that you can model it.

I *uwongo* Am. "clay" (Std. *udongo*). | II See meth.: *uwongo hupatikana ulimai.* | III *mwenana* "kitu laini, kitu ambacho hakijakomaa" (Mau).

13.	*Nami kitovaa sasa*	If I am not wearing it now,
	Wakati utapotasa	When the time comes
	Sitoliweza kabisa	I will not be able to wear it at all,
	Kiwa sitolizoweya	If I do not get used to it now.

14.	*Baba:*	Father:
	Mwana hilo si lazima	My daughter, this is not a must;
	Bora usimame wima	You better stand firm,
	Ndiya njema kuandama	Following the right path,
	Na mbovu kuikimbiya	Running away from evil.

15.	*Binti:*	Daughter:
	Baba shuga ndiyo kinga	Father, the veil is a protection.
	Na waovu hukutenga	It keeps one away from bad people.
	Baba kitovaa shuga	Father, if I do not wear a veil,
	Mate watanimiziya	They will desire me.

16.	*Kizunguka wazi wazi*	If I stroll around without it—
	Kuna wengi majambazi	There are many robbers
	Wabakaji siku hizi	And rapists these days.
	Miini wameeneya	They have increased in the towns.

17.	*Lakini kiisitiri*	But if I cover myself
	Kama ya Mola Amri	According to God's will,
	Nitaepuka khatari	I will avoid danger
	Salamani nitangiya	And be on the safe side.

18.	*Baba:*	Father:
	Basi enenda dukani	So go to the shop
	Kaangalie fesheni	And look at the fashions
	Zitokazo Arabuni	Coming from Arabia,
	Nipate kununuliya	So that I may buy it for you.

19.	*Binti:*	Daughter:
	Baba shuga si fesheni	The veil is not a fashion item.
	Mashuga ya madukani	The veils from the shops
	Siyo kwenye Qurani	Are not those of the Qur'ān,
	Mola aliyotwambiya	Which God told us about.

1 *shuga* Am. "sheet," here "veil" (Std. *shuka*)

HURUMA: SOCIAL ROLES AND RESPONSIBILITY

20. *Baba:*
   Kwani wewe utakalo
   Ni lile liambiwalo
   Junijuni[1] hilo ndilo
   Kwa mbali akitokeya

Father:
Which one do you want?
Like the one called
"This is Junijuni"
When s/he appears from afar?

[1] In this stanza, *junijuni* refers to a figure that forms part of a children's game typically played during Ramadan. A rough bag is placed over a child's head so that s/he cannot see anything. Afterwards, other children make fun of him/her, shouting "Junijuni lataka bembe" ("Junijuni wants *bembe* food"). (*bembe* food is a kind of food consumed during Ramadan.) Thus, in this stanza, the father makes fun of the daughter's wish, since the *junijuni* is an ugly bag. It has become a common derogatory term, used to refer to the veil by those who do not approve of it.

21. *Binti:*
   Baba sifanye dhihaka
   Hilo ndilo la hakika
   Mola analolitaka
   Shuga analoridhiya

Daughter:
Father, do not joke—
That one is the right one,
The one God wants,
The one God agrees with.

22. *Amri yake Wahabu*
   Ni kuvaa jilbabu
   Angaliya ah'zabu
   Imenena wazi aya

The command of the Generous One
Is to wear the veil.
Look at the *Sūrat al-Aḥzāb*—
The verse says so clearly[1].

[1] The reference is to sura 33:59, which reads as follows: "O Prophet, say to thy wives and daughters and the believing women, that they draw their veil close to them; so it is likelier they will be known, and not hurt. God is All-Forgiving, All-Compassionate" (Abr., 434).

23. *Baba:*
   Mwanangu nasikitika
   Wendiyo watakuteka
   Na kwa joto kadhalika
   Utazidi kuumiya

Father:
My daughter, I am sorry.
Your companions will laugh at you,
And the heat
Will make you suffer even more.

24. *Binti:*
   Kitekwa siandi mimi
   Hata wake wa mitumi
   Walikiliwa kwa ndimi
   Na kuzuliwa mabaya

Daughter:
I am not the first to be laughed at.
Even the Prophets' wives
Were slandered
And defamed[1].

[1] See for instance Qur. 24:2.

25.	*Ama kunena ni joto*	And as for the heat,
	Joto ni kitu kitoto	Heat is a minor thing
	Kuliko akhira moto	Compared to the hellfire
	Mtu kwenenda kungiya	One will be thrown in.
26.	*Baba:*	Father:
	Mwanangu umenishinda	My daughter, you have defeated me
	Hoja zako kuzivunda	With your counterarguments;
	Ingawa nimeipinda	Though I made an effort,
	Sikuweza hata moya	I did not succeed, not even once.
27.	*Kalishone jilbabu*	Go and sew your veil.
	Uvae wangu muhibu	Wear it, my beloved daughter,
	Kwani radhi za Wahabu	Since it is necessary
	Yapasa kuzizengeya	To seek to please God.
28.	*Binti:*	Daughter:
	Nakushukuru babangu	I thank you, my father,
	Kunikubaliya yangu	For giving me your permission.
	Hini amri nda Mungu	This is God's order;
	Ndiye amezotwambiya	He is the one who told us so.

3   *Mchezo wa kuigiza* ("Play")

This is a poem in *wimbo* form that Ustadh Mau composed in 2011, and his daughter Azra Mau prepared the first translation, which we have revised here. It was inspired by a prose version of the same story that he read in an Arabic textbook for class six in Saudi Arabia, where the story bore the title *Bayna al-ghanī na al-faqīr* ("Between the Rich and the Poor"). Because he liked the content, he decided to adapt it to poetic form in Swahili. He presented his adaptation to his own pupils at the madrassa as a poetry exercise for reading and comprehension. As in the poem *Jilbabu*, this poem is one of several composed in the form of a dialogue, a "play" (*mchezo*) in verse form. In the play, the two voices—that of the Miser, on the one hand, and the Pauper (also referred to as "Shekhe"), on the other—are not rounded characters, but are allegories of richness and poverty. They represent groups defined by their socioeconomic differences and their outlooks—in the form of the miser and the poor man—rather than individuals. This dialogic form allows for an exchange of arguments to finally arrive at a conclusion that includes the moral message that the audience should keep in mind.

HURUMA: SOCIAL ROLES AND RESPONSIBILITY

1. *Bakhili:*
Mali yangu, mimi nakupenda sana
Wewe kwangu, hushinda mke na wana
Nautungu, kwako mwingi nauwona

Miser [addressing his wealth]:
My wealth, I love you so much.
You are better than my wife and children.
I suffer so much for you.

2. *Yangu raha, ni mali kuyatizama*
Si mzaha, haya ninayoyasema
Ndiyo jaha, kwenye duniya nzima

My pleasure is looking at my wealth.
It's not a joke, what I am saying:
This is the greatest joy in the whole world.

3. *Masikini:*
Ewe bwana, tajiri mwenye nafasi
Tangu yana, mimi riziki siisi
Hela fanya, hisani wema hukosi

Pauper:
O master, rich man who can afford a lot,
Since yesterday I have not eaten.
Please, do me a favor, and you will not lack any blessing.

4. *Ukinipa, na mimi kitu katiti*
Takulipa, Mola ziviye senti
Tangu hapa, na baada ya mauti

If you also give me a little bit,
God will pay you, your savings will grow
Here in this world, and also after death.

5. *Bakhili:*
Enda zako, sinitiliye nuhusi
Haja yako, wataka zangu fulusi
Na sumbuko, nilopata huliisi

Miser:
Go away; do not bring me bad luck.
Your wish [is that] you want my money,
But you don't know the troubles I have endured.

6. *Nondokeya, sisimame mbee yangu*
Takutiya, cha kitwa hiki kirungu
Nakwambiya, kutowa mali utungu

Disappear from my sight; do not stand before me.
I will hit you on the head with this club.
I am telling you, giving money away is painful.

7. *Masikini:*
Mabakhili, wenye mali huteseka
Yao hali, ni kama sisi hakika
Kula hali, ni mali huyarundika

Pauper:
Misers who have wealth are in trouble.
Their state is just like ours:
They do not eat; instead, their only ambition is to amass wealth.

8. *Hufaani, zake nyingi miliyoni*
Masikini, hawafanyii hisani
Zibengini, mwenyewe huzitamani

How are his millions of any use to him?
To the poor, they are of no benefit;
They just stay in the bank, because the owner wants them there.

9. *Shekhe:*
Hodi[1] bwana, ewe nduyake Karuni[11]
Nimeona, nikutowe uwingani
Wakusanya, mali wamwekeya nani

Sheikh:
Hodi master, oh brother of Karuni,
I thought that I had helped you out of your ignorance.
You are collecting wealth, but for whom are you saving it?

HURUMA: SOCIAL ROLES AND RESPONSIBILITY

1 *hodi* a call-word used by someone outside the door who wants to enter a house; similar to knocking at someone's door. | 11 The rich tyrant Qarun, who appears in the Qurʾān, sura 28:76–84, is the prototypical careless and powerful man who is interested solely in high rank and wealth, exploiting others. He does not think about the afterlife, but merely tries to accumulate as much wealth and status as he can in this world. There is also a reference to him in stz. 100 of the poem *Hapo zamani za yana*.

10. *Angaliya, mali mengi umeweka*
    Zingatiya, kuna wengi huteseka
    Wanaliya, kwa kuwazidi mashaka

    Look, you have kept a lot of wealth;
    Consider how many people are suffering.
    They are crying in their great sorrow.

11. *Mayatima, waliokosa mababa*
    Kina mama, wasokua na akiba
    Fanya hima, uwape japo kibaba

    Orphans who have lost their fathers,
    And mothers who have no savings—
    Make an effort; at least give them a dime.

12. *Na maradhi, wangine huwasumbuwa*
    Na baadhi, hamudu kupata dawa
    Mwenye hadhi, towa utabarikiwa

    And sickness: some are afflicted by it,
    And some cannot even afford to buy medicine.
    Oh, you of high honor, donate and you shall be blessed.

13. *Bakhili:*
    Yangu mali, ndiyo wewe wayataka
    Si kauli, hiyo uliyotamka
    Na akili, nadhani imekuruka

    Miser:
    My wealth, that is what you want.
    It is not proper, what you have just said,
    And I think you are out of your mind.

14. *Wanekeza, mimi kutowa sadaka*
    Nimeiza, sitaki na sitotaka
    Nitasoza, shauri lako kishika

    You tell me to give alms;
    I refuse—I do not and shall never want to.
    I will perish if I take your advice.

15. *Wanidhiki, kwa maneno ya upuzi*
    Siyataki, hayo yako siyawezi
    Sigeuki, mali yangu sipotezi

    You are annoying me with your useless words.
    I do not accept them; I cannot stand them.
    I will not change; I shall not lose my wealth.

16. *Nitokeya, nyumbani kwangu haraka*
    Nondokeya, usisimame dakika
    Yako niya, ni mimi kufilisika

    Get out of my house quickly.
    Vanish; do not stand before me, even for a second.
    Your intention is to bankrupt me.

17. *Shekhe:*
    Umekosa, walodhani wewe siyo
    Zako pesa, siyo mimi nitakao
    Takutesa, ufahamu siku hiyo

    Sheikh:
    You have erred; what you think is not true.
    Your money is not what I want;
    It will burden you, remember, on Judgment Day.

18. *Mepofuka, wewe kwa kupenda mali*
    Kuongoka, kwako ni kama muhali
    Takumbuka, kiadiya zilizali[1]

HURUMA: SOCIAL ROLES AND RESPONSIBILITY

You are blinded by your love of wealth.
Becoming righteous is not possible for you—
You will remember when the earthquake comes, right on time.

I *zilizali* "earthquake." This too is a reference to Judgment Day, when the earth will tremble (see also sura 99).

19. *Yako dini, umetupa kwa duniya*
     Na motoni, maliyo yatakutiya
     Mayutoni, siku hiyo¹ tasaliya

Your religion: you have given it up for love of this world.
It is into hellfire that your wealth will throw you;
You will remain in regret on that day.

I *siku hiyo* "that day," another reference to Judgment Day.

20. *Mali yako, yatakuwa ndizo kuni*
     Nyama yako, yakiiyoka motoni
     Nasumbuko, likikutesa mwendani

Your wealth will be firewood in hell;
Your flesh will be roasted in the fire,
And pain will put you in agony, my friend.

21. *Bakhili:*
     Tumo langu, la nyezi nyingi na nyaka
     Ruhu yangu, ile ndiyo huchomeka
     Bure yangu, bure nalihadaika

Miser:
My savings of many months and years are gone—
And my soul is burning.
Alas, for nothing, I have been deceived!

22. *Yamekwenda mali, mebaki mayuto*
     Zote zanda, huuma kiliya mato
     Imevunda, jahazi ya langu pato

My wealth has disappeared; only regrets remain.
I bite my nails in regret, crying many tears.
It has been broken, the dhow that brought me my income.

23. *Laitani, nangalikula vizuri*
    Muilini, kavaa nikanawiri
    Ni shetani, ndiye aliyonighuri

    If I had known, I would have eaten well;
    I would have put shining clothes on my body.
    It was Satan who deceived me.

24. *Masikini:*
    Tulingene, tumekuwa hali moya
    Na lingine, huna lililosaliya
    Twandamane, tushike moya ndiya

    Pauper:
    We have become equals; we are in the same state.
    Anything else? You have nothing that has remained.
    Let us walk together; we take the same path.

25. *Hafaidi, mtu bakhili kwa mali*
    Ni hasidi, mwenyewe kwa yake hali
    Akizidi, humrusha na akili

    He will not derive any benefit, a miser saving his wealth.
    He is envious; he does not allow anything, even to himself.
    If he overdoes it, it can even make him lose his senses.

4   *Haki za watoto* ("Children's Rights")

Ustadh Mau wrote this 257-stanza poem in May 2001. At the time, his last-born son, Aboud, to whom he dedicated the poem, was three years old. In total, Ustadh Mau has eleven children from two wives, as well as thirty-four grandchildren. His first wife, Mama Tunda, gave birth to three girls and five boys. The second wife, Mama Azra, gave birth to two girls before finally giving birth to Aboud. According to Ustadh Mau, he composed the poem after having read various books in English and Arabic on childcare and developmental psychology. He gradually became aware of children's special needs and concerns. He recognized his own failures, misconceptions, and mistakes, as well as problems in society at large. Furthermore, according to him, his first wife was too rude toward the children, while his second wife was very dedicated to her work. She first worked as a schoolteacher and later at the Lamu Museum, so she did not have much time for the children. Ustadh Mau says that he was very close with the children. As he recounts, even at the hospital, the nurses would give the babies to him so that he could hold them. Even nowadays, his grandchildren always come to his library, where they get sweets or some small coins from him.

Ustadh Mau himself was brought up by his paternal uncle. He has five siblings. All the others were brought up by his mother and their father. But since his uncle's children did not survive, his father decided to give Mahmoud to his uncle to raise him. His uncle treated him well; he was never beaten, in contrast to many other children at the time. He also arranged for his education and made him study. His wife was well learned in the Qurʾān, so Mahmoud already knew how to read the Qurʾān before starting school.

Furthermore, Ustadh Mau is also a teacher, and loves to teach children at the madrassa. He is a member of the committee (*wizara*) for children's rights in Lamu, which now seems to be largely defunct. Previously, he also used to be called to court if there were cases of child abuse or, in cases of divorce, when a father would not provide for his children.

On the one hand, the poem is also a didactic and personal poem, a *wasiya* dedicated to his son Aboud—like the one Ustadh Mau's father composed for him (see *Hapo zamani za jana*). On the other hand, the poem is not a typical *wasiya*, addressing children and advising them on how to live in the world. Rather, it speaks to a wider audience, and more particularly the parents, not

 A recorded audio version of the poem is freely available online at https://doi.org/10.6084/m9.figshare.20200514.

the children. His concern for the children and his way of addressing the parents has been noted as quite unusual by his Lamuan audience, since typically it is the children who are taught through such poems.

In the poem, he makes a plea to treat children based on their needs and rights (see also Vierke's contribution "How Ought We to Live?" in Part 1 of this volume). He systematically goes through various elements of children's life-worlds, progressing by age group. He starts by considering babies and infants before moving on to children and adolescents. Later in the poem, he makes a plea for educating children properly, which reflects his general concern with proper education as the key to individual and societal progress. The media in particular has a bad influence on children in his view: it makes children go astray and lose interest in studying. In the poem, he does not refer to social media or the internet, as in 2001, the former did not exist and the latter hardly played a role in everyday life in Lamu. In the context of the poem, it is TV that he is condemning: satellite TV, which came with many additional channels, arrived in Lamu in the 1990s. According to him, the TV programs not only caused children to lose focus on their studies, but also introduced them to harmful content.

1. *Bismillahi Latwifu*   In the name of God, the Kind One,
    Kwa ina lake tukufu   In His glorious name,
    Naanda kuyaswanifu   I begin composing.
    Ya Rabbi nitimiziya   May you, God, help me complete this!

2. *Nitimiziya yatimu*   God, make it complete,
    Rabbi niliyoazimu   What I intend to compose,
    Nieleze wafahamu   So that I can reach
    Watakao kusikiya   Those who listen to my words.

3. *Shabaha na langu lengo*   My target and my aim
    Nataka tunga utungo   Is to compose a poem;
    Asaa uziwe pengo   Maybe it can fill a gap
    Kwenye maudhui haya   When it comes to this topic.

4. *Nitakayo kuyanena*   What I am about to say
    Ni mambo kuhusu wana   Concerns children,
    Khususa walo wanuna   Especially the young ones:
    Haki zao za shariya   It is about their legal rights.

HURUMA: SOCIAL ROLES AND RESPONSIBILITY

5. *Haki za walo watoto* — The rights of those who are young
   Ni kuu mno si toto — Are essential and not minor,
   Zimepowa na uzito — And religious and secular laws also
   Kwa dini kanuni piya — Grant them importance.

6. *Nami tatiya mkazo* — And I also emphasize their rights
   Kuzitaya haki hizo — By mentioning those
   Kwenye shariya ambazo — Of the sharia laws that
   Mola amewapangiya — God has put in place for children.

7. *Tazizungumza haki* — I will talk about the rights
   Alizowapa Khallaki — That the Creator has bestowed on
   Hawa wana makhuluki — Children created by Him
   Kwenye hadithi na aya — Through the hadith of the Prophet and the
   Qur'ānic verses.

8. *Hadithi sitoandika* — I will not quote the hadith
   Aya sitozitamka — Nor recite the verses,
   Muwanga wake hakika — But certainly they enlighten
   Ndiwo taomulikiya — My perspective on the topic.

9. *Uisilamu ni dini* — Islam is a religion
   Mno inayothamini — That values
   Wana tangu matumboni — Children, from the time they are in the
   Bali kabula kungiya — womb
   And even before their conception.

10. *Ni haki ya alo mwano* — It is the right of your child
    Kumpa mama mfano — To have an ideal mother,
    Aliyo mzuri mno — Who is excellent
    Si kwa sura kwa tabiya — Not in appearance, but in character.

11. *Kabla ya kuamuwa* — Before deciding
    Ni upi wa kumuowa — Whom you will marry,
    Upike ukipakuwa[1] — Consider it carefully
    Mama mwema kwangaliya — And look for the qualities of a good mother.

[1] *upike ukipakue* idiomatic for "consider carefully"; as Mau notes (*ufikirie sana, kwa maki-ni*), literally "cook [your thoughts] before you serve them."

12.	*Ni lazima ufikiri*	You should try to imagine
	Mambo yatakayojiri	How things will be
	Kiwatunuku Qahhari	If the Powerful One rewards you
	Wana akawaptiya	With children.
13.	*Fikiri uwaze mno*	Ponder carefully
	Kuhusu mama wa wano	The mother of your future children;
	Usiwe wako mkono[1]	Don't select her hastily
	Kizani utautiya	Or blindly.

1 *-tia mkono gizani* "to do something without first thinking about it."

14.	*Usiutiye kizani*	Don't choose blindly
	Kwa kuteuwa mwendani	By selecting a partner
	Alokungiya matoni	Who attracted you at first sight
	Moyo wako kavutiya	And seduced your heart.
15.	*Mama mno ni muhimu*	The mother is very important.
	Taka mama alotimu	Look for a perfect mother
	Wana wasikulaumu	So that the children will not blame you
	Mambo takapo weleya	When they reach the age of understanding.
16.	*Mteuwe mama bora*	Choose the best mother,
	Si kwa kabila na sura	Not for her tribe nor for her beauty,
	Bali ni kwa njema sera	But for her good conduct
	Mwenye dini na tabiya	In religion and etiquette.
17.	*Wape mama wa fakhari*	Give them an admirable mother
	Mwenye mayezi mazuri	Who can raise them well,
	Wanao waifakhiri	So that your children can be proud
	Kwa mama kuivuniya	Of their mother.
18.	*Siwape mama mtango[1]*	Don't give them a mother who likes to stroll about,
	Na mwenye tabiya jongo	
	Hoyo tawatiya pengo	One with a bad character;
	Ya milele kusaliya	She will leave a hole
		That will remain forever.

1 *mtango* < *-tanga* "to stroll about." "Se promener de long en large, errer ou aller çà-et-là, à l'aventure de côté et d'autre; vagabonder." (Scl. 866).

HURUMA: SOCIAL ROLES AND RESPONSIBILITY 239

19. *Wape mama mtulivu*   Give them a calm mother
    Asiyo mtepetevu   Who is not idle,
    Muyuzi alo mwerevu   But knowledgeable and smart—
    Si mama wa kuukiya   And not a mother who likes to shout.

20. *Alokomaa akili*   Someone who is mature;
    Aso mengi mashughuli   Who is not too busy,
    Tawatunga kwelikweli   But will truly look after
    Wana na kuangaliya   And take care of your children.

21. *Ni bora kiwa mesoma*   It is better if she is educated,
    Wala sambi ni lazima   But I do not say this is a must—
    Kwani alosoma mama   Because an educated mother
    Ni mengi yatamweleya   Understands a lot more.

22. *Mama akiwajibika*   If she is concerned about them,
    Na wana hunufaika   The children will benefit,
    Na mambo mengi hunyoka And many things will go well
    Yakandama sawa ndiya   And take the right course.

23. *Kwani mama ni mwalimu* Because a mother is
    Wa kwanda mno muhimu   A child's first important teacher.
    Athariye nda kuudumu   She makes a lasting impact
    Kwa wanawe husaliya   On her children.

24. *Kiwata athari njema*   If she has a good influence,
    Itasaliya daima   It will always remain.
    Na piya mbovu alama   Likewise, negative impressions
    Hayondoki hubakiya   Don't disappear, but remain.

25. *Nimeyafanya marefu*   I've elaborated extensively
    Ya mama kuwaarifu   Upon the qualities of a mother:
    Mama kiwa mwuongofu   If the mother is virtuous,
    Huongoka na dhuriya   The children will be too.

26. *Ya pili haki ya mwana* The second right of a child
    Kizawa handikwa ina   Is to be given a name after birth:
    Binti au kijana   Girl or boy,
    Lake la kukusudiya   Children should have their own name.

27. *Ina haandikwi lolote*	Children should not be given just any name:
Ni haki yake apate	It is their right to have a name
Ina kama wende wote	Like all other children,
Ambalo tafurahiya	One that will make them happy.

28. *Simwandike ina ovu*	Don't give them a bad name
Kwake itakuwa kovu[1]	That will remain like a scar
Na ya moyo maumivu	And cause pain in their heart
Siku zote tasikiya	Every time they hear it.

1 *kovu* "scar." "Cicatrice, balafre; *Mwenye k.*, balafré. *Mtu wa makovu-kovu*, personne toute couverte de cicatrices" (Scl. 443).

29. *Mpe ina lilo zuri*	Give them a good name,
Kwa wende aifakhiri	To be proud of around other children—
Kiitwa awe hajeri	When called, they will not be ashamed
Bali huliteremeya	But be happy about it.

30. *Ni haki kumwandikisha*	It is their right to be documented,
Mwana kumuorodhesha	To be listed in the census,
Siwe tamuhangaisha	So that it will not cause them trouble
Sikuze zikiadiya	In the future.

31. *Ni haki kumsajili*	It is their right to be registered
Rasmi kwa sirikali	Officially at the local administration.
Wanawake na wavuli	Girls and boys alike—
Ni haki kwa wote piya	It is the right of each of them.

32. *Hili yambo ni muhimu*	This issue is important
Kwa watu wote fahamu	For everyone, understand—
Nawe usione wumu[1]	Don't think that it is difficult
Mwanao kumwandikiya	To register your child.

1 *wumu* Am. "hardness" (Std. *ugumu*)

33. *Mmwandikiye karatasi*	Have a certificate issued
Mwano kizawa upesi	Right after the birth of your child;
Usipoteze nafasi	Don't waste any time,
Kisa utaiyutiya	Otherwise you will regret it later.

HURUMA: SOCIAL ROLES AND RESPONSIBILITY

34.   *Kitoandika haraka*   If you don't get them registered early,
       Hata mwano katukuka   And wait until they are grown up,
       Ni mno utasumbuka   You'll have great difficulty
       Baadaye kuzengeya   Getting it later.

35.   *Ni haki kulla mwanati*   It is the right of every citizen
       Kizawa kupowa cheti   To have a birth certificate;
       Khaswa kwa wetu wakati   Especially nowadays,
       Ni dharura mambo haya   This is necessary.

36.   *Ni haki yake kupendwa*   It is their right to be loved,
       Na kwa mapendi kuundwa   To be brought up with love:
       Wazazi wengi hushindwa   Many parents fail
       Haya kuwatimiziya   To do this.

37.   *Wana wahitaji hili*   Children need
       Mapendi ya kwelikweli   A lot of love.
       Mapendi na maakuli   Between love and food,
       Mapendi hutanguliya   Love comes first.

38.   *Tuwaoneshe ruhuma*   Let us show them softheartedness
       Na kuwapenda daima   And let us always love them;
       Kwa wote baba na mama   Children demand this
       Wana hili huzengeya   From both father and mother.

39.   *Tuwaoneshe imani*   Let us show them kindness;
       Twambe nao kwa makini   Let us talk to them gently.
       Tusizowee wendani   Let us not adopt the bad habit, my friends,
       Wetu wana kurukiya   Of shouting at our children.

40.   *Wana wakiwa wanuna*   When the children are still small,
       Hilo hawapendi sana   They don't like this at all.
       Akiukiwa huwona   When they are shouted at, they feel
       Ni mno memuoneya   That you are abusing them.

41.   *Wana wakizungumza*   When children address us,
       Yataka kuwasikiza   We should listen to them.
       Wana tukiwapuuza   When we ignore them,
       Huwapa fikira mbaya   We make them feel bad.

42.	*Wana na tuwasikize*	Let us listen to our children
	Watakayo watweleze	And let them explain to us what they want.
	Wana na tusiwapuze	We should not neglect them;
	Hiyo si njema tabiya	This is not a good habit.
43.	*Tukiwapuza zijana*	If we neglect the children,
	Huwavunda moyo sana	We discourage them greatly.
	Ni dharura wakinena	It is a must to pay attention
	Akilini kuwatiya	When they talk to us.
44.	*Na wana wetu tuteze*	Let us play with our children;
	Kwa ziswa tuwapumbaze	Let us entertain them with stories.
	Mazoweya tuyakuze	Let us build good bonds
	Na kwao kukaribiya	And let us be close to them.
45.	*Wana na tuwakumbate*	Let us hug them,
	Yuuyuu tuwangate	And let us carry them high on our shoulders.
	Tuwaoneshe ya kite	
	Mahaba na mazoweya	Let us show them unconditional love, Affection, and closeness.
46.	*Tuwape wana wakati*	Let us dedicate time to our children.
	Sisi na wao tuketi	We should spend time with them;
	Tunene yapo katiti	Let us talk to them, even if it is only for a short while,
	Tashamiri mazoweya	To strengthen our bonds.
47.	*Tuwape wana nafasi*	Let us give them a chance
	Wao kuteza na sisi	To play with us
	Kusudi nao wahisi	So that they feel
	Hisabuni huwatiya	They are taken seriously.
48.	*Tuwabusu wana wetu*	Let us kiss our children:
	Ni sunna ya tumwa wetu	This is according to our Prophet's rules,
	Tangu zingali zitutu[1]	From the time when they are still small
	Mpaka kuinukiya	Until they grow up.

---

1 *kitutu* (pl. *zitutu*) Am. "small child" (Std. *mtoto mdogo*; pl. *watoto wadogo*)

HURUMA: SOCIAL ROLES AND RESPONSIBILITY

49. *Tungayaona matoto* Even if we think this is of minor import-
    Yana ndani na ukweto[1] ance,
    Athariye ni mzito These things run deep.
    Hayondoki hubakiya Their impact is great:
    They do not vanish, but linger.

1 *ukweto* "depth."

50. *Wana haya wapatao* The children who experience this
    Si sawa na wakosao Are different from those who don't;
    Hawafani wana hao They do not resemble each other
    Kwa nyendo na kwa tabiya In behavior or character.

51. *Wana haya wakipata* When children receive this,
    Hukuwa pasi matata They grow up without difficulties,
    Akili humetameta With bright minds
    Kimawazo hutuliya And mentally stable.

52. *Mwana haya akosapo* If a child lacks this,
    Kasoro nyingi huwepo There will be deficiencies:
    Wana hunenda mapopo Those children go astray;
    Hawandami sawa ndiya They don't follow the right path.

53. *Ndipo wawapo wakora* That is how they become troublemakers
    Wazazi wakawakera Who upset their parents.
    Tewengo[1] mara kwa mara Trouble again and again—
    Na hawatindi udhiya They don't stop causing problems.

1 *tewengo* Am. "trouble" (Std. *maudhiko*)

54. *Mwana mapendi kikosa* If children lack love,
    Enga mte kutonosa[1] They are like a seedling that is not watered.
    Ukitokufa kabisa If they do not die,
    Utasononeka[11] ghaya They will suffer a lot.

1 *-nosa* Baj. = *-nosha* Am. "to water" | 11 *-sononeka* "to suffer" (Mau: *kutokuwa na raha* "to be without happiness")

55.	*Atasononeka mno*	They will suffer a lot,
	Kikosa mapendi mwano	If your children lack love.
	Hono wa mte mfano	Take the example of the seedling,
	Zidi kuufikiriya	And keep pondering it.
56.	*Mwana kitokwisa mwako*	If children do not quench their thirst
	Kupata mapendi yako	For your love,
	Huwa hesi babaiko	They will not be able to stop worrying
	Kwenye moya kutuliya	And calm down.
57.	*Hatui hatamakani*	The children will not be calm and settled;
	Hastakiri nyumbani	They will not find comfort at home,
	Na hata penye wendani	And even among their friends
	Mara huzuwa balaya	They will suddenly pick quarrels.
58.	*Huwa kama ibilisi*	[Such children] are like the devil,
	Au kama mwanachisi	Or like the bastard who is also the child of a
	Zikiri¹ kwake hazisi	bastard.
	Kitinda handa zipiya	Their misdeeds never end,
		As soon as they stop, they begin again.

1 *zikiri* Am. "mischief" (Std. *vitimbi*)

59.	*Hayo yote ni athari*	This is all the result
	Ya alopata dothari	Of their experiences of being stigmatized
	Ya makosa yalojiri	And being mistreated
	Muda wa kuinukiya	In early childhood.
60.	*Basi natutahadhari*	So, let us be careful:
	Tuwepuwe na khatwari	Let us protect them from danger.
	Wana tuyee uzuri	Let us bring them up well
	Bila kuwakaripiya	Without mistreating them.
61.	*Na haki nyingine tena*	And our children also have a right,
	Alo amuru Rabbana	According to God's command,
	Ni kula kwa wetu wana	To be nourished
	Kunwa na kuvaa piya	And dressed.

HURUMA: SOCIAL ROLES AND RESPONSIBILITY

62. *Mwana akisa kuzawa*　　When a child is born,
    Ni haki yake kupowa　　It is the child's right
    Ya kushibisha maziwa　　To be fed with enough milk:
    Kwa amri ya Jaliya　　This is the order of the Magnificent One.

63. *Maziwa haswa ya mama*　　Especially mother's milk,
    Mwana kunwa ni lazima　　The child needs to drink.
    Ya mamake yakikoma　　If the mother's milk dries up,
    Ya ng'ombe husaidiya　　That of the cow will help.

64. *Maziwa ya mama yake*　　The mother's milk
    Ni dharura kuu kwake　　Is of the utmost priority.
    Akishiba kwayo pweke　　If children drink only this milk,
    Huwa na njema afiya　　They will stay in good health.

65. *Wala sipende kumpa*　　Don't prefer to feed your baby
    Mwana maziwa kwa tupa　　With milk from the bottle.
    Dakitari huzitupa　　Even doctors throw this away;
    Hawapendi kusikiya　　They do not like to hear of it.

66. *Tupa si chombo kizuri*　　The bottle is not a good container:
    Ina na nyingi khatari　　It brings many dangers.
    Mwana hesi utiriri　　Children do not stop whining
    Tupa akiizoweya　　If they get used to bottles.

67. *Na tupa husababisha*　　And the bottle causes
    Maradhi na hurarisha　　Sickness and diarrhea;
    Si sahali kuiyosha　　It is not easy to clean it,
    Burashi ungatumiya　　Even if you use a brush.

68. *Sharuti kuichemsha*　　You have to boil
    Na kisa kuikausha　　And dry it
    Mwana hukubabaisha　　While your child is fussing.
    Lini utatenda haya　　How will you manage all this at once?

69. *Tena ya mama maziwa*　　Furthermore, the mother's milk
    Ameyaumba Moliwa　　That God has provided
    Si moto hayakupowa　　Is neither too hot nor too cold,
    Ni tayari kutumiya　　But ready for consumption.

70.	*Hayana nyingi harara*	It is neither too hot
	Si baridi ya kukera	Nor harmfully cold;
	Mwana hukuwa imara	Children grow strong
	Ya mama akitumiya	If fed with mother's milk.
71.	*Yameumbwa kwa kipimo*	The milk is well balanced
	Haja zake zote zimo	And provides for all their needs.
	Hakuna kiso kuwemo	There is nothing lacking;
	Madini sukari piya	It contains minerals and sugar as well.
72.	*Huhitaji kuyaonda*	You do not need to taste it,
	Wala kudara kwachanda	Nor use a finger to test its temperature;
	Popote unapokwenda	Everywhere you go,
	Huwa na wewe pamoja	You have it with you.
73.	*Huwa ndani mwa matiti*	It is in the breasts,
	Tayari kula wakati	Ready at any time;
	Mwana taabu hapati	The child does not need to suffer,
	Na mama huna udhiya	And you, mother, are never in trouble.
74.	*Kuyasahau huwezi*	You cannot forget it,
	Wala hayakupi kazi	And it does not cause much work.
	Kimwakiza mitilizi	As soon as you put the baby to your breast,
	Huwa ichandama ndiya	the milk starts to flow
		And finds its way.
75.	*Wala hayana gharama*	It does not bear any cost;
	Kununuwa si lazima	You do not need to buy it.
	Neema yake Karima	The Generous One, in His bounty
	Wana amewaekeya	Has provided it for the children.
76.	*Basi kwani kuwawasa*	So why do you deprive them,
	Wana wetu kuwamsa	Weaning our children
	Kab'la ya mwida kwisa	Before the time has come[1]
	Kwa urembo kutapiya	Out of fear of losing attractiveness?

1 In the Islamic context of Lamu, it is common to breastfeed children for two years.

HURUMA: SOCIAL ROLES AND RESPONSIBILITY

77. *Mamama huwadhulumu* The mothers inflict harm
    Wana pasi kufahamu On their children unconsciously,
    Ati ujana udumu Believing their youth should remain,
    Yasimeme kusaliya And keeping their breasts' form.

78. *Mwana piya kadhalika* Likewise, it is the right of children
    Ni hakiye kumpeka To be taken to the clinic
    Kwa tarikhi kutochoka Regularly, without their parents tiring of it,
    Kupima kudunga piya So that they may be vaccinated and weighed.

79. *Mpeke chanjo apate* Take them to be vaccinated
    Na ratiba afuwate Following the schedule.
    Sindano moya siwate Don't miss even one vaccination;
    Ni muhimu kutumiya It is important to get them.

80. *Usidharau sindano* Don't neglect the injections
    Za ziweo na mikono In the thighs and arms;
    Ni kinga hizo kwa mwano They protect your children
    Muwili husaidiya And help their bodies.

81. *Mwana umpe chakula* Give your children food
    Na palo pema kulala And a proper place to sleep.
    Ni hakize kwa jumla In sum, these are the rights
    Sisi mbwa kuwatendeya We should provide for them.

82. *Wape chakula kizuri* Give them healthy food
    Nguo za kuwasitiri And proper clothes;
    Wapokowe[1] wanawiri Wash them so that they may shine
    Ulinde yao afiya And to protect their health.

1 *-pokowa* Am. "to wash" (Std. *-ogesha*)

83. *Wana kula wahitaji* Children need food
    Na ya kunwa safi maji And clean drinking water.
    Afiya bora haiji Good health does not come
    Illa kwa kuizengeya Unless you make an effort.

84.	*Si sharuti kuwa ghali*	Healthy food
	Ya afiya maakuli	Does not need to be expensive;
	Mahitaji ya muwili	The needs of the body
	Ndiyo ya kuzingatiya	Should also be considered.

85.	*Wape matunda na mboga*	Give them fruits and vegetables
	Piya wimbi wa kusaga	As well as millet porridge.
	Kuku mayai kitaga	When the chickens lay their eggs,
	Wana na wapate piya	Children should also get their share.[1]

1 In former times, particularly on Pate, people would sell all their eggs without providing any to the children.

86.	*Nyama ikiwezekana*	If possible, also provide meat
	Samaki ni bora sana	And fish, which is much better.
	Hupata swiha[1] zijana	Children will be healthy
	Zitu hizi kitumiya	If they consume these things.

1 *swiha* Ar. "health" (Std. *afya*)

87.	*Nalo ziwa wasikose*	And don't let them lack milk—
	Wala mno sitokose[1]	And don't boil it too much,
	Ili nafuu isise	So the minerals shall not be destroyed
	Yangani ikapoteya	And evaporate into thin air.

1 *-tokosa* Am. "boil" (Std. *chemsha*)

88.	*Kutokosa ni lazima*	To boil the milk is a must
	Ziwa lisilo la mama	If it is not mother's milk,
	Kwani ndiyo usalama	Because this maintains well-being.
	Ni kanuni za afiya	These are the requirements for health.

89.	*Na mno likitokota*	But if boiled for too long,
	Faidaye hutopata	You cannot benefit from it.
	Moto likisa kwambata	When you see the milk is hot enough,
	Puwa kiona huwiya	Remove it when you see it boiling.

HURUMA: SOCIAL ROLES AND RESPONSIBILITY 249

90. *Mai sana ni muhimu*   Water is of utmost importance
    Kwa sisi wana adamu   For us human beings.
    Sipende mno ya tamu   Don't give too much preference to juice;
    Yalo swafi angaliya   Look for clean water.

91. *Wana wape mai swafi*   Give your children clean water.
    Wala sambe mbona sifi   Don't say, "Why? I have not died
    Nami hunwa mai ghafi   From drinking dirty water
    Nyaka toka nyaka ngiya   Year in and year out."

92. *Yuwa wana ni dhaifu*   You should know, children are sensitive;
    Tumbo zao ni khafifu   Their intestines are feeble.
    Mai yakiwa machafu   When the water is dirty,
    Mara huzuwa balaya   It can cause sudden problems.

93. *Na uchafu si tototo*   And this dirt is not a mud puddle
    Kuwa taona kwa mato   That you can see with the naked eye;
    Kuna zilulu zitoto   There are tiny bacteria
    Kwazo maradhi heneya   Through which sickness spreads.

94. *Zitutu mno zibombwe[1]*   These germs are so tiny,
    Ukiteka kwa kikombe   When you scoop up water in a cup,
    Huziyoni nazo kumbe   You cannot see them.
    Zimo tele huoweya   But—alas—plenty are swimming in it.

1 *kibombwe* (pl. *zibombwe*) Am. "tiny germ."

95. *Hizo mno ni khatari*   They are so dangerous;
    Watu sana hukhasiri   They harm many people.
    Sharuti kutahadhari   You must be careful;
    Mara hukushambuliya   They attack you suddenly.

96. *Maradhi yakimswibu*   If sickness befalls the child,
    Mwana yangawa hububu   Even if it is a small thing,
    Fanya kula taratibu   Make every effort
    Penye dawa kutapiya   To run to a health center.

250 HURUMA: SOCIAL ROLES AND RESPONSIBILITY

97. *Uwee siudharau*   Don't ignore illness;
    Mtoto huwa mkuu   A small thing can grow big,[1]
    Ukawa na wayukuu   And can be passed to grandchildren
    Na zitukuu zikaya   And even great-grandchildren.

1 An illness that is not cured can have long-term effects.

98. *Na mwana kiwa huhara*   And if children have diarrhea,
    Mpe mai kulla mara   Constantly give them water,
    Na dawa zilizo bora   And don't delay
    Sichelewe kuzengeya   Looking for good medicine.

99. *Hata kama hutapika*   Even if they vomit after drinking,
    Mpe mai kadhalika   Continue giving them water.
    Yangawa mengi hutoka   Even if a lot comes out again,
    Machache yatasaliya   Some will remain.

100. *Mai yakiwa katiti*   If the water is not enough,
     Muilini ni mauti   This means death for the body.
     Bila ya mai huketi   Listen, without water
     Muda mrefu sikiya   You cannot survive for long.

101. *Wana kupowa ilimu*   Understand, to have an education
     Ni haki kuu fahamu   Is a great right for children.
     Ilimu nguzo muhimu   Education is an important pillar
     kwa wana waadamiya   For all human beings.

102. *Ilimu kitu dharura*   Education of all kind
     Kwa jamii yake sura   Is absolutely necessary.
     Ilimu akiba bora   Education is a good investment
     Ya mwana kumuwatiya   To make for your child.

103. *Wana lazima wasome*   Children must learn
     Maarifa wayatume   To gain knowledge;
     Wayezi tufanye shime   Parents, let us make an effort
     Ilimu kuwapatiya   To offer them education.

HURUMA: SOCIAL ROLES AND RESPONSIBILITY

104. *Wana tuwasomesheni*
Uwinga tuepusheni
Wana tusimamiyeni
Kuwekeza sawa ndiya

Let us teach our children
To do away with ignorance.
Let us support our children
To show them the right way.

105. *Ilimu wana wapate*
Ilimu namna zote
Tusiwafanye mapite
Ilimu kuwaziwiya

They should receive education—
Education of all kinds.
Let us not make them dummies
By depriving them of education.

106. *Wana tusomeshe dini*
Na msingi Qur'ani
Wakisaa uwingani
Dini itatupoteya

Let us give our children a religious educa-
tion
Whose foundation is the Qur'ān.
If they remain ignorant,
We will lose our religion.

107. *Hilo ni kuu jukumu*
Wazazi tulifahamu
Na mungu tatuhukumu
Tukiwakhini dhuriya

This is a large responsibility
That we, the parents, should be aware of.
God will judge us
If we deprive our children.

108. *Na ilimu za maisha*
Lazima kuwasomesha
Waweze kuifundisha
Wao kuisimamiya

We also have to train them
In the skills of everyday life
So that they learn
To rely on themselves.

109. *Tuwasomeshe skuli*
Tusioneni ni ghali
Ni adui ujahili
Tuupijeni pamoya

Let us send them to school,
And let us not think it is too expensive.
Ignorance is our enemy;
Let us fight it together.

110. *Ujahili ni khatwari*
Kuu mno lake shari
Hata akili hodari
Kwa uwinga hupoteya

Ignorance is a danger;
Its ills are great.
Even a sharp mind
Becomes useless without education.

111. *Tuwafunde za mikono*
Kazi ni nafuu mno
Msumeno na sindano
Wazowee kutumiya

Let us train them in handicrafts
That are very useful;
They should get used to handling
A saw and a needle.

112. *Wana wakiilimika*
     Nafuu hiyo hakika
     Huweneya bila shaka
     Na kwetu husikiliya

     If our children are educated,
     For sure, the benefits
     Will certainly spread
     So that we can also profit from them.

113. *Tuwapeni makawanda[1]*
     Masomoni mbee kwenda
     Wakisoma shindashinda
     Faidaye hupoteya

     Let us give them opportunities
     So they can make progress.
     If they learn irregularly,
     There will be no benefit.

     1 *kawanda* "arena, square" (Std. *uwanja mkubwa*)

114. *Faida hatutoona*
     Ila wakisoma sana
     Wende mbali wetu wana
     Sharqi na gharbiya

     We will not see any good results
     Unless they work hard.
     Our children should travel far,
     To the West and to the East.

115. *Kwenye hizi zetu zama*
     Hauthamiiniwi umma
     Illa kiwa wamesoma
     Zaidi kupindukiya

     In our era,
     People aren't valued
     Unless they are learned
     And well-educated.

116. *Ilimu hiyau sasa*
     Ndiyo hongoza siyasa
     Ndiyo chando cha mapesa
     Hufunguwa zote ndiya

     Now it is education
     That guides politics.
     It is the source of wealth;
     It opens all the doors.

117. *Hela ngaliya Japani*
     Ina ina duiyani
     Nti nyingi uzunguni
     Mate hiyo humiziya

     Take Japan as an example:
     It has a global reputation.
     Many countries in the West
     Envy it.

118. *Walipata kwa uyuzi*
     Na kwa ufundi wa kazi
     Ilimu hizi na hizi
     Kitambo walizengeya

     They have achieved this through knowledge
     And skillfulness in their work.
     They started long ago
     To look for various kinds of knowledge.

HURUMA: SOCIAL ROLES AND RESPONSIBILITY

119. *Na nti zilo tajiri* — As for the rich countries,
Ni zipi hela fikiri — Which are they? Just give it a thought!
Ni zile zilonawiri — They shine
Kwa ilimu kwendeleya — Due to advanced education.

120. *Na lingine nambe sasa* — Let me talk about another matter now.
Si haki na ni makosa — It is not fair—it is a crime
Walowana kuwatesa — To abuse children
Ngumu kazi kuwatiya — And leave hard work for them.

121. *Wana tusilazimishe* — Let us not force our children,
Wala tusikalifishe — Nor overburden them.
Wana tusiwateushe — Let us not chase them
Kama punda ni hatiya — Like donkeys; this is a mistake.

122. *Wana wataka wakati* — The children want the time
Wateze teze katiti — To play a little;
Kuwakaza kama nati — Tightening them like a bolt
Huwavuruga tabiya — Means destroying their character.

123. *Kuwapa kazi nzito* — Making them work hard
Wana wangali watoto — While they are still young
Na kwa tamaa ya pato — Because you want more income
Ni yambo lisilo ndiya — Is not the right way.

124. *Wala sambi ni makosa* — I do not mean that it is a mistake
Wana kutumwa yapasa — To send children on errands;
Si kwa tamaa ya pesa — However, not out of greed for money,
Ni kuwapa mazoweya — But to gradually get them used to it.

125. *Mwana si bibi arusi* — A child is not a bride
Hapei wala haosi — Who does not sweep nor clean the dishes.
Kimtuma kwa kiyasi — If you send them on small errands,
Huwi umemuoneya — You are not abusing them.

126. *Kazi za kwao nyumbani* — Domestic work is fine for them.
Na hata wake jirani — And even if the neighbor
Akimtuma dukani — Sends them to the shop,
Sawa kimtumikiya — It is alright to be at her service.

127. *Kazi kiwa atafanya* If they do work
Kama bajiya kuzanya Like selling *bajiya*[1],
Hatuwezi kulikanya We cannot reject it,
Kwani ni yambo la ndiya Because it's the right thing to do.

1 *bajiya* "a small fried cake of mixed beans"; "Badyia. Sorte de beignet consistant en une boulette de pâte pimentée et frite, que les Indiens préparent avec de la farine additionnée de haricots et de qqs découpures d'oignon, d'aubergine, etc." (Scl. 85).

128. *Mpangiye kwa wakati* Plan the time for them
Afanye kazi katiti So that they do only a little work
Na tena awe hawati And do not miss
Masomo kuhudhuriya Any lessons.

129. *Bajiya zikitotoka* If not all the *bajiya* are sold,
Ziyazi zikimwaika And the potatoes fall to the ground,
Au mwende kampoka And a friend steals from them—
Simziwiye kungiya Don't ban them from the house.

130. *Simwambiye nenda zako* Don't tell them, "Go away—
Sitaki maneno yako I don't want your excuses.
Rudi koko utokako Return to where you came from
Pesa ukitoneteya If you do not bring me money."

131. *Huwa umemwekezani* What lesson are you trying
Mwana una ndiya gani To teach your child?
Ya kupatiya mapeni Why should children earn money for
Nae hukutegemeya you?
They should rather depend on you.

132. *Mwenye kumpa ni wewe* You are the one who should give to them;
Kiya kwako umtowe Instead, when they come to you, you chase
Ende pwani katondowe them away.
Deni yako kulipiya Should they go to the port to collect salvage
To pay your debts[1]?

1 In former times, when *mashua* ("a kind of boat of boards for embarking or disembarking goods"; Krp. 205) arrived on the beach and goods were discharged, if some happened to fall on the ground, children were allowed to pick them up without being scolded or having to pay. Ustadh Mau still remembers how he went to the beach when he was a child, hoping to find a banana or some dates that had fallen from a *mashua* coming from Somalia or Arabia.

HURUMA: SOCIAL ROLES AND RESPONSIBILITY

133. *Huwa memfunda nini*
Huyo mwano masikini
Huyamtiya ndiyani
Huyamwambiya poteya

What have you taught them,
Your poor children?
Have you not put them out on the streets?
Have you not made them go astray?

134. *Mwana kitenda la jongo*
Kurudiwa ni kwa ngongo
Simrudi kwa zigongo
Na makonde kumtiya

If your children misbehave,
Respond to them with one lash of a
whip.
Don't beat them with a stick
Or with punches.

135. *Hata ukighadhibika*
Subira mno yataka
Mkono siwe haraka
Kilo mbee kwatiliya

Even if you are enraged,
You need to be patient.
Your hand should not be too quick
To slap whoever is in front of you.

136. *Mwana utamkhasiri*
Umtiye na dothari
Ya milele na dahari
Nawe uiyute piya

You will intimidate
And humiliate your child
Once and forever,
And you will also regret it.

137. *Mwana adabu mfunde*
kutangamana na wende
Watu wote awapende
Na kuwa safiya niya

Teach your children good manners,
How to behave with peers,
So that they like all kinds of people
Because of their good intentions.

138. *Mfunde kutangamana*
Na wakuu na wanuna
Aitenge kimuona
Sitaha humondoleya

Teach them how to interact
With adults and with children.
Teach them: if they find that someone has
disgraced them,
They should better stay away.

139. *Ayuwe kuna mipaka*
Haifai kuiruka
Kwa amri ya Rabbuka
Na kwa mila na shariya

That is why they should know that there are
boundaries,
That one is not allowed to transgress
By God's command
And custom and law.

140. *Mfunde mwana mfunde*
    Yalo mema ayatende
    Mbeu njema uzipande
    Tangu akiinukiya

Teach the children, teach them
To do only good,
So that you may plant good seeds
From childhood onward.

141. *Mfundishe kwa zitendo*
    Kwa ulo mzuri mwendo
    Maneno yasiwe kando
    Yende sambamba pamoya

Teach them by your good example,
Through your good deeds.
Your words should not contradict,
But be in harmony with them.

142. *Maneno na yako hali*
    Yaandamane mawili
    Yeye simuase hili
    Wewe ukaendeleya

Your words and your behavior
Should go together;
Don't forbid something
That you continue doing.

143. *Kiwa hayatofanana*
    Basi hayana maana
    Maneno ungayanena
    Yangani yatapoteya

If your words don't match your actions,
They have no meaning.
Although you speak,
Your words will vanish into thin air.

144. *Hayatowata athari*
    Kwa mwano ilo mzuri
    Bali itakuwa kheri
    Hayo kutomtaiya

They will not have a good effect
On your child,
So it is better
Not to say them at all.

145. *Sifa hini ni lazima*
    Kwa kula mfunda mema
    Awe baba awe mama
    Mwalimu hukaza niya

This concern is essential
For anyone who teaches good behavior,
Be they a father or a mother—
And it is more important still for the
teacher.

146. *Zijana wana akili*
    Na mambo hutaamali
    Wana zipimo zikali
    Za watu kuwapimiya

Children are clever,
And observe things.
They have a sharp way
Of assessing people.

147. *Wanazo zao mizani*
    Za kumuyuwa fulani
    Hutuondosha ndiyani
    Au kweli hutwambiya

They have their own way of
Knowing someone:
"Do they wish to betray us,
Or are they telling us the truth?"

HURUMA: SOCIAL ROLES AND RESPONSIBILITY

148. *Haki nimezozinena* The rights that I have mentioned
    Nda wote walo zijana Are for all children,
    Awe mume au mwana Be they boys or girls—
    Ni hakiye kwa shariya These are their rights guaranteed by law.

149. *Awe mume au mke* Be the child a boy or a girl,
    Haki hizi yeye ndake These rights are theirs.
    Tuwape tusiwapoke Let us grant them and not deprive them,
    Wenyewe kufurahiya So that they can enjoy them.

150. *Nilotaya kwa bayana* The ones I have mentioned explicitly
    Ndizo maarufu sana Are those that are well known.
    Kuna na nyingine tena There are others
    Napenda kuzishiriya That I would like to point out.

151. *Kuna mambo maalumu* There are some issues
    Mzazi kuyafahamu That a parent should know,
    Mno hayo ni muhimu That are very important,
    Sana humsaidiya And will help them very much.

152. *Marafiki kuwayuwa* To know your child's friends
    Wa mwano kuwatambuwa And assess them
    Hili yambo limepowa Is very important.
    Muhimu nambari moya It should be number one on your agenda.

153. *Marafiki huathiri* Friends have influence,
    Kwa wema au kwa shari For better or worse.
    Rafiki waso wazuri Friends who are no good
    Humpa utwa twabiya Will have a bad influence on their character.

154. *Rafiki kiwa waovu* If their friends are bad,
    Fanya kuwa uwerevu Be clever:
    Umwepuwe si kwa nguvu Do not separate them by force,
    Kwa busara kutumiya But act wisely.

155. *Yaso mema humfunda*
Na mazuri huyaponda
Na kisa kuuma zanda
Ndilo litalosaliya

They will teach your children
what is not good
And destroy their good behavior,
And in the end, it is only regret
That will remain.

156. *Wa mwanao maswahibu*
Kuwa na wao karibu
Uziyuwe taratibu
Tabiya na nyendo piya

So be close with
Your child's friends
So that you get to know them well,
Both their character and their conduct.

157. *Ukiziona si njema*
Mwepuwe mwano salama
Kab'la huyaziuma
Zanda kwa kuiyutiya

When you see they aren't good,
Find a gentle way to keep your child away
Before you bite
Your nails in regret.

158. *Muweke mwano kitako*
Umpe shauri lako
Kwa matamu matamko
Umuekeze ya ndiya

Make your child sit down,
And give him your advice.
With sweet words,
Show him the right way.

159. *Na wala wewe sichoke*
Mnaswihi aepuke
Marafiki asishike
Wa nyendo za kupoteya

Don't get tired;
Persevere in your advice to avoid
Having friends
With bad conduct.

160. *Marafiki ni lazima*
Kwa umri maaluma
Nazengee walo wema
Tapata yapo mmoya

Friends are very important
At a certain age;
Let your children find good ones.
They will find at least one.

161. *Mtu huhitaji watu*
Hili ndilo umbo letu
Metuumba Mola wetu
Ni kiungo metutiya

Everyone needs people.
This is our nature;
This is how our God has created us.
It is a part of the human nature that He put
into us.

HURUMA: SOCIAL ROLES AND RESPONSIBILITY

162. *Hutokeya kwa nadira* It happens sometimes,
    Si ghalibu kula mara But it is not very common,
    Mtu watu humkera That someone is afraid of people
    Penye watu hukimbiya And avoids crowds.

163. *Ni kasoro maalumu* It is a particular defect
    Tunazo wanaadamu That we human beings have,
    Na kwa wangine hudumu And for some it remains
    Zikawa ni mazoweya And becomes habitual.

164. *Marafiki wanautwa* Friends are infectious;
    Hukungiya kama mtwa They infest you like termites.
    Mara na wewe hukutwa Suddenly, you find
    Shimoni metumbukiya You have fallen into a pit.

165. *Na marafiki baadhi* And some friends
    Wenye nyendo za kuudhi With annoying conduct
    Utwa kama wa maradhi Are infectious like a disease;
    Hukupasa mara moya They pass it on to you immediately.

166. *Mwenye afya mtwae* Take a healthy person,
    Pa wawee umtie Leave him among sick people,
    Wangaliye takuwae And see what happens:
    Afya tawaatiya Will he pass his health on to them?

167. *Utaona bila shaka* Of course, you will see
    Maradhi yatamshika That sickness will befall him;
    Afya haitotoka Health cannot spread
    Na waweze kuwaingiya And infect the sick.

168. *Basi hini ndiyo hali* This is how it is
    Ya marafiki batwili With bad friends:
    Alo mwema hubadili The good one is infected
    Wakawa ni hali moya And they all become the same.

169. *Na mangine ya kisasa* And another modern thing
    Ya haribuwo kabisa That is completely destructive
    Ni zifaya za anasa Are the media of entertainment
    Miini zimezongiya That have spread to every town.

170. Khususa haya madishi
Hufuja hayabakishi
Yangiyapo hayabishi
Hufuza moya kwa moya

Especially TV programs
That ruin everything, leaving nothing of value:
You have easy access to them,
You can get them directly from home.

171. Madishi ni mitaimbo
Huvunda mazuri mambo
Ni zaidi ya ulimbo
Hukunasa mara moya

Satellite TV is a crowbar
That smashes all morality.
It is worse than a bird trap;
It seizes you immediately.

172. Ni zitu haya hondosha
Maovu huamirisha
Nyendo mbovu hufundisha
Na huweneza balaya

It curbs good values
And enforces evil,
Teaching bad manners
And spreading mischief.

173. Madishi mambo hufuja
Yalo mema moja moja
Ipo kuu mno haja
Wana kuwateuliya

Satellite TV damages
All that is good, one thing after another.
It is of great importance
To choose the right programs for your children.

174. Imekuwa ni dharura
Kuteuwa kwa busara
Ni zipindi gani bora
Za faida kwangaliya

It has become necessary
To carefully select
Good programs
That are beneficial to watch.

175. Kuna baadhi zichache
Ni zizuri tusiziche
Ziyovu tusiwaliche
Wana kuzishuhudiya

There are a few programs
That are good; let us not hesitate to watch them,
But we should not allow our children
To watch the bad ones.

176. Madishi yana malengo
Kuu ni tabiya jongo
Kuzeneza kwa mipango
Zitapakaze duniya

The central aim of TV
Is to promote immorality
And to spread it according
To well-made plans worldwide.

HURUMA: SOCIAL ROLES AND RESPONSIBILITY

177. *Na nyendo za ulanisi* And all types of perversion
Zisofanana na sisi That do not suit us
Zimeeneya upesi Have spread rapidly
Na madishi ndiyo ndiya Through TV programs.

178. *Na madishi huwekeza* TV programs cause people to
Watu kwenye yakusoza Be morally shipwrecked,
Na nyendo mbovu huviza And increase bad conduct,
Na kuondosha ya haya And do away with our sense of decency.

179. *Huketi baba na mama* The mother, the father,
Na wana wakitizama And the children, all together, watch
Mambo hata kuyasema Scenes that, according to our culture,
Kwa kikwetu ni hatiya Would be an offense even to talk about.

180. *Hutufundisha machafu* They teach us dirty things,
Mengi ya uharibifu And much that is destructive.
Wazungu hutuswarifu Westerners manipulate us and
Kama unga kutezeya Shape us like dough.

181. *Angaliyani mavazi* Look at the dresses
Yavawao siku hizi That people wear nowadays.
Ni sawa na kwenda wazi It is the same as going naked,
Na watu hushangiliya Yet people still praise them.

182. *Ya waso haya mishono* The fashion of the shameless
Kandu ziso na mikono Includes sleeveless tops
Wazi mbavu na ziuno And ones that reveal the belly,
Hadhirani hutembeya Which they openly walk around in.

183. *Hizi ni zake athari* These are some of the effects
Madishi yana khatwari Of these dangerous TV programs;
Wazazi na tusikiri Parents, let us not allow our children
Wana yote kwangaliya To watch all these programs.

184. *Zitabu na magazeti* We need to have a closer look
Sharuti tuzitafiti At books and journals,
Wasipoteze wakati So that our children will not waste their time
Wana kwa kusoma haya Reading the wrong ones.

185. *Kuna mengi siku hizi*	There are many useless
Magazeti ya upuzi	Magazines nowadays
Kwa hayo mwana hawezi	From which children
Kupata faida moya	Do not benefit at all.

186. *Zitabu za ulanisi*	Books promoting perversion
Zi tele pasi kiyasi	Are plentiful, without limit.
Riwaya za kipolisi	Crime stories
Na za ngono meeneya	And pornography have spread.

187. *Haya yote kwa zijana*	All of this is of no use
Mambo hayana maana	To the youth.
Hupoteza mwingi sana	They only waste a lot of
Wakati na pesa piya	Money and time on it.

188. *Mwanao mpeleleze*	Observe your children carefully,
Umfahamu nyendoze	So that you know their habits.
Yalo sawa umwekeze	Guide them on the right path,
Nasaha kumpatiya	And give them advice.[1]

1 *nasahah* "advice"; the Arabic term is seldom used in Swahili. Commonly, as Ustadh Mau notes, *nasaha* is translated as *wasiya* in Swahili, another term originally derived from Arabic. For instance, as Mau notes, the phrase النصيحة لدين *ad-dīn al-nasīha* "religion is advice," from a hadith of the Prophet Muhammad, is rendered as follows in Swahili: *dini ni watu kupana wasiya* "religion means people giving each other advice (*wasiya*)." Thus, the meaning of *wasiya* has changed in Swahili. Originally, in Arabic, *wasiya* meant "testament, the last worlds left down in a written format." This meaning can still be discerned in the sense of *wasiya* as a Swahli poetic genre (see, for instance, the *Wasiya wa mabanati* in this volume).

189. *Kwanda situmiye nguvu*	First of all, don't use force;
Kumkanya mwana ovu	If you want to forbid them from something bad,
Jaribu kuwa mwerevu	Try to be smart,
Kumnyenya tanguliya	And first, ask them carefully.

190. *Mwana simuwate rebe*	Don't leave your child unattended,
Wala mno simkabe	But don't be too strict either.
Siwe kama tupu debe	Don't be noisy as an empty tin[1]
Mayowe ukazoweya	Or get used to shouting.

1 An empty tin is very noisy if you beat it.

HURUMA: SOCIAL ROLES AND RESPONSIBILITY

191. *Kwa mayowe na ukali*
    Haitogeuka hali
    Mwana kimpa kivuli
    Atakalo tarudiya

Through shouting and anger,
The situation does not change.
As soon as you turn your back on your children,
They will continue doing what they want.

192. *Mwanao mbembeleze*
    Yake ndani akweleze
    Na wewe yako mwekeze
    Na kumuonya ya ndiya

Comfort your children
So that they can explain their inner
thoughts to you,
And tell them yours,
And direct them on the right path.

193. *Mwanao mno kikucha*
    Mbee yako atacha
    Akiuvira ukucha
    Tarudiya mazoweya

If your children are afraid of you,
They will stop doing things in front of you.
But just around the corner,
They will resume the old habits.

194. *Yambo kuu na muhimu*
    Ni mwano kukuhishimu
    Hapo takuwa na hamu
    Hapendi kukukoseya

The most important thing
Is that your children respect you.
Then they will make an effort,
For they do not wish to disappoint you.

195. *Na hishima kuipata*
    Kwa wana ni kufuwata
    Ndiya sawa tukapita
    Namna ya kuwayeya

To get respect
From your children, we have to
Follow the right path
In bringing them up.

196. *Mayezi ni kuu somo*
    La mizani na zipimo
    La hitaji misimamo
    Na miko kulishikiya

Upbringing is a lesson of the utmost importance.
It requires good judging and evaluating
As well as principles,
And you also have to stick to your rules.

197. *Yuwa mayezi ni fani*
    Yenye tandu na fununi
    Na muyezi ni fanani
    Kipawa huhitajiya

You have to know, upbringing is an art
That has many forms and modes,
And the parent is an artist
Who needs talent.

198. *Kula mtu si nahuza*
Wa safari kuziweza
Wangine mara husoza
Kwa kupita kombo ndiya

Not everybody is a captain
Who is able to navigate.
Some suddenly hit a rock
Because they take the wrong course.

199. *Si kula mke ni mama*
Mama ni sharuti kwima
Kwa mambo yalo lazima
Wana kuwasimamiya

Not every woman is a good mother.
A mother needs to be steadfast
In the things that are necessary
For supporting the children.

200. *Mayezi yataka miko*
Yana kazi na sumbuko
Mara hutuka zituko
Mtu asotarajiya

Upbringing requires restrictions.
It means work and struggle.
Problems may suddenly emerge
That one did not expect.

201. *Sasa muhukoma pwani*
Katika hunu uneni
Nina zifungu fulani
Napenda kumaliziya

Now I am about to reach
The harbor with my talk,
But I have some remarks
I would like to finish with.

202. *Nikianda la awali*
Taka tuombe Jalali
Walo na njema amali
Wana kututunukiya

To start with my first remark:
We should pray to God
To grant us children
Of good habits.

203. *Na ninenalo la pili*
Ni wana tuwakubali
Tuwatwae kwa miwili
Mno kufurahikiya

And my second remark
Is that we should accept our children
And receive them happily,
With open arms.

204. *Mungu akitupa mwana*
Tumkongowe sana
Tusiwe hununanuna
Mwana tutamtukiya

If God gives us children,
We should welcome them
Without grumbling,
Which would mean despising the child.

205. *Tusifanye kisirani*
Untha na dhukurani
Ni tunu yake Manani
Wote mbwa kufurahiya

We should not be annoyed,
Be the child a boy or a girl—
All are gifts from God
That we should be happy about.

HURUMA: SOCIAL ROLES AND RESPONSIBILITY

206. *Tukiwa upande shingo*
     Na nyoyo tele kinyongo
     Mwana takuwa terengo
     Utiriri na udhiya

     If we hang our heads,
     With hearts full of anger,
     The child will be a burden,
     Torment and annoyance.

207. *Lazima tufurahike*
     Kwa waume na kwa wake
     Kwani wote tukumbuke
     Ni tunu yake Jaliya

     We should be happy
     No matter if the child is a boy or a girl,
     Because we should remember
     That all of them are gifts from God.

208. *Wana mema tuzoweze*
     Tabiya njema tukuze
     Wana tusiwendekeze
     Rebe mno kuwatiya

     We should accustom our children to good
     habits
     And build their characters.
     Let us not spoil our children
     Or give them too much freedom.

209. *Mwana kimpa ahadi*
     Siivunde jitahidi
     Utimize kwa kasidi
     Aone memtendeya

     If you give your children a promise,
     Don't break it; make an effort
     To fulfill it
     So that they see you did it for them.

210. *Mwana ukimzoweza*
     Ahadi kutotimiza
     Nawe shere takuteza
     Wakati ukiadiya

     If your children get used
     To you breaking promises,
     They will also play tricks on you
     In due course.

211. *Kheri umwambiye kweli*
     Yambo ukitokubali
     Mambo huwa ni sahali
     Urongo hatozoweya

     It is better to be frank with them
     In case you don't agree.
     Things will be easier,
     And they will not get used to lies.

212. *Mwana mtiye mahaba*
     Kumpenda Mola Raba
     Hiyo ni kuu akiba
     Mwana utayomwatiya

     Plant in your child
     The love of God;
     This is a great treasure
     That you will pass on to your child.

213. *Mzoweze na kuswali*
     Ili isiwe thakili
     Kikuwa hatokabili
     Nalo kitoinukiya

     Accustom them to praying
     So that it will not be difficult.
     When grown up, they will reject it
     If they did not grow up with it.

214. *Kiwa angali ni mwana*
     Swali nae hukuona
     Tapoelewa maana
     Hatowata mazoweya

When they are still young,
Pray so that they can see you.
Later, when they are able to understand its meaning,
They will not give up this habit

215. *Haja zake zitimize*
     Mapeni simziwize
     Mwate aizoweze
     Kama watu kutumiya

Fulfill their needs;
Don't refuse to give them money.
Let them learn to spend money
As others do.

216. *Mfundishe na kuweka*
     Akiba kitu kitaka
     Asiwe mbwa kusumbuka
     Aweze kuipatiya

Teach them to save,
So that when they want something,
They will not be in trouble
But can buy it on their own.

217. *Kiwa kumi utampa*
     Nasitumiye kwa pupa
     Mwambiye zitiye hapa
     Mbili mbili takwekeya

If you give them ten coins,
They should not spend them hastily.
Tell them, "Put two in the savings box;
I will keep them for you."

218. *Nitakwekeya akiba*
     Uyuwe haba na haba
     Mara huyaza kibaba
     Sikuye husaidiya

"I will keep your savings.
You should know, little by little
Fills up the measure.
It will be of use one day."

219. *Mfunde na ukarimu*
     Kwa wende wanaadamu
     Khaswa walo yake damu
     Ruhuma kuwaoneya

Teach them generosity
Toward their fellow human beings.
Especially those of the same blood,
They should care for them.

220. *Simfunde ubakhili*
     Katawaliwa na mali
     Na piya ubaridhuli
     Simliche kuzoweya

Don't teach them greediness
So that they will be ruled by material concerns,
But also don't allow them
To get used to wasting money.

HURUMA: SOCIAL ROLES AND RESPONSIBILITY

221. *Ushujaa mzoweze*
Hiyo twabiya akuze
Na mno umuhimize
Dhuluma kutoridhiya

Get them used to courage
So that it grows in them.
And emphasize strongly
That they should not endure oppression.

222. *Asiridhike dhuluma*
Kuonewa wake umma
Na wanyonge kusimama
Iwe ni yake twabiya

They should not agree
To their people being oppressed,
But standing by the weak
Should be their character.

223. *Nasitupe haki yake*
Na ya mtu nasitake
Natwae kilicho chake
Cha wangine kuwatiya

They should not throw away their rights,
Nor should they deprive someone else of theirs.
Your children should take what is theirs,
And leave others with their rights.

224. *Tabiya ya unyanganyi*
Hakikisha haifanyi
Usinene simkanyi
Tawata kiinukiya

Make sure they do not develop
The habit of taking what is not theirs.
Don't say, "They will stop it when they grow up,
So I do not need to forbid them."

225. *Mkanye tangu ni mwana*
Kitenda mkanye tena
Ili kusudi maana
Sipende kunyanganyiya

Stop them while they still are children.
If they repeat it, forbid it again
With the intention
Of making them dislike stealing.

226. *Tena mpe mazowezi*
Tangu ali mumaizi
Kuzitenda njema kazi
Jamii kusaidiya

Furthermore, train them,
As soon as they start to understand things,[1]
To do meaningful tasks
That help the community.

1 Acc. to Ustadh Mau, a child starts to understand things at around the age of seven.

227. *Mfunde awe imara*
Penye wende kutojera
Kutowa yake fikira
Au uovu kuziwiya

Teach them to be confident
So that they are not shy in front of their peers,
To tell them their thoughts
And to stop evil deeds.

228. *Mpe sana mazowezi*
Ya kufanya uwamuzi
Mwenyewe asiajizi
Wangine kutegemeya

Train them well
To make their own decisions
So that they shall not be incapable of deciding
Without depending on others.

229. *Na mzazi jitahidi*
Kuzifahamu zaidi
Tabiya za aw'ladi
Kazi takupungukiya

Parent, make an effort
To better understand
The nature of children;
This will make their upbringing easier.

230. *Soma kwa kutaamali*
Mbali mbali zao hali
Kwako takuwa sahali
Kurakibisha tabiya

Read thoroughly
About their various ways of being;
It will be easier for you
To correct your child's behavior.

231. *Na ukitoyuwa kwenda*
Na wano watakushinda
Ubaki kuuma zanda
Na kwa matozi kuliya

And if you don't know how to handle them,
You will find yourself in over your head.
You will bite your nails in regret
And cry many tears.

232. *Uliza yao maoni*
Kwa mambo ya kinyum-
bani
Mfano chakula gani
Yeo mutapendeleya

Ask for their opinion
On matters at home,
Like what kind of food
Would you like to eat today?

233. *Zoweya kuwashawiri*
Wakupe lao shauri
Hili mno ni uzuri
Na hamasa huwatiya

Make it your habit to consult them
So that they give you their opinion.
This habit is very good,
And encourages openness toward you.

234. *Huwapa mawazo bora*
Na hupanuwa fikira
Kiwa wao kula mara
Shaurini tawatiya

It will give them confidence
And will broaden their mind
If you always
Involve them in your decision-making.

HURUMA: SOCIAL ROLES AND RESPONSIBILITY 269

235. *Wao wataiyamini* They will believe in themselves
 Waone wana thamani And will recognize their own value.
 Na kuiyona ni duni They will never consider
 Kwao halitotokeya Themselves inferior or underestimated.

236. *Zijana wape jukumu* Give children responsibility;
 Hili kwao ni muhimu For them this is important.
 Huwafanya sumsumu It makes them self-disciplined
 Shupavu huinukiya And makes them more persistent.

237. *Uzitunge tafauti* Take into consideration
 Za umri na wakati The children's age, as well as the time[1];
 Alo na nyaka katiti Children of a few years are
 Si kama mtanguliya Not like their elder brother or sister.

[1] "Time" referring to age of the child, but also the historical context and its moral standards.

238. *Karibu ya kupevuka* When they become adolescents,
 Wana nyendo hugeuka The behavior of your children changes.
 Jitahidi kuwepuka Make an effort to avoid
 Nguvu kuwatumiliya Using violence against them.

239. *Siwatumiliye nguvu* Don't use force on them,
 Nena nao kwa werevu But talk to them wisely.
 Huwa mno ni wayavu Adolescents are hot-tempered
 Na ghururi huwangiya And overestimate themselves.

240. *Hawaiyoni ni wana* They don't consider themselves children,
 Bali walotimu sana But as fully developed.
 Ni kamili huiyona They see themselves as complete and
 Ni watu wametimiya As mature human beings[1].

[1] *Baleghe*, "puberty," is supposed to start at the age of fourteen. According to Ustadh Mau, this is the time when children and adults quarrel the most.

241. *Wana wafanyie sawa* Treat your children as equals;
 Asili kutobaguwa Never discriminate against them at all.
 Wana utawatomowa You will hurt your children
 Sawa kitowatendeya If you do not treat them equally.

242. *Ukiwapenda wangine*
Kwa ulimi usinene
Kwa zitendo wasiyone
Au utaiyutiya

If you like some more than others,
Don't express it openly,
And do not let your actions show it either,
Otherwise you will regret it.

243. *Hilo wakilifahamu*
Takuwa mbeu ya sumu
Umeyaa za kudumu
Hazondoki husaliya

Because if they realize it,
This will be the seed of poison.
You will have planted lasting seeds.
They don't vanish; they linger.

244. *Naafanyao mazuri*
Mtuze tena dhahiri
Atendao takiswiri
Mweleze yake hatiya

And the ones who do good,
Praise them openly.
And the wrongdoers,
Explain their errors to them.

245. *Mwana kikosa adabu*
Kumrudi ni wajibu
Lakini kwa taratibu
Na kumwekeza ya ndiya

If children misbehave,
It is necessary to discipline them,
But in a careful way,
And show them the right way.

246. *Kikosa mpe nafasi*
Arakibishe upesi
Wala siwete mjusi
Kosa kumkaririya

If they have made a mistake,
Give them a chance to correct it.
Don't scold them
Or be resentful

247. *Simwambie kula mara*
Zangaliye zake sura
Kwani hilo humkera
Usuguni humtiya

Don't speak ill of them all the time,
Or compare their appearance unfavorably to that of others,
Because this hurts them
And makes their bad behavior chronic.

248. *Simwambiye jana jizi*
Au hoyo kikojozi
Huathiri ila hizi
Kula mara kusikiya

Don't call them big thief
Or a bed-wetter!
These abuses affect them
Every time they hear them.

HURUMA: SOCIAL ROLES AND RESPONSIBILITY

249. *Humtonesha jaraha*
     Moyoni hawi na raha
     Hata kama kwa mzaha
     Yeye hatofurahiya

It will irritate their wound,
And they will not be at ease.
Even if you do it jokingly,
They will not be happy about it.

250. *Kuna makosa mangine*
     Ni membamba si manene
     Fumba mato siyaone
     Ifanye hukusikiya

And if other mistakes occur
That are slight and not serious,
Close your eyes; don't look at them.
Pretend you did not hear them.

251. *Jaribu kuikukusa*
     Kwa baadhi ya makosa
     Ni ya mayezi siyasa
     Wayuzi huitumiya

Try to ignore
Some of the mistakes.
This is the best policy for upbringing;
The experienced make use of it.

252. *Hapa ndipo kikomoni*
     Naomba kwenu nyuteni
     Mukiyona punguwani
     Radhi mutaniweleya

Here is the end.
I beg all of you,
If you see any blemishes,
Forgive me.

253. *Hakuna mja kamili*
     Kutokosa ni muhali
     Nawaomba tafadhali
     Nanyi kunisaidiya

There is no perfect human being.
It is impossible not to make mistakes.
I beg you, please
Help me.

254. *Msaada kwenu nataka*
     Muwezao kuandika
     Yale mutayokumbuka
     Nanyi mbee kwendeleya

I want help from all of you
Who can write:
Whatever you consider important,
Continue writing about it in the future.

255. *Nimekoma wasalamu*
     Aloandika nudhumu
     Ni Mahamudu isimu
     Mwenye kite na dhuriya

I have come to the end, *wasalamu*.
The one who composed this poem
Is called Mahmoud by name,
And feels deeply for children.

272 HURUMA: SOCIAL ROLES AND RESPONSIBILITY

256. *Nimeandika kusudi*   I wrote this *utendi* intentionally
     Utendi uwe zawadi   To offer it as a gift
     Kwa bibiⁱ yangu Aboudi To my grandfather Aboud,
     Mama alonizaliya   The father of my mother.

1 bibi (Am.) also "grandfather" (Std. babu). Aboud was also the name of Ustadh Mau's maternal grandfather.

257. *Namtunuku utendi*   I present this *utendi*
     Aboudi changu kipendi To my beloved son, Aboud.
     Wala mimi hili sandi   I am not the first one to write a poem for his
     Baba menitanguliya   child;
                              My father did it before me.

The difference between this *utendi* and Ustadh Mau's other *wasiya* is that in this poem, he advises parents on how to deal with children, rather than advising the children on how to deal with the world.

HURUMA: SOCIAL ROLES AND RESPONSIBILITY 273

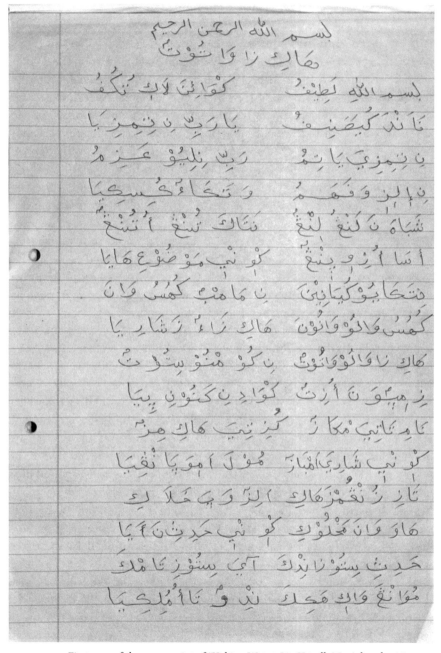

FIGURE 17   First page of the manuscript of "Haki za Watoto" in Ustadh Mau's handwriting

5   *Wasiya wa mabanati* ("Advice to Young Women")

Wasiya wa mabanati was composed in 1974 and is Ustadh Mau's first long poem, of 143 stanzas; he was inspired by the urge to comment on the degradation of customs on Lamu, especially among the youth, sparked, according to him, by the rise of a Western-style modernity reaching their shores. It can be regarded as a didactic poem like the famous *Utendi wa Mwana Kupona*. Yet the poem is not in the classical meter of the *utendi* genre, but was composed in a meter that, as the poet himself remarks, is close to the *dura al-mandhuma* form, made of twelve syllables per line with both an internal and external rhyme. There are very few poems composed in this meter—the classical *Al-Inkishafi* is one exception—as it is so difficult to write. If one also considers that Ustadh Mau composed it without even being aware of the rules of prosody and still only in his twenties, the poem speaks to his innate talent.

The plot of this poem, which largely takes on the form of a realist narrative, follows a tragic story: a cruel man fornicates with a young woman, impregnating her and then abandoning her. The incident causes a tragedy for the young woman and her loved ones. The poet shows great sensitivity in matters of the female psyche, by delving into the woman's psychological and emotional journey, which leads her almost to commit suicide. There is a didactic tone to the voice of the first-person narrator, who predicts the tragedy and warns young women not to be fooled by men like the protagonist. A series of direct speeches constitute the poem, and the narrator lets the man as well as the women's relatives talk about the drama from their own perspectives. Yet, the first-person narrator and the other characters' voices are all silenced in the last part of the poem, in which the woman herself confesses her own tragic history, and begs her savior—the elderly man who has stopped her from committing suicide—to take a book and pen and write her story down so that others may be aware of such dangers. The final goal of the poem and its didactic message is presented in stz. 125, which reads, "Let us complete this writing so as to advise them (the young women)."

The final section of the poem features a flashback and the woman's wish that her own story may spread among her peers. It explains the reasons why the poem is titled and addressed not to a single woman, but more broadly to "young women," referred to as *mabanati* "daughters," *binti Hawaa* "daughters of

Recordings of recitations of the poem are freely available online at https://doi.org/10.6084/m9.figshare.20200889.

Eve," or as the inclusive "we," e.g., *sisi banati* "it is us women." It was precisely this category of young women, that, a decade earlier, the Arabic writer and reformer Sheikh Ali Tantawi was addressing when he composed his pamphlet *Ya-bintī* ("Oh My Daughter"), which Ustadh Mau had read and was inspired by. Like the Arabic pamphlet, which spread widely in the Muslim world, the Swahili poem has been very popular on Lamu, and beyond the archipelago up to the coast of Mombasa: the poem, finally gives a voice to powerless women in a modern world where they are threatened by injustice, marginalization, and exploitation much more than men, who even take advantage of women's weak position. The poem's popularity is also due to the recorded versions of it—performed by the singers Mohammad Kadara, el-Shatry, and Bi Ridhai—that have circulated so widely among Swahili Muslim publics.[2]

The *Wasiya wa mabanati* reflects what Ustadh Mau calls the *mambo ya kidunia* ("ways of life"). *Duniya*, the Swahili term for "world" as well as "life," is a frequent term in the poem, referring to the experiences, challenges, and temptations that all human beings have in this world. In fact, the poem is at times imbued with a critical, sometimes even condenscending or cynical tone toward the cruel people living in this world (cf. stz. 22, *Kumbe duniyani watu ni wabaya* "Alas this world is full of terrible people"), but is also a plea for the poet's fellow man to be more human (cf. stz. 17, *Kuwa insani mwana Adamiya* "Be human, son of Adam!"). As always in his poems and sermons, he emphasizes hope and possibility of a better future. Although the world (*duniya*) is characterized by human failure and ultimately death (stz. 75, "This is the way of the world; Death is a reality created by God"), Ustahd Mau underlines the possibility of improvement for both society and the individual, and gives guidelines for a better future. The poem's first ten stanzas were previously translated and published by Mahazi and Kresse;[3] Azra Mau has continued their work. It should be noted that the poet sometimes switches between singular and plural addresses (for instance, from verse 2 to verse 3), which is difficult to convey in the English translation.

---

2   All these recorded versions are freely available at https://doi.org/10.6084/m9.figshare.2020089

3   See Kai Kresse, "Enduring Relevance: Samples of Oral Poetry on the Swahili Coast," *Wasafiri* 66 (2011): 46–49.

1. | | |
    |---|---|
    | *Sikiza mwanangu* | *nikupe waswiya* |
    | *Mimi ulimwengu* | *ninauweleya* |
    | *Mingi miyaka yangu[I]* | *katika duniya* |
    | *Nawe haya yangu* | *hela[II] zingatiya* |

Listen my child, let me advise you.
I am well versed in the ways of the world.
Many are the years I have spent here on this earth,
So please heed to what I am about to tell you.

I This *kipande* has one syllable more than it should; its reading could be adjusted to Kiamu by using the term *nyaka* rather than the Std. *miaka*, which would reduce the noun from three to two syllables, thus fitting the six-syllable *kipande*. | II *hela* interjection, syn.: *hebu*

2. | | |
    |---|---|
    | *Nawata[I] ujana* | *sito urudiya[II]* |
    | *Mengi nimeona* | *nakuyasikiya* |
    | *Atekao sana* | *mwisowe huliya* |
    | *Ukitaka ona* | *nawe angaliya* |

My youth is behind me, never to return.
There is much that I have seen and heard.
For the one who laughs a lot ends up crying;
If you wish to understand, you need to contemplate.

I -ata Am. "to leave" (Std. -*acha*) | II *sitourudiya*—Negative future tense written by the poet as two separate syntagma: *si* neg. 1st-pers. sg., *to* neg. future temporal marker infix + *urudiya* obj. infix + verb.

3. | | |
    |---|---|
    | *Wengi wamenena* | *hamu kusikiya* |
    | *Wamesema sana* | *koo zikapweya* |
    | *Faida hapana* | *ilio tokeya* |
    | *Usiku mtana[I]* | *muna jiaswiya* |

Many have spoken, but you didn't listen.
They continued to talk until their throats were hoarse,
But that was all in vain;
Night and day, you continue to sin.

I *mtana* Am. "daylight" (Std. *mchana*)

HURUMA: SOCIAL ROLES AND RESPONSIBILITY

4. *Maovu mabaya*   *yana endeleya*
    Kula miyaka huya   *michinjo mipiya*
    Munajivaliya   *mavazi mabaya*
    Muna elekeya   *kwenda dudumiya*

Wrong and bad things continue to happen;
With each coming year, new trends appear.
You dress indecently,
Heading right into destruction.

5. *Watu wa Mombasa*   *waliki twambiya*[1]
    Shetwani wa sasa   *Amu hajangiya*
    Wakija kuposa   *wake kuzengeya*
    Ghafula mkasa   *ume tungiliya*

The people of Mombasa kept telling us,
"The devil of modernity hasn't reached Amu yet";
So they came here in search of brides to propose to,
And all of sudden tragedy befell us.

1 As the poet explains, "us" is an inclusive we and refers in this passage to the people of Lamu.

6. *Tumevuwa nguo*   *wazi twatembeya*[1]
    Tumetupa zuo[2]   *twalokisomeya*
    Tumeshinda hao   *walotanguliya*
    Wana mama zao   *wataka kuliya*

We have undressed, walking without a veil.
We have forsaken the scriptures that we so diligently studied.
Our actions have surpassed those who took up these habits before us,
Making mothers weep over their children's transgressions.

1 As the poet explains, "we" means the people of Lamu in this passage. | 11 *zuo* Am. "traditional old books for Islamic learning" (Std. pl. *vyuo*).

7. *Binti Hawaa*   *kwa Mola rejeya*
    Sandame hawaa   *itakutongeya*
    Hawa tokutwaa   *ukishapoteya*
    Wana kuhadaa   *wata kukimbiya*

Oh daughter of Eve, return to your God.
Do not follow your desires; they will get you into trouble.
They[1] will not take you in once you have gone astray;
They are deceiving you and they will desert you.

1 "They" refers to "men" in this passage.

8.   *Tahadhari sana*   *na kumridhiya*
     Hata ukiona   *mwendo analiya*
     Hawana maana   *hao nakwambiya*
     Mukisa[1] pambana   *atashika ndiya*

Be very cautious about fulfilling men's desires.
Even if you see him, crying tears of sorrow,
They are worthless, I am telling you—
He will desert you as soon as you have fornicated.

1 *mukisa* Am. "when you (pl.) finish" (Std. *mtakapokwisha*)

9.   *Mara utaona*   *mimba mekutiya*
     Hapo huyo Bwana   *atakuambiya*
     Usijali sana   *sisi tu pamoya*
     Ukizaa mwana   *takusaidiya*

You will suddenly realize that he has impregnated you.
That is when the man will tell you,
"Don't worry, we are together;
Once you have the baby, I will help you."

10. *Kitumbo kipana*   *chaanza tokeya*
     Mzigo wa Bwana   *una kulemeya*
     Takwambiya nana   *kwaheri sikiya*
     Hapo utanena   *siku kudhaniya*

And then the belly starts to show;
The man's burden is overwhelming.
He will tell you, "Woman, good bye,"
Then you will say, "I didn't think that of you."

HURUMA: SOCIAL ROLES AND RESPONSIBILITY

11. *Fahali[I] endao* *ameshika ndiya*
    Uko zake kwao *apija nambiya*
    Alinipa ngao[II] *kampasuliya*
    Na wiki ijao *ainda mpiya*

    The bull has taken off, following on his trail;
    He has returned home, announcing to the world,
    "She gave me her shield and I broke it into pieces";
    And the coming week, he hunts for a new one.

    I *fahali* lit. "bull." Mau: "This is a metaphor for referring to a careless man, a presumptuous man." It also symbolizes strength, male sexual prowess, and rampant masculinity. | II This *kipande* features *ngao* ("shield") as a metaphor of the woman's virginity.

12. *Uinuke hima* *ufuwate ndiya*
    Wenda ukikoma *tumbo la kwemeya*
    Na ukisimama *waona udhiya*
    Umuwite Mama *kuto kusikiya*

    You stand determined, forging the way.
    You stagger along; the belly has burdened you.
    When you take a break, you ache;
    You call your mother, but she does not hear.

13. *Umo safarini* *wenda mzengeya*
    Na watu ndiyani *wana kwangaliya*
    Wateka kwandani *nadhiri piya*
    Umo matumboni *mwana wa bandiya*

    You have embarked on a journey, going to search for him,
    And people on the street are giving you stares.
    They laugh both overtly and in secret;
    Are you carrying a doll in your belly?

14. *Umrange sana* *nakumwangaliya*
    Wende kumuona *na bui[I] mpiya*
    Ukitaka nena *amekurukiya*
    Mimba hiyonana *mimi sikutiya*

And after much scouting and looking for him,
You go to find him with a new lover.
When you attempt to speak, he barks out at you,
"That pregnancy, lady, is not mine.

1 *bui* "friend." Mau: especially with reference to friendship among women.

15. *Mimi sikubali*   *utalo nambiya*
    Si mimi awali   *nilokata ndiya*
    Kuna mafahali   *walo tanguliya*
    Nami kikabili   *nikadudumiya*

I shall not accept anything you tell me;
I was not the first to pass through.
There were other bulls that came before me,
And when I approached, I just sank in.

16. *Tena hapa mbele*   *hebu nondokeya*
    Katafute yule   *alokuanziya*
    Mengi makelele   *ukampijiya*
    Ndio tamu ile   *leo vumiliya*

Get away from me;
Go and find the one who did it!"
You moaned so loudly for him;
Because of that pleasure, you now have to bear with this.

17. *Hapo masikini*   *uwande kuliya*
    Ni wewe fulani   *ulotenda haya*
    Mngine sidhani   *kwangu alikuya*
    Kuwa insani   *mwana Adamiya*

At this point, poor you, you start crying:
"You are the one who did this!
Don't think that anyone else came to me;
Be human, son of Adam!"

18. *Tena umrai[I]* *na kumwangukiya*
 Wewe haifai *kunitenda haya*
 Kwani huniyui *ni mwando wa kuya*
 Umekama tui *chicha[II] wanatiya*

You beg him and fall at his feet:
"It's not right to do this to me;
Don't you know me? Is it your first time to come and see me?
Have you squeezed out the coconut milk and left me with the dry flakes?"

I *kumrai mtu* "to coax/soothe someone" (see also Std. *kumbembeleza* "to calm a child down") | II *chicha* Kiung. "grated coconut"; Krapf: "the squeezed substance of a cocoanut, the scraped cocoa-nut after the oil has been squeezed out; it is sometimes rubbed on the hand to clean them of smut or dirt; but more generally it is cast away as refuse" (Krp. 39). In medical and metaphorical language, also used to refer to smegma.

19. *Hapo kwa ghadhabu* *atakwangaliya*
 Hakupi jawabu *kofi takutiya*
 Si la taratibu *atakwatiliya*
 Zizidi taabu *kwako na udhiya*

At that point he will look at you angrily;
Without giving you an answer, he will slap you.
A hard slap he will throw at you;
This will increase your troubles and aches.

20. *Ndipo hapo sasa* *akili kungiya*
 Yalo ya makosa *kuyafikiriya*
 Mwida[I] umekwisa *walotanguliya*
 Ni kama mapesa *ukiyatumiya*

And now is when you come to realize:
You contemplate on all the wrongdoings.
Time is up, and what is gone can't come back;
It's like money once you have spent it.

I *mwida* Am. "time" (Std. *muda*)

282 HURUMA: SOCIAL ROLES AND RESPONSIBILITY

21. *Maji yamekwisa*   *kukumwagikiya[I]*
 Ni zile anasa   *zilokutongeya[II]*
 Hayafai sasa   *ungazingatiya[III]*
 Umekuwa kiswa   *watu wakutaya*

You have already spilled the water;
It's those pleasures that got you in trouble.
It's of no use now, despite your contemplation;
You have become a story that people gossip about.

I Mau uses the metaphor of water to explain that what has happened cannot be changed, and has had an impact on the woman. | II *kutongeya* syn.: *kuletea shida* "to cause trouble." | III *ungazingatia* "even if you think about it now."

22. *Hapo mke shani*   *uwande rejeya*
 Na mwako moyoni   *unashawiriya[I]*
 Nangojeya nini   *sendi kujifiya*
 Kumbe duniyani   *watu ni wabaya*

Now you, beautiful woman, start to depart,
And in your head, your thoughts go back and forth:
"What am I waiting for? Why don't I just go and die?
Alas, this world is full of terrible people."

I *shawiriya* "doubts," referring to thoughts, also expressed by the Swahili utterance *nifanye nisifanye* "shall I do it or not," showing hesitation and insecurity.

23. *Ushawiri sana*   *na kufikiriya*
 Moyoni wanena   *ni pana duniya*
 Mimi ninaona   *kheri kukimbiya*
 Nitaepukana   *na maneno haya*

You constantly ponder and continue to think;
You tell your heart, "This world is vast;
It is better to run away.
I will distance myself from these rumors."

24. *Ingawa wanenda*   *huiyoni ndiya*
 Mawazo kwa inda[I]   *yanakuiliya*
 Hili ukitinda   *na lingine huya*
 Sana utakonda   *kwa mawazo haya*

HURUMA: SOCIAL ROLES AND RESPONSIBILITY   283

Even as you walk, the road is blurred.
Your head is clouded with too many thoughts;
As each one ends, another begins.
You will lose a lot of weight from these worries.

ı *inda* "insensitivity," "spite," "meanness of spirit"; here, *mawazo wa inda* "to have too many thoughts," "to be pensive," "to mull over problems."

25. *Mara kwa ghafula*   *Itakuingiya*
     Fikra ya kula   *sumu kujifiya*
     Au kwenda Shela   *pwani kujitiya*
     Ukiwaza Mola   *wabadili niya*

Then, all of a sudden, it dawns on you:
A suicidal thought of ingesting poison,
Or going to Shela to drown yourself.
But when you think of God, you change your mind.

26. *Kipai cha jaha*   *kimekupoteya*
     Huna la furaha   *katika duniya*
     Na mambo ya raha   *hutaki sikiya*
     Kwa Mola Ilaha   *sasa wajutiya*

You have lost your sense of worth.
You are unhappy in this world,
And have lost interest in all joyful things.
You now direct your regrets to the Lord.

27. *Sana unajuta*   *na kuzingatiya*
     Umekisha pita   *wakati wa haya*
     Na wako ukuta   *ulijivundiya*
     Ni mwezi wa sita   *sasa yatimiya*

You now regret and continue to ponder;
The time for this is now long gone,
And you tore down your own wall.
The sixth month is now underway.

284 HURUMA: SOCIAL ROLES AND RESPONSIBILITY

28. *Sasa ya dhihiri*   *nde yatokeya*
    Siyo tena siri   *wote yaweleya*
    Una tahayari[I]   *watu wakimbiya*
    Yaja kuaziri[II]   *tamu mara moya*

[The pregnancy] is now becoming evident and starting to show.
It is not a secret anymore; everyone is now aware of it.
You are ashamed, and people are deserting you;
The one-time pleasure has come back to disgrace you.

I *tahayari* "feel ashamed, feel shy." | II *yaja* implies the nonexplicit subject *mambo* "things"; *kuaziri* "to calumniate, despise" (Krp. 17).

29. *Zamami mamako*   *amelisikiya*
    Kwa masikitiko   *kaja kukwambiya*
    Nini shida yako   *hebu nelezeya*
    Mbona sasa meko   *unayakimbiya*

Your mother had heard it a while back.
With sadness, she came to inquire,
"What is troubling you? Please explain to me,
Why are you running away from the kitchen?"

30. *Umwambie Mama*   *uwate udhiya*
    Mimi ni mzima   *ni kamili ziya[I]*
    Mimi nimesoma   *mambo yaneleya*
    Na wanaosema   *wanisingiziya*

You tell your mother, "Stop bothering me.
I am well; I am not missing a limb.
I am educated and I have a handle on things.
Those who are talking about me are just slandering me."

I *ziya* "part of the body" (Std. *kia*); *kia cha muili* "flesh" (Krp. 135). See also its use in stz. 56 below.

31. *Tatamka tena*   *mama kukwambiya*
    Mbona nakuona   *wajitapikiya*
    Zile nguo pana   *wazipendeleya*
    Na hutoki tena   *nde[I] kutembeya*

Your mother spoke up again to inquire:
"Why do I see that you are vomiting?
You now prefer baggy clothes,
And I don't see you going out for walks."

I *nde* "outside" (Std. *nje*)

32. *Mama nipulika*   *nitalokwambiya*
     Yai[I] uloweka   *ukaniusiya*
     Amekuja nyoka[II]   *amenidomeya*
     Limebaki kaka[III]   *sasa laoleya*

"Mom, please pay attention to what I am about to tell you:
The egg that you bestowed upon me to protect,
A snake came and bit it.
All that is left now is an empty floating shell."

I *yai*—Literally an edible egg, used in this context to refer to the woman's ovary. | II *nyoka*—Used as a metaphor of evilness to refer to the cruel man who fooled the woman. | III *kaka* "egg's shell, also known as *gamba la yai*" (Krp. 125).

33. *Paka hapa Mama*   *umeshamwambiya*
     Aliyoko nyuma   *ni baba hayaya*
     Mekwenda kutoma[I]   *kamba kuzamiya*
     Au ni kulima   *tonge[II] kuzengeya*

At this point you, have informed your mother.
The only one still unaware of the news is your father, who is yet to return.
He has gone diving for prawns
Or is farming in search of sustenance.

I *kutoma* Baj. "to fish" (Std. *kuvua samaki*) | II *tonge* "lump of food" > *tonge la wali* designates, for instance, a handful of boiled rice, taken and compressed with the hand before it is put in the mouth; *tonge* alone refers to a "morsel, bit, soap," similar to the term *pumba*, which rather refers to something claylike, for instance *pumba la udongo* "clod of clay" (Krp. 377).

34. *Au ni mwalimu*   *ajisomesheya*
    Huja kwao Amu   *mwaka mara moya*
    Mwezi ukitimu   *pesa huweteya*
    Uwengete[1] hamu   *kama ya duniya*

Or maybe he is a teacher who is teaching;
He comes home to Amu once every year,
Bringing home money at the end of every month.
He is carrying a burden with the weight of the world.

1 *uwengete* perfect form of *-angata* "to carry."

35. *Yeye kula mtu*   *huwa kimwambiya*
    Ninae bintu   *kama kamariya*
    Sitompa mtu   *ila kwa rupiya[1]*
    Ni alifu tatu   *zilizotimiya*

He boasts to everyone, telling them,
"I have a daughter like the moon;
I will not give her hand except for rupees
In the amount of three full thousands."

1 *rupiya* "rupee." As Mau says, this Indian currency was used on Lamu before the shilling arrived; the rupee was considered to be more valuable at the time, the equivalent of saying "US dollar" today, as Azra Mau says. The term is used in this line for its rhyme in *-ya*, which was needed here; in another context, a more fitting term would be *pesa* "money."

36. *Haisi hadhani*   *yaliotokeya*
    Mwake akilini   *halijamngiya*
    Ajuwa nyumbani   *mambo hendeleya*
    Anayo yakini   *mwane metuliya*

He doesn't know, and he doesn't have a clue what has happened.
In his mind, it has not dawned on him;
He knows that things are going well back home.
He is sure that his daughter is well settled.

37. *Mara kwa ghafula*   *amemuendeya*
    Bwana wa jamala   *aliotimiya*
    Ya kwanda kaula   *akamuambiya*
    Sinipe muhula[1]   *jawabu neteya*

All of a sudden, he came to him:
A perfect, handsome gentleman.
And the first thing that he told him was,
"Don't take too long to give me a response."

I *muhula* (Ar.) nowadays used to designate a term at university. "An appointed space of time when borrowed goods are to be returned to its owner" (Krp. 264).

38. *Namtaka mwano*   *ulonisifiya*
    Sizinde[I] mkono   *nakupa pokeya*
    Ni alifu tano   *mahari[II] ni haya*
    Na mfungo tano[III]   *Amu nitakuya*

"I am asking for the hand of your daughter, the one you have praised.
Don't hold back your consent; please take what I am giving you,
Five thousand dirhams as a dowry payment,
And in the fifth month I will come to Amu."

I *-zinda* (Std. *-dinda*), syn.: *-kaza* "to refuse" | II According to Mau, with regard to dowry (*mahari*), it is nowadays distributed among the elder relatives (*wazee*); the dowry mainly concerns the bride's side, which has to care of buying utensils and appliances for her. | III *mfungo tano*—The month is referred to based on the Islamic calendar. As Mau tells us, in the past, weddings used to take place in the sixth month, or before the month of Ramadan, while nowadays they mainly occur in December, August, and April (these are the months when schools are closed, outside the three terms).

39. *Baba kakubali*   *hayo karidhiya*
    Kanyosha miwili   *akazipokeya*
    Zali ni kamili   *zilizotimiya*
    Katowa kauli   *ya kufurahiya*

The father agreed, and was satisfied with that.
He extended his two hands to receive the money;
The amount was complete, not missing [a cent].
He extended words of happiness.

I *kanyosha miwili* implies the obj. *mikono* "the two hands." The verb is also used with reference to *miguu* "feet," with the meaning "to stretch one's feet", walking; also it applies to *nguo* "clothes," with the meaning "to hang the laundry," in opposition to *-kunjakunja nguo* "to fold the laundry."

40. *Baba kasafiri*   *kenda kuzengeya*
     Kulla cha fakhari   *mwane kamweteya*
     Kaliyaza gari   *shehena¹ katiya*
     Mkewe habari   *hajampekeya*

The father traveled in search of
Everything that was fancy enough to bring to his daughter;
He filled his vehicle to the brim,
But didn't inform his wife.

1 *shehena* (Ar.) "freight, load, cargo"

41. *Baba akifika*   *nyumbani kingiya*
     Mwane mefunguka   *amejizaliya*
     Akafanya shaka   *aliposikiya*
     Kama mwana paka¹   *chumbani huliya*

When the father arrived and entered the house,
His daughter was in labor for delivery;
He was doubtful when he heard
A kitten-like cry coming from the room.

1 *kama mwana paka* alludes a sound like the one made by a kitten, vaguely like that of a child.

42. *Mama akatoka*   *kumuelezeya*
     Sana kashutuka   *aliposikiya*
     Mwisho hajafika   *kumuhadithiya*
     Baba mekauka¹   *mewaga duniya*

The mother came out to explain to him.
He was shocked when he heard the news;
Before she could finish telling the story,
The father had a stroke and died on the spot.

1 The verb *-kauka* lit. "to get dry" is used here to convey the image of a heart that has stopped pumping.

HURUMA: SOCIAL ROLES AND RESPONSIBILITY

43. | *Akababaika* | *akiona haya* |
Mama kaanguka	*na akazimiya*
Hawezi tamka	*wala kusogeya*
Amebadilika	*hata rangi piya*

She was frightened when she witnessed this.
The mother fell and lost consciousness;
She couldn't utter a sound or move an inch.
Even the color of her face had changed.

44. | *Na hapo nyumbani* | *mwingine hakuya* |
wali ni thineni	*mebaki mmoya*
Na mwana nyongani[I]	*anamliliya*
Mui matumboni	*umemsaliya*

And at home, there was no one else;
They were two, but only one is left,
With a baby at her perineum
And the placenta still in her uterus.

I *nyonga* "perineum"; as explained by Azra Mau, who holds a specialization in gynecology, this term designates the area between the anus and the vulva in the female body.

45. | *Bado hayayuwa* | *yaliotokeya* |
Amejitanuwa[I]	*angali[II] ngojeya*
Kuja kutolewa	*zilizobakiya*
Na aliyezawa	*azidi kuliya*

She was still unaware of what had transpired,
Her legs wide apart while she was still waiting
For what was left inside to be cleaned and removed,
And the newborn kept on crying.

I *-jitanua*—As explained by Azra Mau, this verb means "to divaricate one's legs like when practicing splits." | II *angali* stands here for *bado* "still, yet."

46. | *Kwalina kizere[I]* | *kikipita ndiya* |
Hiko kitiriri[II]	*akakisikiya*
Ruhu isikiri	*kenda kutungiya*
Hayo mandhari	*kayashuhudiya*

There was an old woman passing by;
She heard the continued cries of the baby.
Her heart was not at ease, so she went and peeped in;
She witnessed the scene.

I *kizere* is used to refer to a very old person (*mzee sana* "very old"), usually a woman. | II *kitiriri* something that disturbs; as Mau explains, *mtu ambaye wasumbua, mtu aliyekuwa msumbufu*, "a person who disturbs, a person who is a disturbance."

47. *Bibi kadangana*   *kwa kuona haya*
    Na akili hana   *imempoteya*
    Mekuwa hunena   *kwa lugha mpiya*
    Hajui maana   *anajisemeya*[I]

The old woman was confused at this sight;
It was as if she had lost her mind.
She started speaking in a foreign language;
She did not comprehend what she was mumbling.

I *-jisemeya* lit. "to utter words without knowing their meaning."

48. *Uko kitanduni*   *mzazi huliya*
    Zilo matumboni   *zampa udhiya*
    Mwake akilini   *hayajamngiya*
    Msiba nyumbani   *uliotokeya*

The new mother was on the bed, crying;
What was left in her uterus was causing her harm.
She was yet to acknowledge in her mind
The sad events that had befallen their home.

49. *Ilahi Mwenyezi*   *hapo kamtiya*
    Akili ajuzi   *ilompoteya*
    Kenda kwa mzazi   *kamuangaliya*
    Kamaliza kazi   *zilizobakiya*

At that moment, God restored
The sense of the old woman that had been lost.
She went to the new mother to check on her;
She took care of what was left of the delivery.

HURUMA: SOCIAL ROLES AND RESPONSIBILITY   291

50. *Kisa kumtowa*   *zilizosaliya*
     Ndipo hapo kawa   *meanda tuliya*
     Kisa kachondowa   *kiumbe kipiya*
     Chenda kipokowa   *na kuchadhiniya[1]*

Once she removed the retained placenta,
She started feeling better.
She took the new baby,
Cleaned him, and called *adhan* for him.

[1] *kuchadhiniya* "to call *adhan* for the baby (*kijitoto*)"; here, *-adhinia* refers to the ritual practice of reciting the call of the muezzin into the child's ear.

51. *Hapa nimekoma[1]*   *ya mimba kutaya*
     Tarudi kwa Mama   *kwenda mwangaliya*
     Nipate kusema   *lililotokeya*
     Ameshatuhama   *au mesaliya*

I have now finished recounting the pregnancy;
We will now go back to check on the mother
So that I can say what happened to her.
Has she left us already, or is she still alive?

[1] This is the first-person narrator speaking.

52. *Kwake nikifika[1]*   *kamshuhudiya*
     Hawezi inuka   *mekosa afya*
     Ndipo kamshika   *kamsaidiya*
     Nae kitamka   *kaanza kuliya*

When I reached her,
She was unable to get back up; she had become weak.
Then I took hold of her to help her up;
When she wanted to speak, she started to weep.

[1] This too is the first-person narrator, whom we have to imagine as having paid a visit to the mother and describing the state she was in.

53. Akaliya sana   na kuomboleya
Nami kimuona   sikujiziwiya
Kamwambiya nana   ndio kiduniya
Watu hupambana   na zaidi haya

She wept so much, and lamented,
And the sight of her, I couldn't hold back;
I told her, "Lady, such is life.
People are faced with tougher challenges than these."

54. Na wake binti   aliposikiya
Ya mama sauti   yazidi kuliya
Ziliyo¹ za dhati   zimekazaniya
Kaja kutafiti   nde katokeya

And when the daughter heard
The sound of her mother crying ever more hysterically—
It had become loud, effusive weeping—
She came out to see what was happening.

1 ziliyo "weeping, crying" (Std. kilio)

55. Kule kuja kwake   nde kutungiya
Na kwa mato yake   akashuhudiya
Kuwa ni babake   aliojifiya
Na akili yake   ilimpoteya

When she came to look outside,
She witnessed with her own eyes
That it was her father who had passed away.
She lost her mind.

56. Kisu kaangata   taka kujitiya
Kawahi kutaka   baadhi ya ziya¹
Hapo akapita   kijana mmoya
Akamkamata   ndani kamtiya

She took a knife to kill herself with;
She managed to cut some parts of her body.
At that moment, a young man passed;
He got a hold of her and returned her to the house.

1 This term has already occurred above, in stz. 30. In the context of this stanza, Mau recalls the Swahili saying *tabia ni kia* "habit is like a part of your body."

57. *Na huko chumbani*   *alipoingiya*
    Hakuketi tini   *na akatuliya*
    Ni hapo jununi   *ilimzidiya*
    Akapanda jini   *na mzuka piya*

When she entered the room,
She did not settle down,
And at that moment her madness only increased;
She began acting as if she was possessed.

58. *Hapo kasimama*   *akakazaniya*
    Na mazishi mama   *kayaandaliya*
    Majirani wema   *kumsaidiya*
    Yakawa timama   *mambo mara moya*

At that point, the mother stood fast, trying to be strong.
She organized the funeral;
With the help of her good neighbors,
Everything was completed in time.

59. *Wakisa kuzika*   *na kumsomeya*
    Watu wakashuka   *wakandama ndiya*
    Wakamalizika   *sibaki mmoya*
    Hapo zilifika   *zombo zikangiya*

After the burial and reciting of the Qurʾān,
The people left and went on their way.
They all left, with no one remaining.
At that point was when the furniture[1] arrived at the home.

1 This is referring to the furniture that the father had bought.

294 HURUMA: SOCIAL ROLES AND RESPONSIBILITY

60. *Mama kashutuka*   *zikimfikiya*
     Hakuyatamka   *mume kama haya*
     Wala hakwandika   *wakashuhudiya*
     Illa ni Rabuka   *mewahifadhiya*

The mother was shocked at the arrival of the furniture;
Her husband hadn't informed her of this.
Nor did he write any testament;
It was the Lord that protected them.

61. *Kasema hamali*   *mama kumwambiya*
     Kochi siti mbili   *na stuli piya*
     Na kitanda ali[1]   *alizipakiya*
     Na piya nauli   *amezilipiya*

The porter began telling the mother,
A two-seater sofa with stools
And a high-quality bed had been shipped,
And [her husband] had already paid the transport fee.

1 *ali* (Ar.) "great, superior" (Std. *bora*)

62. *Mama kafikiri*   *akaangaliya*
     Mambo ya kadari   *yalomfikiya*
     Zaidi ya siri   *hazikumweleya*
     Kasema ni kheri   *yamekuwa haya*

The mother looked at it, and contemplated
How destiny had unfolded for her.
She didn't understand much of the secret[1];
She said, "It is for the best that it happened this way."

1 The husband's secret of the furniture.

63. *Lau alikuwa*   *baba mesaliya*
     Mwane angeuwa   *kisu kamtiya*
     Na yeye akawa   *adhabuni piya*
     Ilahi Moliwa   *yote yamweleya*

Had her father survived,
He would have stabbed his daughter and killed her,
And he would have punished himself too.
The Lord Most High understands best."

64. *Kisha stakiri*   *mama kutuliya*
     Hakutaakhari   *dawa kuzengeya*
     Na madakitari   *alokisikiya*
     Wali mahodari   *aliwaendeya*

When the mother calmed down,
She didn't delay in search of medicine;
And of all the doctors that she had heard of,
She chose the best ones and went to consult them.

65. *Akahangaika*[1]   *kuwaandamiya*
     Walokisifika   *dawa zaweleya*
     Muwishowe Rabuka   *kamjaaliya*
     Mwane kutopoka   *akili kangiya*

She went back and forth in search of doctors,
The praiseworthy ones who were competent.
In the end, God made it happen:
Her daughter was cured, and her sanity returned.

[1] *-hangaika* syn.: *kupata shida* "to have troubles" > *mahangaiko* "troubles."

66. *Mara siku moja*   *akamuiliya*
     Kijana mmoja   *akamuambiya*
     Mimi nimekuja   *mke fuwatiya*
     Siwezi kungoja   *nataka rejeya*

One day, there came
A young man, who told her,
"I have come for my wife.
I cannot wait any longer; I want to return."

67. *Mama katamka*   *akamuambiya*
     Wewe ulofika   *sijakueleya*
     Wapi umetoka   *hebu nelezeya*
     Lini ulitaka   *mambo kama haya?*

The mother spoke, asking him,
"You who have just arrived; I don't understand.
Where are you from? Please explain to me,
When did you make this request?"

68. *Kijana mgeni*   *mbele kasogeya*
    Kwa yake lisani   *mama kamwambiya*
    Mimi ni fulani   *jina kalitaya*
    Na kwao nyumbani   *akamutajiya*

The young guest came forward,
And with these words he told the mother,
"I am so-and-so"; he mentioned his name
And he told her where he was from.

69. *Mama karadidi*   *mwana kumwambiya*
    Yako makusudi   *bado kuneleya*
    Katika fuwadi   *hayajatuliya*
    Neleza zaidi   *henda yakangiya*

The mother reiterated to the young man,
"Your intention is not clear to me;
It has not settled in my heart.
Please explain further so that I might comprehend it."

70. *Kaanda ghulamu*   *kumuhadithiya*
    Ya tangu kadimu[I]   *kamtondoleya*
    Hata dirihamu[II]   *akamtaiya*
    Mama kafahamu   *alilolijiya*

The young man began telling her.
He explained his story from the beginning,
And he mentioned even the dirhams he paid;
Then the mother understood what he had come for.

I *kadimu* (Ar.) "beginning" (Std. *mwanzo*) | II *dirihamu* (Ar.) stands for an old unit of weight, corresponding to the Greek and Persian drachma (Scl. 168–169).; see Qur. 12:20 and the note below.

HURUMA: SOCIAL ROLES AND RESPONSIBILITY

71. *Hapo kainama*   *kaanda kuliya*
  Hana lakusema   *huyo kumwambiya*
  Bintiye mwema   *mekuwisha poteya*
  Wala dirihama[1]   *hazikusaliya*

She then bowed her head and began weeping;
She had nothing to say to him.
Her pious daughter had transgressed,
And the money was spent.

[1] *dirihama*—The common Swahilized form is *dirahamu*; in this line, the ending in *-ma* is used to conform to the internal rhyme in *-ma*.

72. *Kasubiri sana*   *jibu kungojeya*
  Hata akiyona   *mambo yendeleya*
  Hapo akanena   *kujiuliziya*
  Kwani yule Bwana   *hakuwaambiya*

He was very patient, awaiting her answer,
Until he realized that the scene was going on.
He then spoke to inquire,
"Didn't your husband inform you?"

73. *Sikiza mwanangu*   *sasa takwambiya*
  Mimi mume wangu   *hakunielezeya*
  Akifika kwangu   *bado kutuliya*
  Ajali ya Mngu   *ilimfikiya*

"Listen my child, I will now tell you:
My husband didn't inform me.
When he arrived at my home, before he could settle in,
God's decree befell him."

74. *Kijana mgeni*   *hapo akaliya*
  Matozi usoni   *yaka mueneya*
  Mwisowe nguoni   *yakamuingiya*
  Hata majirani   *wakamsikiya*

The young guest began weeping,
His face filled with tears,
And by the end, [tears] were falling on his clothes.
Even the neighbors heard him crying.

75. *Katowa kauli*   *huku analiya*
    Hini ndiyo hali   *yahini duniya*
    Mauti ni kweli   *meumba Jaliya*
    Wake na rijali   *yatawafikiya*

Between his cries, he uttered,
"This is the way of this world;
Death is a reality created by God.
It will befall both women and men."

76. *Kisa kabaini*   *hapo kawambiya*
    Sasa kwaherini   *kwetu narejeya*
    Na jamii deni   *nimewawatiya*
    Nanyi kumbukani   *duwa kunombeya¹*

He then spoke clearly, and told them,
"I now bid you farewell; I shall return home,
And I have forgiven the family's debt.
Please remember to pray for me."

1 *duwa* (Ar. *duʿāʾ*) (Std. *dua*). With this term, in conjunction with the verb *kuomba* "to pray,"
a Swahili Muslim devotee enacts his or her supplication to God.

77. *Kapanda garini*   *kajisafiriya*
    Na huku nyumbani   *mama kasaliya*
    Umo huzunini   *hatindi kuliya*
    Hata duniyani   *kukamtukiya*

He got into his vehicle and traveled back,
And the mother was left back home;
She was in so much sadness, she couldn't stop crying,
And she hated to exist in the world.

HURUMA: SOCIAL ROLES AND RESPONSIBILITY

78. *Ingawa aishi*   *hataki duniya*
  Hajifurahishi   *hata siku moya*
  Wala hajilishi   *akajishibiya*
  Kama kifurushi   *amejitatiya[I]*

Even though she is alive, she rejects the world.
She doesn't enjoy herself, not even for a day.
Nor does she eat to satisfaction;
Like a bundle, she has tied herself.

I *-jitatiya* "to fold, bend, tangle, wrap." As Mau says, the verb expresses the image of someone who "curles himself up like a weak person who is depressed" (*kujikunjakunja kama mnyonge asiye na raha*); another way to describe its meaning is *kitu ambacho kimevunjika vunjika*, namely "a thing that has been broken."

79. *Mpaka ajali*   *ikamfikiya*
  Kandama rijali   *alotanguliya*
  Mengi yao mali   *alimetumiya*
  Kasaza kalili   *mwane kamwatiya*

She remained like that until death came for her.
She went after her husband who had preceded her;
Having spent most of their wealth,
She left only a little to her daughter.

80. *Mzaa haramu*   *pweke kasaliya*
  Na ngome[I] adhimu   *alotegemeya*
  Ali wake umu[II]   *amemondokeya*
  Zikazidi hamu   *hapo za duniya*

The illegitimate parent was left alone,
And the great strength that she had leaned on
Was her mother, and she too had left her.
Her worries of the world increased at that point.

I Here used as a metaphor with reference to the girl's mother. | II *umu* (Ar.) "mother" (Std. *mama*). The choice of using the Arabic form in this line is for the sake of the internal rhyme in *-mu*.

81. *Huyo[1] mwanamke* *akiangaliya*
 Mebakiya pweke *na wake udhiya*
 Kijitoto chake *cha mwaka mmoya*
 Yeye ni mamake *na baba pamoya*

It now dawns on the woman that
She is alone with her suffering;
With her, a one-year-old infant
To whom she is both mother and father.

1 *huyo* "that" (Std. *huyu*)

82. *Wote watu wake* *wamemkimbiya*
 Na makosa yake *alowakoseya*
 Ni kuteya kwake *shimoni kangiya*
 Akazaa wake *mwana haramiya*

All of her kin have deserted her,
And the mistake that she had wronged them with
Was to slip and fall into a ditch
And give birth to an illegitimate child.

83. *Sana kafikiri* *kazengeya ndiya*
 Mwisho kakhitari *kwenda kujiftya*
 Shetwani mshari *hilo kamwambiya*
 Kangata swaghiri[1] *akashika ndiya*

She pondered for long, looking for a solution.
Finally, she decided to commit suicide.
The evil Satan persuaded her to do so;
Carrying her young one, she went on her way.

1 *swaghiri* (Ar.) "small" (Std. *mdogo*)

84. *Akenda haraka* *mbio kikimbiya*
 Henda kizungura *watu changaliya*
 Wasije mshika *wakamziwiya*
 Kabla kufika *penye yake niya*

HURUMA: SOCIAL ROLES AND RESPONSIBILITY

She went hastily, running fast.
She kept on turning to check for people
So that they didn't get hold of her and restrain
Her from reaching her goal.

85. *Ngomeni kifika*   *hakushawiriya*[1]
     Alirukaruka   *kajiatiliya*
     Mwane kamshika   *kamkumbatiya*
     Kizama kizuka   *na yeye pamoya*

Upon arriving at the seawall, she didn't think twice:
She jumped and threw herself into the sea,
Holding her child in a tight embrace,
Together submerging in the water and coming up again.

1 *shauria* (Ar.). As explained by Mau, in Swahili, the meaning of this root is "to consider, not to have decided yet"; for instance, if you say *mimi nashawiriya kwenda Mambasa*, it translates to "I have not yet decided whether to go to Mombasa" (i.e., I am still thinking about whether to go to Mombasa).

86. *Kwalina kuhuli*[1]   *akipita ndiya*
     Kaona kwa mbali   *kitu chaoleya*
     Kakita amali   *na kuchangaliya*
     Kajuwa muili   *mwana adamiya*

There was a middle-aged man passing by.
He saw something floating from afar;
He carefully looked and examined it.
He recognized it to be a human body.

1 *kuhuli* (Ar.) "middle-aged person" (Std. *mzee*)

87. *Majini kashuka*   *na nguo pamoya*
     Kenda kwa haraka   *kumfuwatiya*
     Hata akifika   *kamshuhudiya*
     Ruhu muhutoka[1]   *kuwaga duniya*

He descended into the water with his clothes on.
He went hurriedly to get her;
Upon reaching her he observed that
Her soul was about to leave her and abandon this world.

1 *muhutoka* Am. "to be about to leave," a verb with a locative subject prefix (*mu-*) used in Kiamu to express "to be about to." See also *Hafi asiye timiwa*, stz. 7.

88. *Hapo kamshika*   *na mwane pamoya*
     Dau kalitaka   *kumsaidiya*
     Nalolikafika   *kwenda mpokeya*
     Ndani kawaweka   *na yeye kangiya*

At that point, he got a hold of her and her child.
He signaled for the dhow to come to their rescue,
And it arrived to get them;
He put them inside and then he boarded too.

89. *Kisha wapandisha*   *nae kurukiya*
     Akawatapisha   *mai kayamwaya*
     Akahakikisha   *haya kusaliya*
     Hapo kamwamsha   *fahamu kangiya*

After he had gotten them into the boat and he too had jumped in,
He induced vomiting to remove the water they swallowed.
He made sure none remained;
That is when he woke her up, returning her to consciousness.

90. *Bwana kwa makini*   *akamuandiya*
     Kataka undani   *ulomfikiya*
     Kwa sababu gani   *amefanya haya*
     Hata baharini   *kenda kujitiya*

The man began talking to her attentively,
Wanting to know depths of what had befallen her.
Why was it that she did this,
To the point of throwing herself into the ocean?

HURUMA: SOCIAL ROLES AND RESPONSIBILITY

91. *Akamba mwanangu*   *usione haya*
    Yote ya matungu   *mimi nelezeya*
    Kwa uwezo wangu   *takusaidiya*
    Kulla lema Mngu   *atatwegesheya*

He told her, "My daughter, don't be ashamed;
You can tell me all the bitterness that's bothering you.
I will help you to the best of my ability,
And God will bring forth all goodness."

92. *Kamwambia Babu*   *ukitaka haya*
    Tafuta kitabu   *na kalamu piya*
    Kiswa¹ ukutubu   *kipate eneya*
    Kisije wasibu   *wanoinukiya*

She told him: "Oh grandfather, if you are interested in this,
Go find a book and a pen.
Then write the story so that it may spread,
So that the same thing doesn't befall those who are still growing up.

1 *kiswa* (Ar. *qiṣṣah*) "story" (Std. *kisa* or *hadithi*)

93. *Naanda usemi*   *babu kukwambiya*
    Nalizawa mimi   *pwekee mmoya*
    Wala wangu umi   *hakujipatiya*
    Mngine ghulami   *wala bintiya*

I am starting this speech to tell you, oh grandfather,
I was born as the only child,
And my mother didn't get
Any other boy or girl.

94. *Mama na babangu*   *wote kwa pamoya*
    Nyonda mola wangu   *alimewatiya*
    Mkononi mwangu   *wakanitiliya*
    Kulla haja yangu   *nilokizengeya*

Both my mother and father in unison,
God had given them immense love for me.
They delivered into my hands
Each and every need that I sought.

95.

Salina taabu	*na wala udhiya*
Bila ya hisabu	*wakaniatiya*
Mali ya ajabu	*nikiyatezeya*
Sina matulubu	*yasiotimiya*

I had neither any problems nor any suffering.
Without counting, they left lots of money for me,
Immense amounts of wealth to toy with;
I had no wish that didn't come true.

1 *salina* Am. "I did not not have" (Std. *sikuwa na*)

96.

Kipata akili	*mambo kuneleya*
Katiwa skuli	*kenda jisomeya*
Chumba cha awali	*nikakianziya*
Wala sikufeli	*hata mara moya*

When I became of age and started to comprehend things,
I was taken to school to pursue my studies.
From the first grade I started,
And not even once did I fail.

97.

Kasoma kwa hamu	*nikakazaniya[1]*
Ili nikhitimu	*nipate ingiya*
Chuo cha walimu	*na kuendeleya*
Neneze ilimu	*nilojipatiya*

I studied passionately and hard,
To graduate and enroll
In the teachers' college to further my studies,
To spread the knowledge I received.

1 *-kazaniya* syn.: *kufanya kwa bidi* "to put effort into sth."

HURUMA: SOCIAL ROLES AND RESPONSIBILITY

98. *Lakini babangu*   *hakuniridhiya*
    Na mipango yangu   *hakufurahiya*
    Kasema mwanangu   *nyumbani rejeya*
    Kama radhi yangu[1]   *unaizengeya*

But my father didn't accept this,
And wasn't happy with my plans.
He said, 'My child, please return home
If you are searching for my blessings.'

[1] *radhi* "blessings, approvals." In stz. 22–23 of the *Utendi wa Mwana Kupona*, the approvals are recalled to Mwana Kupona's daughter and considered to be five in number: the approval of God, the Prophet, father, mother, and husband. The stanzas reads as follows: *Mama pulika maneno / kiumbe ni radhi tano / ndipo apate usono / wa akhera na dunia*, stz. 22; *Nda Mngu na Mtumewe / baba na mama wayuwe / na ya tano nda mumewe / mno imekaririwa*, stz. 23; "Listen to me, my dear; a woman requires the approval of five before she has peace in this world and the next: Of God and His Prophet; of father and mother, as you know; and the fifth of her husband as has been said again and again".[4]

99. *Kakoseya budi*   *kabadili niya*
    Nyumbani karudi   *kenda jikaliya*
    Katika fuwadi   *huzuni kangiya*
    Yangu makusudi   *yalipofifya*

I had no other choice but to change my plan.
I went back home and settled down there;
In my heart, there was a sadness
When my goals began to fade.

100. *Na siku za kwanza*   *nyumbani kungiya*
    Sana kajikaza   *ndani katuliya*
    Kaanza jifunza   *mambo moya moya*
    Yote kamaliza   *yakanieleya*

And from the first day I arrived home,
I tried my best to feel settled inside.
I started to learn one thing after the other:
I completed everything, and I mastered it all.

---

4 John Williamson T. Allen, *Tendi: Six Examples of a Swahili Classical Verse Form with Translations & Notes.* (New York: Africana Pub. Corp. 1971), 70–71.

101. *Pale jiranini*   *kwalina jariya*
    Tangu skulini   *twaliko pamoya*
    Akija nyumbani   *kuniangaliya*
    Kinena fulani[1]   *twende kutembeya*

In the neighborhood, there was a young woman;
Ever since our school days, we would be together.
She used to come home to visit me;
She said 'So-and-so, let's go out for a walk.'

1 *fulani* (Ar.) "such-and-such man or thing," "quidam, quaedam" (Krp. 73).

102. *Katowa kauli*   *kamrudishiya*
    Tena kwa ukali   *nikimuambiya*
    Na mara ya pili   *sambe kama haya*
    Mimi afadhali   *hapa kubakiya*

I uttered some words in response to her,
And harshly I told her,
'Don't ever say that again;
It's better for me to stay here.'

103. *Tukitoka sana*   *nde kutembeya*
    Twenda kupambana   *na watu wabaya*
    Wasio maana   *wasoona haya*
    Mengi tutaona   *tusoyaridhiya*

If we go meandering a lot,
We will meet bad people,
Without worth or shame,
And we will see a lot that we disagree with.

104. *Lakini swahibu[1]*   *kanikazaniya*
    Kanza niatibu   *na kunangukiya*
    Katika kalibu   *imani kangiya*
    Kasema twayibu   *twende mara moya*

HURUMA: SOCIAL ROLES AND RESPONSIBILITY 307

But my friend kept insisting.
She started making me feel guilty, begging me,
And my heart softened for her.
I said, 'Alright, let's go, just this once.'

1 *swahibu* Ar. "friend" (Std. *rafiki*).

105. *Sute tukatoka*   *tukandama ndiya*
     Tukenda haraka   *tupate rejeya*
     Hata tukifika   *tulokusudiya*
     Ni wa kula nyaka   *watu walokuya*

We left and went on our way.
We went hastily, to be able to hurry back.
And when we arrived at our destination,
There were people of all ages.

106. *Kwaliko na watu*   *walotimiliya*
     Na wana watoto   *handa inukiya*
     Ni ufu kwa tutu[1] *wamejikaliya*
     Kamba twenzetu   *siyawezi haya*

There were mature people,
And young budding adolescents;
Like an ill-assorted group, they were sitting.
I told her, 'Let us return; I can't stand this.'

1 *ufu* "rasped cocoa-nut which has not yet strained (*kununua*) or filtered" (Krp. 394); *tutu* "dish of cowpeas that have been boiled with maize or millet and sometimes mixed with grated coconut juice" (Mam. 768). *Tutu* and *ufu* become mixed in one dish. The metaphorical meaning here is that there is a melee of all kinds of people, including untrustworthy ones.

107. *Kanambiya ngoja*   *kwanza angaliya*
     Tunaanza kuja   *wataka rejeya*
     Ukisha ziyoja   *kuzishuhudiya*
     Wewe hutotaja   *twende kunambiya*

She told me, 'Wait, first have a look!
We have just arrived, and you already want to return.
Once you witness the wonders,
You will not say that you want to return.'

108. *Yakanipendeza* *mimi mambo haya*
  Nami kajikaza   *kibobwe[1] kangiya*
  Kawa ninateza   *na kushangiliya*
  Linkingiya jiza   *tukajirudiya*

I was pleased with these events;
I too made an effort, and tightened my *kibobwe*.
I was dancing and cheering on;
When darkness befell upon us, we went back.

1 *kibobwe* Am. "a strip of cloth, like a *kanga*, worn tightly around the waist by women during dances" (Std. *kibwebwe*).

109. *Na hapo ndiyani* *sasa twarejeya*
  Kaja insani   *kanifuwatiya*
  Akamba fulani   *hebu ningojeya*
  Neno la moyoni   *nataka kwambiya*

While on our way back,
A man came and approached me.
He told me, 'Oh so-and-so, please wait for me;
I want to tell you something from my heart.'

110. *Maneno matamu* *aliniambiya*
  Nusura[1] fahamu   *kuja nipoteya*
  Nikatabasamu   *kamkubaliya*
  Asali na sumu   *nikanwa pamoya*

He told me very sweet things;
I almost passed out.
I smiled and accepted his request;
I drank both honey and poison together.

1 *nusura* "about, nearly"; "a little within a hair's breadth" (Krp. 287).

HURUMA: SOCIAL ROLES AND RESPONSIBILITY 309

111. *Siku hiyo nami*   *niliporejeya*
      Kaanda usemi   *mama kumwambiya*
      Ni wengi kaumi[I]   *pwani walokuya*
      Na hata Warumi[II]   *walihudhuriya*

And on that day, when I returned,
I began talking, recounting to my mother:
'Many people had come to the seafront;
Even white people were there.'

[I] *kaumi* (Ar.) "people," "crowd" (Std. *watu*) | [II] *Warumi* lit. "Romans," but here referring to *Wazungu* "white people," mostly tourists, according to Ustadh Mau. Interestingly, the conceptual blending of "Romans" and "white people" already has a long history. In the oldest known *utendi*, the *Utendi wa Tambuka*, the enemies of the Prophet and his allies are referred to as *Warumi* or *Warumu*, here referring to Byzantine Christians. In later poetry, the term is used interchangeably with Christians, eventually losing its religious connotation to refer to white people in general.

112. *Kashika uradi*   *kiukaririya*
      Henda nikirudi   *kimuandamiya*
      Sijali baridi   *na wala udhiya*
      Mambo yakazidi   *mama kasikiya*

I held fast to this routine, and continued repeating it,
Going back and forth in pursuit of the man.
I didn't mind the cold or the challenges I endured;
Things intensified, and my mother heard about them.

113. *Kanikanya sana*   *na kuniziwiya*
      Akamba kijana   *si njema duniya*
      Hayana maana   *hayo nakwambiya*
      Utajitukana   *na sisi pamoya*

She constantly warned me and tried to stop me;
She said, 'Oh child, the world isn't a good place.
Those things are worthless, I am telling you.
You will bring trouble on yourself and on us, too.'

310 HURUMA: SOCIAL ROLES AND RESPONSIBILITY

114. *Mimi asilani*   *sikumsikiya*
Walinikitwani   *wawili pamoya*
Shetwani na jini   *menisimamiya*
Mwangu akilini   *wameniingiya*

Never did I listen to her.
They had possessed my head, the two together:
Satan and the devil stood before me.
They had completely overtaken my sanity.

115. *Na miwili nyezi*   *ikisa timiya*
Muhibu mpenzi   *alinikimbiya*
Kanatiya kazi   *ya mimba kuleya*
Na kina shangazi   *wakanitukiya*

After two full months,
My dear lover left me.
He left me with the burden of caring for his pregnancy,
And the family of my paternal aunt hated me.

116. *Na wote kaumu*   *kanigeukiya*
Ila wangu umu   *hakunikimbiya*
Majuto adhimu   *yakanifikiya*
Kakonda kwa hamu   *na mwingi udhiya*

And the whole community disowned me,
Except my mother—she never left me.
Immense regret befell me;
I became emaciated from all the trouble and worry.

117. *Yule mvulana*   *alotenda haya*
Mimi kimuona   *alikikimbiya*
Muwisowe kanena   *wanisingiziya*[1]
Si wangu kijana   *mimba sikutiya*

The boy who did this,
Every time I saw him, he would run away.
He finally said, 'You are pinning this on me
That baby isn't mine; I did not impregnate you.'

1 *kusingiziya* syn.: *kumzulia urongo* "pinning a lie on someone"

HURUMA: SOCIAL ROLES AND RESPONSIBILITY

118. *Kastahamili*　　　　　*nikavumiliya*
　　 Ala kulli hali　　　　 *nikajiziwiya*
　　 Mpaka ajali　　　　　*ilipotimiya*
　　 Mwana ni rijali　　　 *nilojizaliya*

I put up with it, and I was patient.
In all matters, I put up with it.
Until the day arrived that
I delivered a baby boy.

119. *Na wala babangu*　　　 *hakujuwa haya*
　　 Mambo ya matungu　　　*yaliotokeya*
　　 Ali Takaungu[1]　　　　*kijisomesheya*
　　 Ninae mwanangu　　　 *watu kiwambiya*

And my father wasn't even aware of them,
The bitter events that occurred.
He was in Takaungu, teaching;
'I have a daughter,' he kept telling people with pride.

[1] *Takaungu* "is the name of a large village close to Kilifi bay in Kenya; it was there the Marsue (Mazrui) dynasty fled after the capture of Mombasa by the Imam of Muscat. The place-name of this village indicates *maji ya utungu*, referring to its previously brackish water that later became drinkable" (Krp. 355).

120. *Mume nikapata*　　　　*kanikubaliya*
　　 Na yaliyopita　　　　 *hakuyasikiya*
　　 Kenda kaangata　　　 *zitu kuneteya*
　　 Khabari kipata　　　　*papo kajifiya*

I got a spouse, and my father accepted him.
What had happened, he had not heard about.
He went and bought furniture for me;
When he heard the news, he died instantly

121. *Akabaki mama*　　　　 *pweke kasaliya*
　　 Huzuni daima　　　　 *zisomwondokeya*
　　 Mpaka kakoma　　　　 *nae kajifiya*
　　 Kabakiya nyuma　　　 *na mwana pamoya*

My mother remained all by herself.
She was always sad; it never left her,
Until she too met her end and passed away.
I remained behind, together with the child.

122. *Nami kaamuwa*   *niwage duniya*
    Nipate pumuwa   *na hunu udhiya*
    Lakini Moliwa   *hakujaaliya*
    Ukaja nokowa   *nipate saliya*

So I too decided to leave this world
So that I too can be relieved from these pains.
But God did not will it;
You came and saved me, and I remained alive.

123. *Hiki ndicho kiswa*   *kilonijiriya*
    Chote nimekwisa   *kukuhadithiya*
    Ni mimi mkosa   *nilomridhiya*
    Mwane ibilisa   *kunikaribiya*

This is the tragedy that befell me;
I have finished recounting it to you.
I am the wrongdoer who gave in
And allowed Satan's child to come near me."

124. *Umefanya wema*   *hili kunambiya*
    Yote ulosema   *nimeyasikiya*
    Nami tasimama   *kukusaidiya*
    Sitokusukuma   *hata mara moya*

[The man speaking:] "You have done well by telling me this.
I have heard everything you said.
I will stand firm to help you;
I will not push you away even once.

125. *Lakini nataka*   *kwako yambo moya*
    Machache tamka   *wendo kuwambiya*
    Yasije wafika   *nao kama haya*
    Utimu waraka   *tuwape wasiya*

HURUMA: SOCIAL ROLES AND RESPONSIBILITY   313

But I want one thing from you:
Say a few things to inform others
So that the same fate doesn't befall them.
Let us complete this writing so as to advise them."

126. *Ninakushukuri*   *hili kunambiya*
    Nami tadhukuri   *machache tataya*
    Wala si kathiri   *tayowataiya*
    Wajitahadhari   *wakiyasikiya*

[The woman speaking:] "I am grateful to you for telling me this,
And I will speak out, mentioning a few things—
And it is not much that I will mention,
So that they can be careful when they hear this.

127. *Mwana mwanamke*   *katika duniya*
    Yeye hadhi yake   *ya kujivuniya*
    Ni umwali wake   *kujihifadhiya*
    Nde asitoke   *kwenda kupoteya*

A girl in this world,
Her virtue to be proud of
Is to preserve her virginity.
She should not go out wandering.

128. *Hiko ni kipai*   *Mngu mekutiya*
    Mtu hakitwai   *akakitezeya*
    Kawapa mabui   *wakupita ndiya*
    Wala hachambui   *akachatiliya*

This is a gift given to you by God
A person shouldn't take it and play with it,
Giving it to friends passing by,
Nor should she remove it and let it go.

129. *Kihifadhi sana*   *na kuchangaliya*
    Sifanye ujana   *kikakupoteya*
    Muwekee bwana   *aje shuhudiya*
    Apate kunena   *nimejivuniya*

Protect it well and take care of it.
Don't hang around with boys, lest you lose it;
Keep it for your husband so that he can witness it,
So that he can say, "I am so proud."

130. *Wala sighurike*   *ukawasikiya*
    Wale wanawake   *waliopoteya*
    Yao usishike   *wakikuambiya*
    Hao lana yake   *Mngu mewatiya*

Don't get tempted to listen
To those women who have lost their way.
Don't trust what they tell you;
They are cursed by God.

131. *Ni sisi banati*   *wazi tawambiya*
    Tujengao nti   *na kuvunda piya*
    Tukijidhibiti   *na kujiziwiya*
    Ni hono wakati   *wa kuendeleya*

It is we, the girls, I am openly telling you,
Who build the country, and we destroy it too.
If we are firm and restrain ourselves,
Only then, we can progress.

132. *Na tuiwatapo*   *ilo sawa ndiya*
    Tukawa upepo   *hatwendi kumoya*
    Aw kama tapo[1]   *zote twapakiya*
    Ndipo nchi hapo   *tunajivundiya*

And when we forsake the right path,
We become like the wind; we fly in all directions.
Or like in a packsaddle, we pack in everything;
At that time, we will break down the country.

1 *tapo* "bât d'âne en sparterie, forme besace" (Scl. 871).

HURUMA: SOCIAL ROLES AND RESPONSIBILITY   315

133. *Musighurikeni*   *wakiwaambiya*
   Ati uzunguni   *kumeendeleya*
   Kwa kutupa dini   *na kuitukiya*
   Wao ruhubani   *wataka kuliya*

Don't be fooled when they tell you
That the West is progressive
Because they disregard religion and hate it.
Their religious leaders want to cry.

134. *Mila ya kizungu*   *mingi ni mibaya*
   Wote ulimwengu   *wametufujiya*
   Wamefanya jungu[I]   *watakatutiya*
   Tuzidi utungu   *kwa kuteketeya*

Most Western customs are bad;
They have ruined the whole world for us.
They have prepared a boiling pot, ready to throw us in
To intensify our pain, burning us.

I *jungu* "an earthen cooking pot" (Std. *chungu*) (Krp. 42); *chombo cha kupikia mithili ya sufuria ambacho hutengenzwa kwa udongo* "a pot to cook in, like a *sufuria*, but made of clay" (see also the picture in Kak. 148).

135. *Hapa namaliza*   *mwiso nawambiya*
   Nimewaeleza   *yote mimi haya*
   Ili kuwafunza   *mambo ya duniya*
   Musije kuteza   *na watu wabaya*

I hereby conclude telling you the end.
I have explained all this to you
So as to teach you the ways of the world,
So you don't mess around with evil people.

136. *Ukiyona mtu*   *aanda kwambiya*
   Mara mbili tatu   *maneno mabaya*
   Mwambie sukutu[I]   *asiposikiya*
   Kivue kiyatu   *na kumpijiya[II]*

If someone starts telling you
Misguiding words, twice or thrice,
Tell the person to shut up—and if he doesn't listen,
Take off your shoe and hit him with it.

I *sukutu* (Ar.) "keep silent" (Std. *-nyamaza*). | II Hemistich adapted from what is also found in al-Ṭanṭawi's *Yā-bintī*.

137. *Atapokuona*   *hukumridhiya*
     Hapo huyo bwana   *tazunguwa¹ niya*
     Kama mbwa maana   *nyumbani takuya*
     Atake owana   *kama kishariya*

When he sees that you didn't give in,
Then that man will change his intentions.
If he is worthy, he will come home,
And he will ask you to marry him according to law."

I *-zunguwa* syn.: *badilisha* "to change."

138. *Asanta sana*   *kwa ulowambiya*
     Yako ya maana   *ulvelezeya*
     Wenziyo zijana   *wapate sikiya*
     Inshaallah Rabana   *tatutimiziya*

[The elder person now answers:] "Thank you so much for what you
have told them,
The meaningful advice that you have explained
So that your fellow youth can hear it.
God willing, the Lord will convey it for us.

139. *Wewe huna mtu*   *aliosaliya*
     Wala huna kitu   *katika duniya*
     Kheri twende kwetu *tukae pamoya*
     Na mwano kitutu   *tutakuyeleya*

You have no one left for you,
Nor do you have anything in this world.
It's better that we go home and live together,
And your little child, we shall care for him.

HURUMA: SOCIAL ROLES AND RESPONSIBILITY   317

140. *Mimi nina mke*   *twaishi pamoya*
     Na kijana chake   *alina mmoya*
     Amekwenda zake   *mewaga duniya*
     Na badili yake   *wewe umekuya*

I have a wife; we live together,
And had one child.
She has passed away and left this world,
And in her place, you have come."

141. *Ninakushukuri*   *yako njema niya*
     Kwa kunisitiri   *katika duniya*
     Nami ni tayari   *kukuitikiya*
     Kwa zote amri   *utazonambiya*

[The woman:] "I am grateful for your good intentions
Of protecting me in this world,
And I am ready to heed your word
In every demand you shall ask of me."

142. *Hapa nimekoma*   *kuwapa wasiya*
     Kwa hini nudhuma   *nilowandikiya*
     Ilahi Karima   *tatuonya ndiya*
     ya kuiyandama   *ilo sawasiya*

Here I conclude, giving you advice
Through this composition I have written for you.
God the Most Gracious will show us the way,
The one that is straight and must be followed.

143. *Ndimi Mahmoudi*   *nilo sema haya*
     Mwane Ahmadi   *Amu mzaliya*
     Namukinirudi   *nilipokoseya*
     Furaha tazidi   *mukiniambiya*

It is me, Mahmoudi, who has conveyed this.
The son of Ahmadi, born in Lamu.
And if you correct me where I have erred,
I will be very delighted if you tell me.

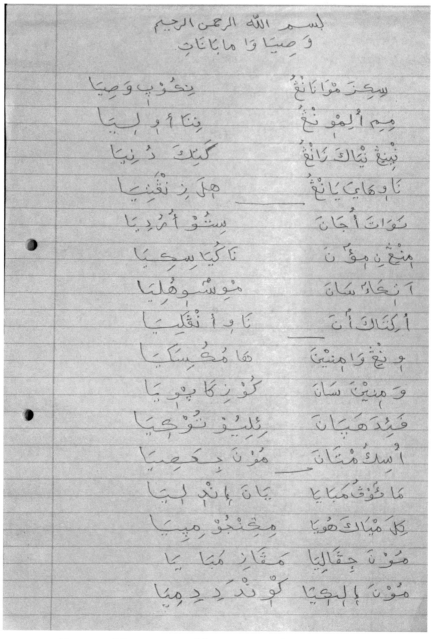

FIGURE 18 First page of the manuscript of the "Wasiya ya Mabanati" in Ustadh Mau's handwriting

Matukio: Biographical Poems

FIGURE 19   Ustadh Mahmoud Mau sitting in front of the oven in his bakery in 1988

1   *Hafi asiye timiwa* ("No One Dies before His Time Is Up")

Ustadh Mau composed this poem in 1999 as a kind of diary entry to remind himself of an incident in which he almost died. He first read it to his mother. He had traveled to Mombasa to visit his child who was studying there. At that time, during an El Niño phase after a long rainy period, the rain had caused the Tana River to swell so large that it destroyed the road in Gharseni. Thus, all the passengers had to get off the bus and board canoes that would take them to the other side of the large current. On the other side, another bus waited to take them to Mombasa. As one of the people on board the canoe tried to stretch his leg, he moved too much and the boat overturned. One man who could not swim grabbed Ustadh by the shoulder to find some support. He was so heavy that he almost made Ustadh Mau drown. Ustadh Mau lost his bag with the school fees for his child inside it. This story is effectively depicted in a dramatic crescendo, but with a happy ending: all six people on the boat survived. After the incident, Mahmoud began fast-

320   MATUKIO: BIOGRAPHICAL POEMS

ing every Monday and Thursday to thank God for saving him from drown-
ing on that day.

1.   *Nataka wapa hikaya, ya mambo yalonipata*
    Kwa utungo tawambiya, kiswache[1] kilichopita
    Mungu kunijaaliya, salimini kunieta
    Hafi asiye[11] timiwa

    I want to tell you a story of what happened to me.
    In verse, I will tell you about a particular incident
    When God protected and saved me.
    No one dies before his time is up.

    1 *kiswache* contracted form of *kisa chake* "its story." | 11 The poet uses the Kimvita (Mv.) and
    Kiunguja (Kiung.) form *asiye* instead of the Lamu *aso*.

2.   *Ni mwaoni twalingiya, kwa idadi watu sita*
    Na mifuko yetu piya, kila mtu kapakata
    Nahuza akatwambiya, hadhari kufurukuta
    Hafi asiye timiwa

    We got into a canoe; we were six in number,
    Everyone holding their bags in their laps.
    The captain told us, "Be careful, do not move too much!"
    No one dies before his time is up.

3.   *Tukaketi hangaliya, kamba alipoiwata*
    Na mtoni kikangiya, na mai kikafuata
    Katika sisi mmoya, guu hawezi kukuta
    Hafi asiye timiwa

    We sat and watched how they untied the rope,
    And the canoe went into the deep water, following the current.
    One of us could not stretch his leg.
    No one dies before his time is up.

4.   *Akitaka kusongeya, hutambaa tatatata*
    Ni yeo! Metwatiliya, maini huparapata
    Hata fahamu kitiya, mzigo nimebingita[1]
    Hafi asiye timiwa

MATUKIO: BIOGRAPHICAL POEMS

And when he wanted to move, he could only do it like a toddler.
Suddenly, we found ourselves in the water, struggling to stay on the
surface.
Before I even realized what happened, I was supporting a heavy
load.
No one dies before his time is up.

I -*bingita* "to carry."

5. *Jibaba la kilo miya, maungoni meikita*
   Kwa dhati meniemeya, mabegani menambata
   Kesa[I] kuisaidiya, kutaka kumkukuta[II]
   Hafi asiye timiwa

   I was carrying a colossus of one hundred kilos on my back;
   He weighed heavily on me, leaning on my shoulders.
   I tried everything to help myself and shake him off.
   No one dies before his time is up.

   I *kesa* < *ka-isa* "to finish." | II -*kukuta* "to shake off."

6. *Nami mkono mmoya, mkoba nimekamata*
   Lakini ukanemeya, sina budi kauwata
   Kauona hupoteya, kashindwa kuufuwata
   Hafi asiye timiwa

   I held my bag in one hand,
   But it became so heavy, I had to let it go.
   I watched it sink, unable to retrieve it.
   No one dies before his time is up.

7. *Hali yangu changaliya, pumzi siwezi vuta*
   Jamaa meniziwiya, mai kwa kasi hupita
   Shahada kaipijiya, na tamaa muhukata[I]
   Hafi asiye timiwa

   When I found myself in a situation in which I could not breathe—
   The fellow prevented me from doing so, and there was a strong
   current—

I pronounced the last creed and was about to give up.
No one dies before his time is up.

1 *muhukata tamaa* Am. "I was about to give up hope," a verb with the locative subject prefix (*mu-*), used in Kiamu to express "to be about to." See also *Wasiya wa mabanati*, stz. 88.

8.   *Kashopoka mara moya, kwa kuwana na kuteta*
    Kitwa nde katokeya, na pumzini nikavuta
    Kawahi yowe kutiya, baba likaniburuta
    Hafi asiye timiwa

For a moment, I managed to surface by fighting and struggling.
My head emerged from the water, and I could inhale;
I managed to shout before the heavy man pulled me down again.
No one dies before his time is up.

9.   *Tukazama kwa pamoya, mai kasi husokota*
    Mungu kanijaaliya, penyenye¹ tena kapata
    Kanena nisaidiya, ukee kaukukuta
    Hafi asiye timiwa

We sank together; the water was swirling quickly.
God granted me another chance to pierce through the surface.
I shouted loudly, "Help me!"
No one dies before his time is up.

1 *penyenye* "loophole."

10.   *Kaiyona naregeya na ziungo huniwata*
   Mwenyewe kashuhudiya ulimwengu hunipita
   Fahamu zikapoteya kisa kwa muda kapata
   Hafi asiye timiwa

I was getting weak, and my joints were failing me.
I could see myself how the world left me behind,
And I lost consciousness, which I regained after a while.
No one dies before his time is up.

MATUKIO: BIOGRAPHICAL POEMS

11. *Fahamu zikiningiya, kijana hunikokota*
    Na kwa mbali hunambiya, jiweni hela ambata
    Kifumbua changaliya, kwenye jiwe meniwata
    Hafi asiye timiwa

    When my consciousness came back, I found a young man pulling me,
    Telling me from afar, "Hold fast to this rock!"
    When I opened my eyes, I saw that he had pulled me toward a rock.
    No one dies before his time is up.

12. *Kamshukuru Jaliya, uhai tena kupata*
    Naye alosaidiya, maini kuniburuta
    Tamlipa Maulaya, kwa dua sitomuata
    Hafi asiye timiwa

    I thanked the Magnificent one for bringing me back to life,
    And the one who helped and pulled me out of the water.
    God will reward him, and I won't abandon him in my prayers.
    No one dies before his time is up.

13. *Baadhi ya abiriya, walikuya nifuata*
    Ili kunisaidiya, mkoba kuutafuta
    Uwapi umepoteya, hata ndiya ulopita
    Hafi asiye timiwa

    Some of the passengers came to me
    To help me look for my bag:
    "Where is it? I do not even know where it was lost."
    No one dies before his time is up.

14. *Hapa kikomo tatiya, kushukuru sitowata*
    Nna na faida moya, ambayo nimeipata
    Mauti kuyakimbiya, si dawa hukufuata
    Hafi asiye timiwa

    I will finish the poem here, but never stop being grateful.
    And there is one lesson that I have learned from it:
    Running from death is not a solution—it still follows you.
    No one dies before his time is up.

2　*Mlango* ("The Door")

Ustadh Mau composed this poem around 2003 or 2004, when he almost had to close down his bakery. The economy was not doing well (see also the poem *Jahazi*), and prices had been rising since the 1990s. His income was not enough to cover his expenses; he had debts of 1,500,000 shillings. Three of his children were at university, which added additional costs to his expenses. So he decided to close the shop for some time, since he no longer had any capital to invest. It was a difficult period for him, since, first of all, no one believed him; secondly, he did not know what to do.

For as long as he could remember, he had worked in the bakery, even when he was just a child and the bakery was run by his uncle. He helped out at the bakery after school until, at the beginning of the 1980s, he took it over from his uncle, to whom he provided some money for his daily provisions. His uncle had taken over the bakery from an Indian (at the time, the bakery was called Amir Bakery), who had ultimately moved away from Lamu, seeking greener pastures.

In 2005, Ustadh Mau retired and handed the bakery over to his firstborn son, Fati, who managed to obtain loans from the bank and to steer the bakery out of its crisis. He could even pay back his debts, but later went bankrupt with a second bakery that he had opened in Malindi. After that, he sold the Lamu bakery to his younger brother, Yassir. The bakery plays a central role in the family: Ustadh Mau calls it "the source of our life"; it earns an income for the whole family, and Yassir still runs the bakery, providing Ustadh Mau with money for his daily expenditures.

1.　*Sitoshunduwa mlango, taushindika[1] wa duka*
　　Kwani mambo henda jongo, hayaekei kunyoka
　　Nimemaliza mipango, siyoni kurakibika

　　I will not open but close the shop's door,
　　Because things are going wrong; they don't seem to be going right.
　　I have tried everything; I do not see any improvement.

　　1 *-shindika* "to close a door without locking it."

2.　*Ni uwamuzi thakili, na wala sikuutaka*
　　Mimi kwenye duka hili, ndipo nilipoinuka
　　Siisi kazi ya pili, illa mikate kuwoka

MATUKIO: BIOGRAPHICAL POEMS

It is a very hard decision, and I did not want it.
This shop is the place where I grew up.
I never learned any other profession except baking bread.

3. *Na adhabu ya kaburi, aiyuwao hakika[I]*
   Zinganga[II] zinazojiri, ni ndani tulomzika
   Wa nde hata khabari, hamba hunena huteka

The only one who really knows the suffering of the grave,
Is one who is buried.
Outside of it, people have no idea; they just gossip, talk, and laugh.

[I] The poem makes reference to a proverb that suggests that only someone who has gone through the same experience can understand the one suffering: *Adhabu ya kaburi aiyuwao ni maiti* "the punishment of the grave, the dead person is the one who knows it." | [II] *zinganga* Am. "trouble" (Std. *dharubu, taabu*)

4. *Na waja mukikutana, usitani[I] hukushika*
   Hufai kunena sina, na sina ukitamka
   Umwambiyao huwona, humfanyiya dhihaka

And when you meet people on the street, they stop you and beg;
You are not supposed to say, "I don't have anything."
When you tell them no, they think you are joking.

[I] *usita* "street," a noun derived from *-pita* "to pass by" (Std. *njia*)

5. *Aswilani hawakiri, hawataki kuridhika*
   Hunena ni ujauri, na twabiya kugeuka
   Ya nyuma yote mazuri, huwata kuyakumbuka

They do not want to accept your answer;
They say it is arrogance and that you have changed in character.
They remember none of your previous favors.

6. *Hata wako wa karibu, huwa nawe wana shaka*
   Wangawa hawakujibu, kwa siri hunungunika
   Hawaziyoni dharubu, ambazo hukuzunguka

Even your close relatives don't believe you;
Though they do not tell you directly, they talk behind your back.
They do not see the problems that have befallen you.

7. *Imekuwa ndake kazi, mtu kitu akitaka*
Humwambiya siku hizi, mambo yameharibika
Hushindana na mkizi, kwa hasira na kuruka

"It has become his habit; when someone begs him,
He says, 'Nowadays, things have gone wrong.'
He is worse than a *mkizi* fish, jumping out of anger."[1]

1 *mkizi* is a kind of fish (like a mullet) that jumps from the sea and that people consider to be very moody and choleric (*mwenye hasira*). Mau: *Ukimwambia kitu ataruka* ("If you tell him something, he will jump"). Mau also refers to a proverb: *Hasira ya mkizi, furaha/tijara ya mvuzi* ("The anger of the *mkizi* is the joy of the fisherman"). In this stanza, which consists of direct speech, Ustadh Mau lets the voices of his neighbors and friends speak about him; they compare him to a *mkizi* fish.

8. *Hayo ndiyo wanenayo, uchenda kuwadirika*
Ulonalo wayo wayo[1], na kwingi kusononeka
Hamba ni kisingiziyo, cha jukumu kuepuka

That is how you find them, talking behind your back.
They say the anxiety and worries you have
Are just an excuse to avoid your responsibility.

1 *wayo wayo* "laments" | 11 *kisingizi* "excuse"

9. *Henda kapata salama, labuda kapumzika*
Zikapunguwa lawama, za wenye kunizunguka
Na utune[1] ukakoma, mlango kiushindika

Perhaps I can get some peace and a bit of rest,
And the reproaches and provocations of those surrounding me
Will stop if I close the shop's door.

1 *utune* "grudges," syn.: *malalamiko*.

MATUKIO: BIOGRAPHICAL POEMS

10. *Hakuna dhiki wa dhiki, mwiso kiza hutanduka*
    Ni yeye pweke Khallaki, atuwao na kutweka
    Makini sibabaiki, kamba yake nimeshika

    There is not just distress after distress[1]; light will do away with the darkness.
    It is only the Creator who can lift the burden or put it on our shoulders;
    That is why I stay calm, holding fast to His rope.

    1 This refers to the saying *Hakuna dhiki wa dhiki, baada ya dhiki faraja*, "There is not mischief after mischief; after mischief there will be delight."

11. *Naamini kwa yakini, kwa hili tafaidika*
    Tamtambuwa ni nyani, mwema wa kuibandika
    Na wa kweli muhisani[1], naye atabainika

    I believe I will certainly benefit from this experience.
    I will recognize the ones who are only pretending to be good,
    And it will be obvious who my true friend is.

    1 *muhisani* Ar. "friend" (Std. *rafiki*)

12. *Mola amenisitiri, tangu nalipoinuka*
    Katika wangu umri, mpaka nilipofika
    Sasa hatoniaziri, inshaallah sitoumbuka

    God has safeguarded me since my childhood,
    Throughout my life, until where I am now.
    Now he will not disgrace me, *inshallah*; I will not be ashamed.

13. *Tammati yangu kauli, kalamu hapa naweka*
    Afuwa haiko mbali, nataraji kuafika
    Na koja la idhilali, shingoni hatonawika

    This is the end of my talk; I put my pen aside.
    Relief is not far; I expect to have it soon.
    He will not put a wreath of misery around my neck.

Maombi: Personal Poems of Supplication

FIGURE 20 Ustadh Mahmoud Mau together with his children, Aboud (in the middle), Hannan (on the right) and Azra (behind)

1 *Hapo zamani za yana* ("Once upon a Time")

This is a poem that Ustadh Mau's father, Ahmad Abdulkadir Abdulatif (1915–1970), composed for him around the time he was born in 1952. Ustadh Mau was the firstborn of his father's six children. Most of his father's poems have been lost; just a few survive. Ustadh Mau read this poem when he was a boy; it even helped him get used to reading Swahili in Arabic script. Ustadh Mau also keeps the copy in Arabic script that his cousin Abdulkadir Muhammad Abdulkadir reproduced from the original. Ustadh Mau had asked him to copy the poem in order to have a copy for himself.

Ustadh Mau's father passed away when he was around fifty-five years old. He was a heavy smoker of cigarettes, which may have contributed to his early death. His father's death marked a substantial change in Ustadh Mau's life, since, being the firstborn son, he had to rearrange his priorities and stop studying in order to take care of the family. From 1971 to 1973, he worked as a shopkeeper in Dar es Salaam. His father had been a marine engineer and the first to have a motorboat (*boti ya machine*), which allowed people to travel from Mokowe, where the buses from Mombasa and Malindi stop, to Lamu. In the last verses of the poem, we find metaphors of sea life: the Prophet is compared to the captain who guides the boat, a metaphor of human life, into the harbor.

In the typical style of an admonitory or advisory *utenzi*, that is a *wasiya*, it is the father's intention to provide his son with guidelines on how to live, drawing from his own experiences as well as the existing lore of advisory poetry, Islamic literature, and popular wisdom. In stanza 17 ff., for instance, he refers to the popular tradition of Nasrudin, widespread in the Islamic world. Nasrudin, though partly fusing with trickster traditions, is also venerated as an exemplary wise scholar and theologian. It was his wisdom that made Ustadh Mau's father wish for a son whom he could name after him. Accordingly, he also addresses his son as both Mahmoud and Nasrudin in the poem. The poem makes reference not only to popular tales, but also to the Qurʾān, and summarizes important tenets of belief for the young Ustadh Mau, which he would take to heart from early childhood onward: the names of the caliphs, the important wars during the Prophet's lifetime, the angels, and the importance of Zakat and Zakat al-Fitr.

The poem echoes the context of its composition but, even more importantly, already outlines many of the concerns that come to assume the utmost import-

 A recording of this poem is freely available online at https://doi.org/10.6084/m9.figshare.20200790.

ance to the son, Mahmoud Ahmad Abdulkadir, and that also recur in his own poetic practice. Even the "format" of passing on one's dearest concerns is the same: for both father and son, the *utendi* is the genre into which one casts the *wasiya*, or intellectual and spiritual heritage.

The poem adopts the personal, caring tone of a father, looking for the right words of lasting meaning, which he wants to pass on to his son. Ahmad's own father passed away in the same year that Mahmoud was born, which probably added to his motivation to write this poem, as a kind of heritage to pass on. Although he does not make reference to his own father, in a number of stanzas he emphasizes the brevity and vanity of life, stressing that death will spare no one, reflecting on his own life. This is a common topic not only in the Qur'ān, but also in Swahili poetry: the rhetorical *wawapi* "where are those" or *wangapi* "how many" questions (stz. 32, as well as stz. 22, 90 ff.) remind the addressee that none of the previous generations, even those in power, were able to avoid death.[1] This is one of the essential cornerstones on which the ethics of the poem are built: all human beings are God's creation and, accordingly, are meant to die. Accordingly, all human beings are equal, since they share the same destiny. This notion, which questions the abuse of power that the hierarchical social structure on Lamu seems to favor, rather urges for solidarity and care. The seemingly parallel tenets of the Riyadha Mosque and the anti-establishment movement around Habib Swaleh played important roles in Mahmoud's family; Ahmad Abdulkadir Abdulatif urges his son not to discriminate against poor people or those of lower social rank. He underlines the importance of caring for his wife, family, siblings, and parents, including visiting the graves of those who have passed away. His son should take care of and give alms to the poor and not mistreat those working for him. The notion of responsibility for the family as well as for the community at large—which his father underlines, also being conscious of his role as a community leader— finds an echo in Ustadh Mau's own poems and his way of caring for and about others.

In this poem, Ahmad takes a look at various facets of life, seeking to advise his son on how to live. To a large extent, the poem also reads as an exemplification of a *mungwana*'s prescribed behavior and social role. He firstly cautions his

---

1 See Clarissa Vierke, "Im Gebälk die Fledermäuse. Figurationen der Vergänglichkeit und der Täuschung in der klassischen Swahili-Dichtung," in *From the Tana River to Lake Chad. Research in African Oratures and Literatures. In Memoriam Thomas Geider*, ed. Lutz Diegner, Raimund Kastenholz, Uta Reuster-Jahn, and Hannelore Vögele, Mainzer Beiträge zur Afrikaforschung (Cologne: Köppe, 2014), 285–309.

MAOMBI: PERSONAL POEMS OF SUPPLICATION 331

son to carefully choose the woman he wants to marry—a concern later echoed in the *Haki za watoto*, which Mahmoud wrote as advice for his own son, Aboudi. The future wife is supposed to be humble and considerate, neither spending too much money nor spreading rumors. Discretion toward one's own wealth, also in times of financial difficulty, is an important quality of the *mungwana* that Mahmoud's father highlights. His son should neither be arrogant nor too outspoken about his own problems—and his wife should be the same:[2] he should maintain his composure no matter how difficult a situation is, being faithful and reliable.

There is another respect in which the poem resembles many of Ustadh Mau's own: it stresses education, *elimu*, and reading, *kusoma*, as important values also for the next generation. In stz. 78, the father warns the son not to study "devilish" writings. According to Mahmoud Ahmad Abdulkadir, the father was referring to secular or Christian education, of which he was deeply suspicious—like many others of the local Islamic elite, who would proudly stick to their own, erudite tradition of learning. Therefore, he never let his son study at a colonial school, but only at the madrassa, which Mahmoud is proud of. However, in his poetry (see for instance *Kiswahili*), Mahmoud does not stick to the same ideal, but rather stresses the importance of all kinds of education, including the natural sciences (see also the poem *Bandari ina mawimbi*), while also highlighting the value of local knowledge, language, and Islamic education in Swahili and Arabic. Times have been changing: while in his father's time, many more traditional institutions of learning existed and there was a high level of Islamic scholarship, the nationalization of Kenya and the compulsory implementation of secular school education after independence has had a damaging effect on many local institutions as well as the value of education. It is the fall of this high culture and local forms of learning and studying, that Ustadh Mau fights against in many of his poems.

1.	*Hapo zamani za yana*	Once upon a time,
	Nalopokuwa kijana	When I was still a boy,
	Hata ndevu siyavuna	When I had not yet even grown a beard,
	Haya naliyasikia	I heard these words:

---

2 The dilemma of the mungwana, who cannot speak about his financial crisis and is accordingly judged as arrogant, is the topic of the poem *Mlango*.

MAOMBI: PERSONAL POEMS OF SUPPLICATION

2. *Mtu akipija fali*[I]
   Ghalibu yake hunali[II]
   Tumeona na dalili
   Nyingi na kuzisikia

   If a man chooses a good omen,
   Mostly he gets what he wishes;
   We have seen and heard of
   Much evidence.

   I *fali* "good omen, auspice." Ustadh Mau: *Kuna mithali isemayo "fali hunali" kwa mfano mimi nilimuita binti yetu mmoja Azra ambalo ni lakabu ya Maryam mamake mtumi Issa. Kwa hivyo, nalipija fali binti huyu awe mfano wa Maryam katika ucha Mungu na utiifu wake. Na baba aliniita mimi Nasurdin akipija fali. Baada ya kusikiya hadithi au kiswa kumuhusu mtoto hoyo Nasrudin nae akapenda apate mtoto awe kama hoyo Nasrudin* ("There is a proverb that says: 'a good omen comes true.' For instance, I called one of our daughters Azra, which is a nickname of Maryam, the mother of the Prophet Issa. Therefore, I chose the name as a good omen for our daughter, so that she will be as God-fearing and obedient as Maryam. And my father wanted a good omen for me, and called me Nasrudin. After hearing the story or tale of Nasrudin, he also wished to have a child who would be like Nasrudin" (see stanza 17 below).) But his aunt later objected: she had lost her child, Mahmoud, and insisted that the baby should have his name. | II *-nali* "to receive" (Std. *-pata*)

3. *Baba ingawa ni mwanga*[I]
   Kijana chake hutunga
   Kula yambo la muanga
   Hupenda kumuuswia

   Even if a father is evil-minded,
   He takes care of his child.
   Every clear bit of advice,
   He likes to pass on to his child.

   I *mwanga* "an evil person, a witch doctor" (Std. *mganga*)[3]

4. *Ukiitaka harusi*
   Mke kwanda mdasisi
   Ulimi ukiwa mpesi
   Wata kumkaribia

   If you want to get married,
   First investigate the woman;
   If she is a gossiper,
   Avoid approaching her.

5. *Mambo twalia mfano*
   Hutaupata usono
   Utaziuma zitano[I]
   Kimoya kutosalia

   Consider other cases:
   You will never find any rest.
   You will bite your five fingers in regret;
   Not even one will be spared.

   I *-uma zidole* "to bite one's fingers" is a sign of regret.

---

3 See also Mohammed H. Abdulaziz, *Muyaka: 19th Century Swahili Popular Poetry*. (Nairobi: Kenya Literature Bureau, 1979).

MAOMBI: PERSONAL POEMS OF SUPPLICATION

6.   *Mke simuonye mali*   Don't show a woman your wealth,
     Ingawa kitu akali   Even if it is just a little;
     Taitia mashughuli   It will be her only concern,
     Apate kukwandolea   Taking everything away from you.

7.   *Ataifanya mwalimu[1]*   She will pretend to be well educated.
     Hazitokoma karamu   She won't stop organizing banquets;
     Nduze wakazi wa Amu   Her relatives living in Lamu
     Na wangine wa kungia   And others will also come.

1 *mwalimu*, lit. "teacher"; here it refers to the social status of a learned person, which she will pretend to have.

8.   *Mtu akikosa chake*   If a person loses his wealth,
     Hutukiwa na nduzake   He is hated by his companions.
     Ina hitwa mwendazake   By name, he is called "Go Away";
     Wendani hukukimbia   Good friends run away from you.

9.   *Mpe chakula kizuri*   Give her good food
     Na libasi ya fakhari   And prestigious dresses
     Nduze wakaa madari[1]   So that her relatives living in elegant, many-
     Ito wakimzindia   storied houses
                                   Will cast an envious eye on her.

1 *madari* "floor, attic"; "étage, espace entre deux planchers ou terrasses" (Scl. 164), here referring to Lamu's elegant, many-storied houses, an architectural style that became prominent in the eighteenth and nineteenth century, and that only rich people could afford.

10. *Mfanye na bangili*   Give her bracelets
     Na mkufu ulo mali   And an expensive chain necklace,
     Phete na hizo zipuli   Rings and earrings
     Kama na majasi[1] pia   As well as a flesh tunnel.

1 *jasi* "flesh tunnel," a hollow piece of jewelry worn in a hole made in the earlobe (Scl. 183)[4]

---

4 See also the picture in James Vere de Allen. (ed.). *Al-Inkishafi. Catechism of a Soul by Sayyid Abdalla Bin Ali Bin Nasir*. With a translation and notes by James Vere de Allen. (Nairobi, East African Literature Bureau, 1977).

MAOMBI: PERSONAL POEMS OF SUPPLICATION

11. | *Mfunge na marijani* | Adorn her with red corals, |
Sukurubu[1] shikioni	Earrings for her ears,
Na kipini cha puani	And you should also give her
Ni sawa ukimtia	A ring for her nose.

1 *sukurubu*; Mau: *aina ya urembo unaotiwa shikiyoni la mwanamke. Wangine waita stadi huwa ni ya dhahabu au fedha* ("a kind of jewelry that is worn on the ears of a woman. It is also called *stadi*. It is made of gold or silver").

12. | *Mtu wa sirakalini[1]* | A government official, |
Usimfanye mwendani	Don't make him your friend.
Mwana haramu[11] nyum-	A child born outside of marriage,
bani	Do not bring him home to raise him.
Usiweke kumyea[111]	

1 According to Ustadh Mau, on Lamu at that time, a representative of the colonial government was considered a spy and hence could never become a trustworthy friend. | 11 *mwana haramu*, lit. "an illegal child," "a bastard." There are many stereotypes with regard to children whose fathers are not known. It is said that they don't hear well or they are not clean people. However, as Ustadh Mau adds, according to Islam, no one can be blamed for the mistake of someone else. Before claiming that a person is a *mwana haramu*, one needs to have real evidence. If it is not true, the one who claimed it is beaten eighty times for disrespecting the other. | 111 *-yea* "to bring up" (Std. *-lea*)

13. | *Na iwapo huna budi* | And if you have no choice, |
Ni kadhwa si makusudi	If it happens, but not intentionally,
Tasahilia wadudi	God will make it easier for you,
Muyuzi wa siri pia	The one who knows all the secrets.

14. | *Na kama hukuswadiki* | And if you don't believe in it, |
Jaribu wangu rafiki	Try it, my friend:
Utaiona hilaki	You will see the tragedy
Itakayokushukia	That will befall you.

15. | *Nduzangu nisaidini* | Help me, my brothers, |
Katika wangu uneni	In my speech.
Mngu atie auni	May God offer his help
Mahmoudi kutumia	For Mahmoud's benefit.

MAOMBI: PERSONAL POEMS OF SUPPLICATION

16. *Asili yake yuani*
    Nalikuwepo dukani
    Mimi na wangu wendani
    Hadithi nikasikia

    I will let you know the reason for this poem:
    I was in a shop
    With my friends,
    And then I heard a story.

17. *Alinena Bahasani[I]*
    Kisa cha Nasurudini[II]
    Moyo wangu katamani
    Ina hili kutumia

    Bahasani told
    The story of Nasrudin.
    My heart longed to
    Use this name.

I *Bahasani* was an Islamic scholar who lived on Lamu. His real name was Muhammad bin Said Ali Badawy. He was the greatgrandchild of the renowned Habib Swaleh, who founded the Riyadha Mosque on Lamu. | II According to Ustadh Mau, Nasrudin was an Arab or Turk renowned for his cunning. He was like Abu Nuwas. In fact, stories about him are widespread in the Middle East and Central Asia as well as in Turkish tradition. He is a kind of trickster character: an apparent fool, who, however, often unravels the truth. His stories also merged with the Juha trickster tradition. Historically, Nasrudin was an important theologian (see Shah, Idries. *The Pleasantries of the Incredible Mulla Nasrudin*. (London, Jonathan Cape, 1968).)

18. *Akajirisha Azizi*
    Mtukufu wa ujuzi
    Isitimu hata mwezi
    Kabuli[I] ikatimia

    God made it happen
    The most Knowledgable
    Not even a month passed
    Before the wish was fulfilled.

I *kabuli* "God's acceptance of an invocation"[5]

19. *Nikamuoa mamako*
    Akapata mimba yako
    Kakwandika ina lako
    Nasurudini sikia

    I married your mother.
    She became pregnant with you.
    I gave you your name.
    Nasrudin, listen.

20. *Litimize ina lake*
    Na zote zitendo zake
    Yambo ovu usishike
    La kukhalifu sharia

    Live up to this name,
    Together with all his deeds.
    Don't adopt evil manners
    That violate the sharia.

---

5 See Abulaziz *Muyaka*, 272.

336   MAOMBI: PERSONAL POEMS OF SUPPLICATION

21. *Kikuilia[1] shetwani*
    Soma daftari hini
    Ufuate yalo ndani
    Henda yakakwapukia

    If the devil comes to you,
    Read this writing;
    Follow what is inside
    So that evil will stay far away from you.

    1 *ilia* < *-ya* "to come" (Std. *-ja*)

22. *Keti sana[1] duniani*
    Ni ndia si masikani
    Wangi walo washindani
    Wamezie kwangamia

    Live in this world in a decent way,
    Which is transitory, not a place to stay.
    Many who have looked for competition
    Have already perished.

    1 *sana*, here "well," syn.: *kwa uzuri*; "well" does not mean "so as to enjoy oneself," but rather has the moral connotation of behaving appropriately. Ustadh Mau refers to a similar use of *sana* in the famous didactic poem *Utendi wa Mwana Kupona*. He quotes the following stanza from memory: *jambo ukitaka nena / washawiri wa maana / wakikuambia si sana / kheri kuinyamalia* ("If you want to say something addressing important people, and if they tell you it is inadequate, it is better to keep quiet.") We could not trace the stanza Mau quotes in either Allen's or Werner's editions of the *Utendi wa Mwana Kupona*, which hints at a later oral variation. Werner gives the following similar stanza 18: *Neno nao kwa mzaha / Yawatiayo furaha / Yawapo ya ikiraha / Kheri kuinyamalia* ("Talk with them cheerfully / Of things which give them pleasure / But when the words might give offense /it is better to hold oneself silent")[6]

23. *Hakutumiki kizazi[1]*
    Wala uyuzi wa kazi
    Lifuate la Azizi
    Bwana wa amri pia

    No lineage is of use,
    Nor your professional skills.
    Just follow His Majesty,
    The Lord having the power.

    1 According to Mahmoud, this is an intertextual reference to sura 23, *āyah* 101 of the Qur'ān, which refers to Judgment Day: "For when the Trumpet is blown, that Day that shall be no kinship, any more between them, neither will they question one another" (Abr., 350). The stanza reminds the audience to trust primarily in God and not in one's relationships, family background, or skills.

24. *Wangapi walo na mali*
    Na ushujaa kamili
    Afia na ikibali
    Wameiwata dunia

    How many of the wealthy
    Who were also really brave
    Healthy, and lucky
    Have left this life?[1]

---

6   Allen, *Tendi: Six Examples of a Swahili Classical Verse Form*, 69, stz. 18.; Werner, Alice and William Hichens. *The Advice of Mwana Kupona upon the Wifely Duty*. The Azanian Classics 2. (Medstead: Azania Press, 1934).

MAOMBI: PERSONAL POEMS OF SUPPLICATION

ı This rhetorical question is a productive trope that recurs in Swahili poetry, evoking the brevity and vanity of life. The most renowned poem in which a whole series of stanzas is constructed around the question is the *Al-Inkishafi*.[7]

25.	*Sikia yangu lisani*	Listen to my words
	Ya shehe Nasurudini	About Sheikh Nasrudin;
	Usizungue sukani	Do not turn the rudder,
	Mwambani ukaitia	Or you will end up on a reef.
26.	*Wewe ndie awali*	You are the firstborn.
	Ituze yako akili	Be sober-minded;
	Ufahamu na ahali[ı]	Mind your relatives,
	Wako na jirani pia	And also your neighbors.

ı Mau: *ahali* "family,", used here primarily to refer to his wives.

27.	*Ukitumwa mtaani*	If you are sent to the neighborhood
	Usifanye kisirani	Don't object;
	Asokabili sokoni	It is only fair to help someone
	Sawa kumtumikia[ı]	Who is not allowed to go to the market.

ı In his father's time, women were not allowed to go to the market. Thus, boys were asked to take over that task.

28.	*Wafahamu na nduzako*	Take care of your siblings,
	Walio wanuna[ı] *zako*	Those who are younger than you,
	Na sute wazee wako	And of us, your parents.
	Siwate kutujulia	Do not forget to inform us.

ı *wanuna* Baj. "the small ones" (Std. *wadogo*). On Lamu, the word appears only in literary works and is part of an elevated style.

29.	*Ukifanya yako kazi*	Even if you are busy with your work,
	Usisahau wazazi	Don't forget your parents.
	Yapokuwa ni kwa mwezi	Even if [just] once a month,
	Ziarani kupitia	Pass by to visit their graves.

---

7 William Hichens. *al-Inkishafi: The Soul's Awakening*. (London: Sheldon Press, 1939).

338 MAOMBI: PERSONAL POEMS OF SUPPLICATION

30. *Usidharau sadaka* — Do not look down on alms.
    Hata kikanda¹ kwa mwaka — Even if it is a small amount per year,
    Ndio taa iso shaka — This is the light, without any doubt,
    Ya akhira na dunia — For this world and the afterlife.

    1 *kikanda* "small amount," literally, a traditional tax that farmers pay to landowners.

31. *Sighurike na ujana* — Don't be deceived by boyish pranks
    Ovu yambo ukanena — So that you utter evil words;
    Mkumbuke wako Bwana — Remember your Lord,
    Au utaiyutia — Or you will regret it.

32. *¹Walinae bibi yako* — You had your grandmother
    Na bibi wa bibi yako — And your great grandmother;
    Wawapi matoni mwako — Where are they before your eyes?
    Wote wametangulia — They have all gone ahead leaving this world.

    1 This stanza again is meant to remind him of the fragility of life.

33. *Kuna hayo mambo mane* — There are four things
    Kabisa usiyaone — That you should not try;
    Mziwie na mngine — Also restrain someone else
    Akitaka kutumia — If he wants to do them:

34. *Usitumie kulewa* — Don't drink alcohol;
    Urongo mwingi na kwiwia¹ — Don't be a liar, or steal.
    Na lane sitofunua — The fourth one, I will not reveal it to you;
    Mwenyewe yatakweleya — You will discover it on your own.

    1 *kukwiwia* "to steal" (Std. *-iba*). Ustadh Mau assumes that the fourth sin, which his father did not want to warn him about explicitly because he was addressing his son as a child, was adultery.

35. *Wangapi walokirisi* — How many of those who inherited
    Walo na nyingi nafasi — And had a lot of wealth
    Wameziwata julusi — Had to abandon the sitting room
    Kaburini wameingia — And went to the grave?

MAOMBI: PERSONAL POEMS OF SUPPLICATION   339

36. *Yepue yambo la wandi[I]*   Keep yourself far from backbiting;
    Kazi hio siwe fundi   Do not master this habit,
    Au utakuwa pandi[II]   Or you will be like a grasshopper:
    Motoni utaitia   You will throw yourself into the fire.

I *wandi* "to backbite," "to gossip" (Std. *-sengenya*) | II *pandi* "grasshopper" (Std. *panzi*), an
insect that symbolizes stupidity and vanity, since it is attracted to fire.

37. *La kwamba na kunongona*   Backbiting and revealing secrets
    Ameziwia Rabana   Is rejected by God.
    Ghalibu hukusanyana   Mostly, they come together
    Mambo hayo kutumia   And are used together.

38. *Situmie ujeuri*   Don't be arrogant;
    Ndio shina la kiburi   This is the root of pride.
    Mja kwake ni khatwari   This is dangerous for a human being
    Mara hupotea ndia   Who easily loses his way.

39. *Mtu kitaka shauri*   If someone needs advice,
    Mpe lema lenye kheri   Give him good and virtuous counsel.
    Haifai kumghuri   It is not good to deceive someone,
    Kizani ukamtia   Leaving him in darkness.

40. *Mtu akikupa siri*   If someone tells you a secret,
    Simtolee khabari   Don't spread it.
    Mtu atatahayari   He will feel ashamed
    Kwa watu wakisikia   When people hear it.

41. *Upitapo barazani[I]*   If you pass by a *baraza*
    Penye watu na wendani   Where people are sitting with their friends,
    Salamu uibaini   Greet them loudly.
    Ndio sawa fahamia   That is the right way—understand it.

I *baraza* "verandah," "porch"; "a stone seat or bench table, either outside of the house or in
the hall, where the master sits in public and receives his friends" (Krp. 22).

42. *Usihishimu mungwana*   Do not respect the patrician
    Ukadharau mtumwa   And despise the slave;
    Wote mbwake Subhana   They all belong to God.
    Ewe kijana sikia   Oh my son, listen!

340 MAOMBI: PERSONAL POEMS OF SUPPLICATION

43. *Masikini kia¹ kwako*   If a poor man comes to you,
Simwambie nenda zako   Do not tell him, "Go away!"
Mmoya mkate wako   Rather, give
Sawa ni kumvundia   Some of your bread to him.

1 *kia* < *-ya* "to come" (Std. *akija*)

44. *Wala usishike tama¹*   And never hang your head,
Kwa yoyote ukasema   Whatever you say.
Ihimidie Karima   Praise the Generous One
Ndio hali ya dunia   This is how life is.

1 *-shika tama* lit. "to hold the cheek," a sign of sadness

45. *Ukiya kwako nyumbani*   When you come home,
Pija hodi mlangoni   Knock at the door
Mtu alioko ndani   So that the one who is inside
Nguo akiivutia   Can get properly dressed.

46. *Singie kama kijana*   Do not enter like a child
Asiyejua kunena   Who can't speak;
Utakosa luko ina   You will spoil your name.
Fahamu nimekwambia   Understand what I am telling you.

47. *Mtu akipowa siri*   If someone is given a secret,
Kuisita¹ ni khiari   It is his choice to keep it hidden,
Mtu ni kukuaziri   But he will disgrace you
Khabari kukutolea   If he reveals your secret.

1 *-sita* "to hide" (Std. *-ficha*). The stanza warns the addressee to choose wisely the one whom to share a secret with (see also the following stanza).

48. *Watu nena nao sana*   Speak wisely to people,
Wazee hata zijana   To elders and the youth,
Siri yako ya maana   With regard to your important secret.
Teua wa kumwambia   Choose whom you want to tell it to.

MAOMBI: PERSONAL POEMS OF SUPPLICATION

49. *Ihifadhi siri yako* — Keep your secret,
    Khaswa ya nyumbani — Especially if it concerns your house.
    kwako — Do not talk about it,
    Usitoe matamko — Divulging it to anyone.
    Yoyote ukamwambia

50. *Ukiwa na siri yako* — If you have a secret,
    Mwambie mzee wako — Tell it to your parent,
    Au alo damu yako — Or to someone else of your own blood,
    Na yoyote kizazi kimoya — Or to anyone of the same descent.

51. *Simpe mtu wa mbali* — Don't tell it to a person who is far from
    Asiokuwa ahali — you,
    Kwake haiwi muhali — Who is not a relative.
    Habari kukutolea — For him, it would not be difficult
    — To spread the news.

52. *Yambo ukitaka nena* — If you want to talk about it,
    Washawiri wa maana — Ask true advisers.
    Wakikwambia si sana — If they tell you that it is not good,
    Yafaa kuwashikia — It is better to agree with them[1].

1 Ustadh Mau adds here that it is important to choose wisely whom to speak to. He adds, *La mtu sishike takughuri kisa akuteke* ("Don't agree with someone's advice who will laugh about you later").

53. *Washawiri na nduzako* — Ask your siblings,
    Ingawa wa nuna zako — Even if they are younger than you.
    Kheri itakuya kwako — The advice's benefit will come to you;
    Ufanyalo kukwendea — Whatever you will do will go well.

54. *Wala situkue dhwana*[1] — Do not become suspicious
    Wenzio wakikunena — That your friends are backbiting you.
    Na dalili ungaona — Even if you have evidence,
    Moyo wako shaka tia — Doubt it within yourself.

1 *dhwana* "suspect," "suspicion." Ustadh Mau paraphrases the stanza as follows: *Ukiona watu wanakusema wewe usifikiriye kuwa watu hao wanakusengenya wewe. Hata ukiona dalili wewe usiamini kuwa hao watu wakusengenya wewe. Moyo wako shaka tiya, yaani labda wanamsengenya mtu mngine sio mimi* ("If you find people talking about you, do

not think that they are speaking ill of you. Even if you come across signs, do not believe that those people are backbiting you. Doubt it by thinking: maybe they are backbiting someone else, not me.") The poet explains that, very often, people are obsessed with the idea that everyone is speaking ill of them. This can turn into a real psychological illness that prevents them from living in peace. So, for Ustadh Mau's father, it is important to stop worrying about other people's behavior and speech. In a way, the father is also urging the son never to think badly of others, but in favor of them, to pardon them or at least not to care too much about gossip.

55. | *Ukipata yako mali* | If you acquire some wealth, |
Usisahau ahali	Do not forget your own family.
Ukaifanya bakhili	If you are a tightwad,
Kesho yatakutongea	It will come back to you in the hereafter.

56. | *Warahamu watu wako* | Be kind to your people, |
Na hoyo mwalimu wako	And to your teacher,
Mekufunda matamko	Who taught you things
Ya akhera na dunia	For this world and the afterlife.

57. | *Usiwatupe nduzako* | Don't neglect your siblings, |
Na wana wa ami zako	Or the children or your uncles,
Hasa wa shangazi yako	Especially those of your paternal aunt:
Sana ni kuwanyalia	Take good care of them.

58. | *Watunge sana wazazi* | Take good care of your parents, |
Kwa yambo la kuwahizi[1]	To avoid things that would shame them,
Kama usiku wa mwezi	Like a beautiful woman walking
Maridadi kutembea	On a bright full-moon night.

Ustadh Mau explains the stanza as follows: the *usiku wa mwezi*, the full-moon night, is a "night without darkness" (*usiku usikuwa giza*), so a beautiful woman needs to take extra care veiling herself well so her beauty cannot be seen, since this would mean bringing shame on the parents.

59. | *Wafahamu walalapo* | Pay attention to them when they sleep, |
Asubuhi waamkapo	And when they wake up in the morning.
Usile chakula hapo	Do not start eating your breakfast
Bila ya kuwayulia	Without greeting them in the morning[1].

1 Mau adds his own reflection: "this is what your parents did for you when you were a child —they fed you first and took you to bed before caring about themselves. So, as an adult, you can pay them back."

MAOMBI: PERSONAL POEMS OF SUPPLICATION   343

60. *Sandamane na muinga*   Do not seek the company of a silly person
    Asoyua kuitunga[I]   Who does not protect your dignity;
    Takuvutia matanga   It will cause you grief,
    Mtu hayakufilia[II]   Even before someone has died.

I *kuitunga* "to take care of it" (Std. *kuichunga*); the object pronoun *-i-* refers to *heshima*, i.e. *-chunga heshima yako* "take care of your dignity." | II According to Ustadh Mau, the second part of the stanza means that a friend who does not protect your dignity, will "cause you shame and disgrace, even before you have committed any mistake" (*takusababishiya mambo ya aibu na fedheha kabla hujafanya makosa*).

61. *Usimwandame dhalimu*   Don't seek the company of tyrants,
    Yapokuwa isilamu   Even if they are Muslims,
    Kwani utakuwa sumu   Because you will be poisonous
    Watu watakutukia   And people will hate you.

I *sumu* "poison," here referring to the "poisonous effect" someone turning into a tyrant has on his or her social environment.

62. *Ukimtuma hamali[I]*   If you give someone a task,
    Mpe ijara kamili   Give him the full payment.
    Usiifanye mkali   Do not be mean;
    Kisakisa kumwambia   Do not delay and say, "Later, later!"

I *hamali* "a minor, additional job (for example, carrying loads)"

63. *Mpe ijara kamili*   Give him the full amount
    Ukisa yako shughuli   When he completes his work;
    Usibadilike hali   Do not change your behavior
    Ukamwambia rejea   By telling him, "Come back later!"

64. *Zungumza taratibu*   Speak deliberately—
    Ndio kistaarabu   This is the civilized way—
    Utakuwa mahabubu   And you will be beloved
    Kula utakapongia   Wherever you enter.

65. *Itangulize awali*   Be the first
    Kuuliza mtu hali   In greeting someone;
    Usiifanye mgoli[I]   Do not think yourself better than others
    Mtu kakutangulia   So that they should greet you first.

I *mgoli* Ustadh Mau: "someone superior" (*mtu bora kuliko wangine*).

344 MAOMBI: PERSONAL POEMS OF SUPPLICATION

66. *Usidharau sharifu* — Do not despise the descendants of the
Prophet,
Kwani ndio watukufu — Because they are the saints,
Wala usifanye swafu — And do not discriminate
Mmoya ukatukia — By hating one of them.

This stanza, on the one hand, reflects the high social status of the *masharifu* on Lamu and Ustadh Mau's father also underlines their particular, unquestionable *baraka*: "they are the saints." But, on the other hand, urging his son not to despise them could possibly refer to a more general change in attitude toward them and the influence of modernist and reformist currents of Islam on Lamu at that time.

67. *Kiwa na haja jirani* — If your neighbor is in need of something,
Siitie shingo ndani — Don't let him down.
Ingawa hana rahani — Although he cannot give you any security,
Yafaa kumtendea — It is good to do something for him.

68. *Fukara na mwenye mali* — The poor and the wealthy,
Wape nzuri kauli — Tend to them equally well.
Uwambie yalo kweli — Tell them the truth;
Urongo kutotumia — Do not tell falsehoods.

69. *Aibu usibaini* — Do not expose the shame
Ya mwendio na jirani — Of your friend or neighbor,
Hata mkeo nyumbani — Even to your wife at home;
Haifai kumwambia — It is better not to tell her.

70. *Hakuna usio tembe*[I] — There is no rice plant that does not have a
Mpunga una uwambe[II] — broken grain of rice.
Na kwetu sute ziumbe — The rice plant is full of dust,
Qadhwa hutusikilia — And all of us human beings,
We each have our fate.

I *tembe* "grain" (Std. *chembe*) | II *uwambe* "dust," meaning that there is no family without anything shameful.

71. *Ukifanya karamu* — If you invite people for food,
Usikhusu waadhamu — Do not target only the respected ones
Kuambia wenye memu[I] — Considered to be of high rank,
Fakhari kuizengea — Looking for prestige.

I *memu*, according to Ustadh Mau: "high rank" (cf. *madaraka, cheo, mtu mtukufu*).

MAOMBI: PERSONAL POEMS OF SUPPLICATION   345

72. *Ifanye kama huoni*   Pretend not to see;
    Cha mtu usitamani   Don't long for something from someone
                                else.
    Muombe Mola Mannani   Pray to God, the Giver;
    Aweza kukutendea   He can do it for you.

73. *Mwekelee Mola wako*   Turn to your God;
    Umuombe haja yako   Ask Him for what you need.
    Situkue cha mwenzako   Don't take it from your fellow man;
    Kitu kitakutongea   This will bring trouble on you.

74. *Ingiapo ramadhani*   When Ramadan comes,
    Siketi sana nyumbani   Do not only sit at home.
    Enenda miskitini   Go to the mosque;
    Mno ukiisomea   Read a lot on your own.

75. *Fitiri[1] usisahau*   Don't forget to pay your Zakat al-Fitr alms,
    Wala usiidharau   Nor despise the task.
    Itapotea nafuu   Otherwise, you will lose the blessing
    Mwezi uloifungia   Of the fasting month.

1 Before the Eid al-Fitr prayer at the end of Ramadan, the "fasting month," every adult Muslim who possesses food in excess of his or her needs must pay Zakat al-Fitr (Fitrana). The head of the household can also pay Zakat al-Fitr for dependents such as children, servants, or any dependent relative. Zakat al-Fitr can be paid during Ramadan, at the latest before the Eid al-Fitr prayers, so that the poor can enjoy the day of Eid. The minimum amount due according to Mau is the equivalent of about 2 kg of wheat flour, rice, or other staple foodstuffs per member of the household, including dependents, even if they do not live in the same house.

76. *Mambo ya ulimwenguni*   The things of the world,
    Wewe mno sitamani   Do not desire them.
    Alitawafa Amini[1]   Even the Prophet passed away;
    Hakuna wakusalia   There is none who will remain.

1 *Muhammad al-Amini*: According to Ustadh Mau, a praise name of the Prophet, "Muhammad, the faithful," which was given to him because of his steadfast character, even before God's revelations.

77.	*Fungamana na kusoma[I]*	Let us embrace reading the Qurʾān,
	Rafiki[II] mwenye hatima	A friend who will be with you until the end.
	Hawezi kukusukuma	He cannot push you away,
	Kaburini ukiingia	Even if you enter the grave.

I *kusoma*—Here the father is referring particularly to reading the Qurʾān. | II According to Ustadh Mau, *rafiki* is used here as a metaphor for the Qurʾān, which accompanies a pious Muslim until his death.

78.	*Usimsome shetwani [I]*	Don't read the devil.
	Wewe soma Qurani	Read the noble Qurʾān;
	Ufuate yalo ndani	Follow what is inside.
	Kheri utaionea	This will be better for you.

I *shetwani* "devil"; here, this means secular education, which in the beginning was considered *haram* ("impure," "illegal") and a wicked strategy to make pupils lose their religion. Ustadh Mau's father strongly supported this view, as did Mahmoud's teacher, Said Hassan Badawi. A primary school was built in Lamu in the '50s, after World War II. Before, there were evening classes for learning how to read and write. These classes were attended, for instance, by his father. Despite his father's own distrust of secular education, Ustadh Mau wanted a good education for all his children, and they all went to school, mostly up to secondary school. Some of his children, such as Nadia, Fatih, Azra, and Hannan, also went to university.

79.	*Nakuombea Wadudi*	I pray to God, the Beloved:
	Utimu hunu mradi	May I accomplish this project[II].
	Ina lake Ahmadi	His name is Ahmad,
	Ndie babake Rabia[I]	The father of Rabia.

I *Rabia* is Ustadh Mau's sister, the third child after him and Aziz; Amina was the last-born. Nuru and Sofia are the fourth and fifth, respectively. | II *This project* here implies the project of composing this poem.

80.	*Usifanye ushindani*	Do not create rivalry
	Uyualo ukakhini[I]	If you know something and withhold it;
	Haifai duniani	It is not appropriate in this world
	Mtu hila kutumia	If you use schemes.

I -*hini* "to prevent others from using what you have in your hand"[8]

---

8 Abdulaziz, *Muyaka: 19th Century Swahili Popular Poetry*, 223.

MAOMBI: PERSONAL POEMS OF SUPPLICATION

81. *Ikiwa ni la makosa*
   Usilifanye kabisa
   Waalimu wa madrasa
   Haya wamezuilia

If there is something wrong,
Do not do it at all.
The teachers of the madrassa,
They don't allow mistakes.

82. *Baba pulika maneno*
   Kiumbe ni radhi tano
   Ndipo apate usono¹
   Wa akhira na dunia

Son, listen to these words:
There are five blessings [that allow] men
To find peace
Here and in the afterlife.

   1 *usono* "rest"

83. *Radhi nitazibaini*
   Upate yua yakini
   Usiulize wendani
   Ni hizi takutajia

I will make these blessing clear to you
So that you may know them in detail.
Do not ask your friends.
I will mention them:

84. *Ni Mungu na mtumiwe*
   Baba na mama wayue
   Na mke ni ya mumewe
   Mno imekariria

There is God's and His Prophet's blessings, and
Those of the father and the mother; take note of it.
A wife gets blessings through her husband;
This has been repeated many times.

   1 See for instance *Mwana Kupona*, which in stz. 24 reminds us, *naawe radhi mumeo/siku zote mkaao/siku mukhitariwao awe radhi mekuwea* "Please your husband all the day you live with him and on the day you receive your call, his approval will be clear"[9]

85. *Wasikize ami zako*
   Na mama na bibi yako
   Wasipate ovu lako

   Muini kulisikia

Listen to your uncles,
And your mother and grandmother.
Do not let them discover any evil of your doing
That they may hear about in town.

86. *Usiitie muini*
   Kwa tarumbeta na beni
   Koti likawa rahani
   Zitakutukia ndia¹

Do not spread it around town
With a trumpet and a band;
If your coat is put in a pawnshop,
The people in the street will reject you.

---

9 Allen, *Tendi: Six Examples of a Swahili Classical Verse Form*, 60–61.

1 *ndia* Am. "way," "street" (Std. *njia*), here referring to the people in the street, i.e. the town.

87. *Utimizapo timamu* — If you stick carefully to what I have told you,
    Ewe kijana ghulamu¹ — You, young boy,
    Mno utaona tamu — You will enjoy the sweetness
    Ya akhira na dunia — Of the hereafter and of this world.

1 *ghulamu* (Ar.) "young boy"

88. *Alozawa na mamake* — The one born of his mother,
    Mwiso wake henda zake — In the end, he will leave this world.
    Huyatupa mali yake — He will throw away his goods,
    Na mamboye yote pia — And everything he has.

89. *Kitokacho matumboni* — Nothing coming from a womb
    Hakidumu duniani — Remains in this world,
    Mwisoe ni mtangani — But finds its end in the sand.
    Nyumba kitakwenda ngia — That is the house it will enter.

90. *Usisahau mauti* — Don't forget about death.
    Yambo halina wakati — You do not know when it comes.
    Siwe mno asharati¹ — Don't be malicious,
    Itakughuri dunia — Otherwise life will mislead you.

1 *asharati* "adulterer"; for Ustadh Mau, "troublemaker," "insurgent." Bakhressa: *Asharati matendo maovu, mambo yasiokuwa na muruwa; mambo ya hasharati yameharamishwa na dini* (Bak. 106): ("*Asharati*: evil deeds; matters that are not virtuous; bad things that have been forbidden by religion").

91. *Hao wenye manuari¹* — The ones with military power,
    Warumu na wa Miswiri — The Romans and Egyptians,
    Hawakupowa khabari — They were not aware
    Ya kuiwata dunia — That they had to leave this world.

1 *manuwari*, lit. "war ships," "military equipment" (< the English expression "man-of-war").

MAOMBI: PERSONAL POEMS OF SUPPLICATION

92. *Yandie tangu Adamu*
    Maana hawafahamu
    Ndio waloona tamu
    Nao hawakusalia

    Death started with Adam,
    But people do not understand its meaning,
    Those who enjoyed life,
    Did not remain.

93. *Nalikiketi na hari*
    Nyumbani nikifikiri
    Kiyatunga mashairi
    Haya nimezokwambia

    I was sitting and sweating,
    Thinking at home
    About composing this poem
    That I am reciting to you.

94. *Ukitembea ndiani*
    Angalia ghorofani
    Na walio makutini

    Wote watapita ndia

    If you walk through the streets,
    Look at those in the multi-storied houses,
    And those in the huts thatched with palm
    leaves:
    They all go the same way.

95. *Waka nyumba ya akhira*
    Kwako itakuwa bora
    Utaona na ishara
    Hapa katika dunia

    Build a house in the hereafter;
    For you, this will be better.
    You will see the signs
    Here in this world.

96. *Utaona moyo wako*
    Waipenda dini yako
    Na kumcha Mola wako
    Alama nimekwambia

    You will see that your heart
    Loves your religion
    And fears your God.
    These are the signs—I am telling you.

97. *Hapa basi nimekoma*
    Siwezi tena kusema
    Yatosha ukiyandama
    Haya nimezokwambia

    Here I have come to an end;
    I can speak no longer.
    It is enough for you to follow
    What I have recommended to you.

98. *Alotunga ni Azizi* [I]
    Kumpa nduye hirizi [II]

    Awapo ni mumayizi
    Apate kuitumia

    The composer of this poem is called Aziz.
    He composed it to give it to his brother as
    an amulet
    When he is a mature
    So that he may use it.

I *Azizi* is another son of Ustadh Mau's father; he is using his son's name as a way to include all his children. In fact, the composer is the father himself: Ahmad Abdulkadir Abdulatif. | II *hirizi* recalls the similar verse uttered in *Mwana Kupona*: *twaa nikupe hirizi/uifungeto kwa uzi/uipe na taazizi/upate kuyangalia* (stz. 8); "Take the amulet that I give you; tie it

350   MAOMBI: PERSONAL POEMS OF SUPPLICATION

firmly with cord; honor it and pay attention to it".[10] The poem teaches the addressee and thus works as a protective charm.

99.	*Na zaka uzifahamu*	Don't forget to give alms
	Wakatiwe ukitimu	When the time arrives;
	Usiifanye mgumu	Do not be stingy with your wealth,
	mali yatakutongea	Otherwise this will cause you problems.

100.	*Ufahamu na Karuni*[1]	Consider the example of Qarun,
	Aliiza ya Mannani	Who rejected God's orders.
	Alitiwa ardhini	He was buried in the soil,
	Na mali yake pamoja	Together with his wealth.

1 The story of the very rich tyrant Qarun is told in the Qur'ān, sura 28, *āyāt* 76–84, as a warning to those who desire high rank and wealth, exploiting others without thinking about their fleeting nature. Qarun was a boastful character who praised his own capacities without fearing God. The ones enjoying this life envied him, and the pious warned him. In the end, "We made the earth to swallow him and his dwelling and there was no host to help him, apart from God, and he was helpless" (*āyah* 81, Abr., 401).

101.	*Maka itie moyoni*	Nourish the intention of going to Mecca
	Na kumzuru Amini	To visit the Prophet.
	Kafu kutounga nuni[1]	Say "be" so that it "is";
	Mungu takutimizia	God will accomplish your wish.

1 *Kafu kutounga nuni* literally "before 'kaf' joins 'nun.'" The two Arabic letters refer to the verbal form كان *kāna* "to be." Thus, before *k* and *n* and thus the whole expression of the wish ("make it come true") is pronounced, the wish will have been accomplished. It is an idiomatic expression underlining how God will immediately answer any good intention.

102.	*Siku hio makureshi*	On that day, the Quraish
	Walipanga nakishi	had a discussion
	Zilo ndiani jaishi	Concerning the caravan
	Msafara ya ngamia	That he found along the way.

Ustadh Mau explains the stanza as follows: when the Prophet told the Quraish that he had traveled from Mecca to Jerusalem and to heaven in just one night, they did not believe him. They asked him about a caravan he found along the way to challenge him and to prove that he was a liar. However, he was able to provide them with details about the caravan and some other things he witnessed to make them see that he had really traveled that great distance all in one night. The stanza underlines the power and veracity of the Prophet, which no one should doubt.

---

10   Allen, *Tendi: Six Examples of a Swahili Classical Verse Form*, 58–59.

MAOMBI: PERSONAL POEMS OF SUPPLICATION   351

103. *Itukuze na miraji[I]*   Honor the day of the Prophet's ascen-
                                          sion,
    Kwani ni siku ya taji   Because it is a supreme day.
    Alipazwa mtumwaji[II]   The Prophet was uplifted
    Kuonana na Jalia   To meet with the Powerful One.

I On the twenty-seventh of Rajab, the story of the Prophet's night journey, the *miraji*, is read in the mosque, and afterwards there is chai for everyone. Ustadh Mau used to participate when he was a child, but no longer. However, he preaches about the *miraji* and what one can learn from it in the sermons that he delivers on or around that day. For Ustadh Mau, one cannot and should not refer to a specific date, because the date is uncertain, and he believes it was added in the course of transmission. | II *mtumwaji* "the one who was sent," referring to the Prophet; unusual nominal derivation (conditioned by the rhyme) from the verb *-tuma* using the derivative of habitual agent nouns in *-aji*.

104. *Umuyue wa awali*   Know the first person
    Aliyetoa kauli   Who began speaking,
    Kumtukuza rasuli   Venerating the Prophet
    Mbee ya makureshia   In front of the Quraish.

105. *Abubakari[I] Swadiqi*   Abubakar, the faithful,
    Mbee watu khalaiki   In front of plenty of people,
    Alivunda wanafiqi   He opposed the hypocrites
    Akamwandama nabia   And supported the Prophet.

I Here the father mentions the Four Caliphs, starting with Abubakar. He was the first man who believed in the Prophet. He had been his close friend even before.

106. *Na Ali Haydar[I]*   And Ali Haydari
    Athmani na Omari   And Uthman and Omari
    Makhalifa mashuhuri   Are the renowned caliphs
    Yafaa kuwayulia   Who deserve to be mentioned.

I Ali Haydar, who is the main protagonist of many *tendi*, was the fourth caliph after the Prophet. He married the daughter of the Prophet, Fatimah. Omari was the second caliph, Athmani the third; nevertheless, in the stanza, the order is subverted in accordance with the rhyme in *-ri*.

107. *Uyue na makureshi*   Consider the Quraish,
    Walipofunga jaishi   When they prepared for battle
    Madina kwenda kughashi   And went to destroy Medina—
    Yaliyowasikiliya   Remember what happened to them.

This stanza refers to the third war in the history of Islam, which is mentioned in sura 33, *āyāt* 10 ff. Before were the battles of Badr and Uhud, in which the Prophet's followers fought against those opposing Islam.

108. *Ufahamu na Huseni*   Remember Hussein
Na ndugu yake Hasani   And his brother Hasan.
Wazee wake ni nyani[1]   Who were their parents?
Mama alowazalia   The mother who gave birth to them?

1 The question is a rhetorical one, because it is widely known that Hassan and Hussein are the two sons of Fatimah, Ali's wife, and are the Prophet's grandchildren.

109. *Takwepulia weusi*   May the Generous One remove the darkness
Moyoni mwako Mkwasi   From your heart.
Akuwashie fanusi   May he light a lantern for you,
Mwanga wa kamaria   Shining like moonlight.

110. *Kuna malaika mauti*   The angel of death[1],
Mtoa ruhu umati   Who removes the soul from the body,
Kula kilicho hayati   Everything that exists in the life,
Henda kuitwalia   He goes and takes it away.

1 Implying the angel of Azrael.

111. *Ndie mpaza[1] majumba*   He is the one who uproots the houses;
Ndie mnyakua simba   He is the one who grabs the lion.
Kijana ndani ya mimba   Even an infant from within the womb—
Henda akiitwalia   He can go and snatch it.

1 -*paza* "to grind maize," "to lift"

112. *Nasurudini sikiza*   Nasrudin, listen
Haya nimezokweleza   To what I have explained to you.
Tuyandame ya nahuza   Let us follow the captain
Bandari tupate ngia   So that we may enter the port.

Here, life is compared to a journey by ship, which will reach the port at the end of one's life. The metaphor of the ship is also widely used by Ustadh Mau himself. The captain, *nahuza* (Std. *nahodha*), refers to the Prophet, who guides and steers the ship.

MAOMBI: PERSONAL POEMS OF SUPPLICATION   353

113. *Tufuate la Amini*   Let us follow the lessons of the Trustworthy
                                        One
Tulihai duniani   While we are still alive in this world.
Kesho tumaiti jizani   Tomorrow we will be dead, lying in dark-
                                        ness
Mahali pakushukia   In the place to which we descend.

The dark place mentioned at the end of the stanza is the grave.

114. *Tuifunde na ilimu*   Let us become educated
Ovu lema tufahamu   So that we can differentiate good from bad.
Askari wa Kiramu[1]   The soldiers take note;
Tuyuwe hutwandikia   Record our deeds.

1 According to Ustadh Mau, the "soldiers" refers to the two angels, which record people's
good and bad deeds. One of them is called Raqib, and the second one Ateed (see also Qur.
sura 50, *āyāt* 17–18).

115. *Hoyo hana kusahau*   He never forgets.
Toto akalidhwarau   Even tiny issues, he does not neglect them.
Zaidi ya Mwanatau   He is more diligent than Mwanatau[1],
Kabuli akipokea   Who reacts when she receives your prayer.

1 According to Ustadh Mau, "Mwanatau was a woman from Siu, a member of the Saggaf
clan, who lived a long time ago. People believed that if you prayed to God using Mwanatau
as an intermediary, God would accept your prayer." (*Mwanatau ni mwanamke wa Siu aliye-
zaliwa zamani—mwanamke wa kabila ya Saggaf. Watu waamini kwamba ukiomba Mungu
kwa kupitia ya Mwanatau, Mungu atapokea dua yako.*)
Ustadh Mau remembers a marvelous tale about her: *Kulikuwa na jahazi iko baharini,
jahazi ikazuka/ikatoboka tundu. Maji yakaingia kwenye jahazi. Watu waliosafiri kwenye
jahazi ile wakapiga kelele wakasema eeh Mwanatau tuokoe! Mwanatau alikuwa ako Siu
chooni, akasikia ile sauti ya wale wasafiri; akarusha kiatu chake cha biti. Kiatu kikenda pale
pale kwenye jahazi kikaziba ile tundu na jahazi ikasafiri salama mpaka ikafika bandarini
pale ilipotoka. Ilipofika Mwanatau akaenda akatoa kiatu chake* ("There was a dhow on the
open sea that sprung a leak. Water entered the dhow. The people traveling in that dhow
started shouting, "O Mwanatau, save us!" Mwanatau was in the bathroom in Siu. When she
heard the voices of those traveling, she threw her wooden slipper—and the slipper arrived
directly in the dhow and covered the hole. The dhow traveled safely until it reached the
harbor it had left. When it arrived, Mwanatau went to retrieve her slipper").
Ustadh Mau does not believe in those tales, but there are people who do still believe in
her, as he says. There is even a person called Mwanatau, belonging to the Saggaf clan, who
lives in Lamu nowadays.

116. *Haghafiliki hakika*
     Hata kwa nusu dakika
     Kazi yake ni kuandika
     Paoni¹ hatopokea

He does not forget, for sure,
Not even for half a minute.
To write is his job;
He does not accept any pounds as a
bribe.

1 *paoni* "pounds," corresponding to 20 shillings at that time.

117. *Maisha mangi hakuna*
     Kama karne za yana
     Yafaa kuuswiana
     Safarini tumengia

Life has not become longer
Than in the last centuries;
It is good to remind each other
That we are on a journey.

118. *Tumekuomba Karima*
     Tupe mashukio mema
     Tutanganye na hashima
     Mwana wa makureshia

We pray to you, Generous One;
Grant us a good stay.
Keep us close to the Prophet,
The son of the Quraish.

119. *Waadhi muufahamu*
     Si wake pweke ghulamu
     Mbwetu sute isilamu
     Wa Hawa na Adamia

You have to understand that this admonish-
ment
Is not meant for boys only:
It is for all of us Muslims,
Descendants of Eve and Adam.

MAOMBI: PERSONAL POEMS OF SUPPLICATION   355

2   *Tunda* ("Fruit")

Ustadh Mau wrote this poem for his firstborn, Fati. He was born in October 1976. The young father was overwhelmed with joy. He compares the son to a long-awaited fruit that has taken time to ripen. The fruit is not an uncommon metaphor for a child, often also a young girl in the context of Swahili poetry.[11] The narrator, the father, compares himself to a gardener, carefully watering the plant every day—also not an unusual metaphor for the endless care and anxiety of a parent who can no longer wait for the child to be born. After the child's birth, the point of narration of the poem, the narrator depicts himself as short of words: the joy taking hold of him makes concentration a difficult task.

1.   *Siyui ninene nni, ili niweze wayuza*
      Niwambiye neno gani, ambalo litaweleza
      Furaha zilo moyoni, yeo tunda kupasuza
      Tunda nilolitamani, nyaka nyingi kiliwaza

      I do not know how to express myself so that I can let you know.
      Which words should I use to express
      The happiness that fills my heart? Because today, the fruit has sprouted,
      The fruit that I have longed for; for many years I have thought of it.

2.   *Tunda hili kwa hakika, limenituza fuadi*
      Sana nimefurahika furaha ziso idadi
      Tunda hili kualika[1], kama uwa la waridi
      Namshukuru Rabbuka kutupa hizi zawadi

      For sure, this fruit has calmed my heart.
      I am so happy; endless joy has taken hold of me.
      For this fruit to blossom like a rose,
      I thank God that he has granted us this gift.

      1 *-alika* "to blossom"

---

11   See Clarissa Vierke. "Frau Betelpfeffer und die lustvollen Stunden. Die Inszenierung sinnlicher Erfahrung, Erinnerung und Erwartung in früher Swahili-Dichtung," In Lena Henningsen, Kai Wiegandt and Caspar Battegay (eds.): *Gegessen? Essen und Erinnerung in den Literaturen der Welt.* (Berlin: Neofelis, 2019), 125–148.

3. *Tunda nililolipenda, na hamu kulishikiya*
   Kula siku kilitunda, kwa hima kilinosheya
   Ni tunda langu la kwanda, ambalo limetokeya
   Rabbi Mola talilinda, alipe njema afiya

   I was so excited about the fruit I loved.
   Every day I looked after it and carefully watered it.
   It is my first fruit to sprout;
   God will protect it and bestow good health on it.

4. *Talihifadhi Mannani, lisikumbwe na uovu*
   Likuwe pake mtini, hata liwe ni komavu
   Wala lisanguke tini, liketi kwa ushupavu
   Lisingiwe aswilani, lidumu na uwangavu

   The Bestower will protect it, so that no evil will befall it,
   So that it can grow on its tree until it is ripe enough.
   It should not fall down; let it stay firmly
   So that it shall not be infested by insects, but continue shining.

5. *Kauli yangu tammati, kwamba mangi sitoweza*
   Nilonazo si katiti, furaha menizlmbiza
   Sina makini kuketi, kalamu kucharaza
   Kwa hizi tano baiti, shairi nalifupiza

   This is the end of my talk; I cannot say much.
   What I have is not little; joy has overwhelmed me[1].
   I am lacking the concentration to sit down and further guide my
   pen;
   That is why I have shortened this poem to these five verses.

   1 -*zimbiza* "to overeat"

3 *Kipande cha ini* ("Piece of My Liver")

Ustadh Mau started composing this poem after the short period of the *maulidi*
celebrations, which he spent with Azra on Lamu before she went back to Faza
with her maternal grandmother. Her grandmother Abuba (Bi Rukiya) raised
her because her mother was studying in Eldoret. Azra was two years and sev-

MAOMBI: PERSONAL POEMS OF SUPPLICATION 357

eral months old when he wrote this poem for her. When her mother returned from Eldoret, Azra also returned to Lamu, also because the school was better.

1. *Az'raa[1] kusafiri mno nimesikitika*
    Kama ni yangu khiyari mwanangu hungeondoka
    Kwani umeniathiri na sitaki kukwepuka
    Saa zote hukumbuka ya mwanangu mazoea

    Azra, your traveling has made me so sad.
    If I could choose, my daughter, you would not depart,
    Because you have captivated me and I don't want to be far from you.
    I always recall the time I used to spend with my daughter.

    1 *Az'raa* epithet of Mary, the virgin. Mahmoud gave his daughter the name Azra after his niece, who, after studying in Saudi Arabia, opened a Muslim school (Muslim Girls Training College) in Pangani, Nairobi. For Ustadh Mau, she was the role model that his newborn daughter should emulate. The name was meant to influence Azra's destiny. In a similar way, Ustadh Mau himself was at first called Nasrudin by his father (as the poem *Hapo zamani za yana* shows).

2. *Niwapo nawe mwanangu na mimi huwa kijana*
    Kasahau ulimwengu kwa raha ninayoona
    Na hupungua tewengu[1] shida zote kawa sina
    Khaswa twapotwanena mimi na wewe pamoja

    When I am with you, my daughter, I also turn into a child:
    I forget the world for the joy I feel.
    Worries decrease and I forget all my problems,
    Particularly when we talk to each other, you and me together.

    1 *tewengu* "worries" (Std. *makero*)

3. *Sauti yako laini na maneno nusu nusu*
    Husikiza kwa makini kila mara kikubusu[1]
    Kukosa langu ini ni kama kutiwa kisu
    Ni wewe nimekuhusu kwenye nduzo wote piya

Your soft voice and half-spoken words,
When I listen to you carefully, always kissing you—
To miss you, my heart, it feels like a knife is stabbing me.
I wrote this poem[II] for you from among all your siblings.

I *kubusu mtoto* "to kiss the child." This is only done when the child is young; the relationship changes once the child grows up, as Mau underlines. | II The title of this poem, *Kipande cha ini*, (Ar. *faldhat alkibdi*) "a piece of liver," is taken from Mau's memory of an Arabic poem by the Arabic poet Hatwan Innu Almualla, with a line reading, "our children are livers walking the earth."

4. *Kuwa nawe ni anasa ni pumbao kubwa sana*
Ni raha isiyokwisa kuwa nawe wangu mwana
Starehe nimekosa na rafiki wa kunena
Dhiki mno nimeona ghafula kunikimbia

To be with you is an entertainment; it is a great delight.
It is an endless happiness to be with you, my daughter.
I have lost interest in all pleasures and have no friends to talk
to;
I am full of agony because of your sudden departure.

5. *Mwanangu nikikulisha ziyazi mayai nyama*
Na niwapo na kunywesha soda matama matama[I]
Mwanangu hunikumbusha mke wangu wako mama
Kawaza mengi ya nyuma siku zilotangulia

My daughter, when I feed you potatoes, eggs, and meat,
And when I give you small sips of soda to drink,
My daughter, you remind me of my wife, your mother.
I have been thinking a lot about our past, in former times before
you.

I *kupiga tama* "to take a sip"

6. *Mwana ukija dukani kumwuliza Amita[I]*
Ukingia hata ndani alipo kumfuata
Hata naye masikini mayondi amempata
Hana tena wa kumwita na maneno kumwambiya

My daughter, when you come to the bakery, you look for Amita.
Whenever you would come in, you would go to where he was.
Even he is now sad, taken by grief;
He has nobody to call him nor speak to him.

I Amita: *mchomaji wa mkate katika duka* "one of the bakers in the bakery" whom Azra liked very much.

7.　*Mwanangu sineni sana kanena yasoneneka*
　　Kipenda Mola Rabbana mwanangu hutosumbuka
　　Na siku ya kukutana natumai itafika
　　Siku hiyo tatushika mno kukukumbatia

My daughter, let me not talk too much, lest I say words that should not be uttered.
God willing, my daughter, you will not suffer.
And I hope the day for us to meet will come soon.
On that day, I will hold you tight and embrace you.

8.　*Yondi lako Azraa litengenye na wengine*
　　Balite[I] sasa hiyau ana hamu akuone
　　Muhudati hasahau kukutaya ukezene
　　Na bibiyo[II] nimuene ungiziye mazoea

When you leave, you also make others sad.
Balite longs to see you immediately;
Muhadati doesn't fail to mention you constantly.
I have seen your grandmother; she has grown used to your presence.

I *Balite* refers to Azra's half-sister Barike, who was born to Mahmoud's other wife and is one year older than Azra. When she was little, Azra could not pronounce her name well; thus, she called her "Balite." Muhadati refers to Azra's half-brother, who is the same age as her. | II Bibiyo here refers to Ustadh Mau's mother.

9.　*Kauli yangu tammati hapa nafunga shairi*
　　Nakuombeya kwa dhati na dua tazikariri
　　Mungu akupe bahati kama mwezi unawiri
　　Uwe na moyo wa ari, wa umma kutumikiya

My words have reached their end; I am concluding the poem here.
I am praying for you with all my heart, and I recite these prayers.
May God grant you good luck so that you shine like the moon
And that your heart is determined to serve the community.

4   *Mola zidisha baraka* ("God Increase Your Blessings")

Ustadh Mau composed this poem in *shairi* form on behalf of his daughter Hannan on the occasion of the one-hundredth anniversary of the school she attended. Kenya High School is one of the most prestigious and traditional boarding schools for girls in Kenya, whose graduates typically hold high-ranking positions in Kenya (see also stanzas 2 and 3). The school, located in Nairobi, traces its beginnings to 1910. Originally a colonial school for British pupils, the first African girl was admitted in 1961. In 1974, the Kenyan government took over the school. It is very rare for children from the coast to attend this school, since enrolment depends on excellent results at school and on the national test.

The poem takes the form of a *dua*, a prayer or invocation, which is emphasized from the first stanza and throughout the chorus—the last line of each stanza. The *dua* gives the poet the opportunity both to express his gratitude and to list the merits of the school, while at the same time praying for a blessed future. The poet refers to different positions in the school; to a large extent, the school has retained functions and institutions that date back to colonial times: the symmetrical architecture of boarding houses supervised by matrons (see stz. 6) and prefects. Mahmoud compares the headmistress to a captain (*nahodha*) in firm control of a ship, i.e. the school. He underlines the importance he attributes to education in a "changing world" (stz. 13) and, particularly, encourages the girls to work hard and not consider themselves different from boys (stz. 14). Concluding the poem (see the last stanza), Mahmoud does not sign the poem in his name, but rather in the name of his daughter Hannan, ascribing the poem's composition to her. This is not unusual: in poems composed on commission, he does not mention himself as the author of the poem. The poem was first translated by Ustadh Mau's daughter Azra, whose translation we have slightly amended here.

1.   *Twamshukuru Mannani Mola wetu msifika*
       Kamili moja karini shule imekamilika
       Kenya High nda zamani bado haijazeeka
       Mola zidisha baraka

MAOMBI: PERSONAL POEMS OF SUPPLICATION

We thank the All-Knower, our Lord, the most exalted.
One full century, this school has reached.
Kenya High is antique, but it has not become old.
God, increase your blessings.

2. *Kupitia shule hini ni wengi wamezotoka*
   Wameenea nchini hata ng'ambo wamefika
   Watele madarakani makubwa wameyashika
   Mola zidisha baraka

   Through this school, many have passed,
   Scattered all over the country, even lands overseas.
   Plenty have reached positions high up in the hierarchy.
   God, increase your blessings.

3. *Walotoka hapa ndani alifu tano hakika*
   Ni kama nyota angani wameta wamemetuka
   Kenya High kwa yakini ni shule ya kutajika
   Mola zidisha baraka

   Those who came out of there, for sure, five thousand in number,
   They are like stars in the sky, shining so bright.
   Certainly Kenya High is a school with a reputation.
   God, increase your blessings.

4. *Uvionavo majini vinaolea kumbuka*
   Vimeundwa kwa makini imara vikaundika
   Hayawi kwa kutamani mambo kwa kuwajibika
   Mola zidisha baraka

   The boats you see floating on the water, remember,
   They were meticulously made; strong they have been built.
   The boats cannot be made by just wishing them into being; producing
   the boats takes responsibility.
   God, increase your blessings.

5. *Kenya High mujueni chombo kisotingisika*
   Kwanza mshika sukani ni nahodha asoshaka
   Rose Mary ni makini na hana kubabaika
   Mola zidisha baraka

Know that Kenya High is an unwavering vessel.
First and foremost, the steersman is a real captain, without a doubt.
Rose Mary[1] is confident, with no apprehensions.
God, increase your blessings

1 *Rose Mary* refers to Rosemary Saina, who was the headmistress of the school from 1999 to 2015.

6.   *Ana na wake wendani pamoja wajumuika*
Walimu madarasani vema wamelilimika
Wasimamizi mabweni[1] ni wazuri kadhalika
Mola zidisha baraka

And she has her colleagues; they all come together.
Teachers in the classrooms, well educated they are.
And the dormitory matrons, they are also good.
God, increase your blessings.

1 Kenya High School still retains the original structure of the school, dating back to colonial times, consisting of ten boarding houses (*mabweni*). There is a resident matron for each block, mostly consisting of two dormitory houses.

7.   *Askari mlangoni kwa kazi hana dhihaka*
Na wale walo jikoni ni mafundi wa kupika
Kadhalika ofisini hisabu wema waweka
Mola zidisha baraka

The watchman at the gate, he takes his job seriously,
And those in the kitchen, they are specialists in cooking.
Also, in the office, the accounts are well kept.
God, increase your blessings.

8.   *Bodi yetu ya shuleni ni sana wahangaika*
Wafanya juu na chini bidii bila kuchoka
Shule hakukosekani kila cha kuhitajika
Mola zidisha baraka

Those on our school board struggle a lot;
They do everything they can, relentlessly making an effort.
The school does not lack anything that is needed.
God, increase your blessings.

MAOMBI: PERSONAL POEMS OF SUPPLICATION

9. *P.T.A. kumbukeni mwito sawa yaitika*
   Wa wajibika kazini mzigo waloitweka
   Hawalumbi asilani na wala kulalamika
   Mola zidisha baraka

   Also think of the PTA;[1] it answers its call.
   Those who have taken over responsibility at work have shouldered a
   burden;
   Yet they do neither proclaim, nor do they complain.
   God, increase your blessings.

   1 PTA = Parent-Teacher Association, one of the oldest committees of its kind in Kenya.

10. *Twakariri shukrani kwenu nyute wahusika*
    Mwaijenga shule hini na kazi yatambulika
    Twawaomba sichokeni na wala kupumzika
    Mola zidisha baraka

    We reiterate our gratitude to all of you concerned.
    You are building this school, and your work is recognized.
    We ask you not to stop, nor to take a break.
    God, increase your blessings.

11. *Tukaribu kikomoni shairi kumalizika*
    Twaomba Bwana mbinguni dua yetu kuitika
    Atubariki suteni Mungu kwa zake baraka
    Mola zidisha baraka

    We are reaching the conclusion; the poem is coming to an end.
    We ask God the Most High in heaven to answer our prayer.
    May God bless us all with his blessings.
    God, increase your blessings.

12. *Tupe nchini amani, tuzidi kumakinika*
    Nchi yetu tujengeni ipate kunawirika
    Kwa shime tumalizeni ufisadi kutoweka
    Mola zidisha baraka

Give us peace in our country; stable we shall become.
Our country we should build, so that it blossoms.
With vigor we must finish it; corruption should disappear.
God, increase your blessings.

13. *Kabla kueka chini kalamu niloshika*
    Wasichana tusomeni tutukue madaraka
    Nyuma tusijiwekeni dunia yenda haraka
    Mola zidisha baraka

    Before I put down the pen I am holding,
    Girls, let us get educated; let us take responsibility.
    Behind we should not stay; the world is moving fast.
    God, increase your blessings.

14. *Hatuna la punguani ametuumba Rabbuka*
    Sawa na wetu wendani wanaume bila shaka
    Tusiiyone ni duni na moyo tukavundika
    Mola zidisha baraka

    We are not deficient in the way God has created us.
    No doubt, we are equal to our fellow men.
    We should not look down on ourselves or be discouraged.
    God, increase your blessings.

15. *Twashukuru wageni kuja tumefurahika*
    Ndenu nyinyi shukrani nyingi zisomalizika
    Na mwisho ni kwaherini karibuni mukitaka
    Mola zidisha baraka

    We thank our guests; we are happy you came.
    You deserve many, even countless thanks.
    Lastly, I say goodbye, and welcome back if you want to return.
    God, increase your blessings.

16. *Jina langu ni Hannani shairi nimeandika*
    Kushukuru wa mbinguni kutimiza mia nyaka
    Shule yetu twathamini daima twaikumbuka
    Mola zidisha baraka

MAOMBI: PERSONAL POEMS OF SUPPLICATION   365

My name is Hannan; I wrote this poem.
I praise the One in heaven; may He let the school reach one hundred years.
We value our school, and will always remember it.
God, increase your blessings.

5   *Yasome na kukumbuka* ("Read and Remember")

Ustadh Mau composed this poem for his daughter Nadya on the occasion of her wedding on May 28, 2010. The poem is composed in *utendi* meter and consists of only twenty-one stanzas. The poet calls it a short letter, which he decided to compose for her because she is departing from home and starting a new life with her husband. Having been composed for a specific occasion, the poem was conceived as a gift that the father and poet Ustadh Mau felt the urge to compose. As in many other poems, Ustadh Mau does not refrain from speaking the truth about the life that his daughter is about to embark on, i.e. the ups and downs, problems, rough tides, and turbulent winds she will have to face. He exhorts his daughter to be ready for all of this, and portrays her as a good captain gifted with calmness, charm, and intelligence. Nadya is the fourth child born from his first wife; she is their second daughter. Ustadh Mau urges his daughter to read and to heed his warnings and wishes. We have revised the previous translation of Mohamed Karama here.

Bismillahi ar-raḥmān ar-raḥīm

1.	*Bismillahi awwali*	In the name of Allah, first and foremost,
	Nakuombawe Jallali	I ask you, Lord:
	Unifanye sahali	Make it easy for me
	Kwamba nalokusudiya	To say what I intend to say.
2.	*Nia na yangu kusudi*	My aim and goal
	Ni machache kuradidi	Is to repeat a few points,
	Kumpa yawe zawadi	To give them as a gift
	Binti yangu Nad'ya	To my daughter Nadya.
3.	*Binti yangu kumbuka*	My daughter, remember,
	Sasa kwenu huondoka	You are departing from your home now.
	Wendao kujumuika	You are going to intermingle
	Na watu wako wapiya	With your new kinsmen.

4.	*Fahamu wangu binti*	Understand, my daughter:
	Watu huwa tafauti	People are different.
	Sharuti uidhibiti	You need to control yourself
	Kuishi nao pamoya	To live with them.
5.	*Ifunde uvumilivu*	Teach yourself endurance.
	Usitamke maovu	Do not utter bad words.
	Wala usiwe mzivu	Do not be lazy
	Wangine kutegemeya	So that you need to depend on others.
6.	*Ya kinya twabiya yako*	Silence is your character trait;
	Siiwate hata hoko	Do not give it up, even there.
	Singiliye liso lako	Do not poke your nose into something
	Angaliya moya moya	that is not yours;
		Take care of one thing at a time.
7.	*Mwendo kitenda makosa*	When your fellow man makes a mistake,
	Jaribu kuikukusa	Try to restrain yourself.
	Yakikushinda kabisa	When you are absolutely not able to,
	Huna budi kumwambiya	You have no choice but to tell him.
8.	*Mwambiye kwa taratibu*	Talk to him softly;
	Sidhihirishe ghadhabu	Do not show anger,
	Wala sikose adabu	And do not lose your good manners,
	Ya matango ukataya	So that you don't utter bad words.
9.	*La wajibu tekeleza*	Fulfill your duties,
	Na zaidi ukiweza	And go beyond them if you can.
	Mwendo kikaza regeza	When your fellow man pulls the rope
	Kushindana siyo ndiya	tightly, loosen it;
		Quarreling is not the right way.
10.	*Mwanangu kula wakati*	My child, every time
	Kukizuka tafauti	A disagreement erupts,
	Sipende kuweka kiti[I]	Do not make any effort to prolong it
	Nguo mai kuvuliya[II]	By rolling your sleeves up to fight.

I -*weka kiti* lit. "to put a chair"—an idiomatic expression that means "to provoke an argument and make it go on." Ustadh Mau notes, *Ikitokea tofauti kukosana na mtu, pengine na mtu yeyote nyumbani, shemeji yake ama mama ya mumewe, asifanye mambo marefu ya kugombana na kujibizana maneno. Yaani usifanye ule ugomvi ukajiandaa na ukataka uendelee* ("If a disagreement surfaces and she has an argument with someone else, e.g. the brother-in-law or the mother of her husband, she should not make any effort to prolong the fight or the exchange of words"). | II *nguo mai kuvuliya* lit. "to take off the clothes to have a bath"; it is an idiomatic expression: "to be eager," "to be prepared for something," here "not to be able to wait," or in this context "to be prepared or even eager to fight." Ustadh Mau notes, *kujitayarisha kwa ugomvi. Ikiwa inatokea kwamba kwa bahati mbaya wamekoseana asiwe amejitayarisha mapema, amejiandaa kugombana* ("to prepare oneself for a fight. If it unfortunately happens that they do wrong to each other; she should not be the one prepared and eager for a fight").

11. *Jaribu sana kwepuka*   Try as much as possible to avoid
    Utesi utapozuka   Indulging in conflict;
    Ndipo utasalimika   Then you will be secure.
    Amanini kusaliya   In peace you shall reside.

12. *Jaribu kumfahamu*   Try to understand him:
    Mwendo ni mwanaadamu Your partner is a human being.
    Hupatwa na hali ngumu He is confronted with hard times,
    Mambo yakamtatiya   And things may trouble him.

13. *Elewa kuwa maisha*   Know that in life,
    Hushusha na kupandisha There are ups and downs.
    Mara huzinya huwasha   Sometimes the fire smolders, sometimes
    Ndiyo yake mazoweya   it's stoked:
      That is its nature.

14. *Kuna jongo na kunyoka*   There is roughness and smoothness in
    Na mambo kubadilika   life,
    Mara miuya huzuka   And things change.
    Shuwari ikapoteya   When huge waves appear,
      Calm waters no longer exist.

15. *Kuwa na sawa zipimo*   Be in good balance,
    Kwa kubisha[I] na ya homo[II] Traveling against or with the wind.
    Aso taa ni tomomo[III]   The one who does not have a small basket,
    Haidumu hali moya   has a long one,
      But they do not persist for long.

I *kubisha* "to cross with a boat," a difficult way of steering a dhow against the wind, since one has to change the sail's position again and again. | II *ya homo*, "an easy journey going with the current and the wind"; Ustadh Mau adds, *Safari haina shida yeyote, upepo mzuri, maji yanasaidia. Wewe unakaa kwenye mashua ama jahazini na huna taabu yoyote* ("Such a journey does not cause any problems, since there is a good wind and the water current also helps. You just stay in the boat or dhow without any problem"). *Kubisha* and *ya homo* are antonyms. Ustadh Mau adds, *Haidumu hali moya. Maisha si sampuli moya kila siku. Siyo siku zote kwamba una furaha, wakati mwingine, mambo ni ya maudhiko* ("The situation never remains the same. Life is not the same every day. It is not that you are happy every day. Sometimes, things are also painful"). | III *taa* "a kind of small, narrow basket with a handle"; *tomomo* "a kind of long basket, primarily used by builders of dhows (*mafundi wa kuunda jahazi*)." *Aso taa ni tomomo* is a saying meaning that one is either in a situation of happiness or despair, but as the last *kipande* adds, neither of them lasts for long.

16. *Mwanangu kuwa tayari* My daughter, be ready
    Kwa mambo yatayojiri For everything that will happen.
    Kuwa nahuza hodari Be a good captain
    Kukitokeya miuya When rough tides come.

17. *Kwa shuwari sighurike* And calm water should not deceive you;
    Kwa wimbi sibabaike High waves should not worry you.
    Sukani yako ishike Hold your steering wheel,
    Na dira kuangaliya And look at the compass.

18. *Muisha yana asali* Life has honey in it,
    Na hayakosi subili And does not lack aloe,
    Na mja mwenye akili And the intelligent human being
    Yote huyatarajiya Expects both.

19. *Mwanangu mwendao mbali* My daughter, who is going away
    Kuishi nae mvuli To live with her husband,
    Tafauti yako hali Your situation is different now:
    Nduzo walotanguliya Your siblings have already gone through it.

20. *Ndipo nami kaandika* That is why I wrote
    Hunu mfupi waraka This short letter,
    Usome na kukumbuka For you to read and remember.
    Nimekupa ni wasiya I have given you a poetic legacy.

21. *Kauli yangu tammati* I conclude my words.
    Hukuombeya kwa dhati Earnestly I pray for you;
    Nyota njema ya bahati A star of good fortune
    Mwanangu kukuwaliya Should be yours, my child.

FIGURE 21   The young Mahmoud in 1964

References of Part 2

Abdulaziz, Mohamed. *Muyaka. 19th Century Swahili Popular Poetry*. Nairobi: Kenya Literature Bureau, 1979.

Ahmed Sheikh Nabahany. *Kandi ya Kiswahili*. Dar es Salaam: Aera Kiswahili Researched Products, 2012.

Allen, James de Vere. (ed.). *Al-Inkishafi. Catechism of a Soul by Sayyid Abdalla Bin Alo Bin Nasir*. With a translation and notes by James Vere de Allen. Nairobi, East African Literature Bureau, 1977.

Allen, J.W.T. *Tendi: Six Examples of a Swahili Classical Verse Form with Translations & Notes*. New York: Africana Pub., 1971.

Arberry, John Arthur. *The Quran Interpreted*. Oxford: Oxford University Press, 2012. First published 1964.

Bakhressa, Salim K. *Kamusi ya maana na matumizi*. Nairobi [etc.]: Oxford University Press, 1992.

Chiraghdin, Latifa. *Shihabuddin Chiraghdin. Life journey of a Swahili Scholar*. Mombasa: Jor's Publishers, 2012.

Chiraghdin, Shihabdin. *Malenga wa Karne Moja: Utangulizi na Ahmed Sheikh Nabahany*. Nairobi: Longman, 1987.

Chiraghdin, Shihabdin. (ed.). *Malenga wa Mvita: Diwani ya Ustadh Bhalo*. Nairobi: Oxford University Press, 1971.

Eastman, Carol & Yahya Ali Omar. "Swahili Gestures." *Bulletin of the School of Oriental and African Studies* 48, no. 2: (1985): 321–332.

El-Maawy, Ali A. The Lamu Hero: The Story of Bwana Zahidi Mgumi [1760–1832]. Unpublished book manuscript, 2008 (1973).

Frankl, Peter J.L. & Mahmoud Ahmad Abdulkadir. 2013. "Kiswahili: a poem by Mahmoud Ahmad Abdulkadir, to which is appended a list of the poet's compositions in verse." *Swahili Forum* 20: (2013) 1–18.

Gicharu, John Mwaura, Nyangoma, Benjamin and Chris Oluoch. *Kamusi Kuu ya Kiswahili*. Nairobi: Longhorn Publishers, 2015.

Gray, Thomas. *An Elegy Written at a Country Church Yard*. London, Dodsley, 1751.

Hichens, William. *al-Inkishafi: The Soul's Awakening*. London: Sheldon Press, 1939.

Kresse, Kai. "Enduring relevance samples of oral poetry on the Swahili coast." *Wasafiri* 2, no. 2 (2011): 46–49.

Krapf, J.L. *A Dictionary of the Suahili Language: With Introd. Containing an Outline of a Suahili Grammar*. London: Trubner, 1882.

Mathieu, Roy. *Mathias E. Mnyampala 1917–1969: Poésie d'expression swahilie et construction nationale tanzanienne*. PhD dissertation. Institut National des Langues et Civilisations Orientales (INALCO), Paris, 2013 http://tel.archives-ouvertes.fr/tel-00778667/

Mohamed, A. Mohamed. *Comprehensive Swahili-English Dictionary*. Nairobi: East African Educational Publishers, 2011.

Raia, Annachiara. "Angaliya baharini, mai yaliyoko pwani: The Presence of the Ocean in Mahmoud Ahmed Abdulkadir's Poetry." In *Lugha na fasihi. Scritti in onore e memoria di/Essays in Honour and Memory of Elena Bertoncini Zúbková*, edited by Flavia Aiello and Roberto Gaudioso, 223–250. Naples: Università degli Studi di Napoli "L'Orientale," 2019.

Sacleux, Charles. *Dictionnaire swahili-français*. Univ. de Paris. Travaux et mémoires de l'Institut d'ethnologie: Vol. 36. Paris: Inst. d'Ethnologie, 1939.

Said, Amira Msellem. *Wasifu wa Ahmed Sheikh Nabhany*. Mombasa: JC Press, 2012.

Shah, Idries. *The Pleasantries of the Incredible Mulla Nasrudin*. London, Jonathan Cape, 1968.

Stigand, C.H. *A Grammar of the Dialectic Changes in the Kiswahili Language: with an Introduction and a Recension and Poetical Translation of the Poem Inkishafi, A Swahili Speculum Mundi by the Rev. W.E. Taylor*. Cambridge: at the University Press, 1915.

Vierke, Clarissa. "Frau Betelpfeffer und die lustvollen Stunden. Die Inszenierung sinnlicher Erfahrung, Erinnerung und Erwartung in früher Swahili-Dichtung." In *Gegessen? Essen und Erinnerung in den Literaturen der Welt, edited by* Lena Henningsen, Kai Wiegandt and Caspar Battegay, 125–148. Berlin: Neofelis, 2019.

Vierke, Clarissa. "Im Gebälk die Fledermäuse. Figurationen der Vergänglichkeit und der Täuschung in der klassischen Swahili-Dichtung." In *From the Tana River to Lake Chad. Research in African Oratures and Literatures. In Memoriam Thomas Geider*, edited by Lutz Diegner, Raimund Kastenholz, Uta Reuster-Jahn, and Hannelore Vögele, 285–309. Mainzer Beiträge zur Afrikaforschung. Cologne: Köppe, 2014.

Werner, Alice and William Hichens. *The Advice of Mwana Kupona upon the Wifely Duty*. The Azanian Classics 2. Medstead: Azania Press, 1934.

Index

Abdalla, Abdilatif   3, 72, 101, 120, 126
Abdalla of Shela, Thinana bin   51
Abdallah, Sayyid Omar   6, 14
'abjād   83
adabu   34, 36, 110, 144
adulte initié   70, 74
ahlul-sunna   24
Al-Azhar University   16, 76
Al-Hussein Original Shop   147
Al-Najah Primary School   52
Alawy, Sayyid Abdulrahman   13
Ali Waleedi, Aisha   59
Amu (poem)   4, 74, 95–96, 126–127, 160, 173–185, 205–206, 277, 286–287
Annaswiha Women Group   21, 223
Answar Sunna   see *ahlul-sunna*
'Aqqād, 'Abbās Mahmūd al-   6, 79–80, 91
Aredy, Swaleh   147
Asilia Bakery   15, 21, 40–41, 51–52, 97, 122–125, 319, 324, 359
'Athar al-'Arab fī al-ḥadārah al-'Urubiyyah   80
Athman, Sayyid 'Idarusi bin   48
āyah (pl., *āyāt*)   32, 83, 85, 173, 336, 350, 352–353

Badawy, Sayyid Hassan   15, 22, 52, 70–71
Bajuni islands   16
Bandari ina mawimbi (poem)   36, 95–96, 117, 174, 186–189, 331
Banna, Hassan al-   18
bara   42–44, 201, 211
Barigoni   196
Bayreuth University   4–5, 7, 11
Baytu Thaqafa   70
bid'a   54
Bul'arāf, Ahmad   76, 92, 377
busara   98–99
Bwana Muyaka   see Hajj, Muyaka bin
Bwanamaka, Sauda Kasim   59

Cairo   6, 71, 76–78, 81, 377
Chinese Communist Party Chairman Mao   11, 101
Chiraghdin, Shihabuddin   140, 206, 209
Comoros   49–51, 69

Dar es Salaam   15, 41, 50–51, 329
District Commissioner   29, 68
dura al-mandhuma   153, 274

Education Trust Committee   30
elimu   26, 42, 55–56, 69, 74, 82, 84, 86, 88–89, 117, 196–217

Faiz Bookshop   83
Farasi (area of Lamu)   70
Farsi, Sheikh Abdallah Saleh al-   6, 14, 57, 81
fasihi   109–110
Fi sabil al-Iṣlāḥ   141
fiqh   52, 81
Fumo Liyongo   109

Ghazali, Abu Hamid al-   80–81
gungu   36

Habib Saleh   15, 24, 49, 51–53, 69, 330
Hadhramawt   23–24, 48–50
Hafi asiye timiwa (poem)   179, 302, 319–323
Haji, Muyaka bin   57, 109, 140, 204, 206, 208, 212
Haki za watoto (poem)   41, 45, 56–58, 61, 63, 95, 98, 106, 108, 110–111, 120, 122, 125–127, 235–273
Hapo zamani za yana (poem)   4, 53, 59, 171, 173, 231, 236, 329–354, 357
hekima   98
heshima   31, 34, 36, 108–109, 125, 343
homme de lettre   110
huruma   58, 171, 218–318

Iḥiyā' 'ulūm ad-dīn   80
ilimu   see elimu
Indonesia   50
Inkishafi, Al-   49, 65, 72, 116–117, 124, 129, 208–209, 211, 333, 337, 371
Islam al-sawti, al-   133, 379

Jahazi (poem)   59, 61–63, 105, 124–127, 172–173, 190–191, 324
Jamhuri Day   29, 72
Jamia Mosque   21, 23
jamii   88, 90, 142, 171, 175–195

Japan   57, 117, 192, 205
Jilbabu (poem)   35, 172, 223–228
Jukwaani Festival   3, 121, 218
Juma Bhalo Sayyani, Ahmad Nassir   3, 13, 20, 209

Kadara   146–147, 154
KANU (Kenya African National Union)   248
Kasim, Sheikh Muhammad   55, 139
Kenya Certificate of Secondary Education (KCSE)   x
Kenya High School   360, 362
Kenya National Union of Teachers   196
Kenyatta, Uhuru   123
Kerala   50
Kezilahabi, Euphrase   159
Khaldun, Ibn   150
Kiamu dialect   3, 41, 43, 47, 57, 61, 64, 138, 145–146, 173, 175
Kibajuni dialect   173
Kijitoni   70
Kijuma, Muhamadi   3
Kikuyu language   139, 211
Kimvita dialect   138–139, 145, 173, 320
Kilio huliya mwenye (poem)   36, 41, 45, 57, 172, 192, 200–205
Kimwondo (genre)   36–37
Kimwondo (poem)   2, 17, 58, 146–148
Kipande cha ini (poem)   59–60, 71, 356–359
kipawa   63
Kishamia   49
Kisumu   211
Kiswahili (poem)   2, 17, 42–43, 45, 49, 57–58, 61, 140, 192, 200, 206–213
kite   112–113, 118, 122, 125, 128, 242
kitendo   13, 26, 220
kiti cha enzi   132
Kiunguja dialect   281, 320
Kiwandeo   46
Kizingitini   16
Krapf, Johann Ludwig   57
kujibizana   17, 35, 105
Kutch   16
kutiwa sauti   154
Kuwait   135, 150

Laisa min al-Islam   54, 81
Lake Victoria   211
Lamu District Education Board   52

Lamu District Magistrate Court   15
Lamu Museum   4, 200, 235
Lamu Muslim Youth   30
Lamu Old Town ("Lamu town")   14–15, 70, 176, 187
Lamu West Constituency AIDS Committee   52
Lamu Youth Alliance   19
Langoni (area of Lamu)   75, 83
LAPPSET (Lamu Port-South Sudan-Ethiopia-Transport Corridor project)   165
Leibniz-Zentrum Moderner Orient   27
loho   73

Ma'alim fi al-Tariq   82
Machakos Muslim Institute   16, 52
Madhubuti, Abubakar   176
Madrasatul Falah   16
mafumbo   6, 104–105, 161, 173
Malabar coast   16
Malaysia   50, 149
Malindi   51, 324, 329
Mama msimlaumu (poem)   3, 59, 61, 63, 95, 97, 119, 122, 125–127, 172, 179, 218–222
Manda   44
Mani Bookshop   83
maombi   171, 328–368
Marxism   100–101
mashairi   36, 104, 106–107, 148, 177
masharifu   16, 24, 344
masharti   60
matukio   171, 319–327
Mau Mau   11
Maulidi   11, 24–25, 53–54
Maulidi Barzanji   48
maweko   26
Mazrui, Sheikh Al-Amin   6, 14, 55, 71
Mbarak, Barka Aboud   51, 153, 168
Mbwana Radio Station   147
Mchezo wa kuigiza (poem)   7, 35, 172–173, 228–234
Mecca   48, 77, 350
mila   54
Mlango (poem)   51, 97, 122, 124–128, 172, 179, 324–327, 331
Mngumi, Zahidi   140
Mohammed-Nagar (Gujarat)   50
Mokowe   44, 51, 329

INDEX   375

Mola zidisha baraka (poem)   7, 35, 172, 174,
  360–364
Mombasa   2–4, 11–14, 26–28, 34–35, 43–44,
  51–52, 55, 57–58, 66, 81, 138–139, 147,
  158, 206, 208–210, 301, 319, 371–372
Msallam, Sheikh Ahmad   16–17, 26, 28
mshairi wa jamii   100–101
msomaji   147, 151–152, 154
Mtamuini (area of Lamu)   30, 51, 143
mtu wa watu   5, 13–27, 374
mtungaji   3, 151
Muhadhari, Ghalib   147
Mukharati (poem)   59
Mumbai   76, 377
mungwana   108–110, 331
Muqaddima   150
Muslim Academy in Zanzibar   14
Muslim Brotherhood   18
Muṣṭafā al-Bābī al-Ḥalabī   76–77
Muṭālaʿāt fī al-Kutub wa-al-ḥayāh   80
Mwalimu (poem)   7, 36, 73, 85–86, 196–
  199
Mwalimu Saggaf   *see* Alawy, Sayyid
  Abdulrahman
mwalimu wa jamii   12–13, 21, 23
Mwengo Athmani   208
Mwengo Bakari   114
Mwcnyc Mansab   48–49
mwimbaji   154
Mzamil, Mzamil Omar   146

Nabahany, Ahmed Sheikh   3, 98, 140, 206,
  208–209, 371
Nairobi   3, 21, 23, 26, 43–44, 52, 72, 218, 223,
  357, 360
Nās wa-al-ḥaqq   79, 82
Nasrudin   329, 332, 335, 337, 352, 357
Neto, Agostinho   100
ngomeni   14, 187
Ngong Forest   218
Nyerere, Julius   13, 100
nyimbo (genre)   36, 224
Nyuma ya Gereza (area of Lamu)   70

Oman   50
Omani Empire   50
Omdurman Islamic University   16
organization, community-based   21

Pakistan   135
Pate   46, 48–49, 59–60, 95, 109, 206, 208–
  209, 248
Persia   57, 172, 204, 214, 216
Portuguese incursion   50, 132, 217
print Islam   39, 77–78
pwani   42, 44, 137, 191
Pwani Mosque   15, 19, 23, 52, 70

Qaradawi, Yusuf al-   6–7, 79, 82, 365
Qurʾān   32, 36, 51, 53–57, 71, 73, 173, 226, 231,
  235, 329–330, 346, 350
Qutb, Sayyid   18, 82

Ramadan   52, 87–88, 175, 227, 287, 345
Ramani ya maisha ya ndowa (poem)   30, 59,
  97, 107, 127
Rashid Rida, Muhammad   71, 81
Risālat al-Jāmiyya   149
Riyadha Mosque   15–16, 24, 49–52, 69, 75,
  330, 335
ruhuma   112–114, 118, 120–122, 125, 127, 221,
  266

Sacleux, Charles   109–110, 112, 210, 238
Saʿīd ul-Būsīrī, Muhammad ibn   48
Salafism   1–2, 16, 24–25, 56, 81–82
Saudi Arabia   25, 52, 54, 135, 150, 173, 228, 357
Sauti ya dhiki   72, 120, 155
Sauti ya haki   14, 71, 139
sauti ya mahadhi   154–155
Sayyid Saleh Alwy Jamalail   *see* Habib Saleh
School of Oriental and African Studies
  (SOAS)   27, 48, 208
Senghor, Léopold Sédar   100
Shafiʾi school   81
Shatry, Abdallah el-   4, 147, 154, 275
Shii Ithnashari Islam   15
Shiite community   24
shiʿr al-ghināʾī, al-   138
shiʿr al-taʿlīmī, al-   138
Shirazi influence on Lamu   214–216
Siraji (poem)   107
sitara   31, 125–126
Siu   59, 143, 154, 173, 208, 353
Six Characters in Search of an Author   134,
  158, 379
Somalia   17, 60, 77–78, 223, 254
Sudan   16, 19, 23, 42, 52, 60, 76, 186

Sufism 2, 24, 54–55, 78, 81, 116, 150, 376
ṣuḥba 71
Sumayṭ, Aḥmad b. 76
Sunni Islam 24, 50
Surat, port of 16
Surti community of Gujarat 50
Swafaa Mosque 15, 24

Tabaraka 48
tabia njema 86
Tabuk 47
Ṭahṭāwī, Rifāʿa Rāfiʿ al- 78
Tana River 319
Ṭanṭawi, Sheikh Ali al- 82, 135–137, 140–141, 144, 148, 150, 275, 316, 379
tathlitha xii
Thamaratul Jannah 21
Thiong'o, Ngũgĩ wa 79–80, 139
Tunda (poem) 59, 355
Tupijeni makamama (poem) 18, 89, 192–195

ubao 73, 85
ujuzi 21, 26, 84, 88, 128
Ukimwi ni zimwi (poem) 18, 37, 58
Umm al-Qurā 48
United Nations Convention on the Rights of the Child 56
Ustadh Harith 11–12, 16, 54, 81

Utendi na Miqdadi na Mayasa 138–139
Utendi wa Mwana Kupona 30–31, 47, 107, 138, 143, 157, 208, 274–275, 336, 347, 349
Utendi wa Tambuka 47, 208, 309
Utendi wa vita vya Uhd 139
Utendi wa Yusuf 4
utu 13, 103
Utu ni vitendo 13

Wahhabism 24–25, 43, 54, 81
wajibu 100, 177, 270, 366
wasiya (genre) 4, 59, 64, 142, 144, 171–172, 235–236, 262, 272, 329–330
Wasiya wa mabanati (poem) 2, 6–7, 18, 20, 58, 60, 97, 133–134, 136, 147, 172, 274–318, 379

Ya-bintī 82, 93, 133, 135–137, 140–141, 143–144, 148, 150, 164, 173, 275
Yasome na kukumbuka (poem) 7, 365–370

Za Washirazi athari (poem) 7, 36, 172, 192, 214–217
Zanzibar 14, 46, 50, 70, 76–77, 149, 214–215
Zarnuji, Burhan al-Din al- 73
Zayn al-Ḥibshī, Aḥmad b. 149
ziyara 24